TECHNOLOGY AND MEASUREMENT AROUND THE GLOBE

T0384646

There have been tremendous advancements in technology-based assessments in new modes of data collection and the use of artificial intelligence. Traditional assessment techniques in the fields of psychology, business, education, and health need to be reconsidered. Yet, while technology is pervasive, its spread is not consistent due to national differences in economics and culture. Given these trends, this book offers an integrative consolidation of how technology is changing the face of assessments across different regions of the world. There are three major book sections: in "Foundations," core issues of computational models, passively sensed data, and privacy concerns are discussed; in "Global Perspectives on Key Methods/Topics," the book identifies ways technology has changed how we assess human attributes across the world; and finally, in "Regional Focus," the book surveys how different regions around the world have adopted technology-based assessments for their unique cultural and societal context.

LOUIS TAY is William C. Byham Professor of Industrial-Organizational Psychology at Purdue University. His research interests are in psychological assessments, measurement, machine learning, and data science. He is also the founder of ExpiWell (www.expiwell.com), a technology-based company that enables researchers to capture real-world experiences.

SANG EUN WOO is Professor of Psychological Sciences at Purdue University. She studies how people's personality and motivation can help explain various psychological phenomena in the workplace. Her focal expertise lies in developing and validating (often new and/or underutilized) techniques of measuring individual differences, as well as in clarifying the theoretical underpinnings and implications of such techniques.

TARA BEHREND is Associate Professor of Psychological Sciences at Purdue University. She is an internationally recognized expert in the psychological effects of workplace technologies. She is also a member of the National Academies Board on Human-Systems Integration and former Program Director for the National Science Foundation's Future of Work and Science of Organizations programs.

EDUCATIONAL AND PSYCHOLOGICAL TESTING IN A GLOBAL CONTEXT

Editor
Neal Schmitt, *Michigan State University*

The Educational and Psychological Testing in a Global Context series features advanced theory, research, and practice in the areas of international testing and assessment in psychology, education, counseling, organizational behavior, human resource management and all related disciplines. It aims to explore, in great depth, the national and cultural idiosyncrasies of test use and how they affect the psychometric quality of assessments and the decisions made on the basis of measures. Our hope is to contribute to the quality of measurement and to facilitate the work of professionals who must use practices or measures with which they may be unfamiliar or adapt familiar measures to a local context.

Published titles:

TECHNOLOGY AND MEASUREMENT AROUND THE GLOBE

EDITED BY

LOUIS TAY
Purdue University

SANG EUN WOO
Purdue University

TARA BEHREND
Purdue University

CAMBRIDGE
UNIVERSITY PRESS

Shaftesbury Road, Cambridge CB2 8EA, United Kingdom

One Liberty Plaza, 20th Floor, New York, NY 10006, USA

477 Williamstown Road, Port Melbourne, VIC 3207, Australia

314–321, 3rd Floor, Plot 3, Splendor Forum, Jasola District Centre, New Delhi – 110025, India

103 Penang Road, #05–06/07, Visioncrest Commercial, Singapore 238467

Cambridge University Press is part of Cambridge University Press & Assessment, a department of the University of Cambridge.

We share the University's mission to contribute to society through the pursuit of education, learning and research at the highest international levels of excellence.

www.cambridge.org
Information on this title: www.cambridge.org/9781316515280

DOI: 10.1017/9781009099813

First published 2024

A catalogue record for this publication is available from the British Library.

Library of Congress Cataloging-in-Publication Data
NAMES: Tay, Louis (Psychologist), editor. | Woo, Sang Eun, editor. | Behrend, Tara, editor.
TITLE: Technology and measurement around the globe / editors, Louis Tay, Purdue University, Sang Eun Woo, Purdue University, Tara Behrend, Purdue University.
DESCRIPTION: 1 Edition. | New York, NY : Cambridge University Press, 2024. | Series: Educational and psychological testing in a global context | Includes bibliographical references and index.
IDENTIFIERS: LCCN 2023022953 (print) | LCCN 2023022954 (ebook) | ISBN 9781316515280 (hardback) | ISBN 9781009096591 (paperback) | ISBN 9781009099813 (epub)
SUBJECTS: LCSH: Psychological tests–Data processing. | Educational tests and measurements–Data processing. | Educational tests and measurements–Computer programs.
CLASSIFICATION: LCC BF176 .T393 2024 (print) | LCC BF176 (ebook) | DDC 150.28/7–DC23/eng/20230627
LC record available at https://lccn.loc.gov/2023022953
LC ebook record available at https://lccn.loc.gov/2023022954

ISBN 978-1-316-51528-0 Hardback
ISBN 978-1-009-09659-1 Paperback

Contents

v

Contributors

KRISTINA ALOYAN Skolkovo School of Management, Russia

THAIS BRANDÃO Ayrton Senna Institute, Brazil

DAVID CHAN Singapore Management University, Singapore

CHULIN CHEN University of Minnesota, USA

MUNMUN DE CHOUDHURY Georgia Institute of Technology, USA

TOON DEVLOO Bondi X, Argentina

FILIP DE FRUYT Ghent University, Belgium

KIM K. GLOYSTEIN Bielefeld University, Germany

CRISTINA GONZALEZ Pennsylvania State University, USA

NIGEL GUENOLE University of London, UK

IVAN HERNANDEZ Virginia Tech, USA

RICHARD N. LANDERS University of Minnesota, USA

VIVIEN LEE University of Minnesota, USA

MENGQIAO LIU Amazon Inc., USA

FABIANO KOICH MIGUEL Federal University of São Carlos, Brazil

HANYI MIN Pennsylvania State University, USA

NICK MODERSITZKI Bielefeld University, Germany

SANDRINE R. MÜLLER Bielefeld University, Germany

LIBERTY MUNSON Microsoft, USA

FRED OSWALD Rice University, USA

LE VY PHAN Bielefeld University, Germany

RICARDO PRIMI Ayrton Senna Institute, Brazil

PETER SAVILLE 10X Psychology, UK

JULIANA SEIDL Longeva, Brazil

HYUN JOO SHIN Johns Hopkins University, USA

Q. CHELSEA SONG Purdue University, USA

CICEK SVENSSON Caveon Test Security, USA

TIMOTHY TEO Chinese University of Hong Kong, Hong Kong

MEAGHAN M. TRACY Purdue University, USA

NAKUL UPADHYA Purdue University, USA

BART WILLE Ghent University, Belgium

HENG XU American University, USA

NAN ZHANG University of Florida, USA

ANA CAROLINA ZUANAZZI Ayrton Senna Institute, Brazil

Introduction

Louis Tay, Sang Eun Woo, and Tara Behrend

Technology, that is, the output of human innovation, has always been central to human progress worldwide. Early on, the ancients developed the wheel, concrete, calculus, and paper, which led to advances in transportation, construction, and communication. Today, the incarnation of technology falls in the realm of the digital and computational, and its progress has been rapid, even arguably exponential. In his chapter, "The Law of Accelerating Returns," Ray Kurzweil writes, "An analysis of the history of technology shows that technological change is exponential, contrary to the common-sense 'intuitive linear' view. So we won't experience 100 years of progress in the 21st century – it will be more like 20,000 years of progress (at today's rate)" (Kurzweil, 2004, p. 381).

We are at a unique juncture of mass adoption of mobile and wearable technology, gobs of internet and communication behaviors among people, artificial intelligence that can rival and surpass human performance on many tasks, and storage capacity for data and computational power hitherto unheard of. The global phenomenon of big data has arrived, and this has led to disruptions across the world and throughout multiple fields. Indeed, the tools and approaches in psychological, organizational, and sociological research have changed with the advent of big data and related technologies (McFarland et al., 2015; Oswald et al., 2020; Woo et al., 2020). The field of human assessments is similarly affected and transformed.

While technology is pervasive, its spread is not consistent across the globe due to differences in wealth and development among countries. It has been noted in the *2020 World Social Report* by the United Nations that inequality continues to pervade, and the average income of people living in North America is 16 times higher than those living in sub-Saharan Africa. This affects the ability of countries to purchase and use advanced technologies. The issue is, of course, not merely one of economics but also culture. Culture affects not only whether technologies are adopted (Ashraf et al., 2014) but how technologies are used, and it can shape the link between attitudes and technology use (Dinev et al., 2009). These kaleidoscopes of dimensions can lead to unique differences between regions of the world in how technology is shaping human assessments.

We (Tay, Woo, and Behrend) had these macro technology trends in mind when conceiving a vision for this book. To this end, we convened a conference in the summer of 2020, hosted virtually at Purdue (www.purdue .edu/hhs/psy/tmag/) with the sponsorship, endorsement, and support of the International Test Commission and Consortium for the Advancement of Research Methods and Analysis, Society for Industrial and Organizational Psychology (SIOP) Foundation, and Purdue Psychological Sciences to generate discussions about various aspects of technology, measurement, and culture. The presentations and conversations from that conference became chapters for the book you are now reading.

This edited book takes stock of how technology is changing the face of assessments in its relentless march around and in different regions of the world. Past technological progress in human assessments, or *measurement*, has primarily been constrained to carefully designed data within surveys or tests. Even when there are advances in the mode of data collection (e.g., paper and pencil to online) or procedure (e.g., static to computerized adaptive assessment), these data are crafted within a system that fits our typical psychometric models (e.g., classical test theory, item response theory). With the rise of big data, we now draw on organic data arising from multiple sources to make inferences about human attributes; we also rely on new computational models for measurement that often do not even have the notion of a latent trait (D'Mello et al., 2022). These new modes of data and measurement models require us to think through the applicability of traditional psychometric issues of reliability, validity, and bias (Liou et al., 2022). For instance, the notion of internal consistency reliability with Cronbach's alpha is less applicable to computational models that use thousands of distinct (and potentially uncorrelated) features to score individuals. Further, the notions of measurement bias need to be expanded to incorporate machine learning models that are distinct from traditional psychometric models (Tay et al., 2022). At the broadest level, new interdisciplinary approaches to designing, implementing, monitoring, and auditing these technology-based assessments are needed (Landers & Behrend, 2023).

We structured the book into three major sections: foundations, global perspectives, and regional focus. In foundations, we consider the core issues of computational models, new passively sensed data, and privacy concerns. In global perspectives, we seek to identify some key ways technology has touched on how we are measuring human attributes across the world. Finally, in regional focus, we survey how different regions around the world have adopted technological advancements in measurement for their unique cultural and societal context.

Foundations

Led by computer and data scientists seeking to apply new technologies, data, and computational models for human assessments, there is a significant need for understanding the intersection between these newer machine learning models and psychometrics. In Chapter 1, Song et al. provide an overview of machine learning algorithms and applications, along with how they advance psychological measurement. Drawing from their expertise, they provide recommendations and resources to researchers and practitioners seeking to apply these new methods in measurement.

A leading edge of pervasive technology is passive sensing. The application of this technology for measurement exemplifies and reflects many of the issues, opportunities, and challenges that newer technology-enabled assessments face. In Chapter 2, De Choudhury illustrates a range of passive sensing measurements (e.g., smartphones, wearable devices, and social media) in the context of the workplace to elucidate the types of assessments that are possible. She also discusses the strengths of such data along with the need to address limitations of generalizability and modeling of such data in future work. In addition, she calls for cross-disciplinary teams to address foundational issues of construct validity, theoretical grounding, research design, and ethics when using passive sensing for assessments.

With big data, privacy and security issues come to the fore as these types of technology-enabled assessment data become pervasive. In Chapter 3, Xu and Zhang discuss the opportunities and challenges of organic data collection from a privacy lens. They show how inferences about individuals can be made even under anonymity due to the abundance and interconnectedness of data. Given these practical limitations, there is a need to rethink and redefine what privacy means and to evaluate it across applications and time. In closing, they describe some state-of-the-art privacy-preserving techniques and their limitations.

Global Perspectives

Social media data, which includes content posted to social networking sites, friend/contact network information, photos, and usage behavior, has been used extensively to make inferences about the characteristics of users. Much has been made of these big data and machine learning approaches to modeling constructs such as personality and cognitive ability. In Chapter 4, Min and Gonzalez offer words of caution and advice for researchers who wish to conduct cross-cultural studies using social media data, as well as advice about how to measure culture-related constructs using data collected from social media.

Games have captured the global public's attention as a means of increasing engagement and increasing applicant reactions, as well as a means of conducting "stealth assessment" by measuring the behavior of game players in order to make inferences about relevant constructs. In Chapter 5, Landers et al. explore the phenomenon of games from a privacy and legality perspective, exploring game vendors' attitudes about the challenges of administering game-based assessments. This chapter also outlines the cross-cultural design and implementation factors that game developers must consider when deploying global game-based assessments.

Like games, mobile sensing has dramatically changed the way that assessment can be done without relying on self-reports. Mobile sensors use devices, including smartphones, badges, RFID (radio frequency identification) tags, or other devices, to capture information about the movements and behaviors of a person. When deployed in groups, this data can be used to generate information about social networks and communication patterns as well. The implementation of these methods has far outpaced research, though, and researchers using mobile sensing risk introducing bias or overlooking cultural differences in how the data should be collected and interpreted. In Chapter 6, Phan et al. provide a thoughtful and thorough approach to thinking about the deployment of mobile sensing in a responsible and ethical manner that accounts for cultural variation.

Regional Focus

In Chapter 7, Song et al. give a helpful overview of current applications and challenges associated with technology and measurement. After describing five major technologies used for psychological measurement (i.e., smartphones, wearable devices, social media, computerized adaptive testing, and game-based assessment), the authors discuss issues of legislation and regulation (e.g., data privacy and security) that are specific to Asian countries such as China and South Korea, and cultural/economic differences within Asia that may influence technology acceptance within a specific region.

In Chapter 8, Chan takes a deeper dive into the country of Singapore. He provides an insightful analysis of various factors surrounding Singapore's quest to become a "Smart Nation," at multiple levels of analysis. Organized by three C's (i.e., contexts, changes, and collaborations), these factors range from global- and industry-level demands and infrastructure development to individuals' well-being and socio-cognitive biases, which are all crucial considerations when designing and implementing technology-enabled measurement tools. The explicit focus on national-level innovation and collaboration driven by strong people-centric values is noteworthy and serves as a useful benchmark for other parts of the globe.

In Chapter 9, Guenole et al. discuss how technology affects measurement practices in Europe. Most noteworthy are the survey results from 182 professionals in Europe who utilize measurement technologies in talent management. Results indicated that emerging assessment technologies such as game-based assessment, text parsing (e.g., resumés), chatbots, digital footprint scraping, and Internet of Things assessment technology are not as prevalent compared to more conventional techniques such as questionnaires, interviews, assessment and development centers, and situational judgment tests. On the other hand, more privacy-related concerns were expressed around the newer technologies. The authors describe more fine-grained trends within each of the emerging technologies and conclude by noting some new challenges associated with them, such as finding and establishing the bridge between scientific (psychometric) principles and "innovative and tech-driven" assessment practices that are increasingly popularized in industry.

Focusing on (but not limited to) the North American region, Munson, in Chapter 10, makes acute observations about legal, ethical, social, and practical challenges related to privacy, accommodations vs. accessibility, and opt-out-of-testing trends. Like Guenole et al., Munson also calls for further development of "computational psychometrics" where traditional psychometric ideas are well integrated with innovations in computer science and newer sources of data. This requires interdisciplinary work that was hitherto the domain of only psychometricians.

In Chapter 11, De Fruyt et al. discuss a couple of technological innovations in developing personalized assessment for educational and workplace applications in the South American region. Similar to Chan, De Fruyt et al. mention the need for technological infrastructure that allows for large-scale (remote) assessment that overcomes discrepancies in accessibility due to economic inequalities in the region. The authors also discuss challenges with user familiarity with technology, which have been noted in other chapters (e.g., Song et al.; Guenole et al.).

Conclusion

In the final chapter, the book concludes with integrative comments and conclusions from Oswald and Behrend, who reflect on themes including privacy, transparency, justice, and emerging technologies and offer future directions for researchers working on the intersection of assessment and technology, placing special emphasis on testing and the policy and societal implications of testing.

REFERENCES

Ashraf, A. R., Thongpapanl, N., & Auh, S. (2014). The application of the technology acceptance model under different cultural contexts: The case of online shopping adoption. *Journal of International Marketing, 22*(3), 68–93. https://doi.org/10.1509/jim.14.0065

D'Mello, S. K., Tay, L., & Southwell, R. (2022). Psychological measurement in the information age: Machine-learned computational models. *Current Directions in Psychological Science, 31*(1), 76–87. https://doi.org/10.1177/09637214211056906

Dinev, T., Goo, J., Hu, Q., & Nam, K. (2009). User behaviour towards protective information technologies: The role of national cultural differences. *Information Systems Journal, 19*(4), 391–412. https://doi.org/10.1111/j.1365-2575.2007.00289.x

Kurzweil, R. (2004). The law of accelerating returns. In C. Teuscher (Ed.), *Alan Turing: Life and legacy of a great thinker* (pp. 381–415). Springer.

Landers, R. N., & Behrend, T. S. (2023). Auditing the AI auditors: A framework for evaluating fairness and bias in high stakes AI predictive models. *American Psychologist, 78*(1), 36–49. https://doi.org/10.1037/amp0000972

Liou, G., Bonner, C. V., & Tay, L. (2022). A psychometric view of technology-based assessments. *International Journal of Testing, 22*(3–4), 216–242. https://doi.org/10.1080/15305058.2022.2070757

McFarland, D. A., Lewis, K., & Goldberg, A. (2015). Sociology in the era of big data: The ascent of forensic social science. *The American Sociologist, 47*(1), 12–35. https://doi.org/10.1007/s12108-015-9291-8

Oswald, F. L., Behrend, T. S., Putka, D. J., & Sinar, E. (2020). Big data in industrial-organizational psychology and human resource management: Forward progress for organizational research and practice. *Annual Review of Organizational Psychology and Organizational Behavior, 7*(1), 505–533. https://doi.org/10.1146/annurev-orgpsych-032117-104553

Tay, L., Woo, S. E., Hickman, L., Booth, B. M., & D'Mello, S. (2022). A conceptual framework for investigating and mitigating Machine-Learning Measurement Bias (MLMB) in psychological assessment. *Advances in Methods and Practices in Psychological Science*, 5(1). https://doi.org/10.1177/25152459211061337

Woo, S. E., Tay, L., & Proctor, R. W. (Eds.). (2020). *Big data in psychological research*. American Psychological Association.

PART I

Foundations

CHAPTER I

Machine Learning Algorithms and Measurement

Q. Chelsea Song, Ivan Hernandez, Hyun Joo Shin,
Meaghan M. Tracy, and Mengqiao Liu

MACHINE LEARNING AND ITS UNIQUE CONTRIBUTION TO MEASUREMENT

Machine learning (ML) is a subfield of artificial intelligence that utilizes data to optimize predictions and discover underlying patterns (e.g., Mitchell, 1997). Compared to traditional approaches for measuring human attributes (e.g., classical testing theory, item response theory), machine learning uniquely contributes to measurement by being better suited to (1) utilize organic data and (2) capture complex relations. Organic data are naturally occurring digital footprints that are collected without reliance on a specific research design or measurement scale; examples include online search records, Twitter posts, and location data collected from fitness trackers (see Groves et al., 2011; Hickman, Bosch, et al., 2022; Xu et al., 2020). Such data convey rich behavioral and psychological traces embedded in everyday contexts, providing valuable information for measurement. However, due to their complexity and lack of structure, they were rarely utilized in psychological measurement – until the introduction of machine learning. With machine learning, we are now capable of analyzing a diverse and complex range of data, from self- and other-reports to audiovisual footprints. To name a few, machine learning is used to measure personality from interview videos (e.g., Hickman, Bosch, et al., 2022), stress and emotions from social media posts (e.g., Wang et al., 2016), and interpersonal relationships from proximity data obtained from wearable sensors (e.g., Matusik et al., 2019). Such capability allows for increased accuracy in measurement as well as ecological momentary assessment of human behavior and cognition – enabling a more comprehensive measurement of human psychology and behavior.

Machine learning can also capture complex relations (e.g., nonlinear relations and interactions), potentially uncovering new insights into psychological phenomena. Recent works utilized machine learning to study personality nuances at the facet and item levels, extending the theoretical and practical understanding of personality traits (e.g., Putka et al., 2018). Unlike traditional parametric methods, ML algorithms do not rely on a priori specification of dimensions, allowing for a more flexible examination of the data (e.g., Jiang et al., 2020). Finally, ML algorithms are capable of handling high-dimensional data (where the number of features is large relative to the sample size), enabling the integration of multiple and complex data types while seeking to maintain the accuracy and generalizability of measurement.

In general, machine learning contributes to measurement in two crucial ways: conceptualization of a construct (via unsupervised learning) and empirical keying (via supervised learning). Unsupervised learning aims to find structure or patterns within data, and it could be used to explore the structure of a construct (e.g., to identify depressive symptoms among a wide variety of mental health symptoms). Similar to factor analysis in classical testing theory, unsupervised learning contributes to the conceptualization of a construct, providing the foundation for measurement. Yet, compared to traditional measurement methods, unsupervised learning has the advantage of identifying patterns from a large set of unstructured data, potentially contributing to broadened conceptual understandings. Supervised learning aims to estimate certain psychological constructs (e.g., ability) from a set of features (e.g., interview transcripts, event logs). Supervised learning, when used in measurement, is effectively an empirical keying method to convert features (or variables) into construct estimates – similar to the empirical keys used in traditional measurement, yet with improved accuracy, scalability, and consistency.[1] Together, machine learning contributes to measurement through conceptualization and empirical keying.[2] In the sections below, we discuss common ML algorithms used in measurement.

---

[1] A construct estimate could be continuous (e.g., ability level) as well as categorical (e.g., depressive symptoms). When supervised learning is used to measure a continuous construct, the process is called *regression*; when it is used to measure a categorical construct, the process is termed *classification*.

[2] The use of unsupervised (contextualization) and supervised learning (empirical keying) ML algorithms in measurement are guided by different approaches, which vary on the theory-data spectrum. Hickman, Song and Woo (2022) provides a systematic discussion of these approaches, which include (1) the theory-driven, hypothetico deductive approach, (2) the construct-driven, data-flexible approach, and (3) the data-driven, construct-informing approach.

1.1 Overview of Common ML Algorithms Used in Measurement

1.1.1 General Procedures of Using ML Algorithms in Measurement

A variety of ML algorithms can be used for measurement, yet their applications follow the same general procedure, which we describe in this section.

Suppose we want to measure the conscientiousness facets that are most relevant to one's performance in a certain job. We start by using unsupervised learning to define the construct and determine its structure (i.e., conceptualize the construct). For example, we ask incumbents to describe characteristics that help them successfully perform the job, and use unsupervised learning (e.g., topic modeling) to identify the common themes mentioned in the textual descriptions. Suppose the analysis identifies two main themes – dutifulness and order.

Next, we use supervised learning to develop empirical keys for measuring dutifulness and order. To do this, we begin by collecting data for model training and evaluation. Supervised learning requires two types of data: features and "ground truth." Features are variables used to estimate the construct. For instance, features for dutifulness and order include video recordings of an individual completing a work sample, email correspondence and log files related to certain work tasks, and human resource records on attendance – they all convey behavioral and psychological traces that reflect the construct. "Ground truth" is an operationalization of a construct provided by an existing, valid measure.[3] For instance, the "ground truth" of dutifulness and order could include self-reported facet-level scores from the NEO Personality Inventory-Revised (Costa & McCrae, 1992).

To train and evaluate an ML model, we split the dataset into two parts: training and test sets. The training set is used for training the model (or finding the empirical keys), and the test set is used to evaluate the performance of the model.

During model training, we first select an ML algorithm, and use the training data to find an optimal set of parameters that most accurately estimates the "ground truth" from the features. Hyperparameter tuning and cross-validation are used to find the optimal parameters, and the resulting model is called the trained model. For example, suppose we want to train an elastic net ML model to measure individuals' dutifulness and order. The elastic net model includes a number of parameters (e.g., feature

---

[3] The choice of "ground truth" is critical for construct validation. For a discussion of this issue, see Braun and Kuljanin (2015) and Tay et al. (2020).

weights) whose value could be adjusted to more accurately estimate the construct. We use hyperparameter tuning and cross-validation to systematically review a range of potential values for the parameters and identify the best set of values that provide the construct estimates most closely resembling the "ground truth" (e.g., self-reported dutifulness and order). These selected parameter values are used to specify the trained model.

Following model training, the next step is to evaluate the model using a test set. For example, we use the trained model to estimate individuals' dutifulness and order from their task completion log files and compare the estimates with self-reported dutifulness and order (the "ground truth"). If the model estimates approximate the "ground truth" well, the model passes the evaluation. The final model could be used to measure dutifulness and order in new samples.

In the following section, we describe the common ML algorithms used for measurement. The algorithms, as well as their example applications, are summarized in Table 1.1.

1.1.2   *Unsupervised Learning Algorithms*

1.1.2.1   *Clustering Methods*

Clustering methods are a type of unsupervised learning that seeks to discover distinct groupings (e.g., types of symptoms, groups of people). Clustering has been used to conceptualize collaborative problem-solving skills from log data of online simulation tasks (Polyak et al., 2017) and identify depressive symptoms from self-rated and clinician-rated depression scale scores (Chekroud et al., 2017).

k-Means Clustering: k-means clustering is one of the earliest and most commonly used clustering algorithms (MacQueen, 1967; Steinhaus, 1956). It first calculates the "mean" of k random sets of observations and uses them to determine k initial center points. Then, for each initial center point, the algorithm identifies a cluster of data that is closest to the center point and updates the location of the center point based on the mean of the new cluster. The algorithm iterates through these steps until the total within-cluster variance is minimized and the center points no longer change substantially (Hastie et al., 2009).

1.1.2.2   *Topic Modeling*

Topic modeling is used to find recurring semantic patterns among texts. One of the most popular topic modeling approaches is latent

Table 1.1 Description of common ML algorithms and their example measurement applications

Algorithms	Brief description	Example	Resources
Unsupervised learning			
k-means clustering	Calculates the "mean" of k random sets of data to determine k initial center points. For each initial center, the algorithm identifies a cluster of data that is closest to the center point, and repeatedly updates the location of the center point until the total within-cluster variance is minimized and the center points are stable.	Classify collaborative problem-solving skills of individuals from log files of online simulation (Polyak et al., 2017)	Steinhaus (1956)
Topic modeling	Identifies themes within documents. A common topic modeling algorithm, LDA, uses the distribution of the keywords in the documents.	Identify facets of job satisfaction from textual reviews (Jung & Suh, 2019)	Blei et al. (2003)
Supervised learning			
Linear regression			
OLS regression	OLS regression models the linear relation between the features and the outcomes of interest by minimizing the squared differences between the estimated and observed outcomes (i.e., the residuals) in the training data.	Measure dark side of personality from social media status updates (Akhtar et al., 2018)	Kenney and Keeping (1962)
Regularization			
Ridge	Ridge regression aims to reduce model overfit by shrinking feature weights *toward* zero without fully eliminating them through regularization.	Measure Big Five personality traits from Facebook profile status messages (Park et al., 2015)	Hoerl and Kennard (1970)

Table 1.1 (cont.)

Algorithms	Brief description	Example	Resources
LASSO	Similar to ridge regression, however, LASSO allows certain feature weights to be shrunk to zero, enabling both feature selection and regularization (shrinking *toward* zero).	Measure HEXACO personality from Facebook activities (Youyou et al., 2015)	Tibshirani (1996)
Elastic net	Improves upon ridge and LASSO regression by including both the penalty terms so that feature weights are shrunk both toward zero (regularization) *and* to zero (feature selection) and allows adjustment of the strength of regularization and feature selection.	Measure Big Five personality from automated video interviews (Hickman, Bosch, et al., 2022)	Zou and Hastie (2005)
Nearest neighbor			
k-NN	Classifies or estimates the value of an unknown observation through its nearest neighbors whose values are known. The final classification or estimate is determined by majority vote or through averaging.	Measure likelihood of a user spreading disinformation on social media by comparing their writing style to other known disinformation spreaders (Cardaioli et al., 2020)	Fix and Hodges (1951)
Tree-based models			
Decision trees	Partitions (or splits) data using if-then decision rules determined by the features. The feature that accounts for the most unexplained variance is introduced first, followed by the next most discriminatory feature, and so on.	Measure leadership style preference using educational degree, major, gender, and marital status (Salehzadeh, 2017)	Quinlan (1986)

Method	Description	Example application	Reference
Bagged trees and random forest	Bagged trees: trains multiple decision trees with bootstrapped samples from the training data. Random forest: trains multiple decision trees with bootstrapped samples, but the features of each decision tree are introduced at random. For both algorithms, the trained trees are separately used to estimate construct scores, and the final construct estimate is the average across (regression) or majority vote of (classification) the decision trees estimates.	Measure job performance from performance appraisal narratives from supervisors (Speer, 2020) Measure suicide intention from individuals' health care registry data (Gradus et al., 2020)	Breiman (1996) Breiman (2001)
Gradient-boosted trees	Trains decision trees that improve upon each other by learning from the previous decision tree. Stochastic gradient-boosted trees use random subsets from the training data to improve estimation.	Measure the degree that a job applicant taking a personality assessment was inflating their true personality trait scores (Calanna et al., 2020)	Friedman (2001, 2002)
Support vector machine	Estimates construct scores from linear and nonlinear relations by finding the optimal hyperplane (or threshold) that denotes the separation between data of different classes (classification) or the best approximation of the relation between outcomes and features within a given margin of error (regression).	Measure emotion from electroencephalography signals (Hassanien et al., 2018)	Drucker et al. (1996)
Neural network	Consists of complex interconnected structures that allow discovery of patterns and underlying relations in a set of data.	Measure psychopathy from tweets (Ahmad et al., 2020)	Hanson and Salamon (1990)

17

Dirichlet allocation (LDA; Blei et al., 2003), which aims to find the thematic structure within text documents. LDA identifies the theme of the documents based on the distribution of the keywords included in the documents (Chaney & Blei, 2012). Other topic modeling approaches include structural topic models (Roberts et al., 2014), which take into account covariates when creating topics; hierarchical LDA (Blei et al., 2003), which identifies topic hierarchies; and Top2vec (Angelov, 2020), which converts each of the N documents into a series of K numbers representing their standing on a variety of underlying dimensions (i.e., a document embedding, e.g., Doc2Vec, Universal Sentence Encoder, BERT) and applies clustering methods to the $N \times K$ data matrix.

Example Applications of Unsupervised Learning Algorithms

Clustering: Polyak et al. (2017) used k-means clustering to identify profiles of collaborative problem-solving skills exhibited in an online simulation game scenario. In the online game, players collaborate with an automated virtual agent to complete various missions (e.g., solve a passcode to unlock a door, discover a sequence of power transfer steps). The players engage in dialogues with the virtual agent, where in each dialogue, the virtual agent provides a prompt, and the player reacts by choosing a response among multiple options. The player's response choices, as well as other behavior data (e.g., number of mouse clicks, keystrokes, dialog selection timing) are recorded in a log file – this log file provides organic data with behavioral traces that reflect the player's collaborative problem-solving skills. The researchers conducted k-means clustering analysis on the log files and identified different profiles of collaborative problem-solving skills among players. These profiles allow researchers to further develop measures (e.g., games, response options) that better capture a comprehensive range of collaborative problem-solving skills.

In general, compared to traditional approaches where researchers manually code qualitative data to distill and categorize patterns (e.g., types of collaborative problem-solving skills), unsupervised learning methods offer more efficiency and scalability. This is especially important for measuring and studying collaborative problem-solving skills under new contexts, such as during remote and hybrid work. For example, researchers could analyze Slack (the online messaging application) data with the clustering method demonstrated in Polyak et al. (2017) to study how coworkers are collaborating with each other to solve problems during in-person and remote work settings.

Topic Modeling: Jung and Suh (2019) used LDA to identify facets of job satisfaction from 35,063 textual employee reviews posted on an online job site (that capture employees' organic description of their jobs). The algorithm identified 30 different facets of job satisfaction, ranging from satisfaction toward organizational culture to work intensity and efficacy. Among these facets, some (e.g., satisfaction toward supervisor and pay) align with existing theory, while others (e.g., satisfaction toward project, interfirm relationship) provide new insights to existing literature. Topic modeling contributed to improved understanding and measurement of employee job satisfaction.

1.1.3 Supervised Learning Algorithms

1.1.3.1 Linear Regression

Linear regression models a linear relation between the features and the outcomes of interest. For example, in simple linear regression, feature X and outcome Y are modeled as: $y = B_0 + B_1 X$, where B_0 represents the intercept of the regression line (i.e., the outcome value when the features are held constant at 0), and B_1 represents the slope of the regression line (i.e., feature weights, or how the outcome changes given one unit increase in a feature). Multiple linear regression consists of multiple features and one outcome and is expressed as: $y = B_0 + B_1 X_1 + B_2 X_2 + \ldots + B_n X_n$.

Ordinary Least Squares (OLS) Regression: OLS regression (Kenney & Keeping, 1962) aims to minimize the squared differences between the estimated and observed outcomes in the training data. This squared difference is termed the least squares error and is calculated as: $\sum_{i=1}^{N} \left(y_i - \widehat{y_i} \right)^2$, where $\widehat{y_i}$ is the estimated outcome obtained using the regression model and y_i is the observed outcome value. OLS regression aims to find a set of intercept and feature weights that minimize the cost function, and the resulting model provides the best linear representation of the relation between the feature and the outcome.

Although linear regression models are simple and commonly used for measurement, they are prone to model overfit (and high bias, as we discuss later). That is, linear regression models have the tendency to capture uniqueness in the training data, resulting in inaccuracy when they are used for measurement in new data or a new sample. For example, in Figure 1.1, Panel 1 shows a regression line (dashed line) that is trained with the training data (triangles). Although the regression line fits the training data well, as shown in Panel 2, it does not accurately model the test set

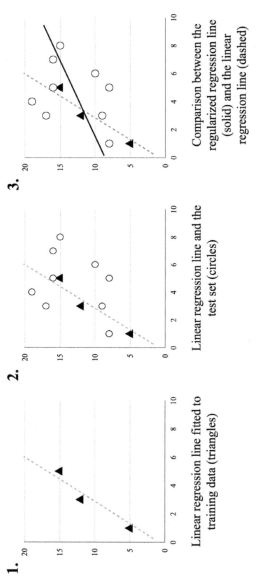

1. Linear regression line fitted to training data (triangles)

2. Linear regression line and the test set (circles)

3. Comparison between the regularized regression line (solid) and the linear regression line (dashed)

Figure 1.1   Comparison of linear and regularized regression models (circles), suggesting that the regression model overfitted to the training data and will not perform well in a new sample.

1.1.3.2 Regularization

Regularization is a family of regression algorithms introduced to overcome the risk of model overfit. Figure 1.1, Panel 3 shows the regularized regression line (solid line). Compared to the overfitted linear regression line (dashed line), the regularized line fits well with both the training and test sets, resulting in higher estimation accuracy in the test set.

This improvement in regularization model accuracy is related to model bias and variance. Model bias refers to the systematic difference between the true population estimate and the model estimate; and variance refers to the variation in model accuracy when the model is applied to different sets of data. The combination of bias and variance determines the overall accuracy of a model: a model has higher accuracy when both the bias and variance are small. When training a model, we aim to lower both bias and variance. However, it is difficult to minimize both bias and variance in a model (a problem known as "bias-variance tradeoff"; Hastie et al., 2009). Regularization algorithms aim to increase estimation accuracy by striking an optimal balance between bias and variance. This is done through the regularization cost function, which includes the OLS least squares error term, a penalty term to regularize bias (and thus variance), and a tuning parameter to find an optimal balance between bias and variance. Regularization includes ridge (Hoerl & Kennard, 1970), LASSO (Tibshirani, 1996), LARS (Efron et al., 2004), and elastic net regression (Zou & Hastie, 2005).

Ridge Regression: Model overfit could be caused by multicollinearity (or redundancy among features) and large feature weights. Ridge regression aims to reduce model overfit by shrinking (regularizing) the feature weights (or regression coefficients) *toward* zero without fully eliminating them (Hoerl & Kennard, 1970). The ridge regression cost function is: $\sum_{i=1}^{N}(y_i - \hat{y}_i)^2 + \lambda\sum_{j=0}^{M}w_j^2$ where w is the feature weight for each j feature and λ is the tuning parameter that determines the regularization strength. The cost function includes a least squares error term, $\sum_{i=1}^{N}(y_i - \hat{y}_i)^2$, and a ridge regression penalty term, $\sum_{j=0}^{M}w_j^2$. The penalty term adds to the overall error of the model, especially for large feature weights, and the strength of the regularization is adjusted by λ. As shown in Figure 1.2, the ridge regression penalty term (represented by the bolded circle border) constrains the feature weights to a limited solution space (represented by the gray-shaded circle area). The intersection between the solution space (gray-shaded circle) and the least squares error (ellipse) provides a solution that minimizes the ridge regression cost function and strikes an optimal balance between bias and variance.

LASSO Regression: LASSO regression, similar to ridge regression, also aims to reduce model overfit; however, unlike ridge regression, LASSO allows certain feature weights to be shrunk *to* zero, enabling both feature selection and regularization (shrinking *toward* zero; Tibshirani, 1996). The LASSO cost function is: $\sum_{i=1}^{N} \left(y_i - \hat{y}_i \right)^2 + \lambda \sum_{j=0}^{M} \left| w_j \right|$, where the penalty term is $\sum_{j=0}^{M} \left| w_j \right|$. Compared to the ridge penalty term $\sum_{j=0}^{M} w_j^2$ (sum of squared coefficients), the LASSO penalty term is the sum of squared absolute coefficients, which allows the feature weights to be zero. As shown in Figure 1.2, the intersection between the solution space constrained by the LASSO penalty term (represented by the gray-shaded diamond) and the least squares error (ellipse) is where the feature weight, β_2, is zero, effectively dropping that feature.

Elastic Net Regression: Elastic net regression combines the characteristics of both ridge and LASSO regressions (Zou & Hastie, 2005). The elastic net cost function is: $\sum_{i=1}^{N} \left(y_i - \hat{y}_i \right)^2 + \lambda \left[\alpha \sum_{j=0}^{M} \left| w_j \right| + (1 - \alpha) \sum_{j=0}^{M} w_j^2 \right]$, and the penalty term consists of both the ridge and LASSO penalty terms, where α determines how much emphasis each term receives. The optimal α value could be specified by the user or found via hyperparameter tuning.

1.1.3.3 Nearest Neighbor Algorithms

Nearest neighbor algorithms are memory-based methods where an unknown point is classified or estimated using information from other data points close to it (i.e., the nearest neighbors). Nearest neighbor algorithms include k-nearest neighbors (k-NN), approximate nearest neighbors (Arya et al., 1998), and t-distributed stochastic neighbor embedding (Van der Maaten & Hinton, 2008), among which k-NN is the most widely used.

k-Nearest Neighbors: k-NN could be used for both classification and regression. When used for classification, k-NN classifies an unknown observation through its "nearest neighbor" whose outcomes are known (Altman, 1992; Fix & Hodges, 1951). k represents the number of nearest neighbors used to classify the unknown observation. As shown in Figure 1.3, Example 1 (top panel), when $k = 1$, we label the unknown

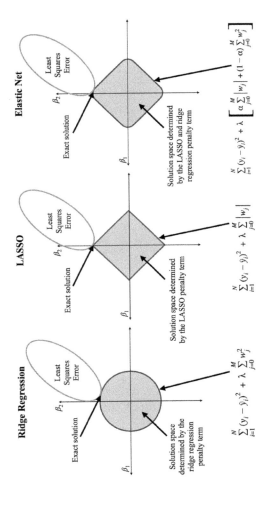

Figure 1.2 Comparison among three regularization algorithms: ridge, LASSO, elastic net

Note. This figure provides a comparison among the three common regularization algorithms. For each algorithm, the penalty term (represented by the black bolded border) constrains the feature weights to a limited solution space (represented by the gray-shaded area). The intersection between the solution space (gray-shaded area) and the least squares error (ellipse) provides a solution that minimizes the cost function of each algorithm (ridge, LASSO, elastic net).

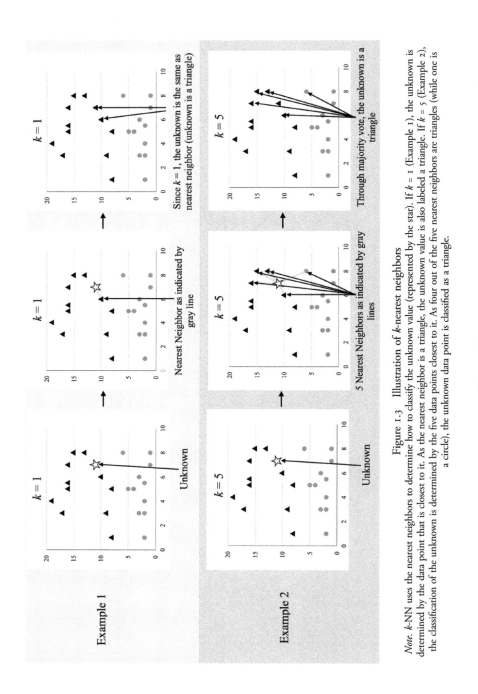

Figure 1.3   Illustration of *k*-nearest neighbors

Note. *k*-NN uses the nearest neighbors to determine how to classify the unknown value (represented by the star). If *k* = 1 (Example 1), the unknown is determined by the data point that is closest to it. As the nearest neighbor is a triangle, the unknown value is also labeled a triangle. If *k* = 5 (Example 2), the classification of the unknown is determined by the five data points closest to it. As four out of the five nearest neighbors are triangles (while one is a circle), the unknown data point is classified as a triangle.

(represented by the star) based on the closest data point, which is a triangle. Thus, the unknown value is also classified as a triangle. If $k > 1$, the classification of the unknown observation is determined by a majority vote from the k nearest neighbors. As shown in Figure 1.3, Example 2 (bottom panel), if $k = 5$, we first identify five nearest neighbors of the unknown point (star). The five nearest neighbors include four triangles and one circle. Thus, through majority vote, the unknown value is labeled as a triangle. For regression models, the predicted outcome of an unknown observation is a weighted average, where the weights are the inverse distance between each neighbor and the unknown observation.

k-NN has a number of advantages. It does not assume linearity, and thus could be used to model different relations flexibly. It is also a memory-based model where no pretraining of the algorithm is required (i.e., "lazy learning"; Bontempi et al., 1999). However, k-NN requires observations from all possible feature combinations, and thus is susceptible to the "curse of dimensionality" (Kouiroukidis & Evangelidis, 2011) and requires high computational power (Kotsiantis, 2007). It also assumes all features are equally important, unlike regularization that allows for feature selection or regularization of less important features.

1.1.3.4   Tree-Based Models

Tree-based models are recursive partitioning methods that are nonparametric and highly flexible. The most common tree-based models include decision trees (Morgan & Sonquist, 1963), bagged trees (Breiman, 1996), random forests (Breiman, 2001), and gradient-boosted trees (Friedman, 2001).

Decision Trees: Decision trees are the simplest of the tree-based algorithms and use if-then decision rules (Quinlan, 1986). The algorithm begins by selecting features that account for the most unexplained variance in the data. It then partitions the data based on different values of the features, and this process is repeated until all the observations are classified or estimated. For classification trees, the outcome is the probability (%) of an observation belonging to a certain group; for regression trees, the outcome is a continuous estimate (James et al., 2013). Figure 1.4 provides an example of a decision tree for classification. In the example, Feature 1 is first used to partition the data. The data points that meet Feature 1's cutoff is classified as "A," and the rest is further partitioned using Feature 2. The remaining features are subsequently introduced to the model, and the process is repeated until the classification is complete.

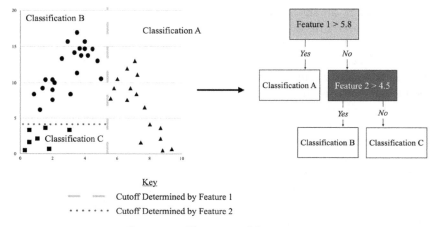

Key
— — — —   Cutoff Determined by Feature 1
· · · · · · ·   Cutoff Determined by Feature 2

Figure 1.4   Illustration of decision tree

Note. Illustrates a classification tree. Data is split based on the cutoffs (or decision rules) determined by the features. For example, Feature 1 (in light gray) is the feature that accounts for the most unexplained variance in the data and therefore is introduced to the model first. The data points whose Feature 1 value is greater than the 5.8 cutoff (as indicated by the dashed line) are classified as "A" and the rest is further partitioned using Feature 2. The data points whose Feature 2 value is greater than the 4.5 cutoff (as indicated by the dotted line) are classified as "B." The rest of the data points are classified as "C."

Decision trees allow for intuitive interpretation and visualization (as demonstrated in Figure 1.4). They are also flexible in detecting non-linearity and interactions between features and outcomes (Quinlan, 1986). However, decision trees are limited in that they exhibit high variance (and are thus susceptible to model overfit): the effect of an error in a decision rule affects all of the following splits. Because of this, a second independent sample of observations is often used to prune the decision rules to reduce overfitting and high variance in estimations (Hastie et al., 2009; Myles et al., 2004).

Bagged Trees: Bagged trees address the limitations of decision trees by aggregating the results of multiple decision trees to find one stable outcome (i.e., lower variance; Breiman, 1996). First, the algorithm trains a number of decision trees using independent bootstrapped samples of the training data. These trained trees are then used to estimate the constructs in the test data, and the individual estimates are aggregated to form the final construct estimate. We demonstrate this process in Figure 1.5. First, decision trees are trained using bootstrapped samples of the training data.

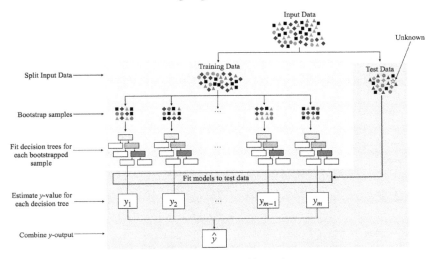

Figure 1.5   Illustration of bagged trees

Note. The aim in this example is to classify or estimate the unknown data point (the star). y is the model estimate and m is the number of decision trees. The light gray area presents the model training process, and the dark gray area presents the process of using the model to estimate constructs in the test set. First, decision trees are trained using bootstrapped samples of the training data. These trained trees are then used to estimate the construct scores in the test set $(y_1, y_2, \ldots, y_m)$. The resulting construct estimates from individual decision trees are then aggregated to form the final construct estimate $(\hat{y})$. For regression, the final construct estimate is the average across the decision trees; for classification, the final construct estimate is a majority vote from the classification outcomes of each tree.

These trained trees are then used to estimate the construct in the test set $(y_1, y_2, \ldots, y_m;$ indicated by the star). The resulting construct estimates from the individual decision trees are then aggregated to form the final construct estimate (y). For regression, the final construct estimate is the average across the decision trees; for classification, the final construct estimate is a majority vote from the classification outcomes of each tree.

Bagged trees are more recommended than decision trees as they account for the latter's tendency to overfit. However, bagged trees are not without limitations. For example, in bagged trees, the estimated values of the individual decision trees tend to be highly correlated with each other, lacking the diversity needed to reflect the full outcome space and, therefore, may result in low estimation accuracy (Quinlan, 1996).

Random Forests: Random forests address the limitations of bagged trees through feature sampling (Breiman, 2001). Similar to bagged trees,

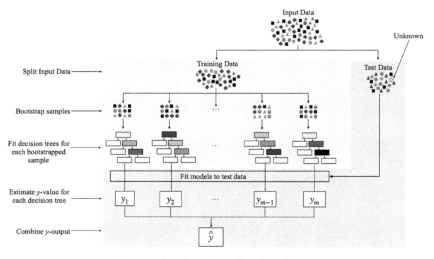

Figure 1.6   Illustration of random forests

Note. y is the model estimate and *m* is the number of decision trees. Similar to our example of bagged trees (Figure 1.5), the aim is to classify or estimate the unknown data point (the white star). The light gray area presents the model training process, and the dark gray area presents the process of using the model to estimate constructs in the test set. First, decision trees are trained using bootstrapped samples of the training data, where the features included in the trees are *randomly selected.* These trained trees are then used to estimate the construct scores in the test set (y_1, y_2, . . ., y_m). The resulting construct estimates from individual decision trees are then aggregated to form the final construct estimate ($\hat{y}$). For regression, the final construct estimate is the average across the decision trees; for classification, the final construct estimate is a majority vote from the classification outcomes of each tree.

in random forests, multiple decision trees are trained using independent bootstrapped samples, and the trained trees are then used to obtain estimates. The final construct estimates are obtained by aggregating the estimates from the individual decision trees. However, unlike bagged trees that use all features to train the trees, random forests randomly choose the features to train each tree (i.e., feature sampling). By randomly sampling the features, the estimates from the decision trees are less likely to be correlated with each other and thus are more reflective of the outcome space, contributing to improved estimation accuracy (Breiman, 2001). Figure 1.6 illustrates a random forest. Compared to bagged trees (Figure 1.5), in random forests, each decision tree is fitted onto boot-strapped samples of the training data using *random* features, as shown in Figure 1.6, where the various features (boxes) are randomly presented across the decision trees.

Gradient-Boosted Trees: While the bagged trees and random forests independently train decision trees, in gradient-boosted trees, the subsequent decision trees improve upon the previous decision trees, further increasing estimation accuracy. The algorithm first trains a decision tree using the full training data. The residuals, or the unexplained variance, from the first tree are then used to train a second decision tree, and this process is repeated until the residuals become smaller than a user-specified threshold. Figure 1.7 shows an illustration of gradient-boosted trees.

Stochastic Gradient-Boosted Trees: Gradient-boosted trees train decision trees using the full training data, and thus could be computationally intense and sensitive to local minima. To address this issue, scholastic gradient-boosted trees (SGBT) randomly sample subsets of the training set to train the individual trees. Each new tree is trained based on previous trees to reduce residuals and improve measurement, especially in areas not well estimated in previous samples. Compared to gradient-boosted trees, SGBT tends to provide more stable and accurate estimates, and is computationally more efficient (Hastie et al., 2009).

1.1.3.5 Support Vector Machines

Support vector machines (SVM) (Drucker et al., 1996) offers a robust method for predicting outcomes with nonlinear relation to the features. SVM does so by using kernel functions to apply mathematical transformations of the feature space to model complex relations. SVM also relies only on a small but critical subset of the training data to guide classification and estimation, and thus is less influenced by outliers. Thus, when there are many features compared to the sample size (i.e., high p to n ratio), SVM tends to perform better compared to regression and tree-based approaches (Kotsiantis, 2007). Finally, SVM uses an "error tube" to allow for a certain level of error in classification and estimation, making it possible to make classification or estimation in cases of complex relations.

1.1.3.6 Neural Networks

Neural networks are inspired by the way the human brain operates. Similar to the way neurons propagate signals, neural networks consist of complex interconnected structures that allow them to discover patterns and recognize underlying relations within a set of data (Hanson & Salamon, 1990). In addition, unlike other ML algorithms that require the data to be

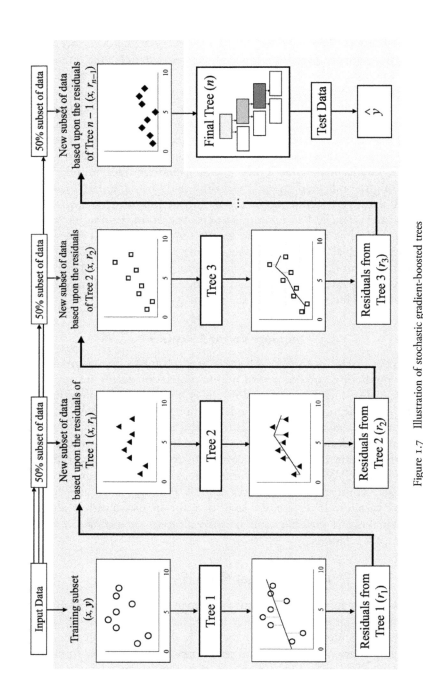

Figure 1.7 Illustration of stochastic gradient-boosted trees

Note. First, a decision tree, Tree 1, is trained with the entire training data (circles) to estimate the outcome, *y*. The residuals of Tree 1, γ_1, are calculated as the difference between the estimated and observed outcomes (*y*). Then, a new decision tree, Tree 2, is trained with a randomly selected subset of the training data to estimate the Tree 1 residual, γ_1. This process (where the residuals from the previous tree are used to train a new tree) is repeated over *n* iterations until the residuals are constant. The last decision tree is the final decision tree and is used to estimate the construct score (*ŷ*).

(a) Perceptron Network   **(b) Feedforward Network**

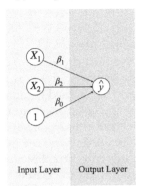
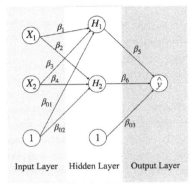

Input Layer   Output Layer   Input Layer   Hidden Layer   Output Layer

Figure 1.8   Illustration of neural networks: a perceptron neural network and a
feedforward network with a single hidden layer

Note. Panel (a) represents the perceptron network, where multiple features connect to one output
layer. X represents the input variables (or features). β represents a weight value which the value of
the connected variable is multiplied by to obtain the output passed to the receiving node. This
weight is adjusted during training to minimize prediction error. $\hat{y}$ represents the estimated
construct score which is computed from multiplying, summing, and transforming the values of
the connected input variables. Panel (b) represents the feedforward network which adds the
additional "hidden layer" between the input variables and the estimate. In this panel, H represents
the value computed from multiplying, summing, and transforming the values of the
connected input variables.

distilled into important features, neural networks perform feature engineering within the network. These properties make neural networks adept
at analyzing unstructured data with ill-defined features, including text,
images, and audio.

The simplest form of a neural network is called a perceptron.
Perceptrons have a series of input nodes (the features) that connect to a
single output node. Figure 1.8a presents a perceptron with two input
nodes that correspond to two features: x_1 and x_2. It also includes a constant
node; if the constant is 1 (as shown in Figure 1.8a), the perceptron is
mathematically equivalent to a linear regression. Each connection has a
specific weight (e.g., β_0, β_1, β_2 in Figure 1.8a) that the neural network can
modify to better estimate the outcome.

Neural networks typically consist of multiple perceptrons, allowing
them to model complex relations. Perceptrons whose outputs are inputs
into another perceptron are called "feedforward neural networks" (Bengio,
2009). As demonstrated in Figure 1.8b, feedforward neural networks add
an additional layer of neurons between the input and the output, called the

hidden layer (in Figure 1.8b, the two nodes in the hidden layer are labeled "H₁" and "H₂"). The hidden layers allow feedforward networks to model complex relations between inputs and outputs (Lu et al., 2017). Networks with many hidden layers are termed "deep neural networks."

The goal of training a neural network is to adjust the weight values in the network so that the transformation of the input features is as close to the desired output as possible. Neural networks are trained in an iterative process. Rather than sending all of the training data at once through the network, the network works on a subset of the training data in each iteration. In each iteration, the weights obtained from the previous iterations are used to estimate outputs in the current subset, and the estimated outputs are compared to the "ground truth." Based on how well the estimated outputs approximated the "ground truth" (i.e., the magnitude of the error), the weights are further updated. After being provided all of the data, the network can revisit the dataset, and continue to adjust its weights, until the errors reach a certain acceptable threshold. This process of using errors in previous weights to inform further weight updates is called "backpropagation." An example of backpropagation is shown in Figure 1.9. The goal of the network is to identify whether the 9 pixel × 9 pixel image (on the left of the figure) is a diamond or a square. The network includes 81 input features (see "Input Layer"), representing the color (gray vs. black) of the 81 pixels in the image. First, the network generates a set of weights through forward propagation. The network uses this set of weights to identify the image, and the output suggests a 20% probability that the image is a diamond, and an 80% probability that the image is a square. Because the image is a diamond (i.e., the ground truth is 100% probability that the image is a diamond and 0% probability that the image is a square), the current outputs are inaccurate. To improve the accuracy, the network revisits the dataset and continues to adjust its weights through backpropagation. Backpropagation allows the network to eventually approximate the data with high accuracy (Lu et al., 2017).

Neural networks can easily overfit to the training data, especially if the model is overly complex. One can mitigate this problem by limiting the number of times (i.e., epochs) the training data passes through the neural network when finding weights or using ridge or LASSO to regularize the weights. Some analysts mitigate overfitting through "dropout," or temporarily removing a random proportion of nodes. Additionally, analysts can control the learning rate so that changes to the weights are gradual and less influenced by individual data points.

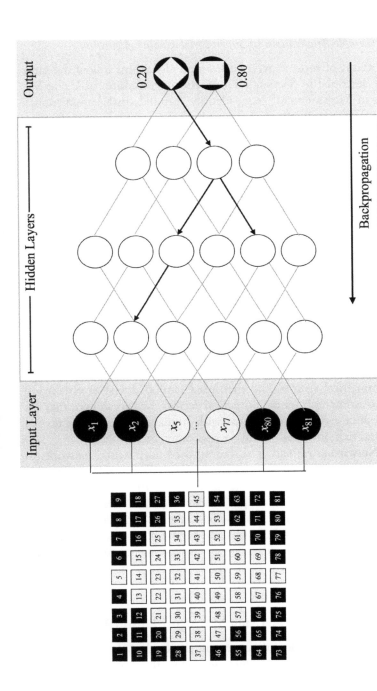

Figure 1.9   Illustration of neural networks: backpropagation

Note. When estimating the shape within the far-left image, data are input into the input layer (pixels) and to the output. As seen in the output layer, the neural network inaccurately estimated that the shape is likely a square (0.80). To correct this error, and forward propagated through the hidden layers the network updates the weights (white circles) in the hidden layers to through back propagation (indicated by the bolded arrows). This process is repeated until the correct shape is estimated the majority of the time.

Example Applications of Supervised Learning Algorithms

The applications of most supervised learning algorithms follow the same procedures described in Section 1.1.1 "General Procedures of Using ML Algorithms in Measurement" (e.g., identify "ground truth," train model, test model). We now briefly describe a number of example applications.

Elastic Net Regression: Hickman, Bosch, et al. (2022) used elastic net regression to measure Big Five personality traits from automated video interviews. The researchers separately trained two kinds of elastic net models, each treating self-reported and interviewer-reported Big Five personality traits as the "ground truth." To train the models, the researchers first extracted verbal, paraverbal, and nonverbal behavior indicators from video clips of individuals responding to interview questions. The behavior indicators were converted to numerical vectors, and elastic net models were trained to obtain personality estimates that approximate the "ground truth."

Random Forest: Speer (2020) used random forest to measure job performance from performance appraisal narratives. Performance appraisal narratives are textual descriptions of employee job performance, typically provided by supervisors; they provide organic descriptions of employees' performance, as illustrated by the supervisor. The researchers first used natural language processing techniques (e.g., n-gram scoring) to convert texts into numerical vectors, and then used random forest to obtain job performance estimates from the numerical vectors. Results showed that the job performance estimates converged with human ratings of the textual narratives and demonstrated validity across different samples.

Neural Networks: Ahmad et al. (2020) used deep neural networks to measure personality dark triads from tweets (from Twitter). Three psychiatrists annotated each tweet in the training set to "dark triad" (e.g., psychopath) and "light triad" (e.g., nonpsychopath); these annotations served as the "ground truth" for model training. To train the neural network model, the researchers first used natural language processing techniques (e.g., work embedding) to preprocess the textual tweets into numeric vectors, and then trained neural network models to obtain personality dark-triad estimates from the numeric vectors.

1.2   Recommendations for Using ML Algorithms in Measurement

A number of factors could influence our choice of ML algorithms for measurement. These factors include: (1) the balance between interpretability and estimation accuracy, (2) the missingness present in the training data, and (3) the computational demands of the models.

I.2.1 Interpretability versus Estimation Accuracy

ML models differ in their interpretability: for some models, it is easy to understand how the inputs are transformed into an output value, while that is not the case for others. Models whose learned relations are easy to infer and describe are called "white-box" models. Models that generate complex rules more difficult to understand are referred to as "black-box"[4] models.

I.2.1.1 White-Box Models
Overview of White-Box Models: Linear regression is an example of a "white-box" model, where the intercept and regression coefficients clearly illustrate the relation between the features and the estimates and provide sufficient information to reproduce the estimates. In a regression model, the intercept represents the expected value of the outcome, when the features are 0. The regression coefficients of a feature represent the amount of expected change in the outcome per one-unit increase in that feature, holding all other features constant. Decision trees are also considered white-box models because the process of obtaining an outcome from the features is expressed using intuitive declarative rules (e.g., whether a feature value is greater or smaller than a cutoff). Comprehension of these rules does not require sophisticated mathematical training, making the model clear and easy to interpret.

Benefits of White-Box Models: The benefits to using white-box models include (1) theoretical development, (2) defensibility, and (3) model evaluation. White-box models provide clear processes that illustrate the relations among variables, which could help derive parsimonious explanations and thus improve the theoretical understanding of the variables. Additionally, white-box models offer clarity on the features used, the relative importance of the features, and the relation between the feature and the outcome, allowing one to defend the conclusions of the model. Finally, white-box models are intuitive, facilitating the evaluation of the model coefficients to what would be expected by theory, thus promoting greater confidence and trust in the model (Winkielman et al., 2003).

---

[4] We restrict this term to opaqueness caused by complexity and not proprietary secrecy (Rudin, 2019).

1.2.1.2   Black-Box Models

Overview of Black-Box Models: Models with architectures that cannot translate to concise explanations are called black-box models. Random forests, SVM, and deep neural networks are considered "black-box" models. Random forests contain hundreds of trees, each with their own set of features and decision rules. SVM projects the feature onto a multi-modal nonlinear surface to create decision boundaries. Neural networks contain dozens of sequential hidden layers that nonlinearly transform the outputs of each prior layer. These models are complex, which can confer many advantages, but at the expense of the interpretability, defensibility, and intuitiveness.

Benefits of Black-Box Models: The benefits of black-box models include (1) potentially higher model accuracy, (2) robustness across different problems, and (3) feature engineering capability. First, compared to white-box models, black-box models have the potential to better capture the relation between features and outcomes because they typically contain many more parameters than their white-box counterparts. Second, black-box models are useful for modeling a wide range of feature-outcome relations, especially when the relation is complex. Black-box models are often useful when one does not yet have an a priori picture of the underlying relation. Third, black-box models can automatically engineer features, allowing the models to capture key higher-order relations. Researchers often seek to generate new feature variables from existing variables, such as by aggregating personality items to form a composite. Models like neural networks and random forests create higher-order representations of variables based on the relations reflected in the data, thus increasing the accuracy of the model.

1.2.2   Data Missingness

Training data commonly consist of missing inputs. For example, participants may forget or refuse to complete a response; they may run out of time or not understand the instructions; and data collection software may experience an error or internet outage. These missing data points could significantly impact the performance of some ML algorithms (Rubin, 1976).

Linear regressions, SVM, and neural networks require the input data to be complete (and without missingness). For those algorithms, researchers are advised to use an imputation approach that approximates the true value of the missing data point (e.g., stochastic model-based imputation) to meet the requirement of the algorithm while preserving information conveyed in the data (Newman, 2014). Decision trees, random forests, and gradient-boosted trees can automatically handle missingness through methods such as surrogate identification (e.g., imputing missing value using complete value from a neighboring/similar case; Batista & Monard, 2002), median imputation (e.g., imputing missing value with the median of the observed data for that column), and more sophisticated sparsity-aware splitting (e.g., building decision trees by assigning missing entries to different split sides and determining which assignment provides the largest maximum gain; Chen & Guestrin, 2016). These algorithms do not require any prior imputation, which is useful for situations where imputation is computationally infeasible. However, these missing data treatments that only impute the single most-likely value for a given set of predictor values tend to demonstrate greater error in reproducing the natural variability within the original data. To more accurately reproduce the variance of the columns, researchers can use stochastic model-based imputation, which applies randomness to the predicted/imputed values. (Newman, 2014).

1.2.3   Computational Resources

Users often have limited computational resources and time for training ML models. Certain models require more advanced computational resources, such as random access memory (RAM), computational processing unit (CPU), and graphics processing unit (GPU).

1.2.3.1   *Memory Requirements: RAM*

RAM is a computer hardware for storing information during computation. Larger RAM allows for more data and parameters to be processed during model training. If the model training requirement exceeds the available RAM, it may result in an error in the model or the computer may terminate the operation. RAM requirement is determined by the sample size, number of features, and the model's parameterization. Larger sample sizes, number of features, and number of parameters require larger RAM. This is especially likely when the model is complex. For example, a large RAM is necessary for random forests with large numbers of trees, SVM with complex kernels, and neural networks with multiple hidden layers; while small to moderate RAM could generally satisfy the needs of linear regression models. When the model requires large RAM for training, one could consider using batched training (e.g., learning from 50 to 1,000 instances at a time via stochastic gradient descent optimization; Zhang, 2004) to make memory usage flexible and reduce the RAM needs. Similarly, bagged methods can minimize RAM usage by modifying the number of features and bootstrap proportions in each iteration.

1.2.3.2   *Computation Speed Requirements: CPU*

CPU is responsible for carrying out the model training process. A CPU with faster computational speed (i.e., clock rate) can train a model in a shorter amount of time. While insufficient RAM will introduce errors to model training, an underpowered CPU will prevent a model from being trained altogether. Typically, faster CPUs are beneficial for complex models (that require numerous parameters to estimate) and models with large sample size and number of features. Models that are simple and require a few computational steps are the least CPU intensive. Linear regression and *k*-nearest neighbors generally require less CPU, whereas random forests, SVM, and neural networks are more CPU intensive. In cases where the model training requires large CPU capacity, one could consider using parallel processing (Brownlee, 2020; Kuhn, 2019). Parallel processing partitions a computational task into multiple smaller tasks (e.g., constructing a single tree of the random forest) and distributes them to multiple cores on a computer to work on simultaneously, therefore shortening the total time to complete the task.

1.2.3.3   *Graphics Computation Requirements: GPU*

GPUs are a component of the computer that is specialized at graphical computations (e.g., calculating lighting angles, movement trajectory, and collision). These tasks require linear algebra computations that often take CPUs weeks, months, or even years to complete, while GPUs could perform the computation in parallel, greatly reducing the computation time (Fujimoto, 2008). For example, neural networks typically require GPUs when the features include text, audio, timeseries, and image analysis. GPUs are equipped with their own memory storage functionality, yet just as with RAM, it might not be sufficient for certain applications when the model is complex or the number of features is large. To address this limitation, one might use smaller batch sizes or switch the precision of the calculations to 16-bit instead of the typical 32-bit (akin to rounding a long decimal number). This precision change negligibly changes the model coefficients, but allows the calculations to proceed within memory capacity.

1.2.4 How to Learn More?

There are many readily available resources to help researchers and practitioners apply ML to measurement, which includes click-and-point programs (e.g., IBM SPSS Statistics for Windows, IBM Corp., 2020; Shiny R package, RStudio, 2020), as well as more flexible programming languages – R and Python. Both R and Python are free and open-source programming languages that are widely used for machine learning. Yet, they are distinct in terms of (1) purpose, (2) usability, and (3) flexibility (Krajewski, 2020). First, the two languages' *purpose* is different. R is specifically developed for statistical analysis, while Python is developed for more general programming. If your focus is data analysis or statistical modeling, you may prefer R. However, if your focus is to integrate data analytics and statistical capabilities into a production workflow, you may prefer Python. Second, in terms of *usability*, R is equipped with a wide variety of packages for statistical analyses and measurement (e.g., general linear modeling, item response theory); while Python offers packages focusing on data processing and machine learning (e.g., for natural language processing and computer vision). Third, Python is generally more *flexible* than R. Python codes can easily be integrated into existing software architectures including back-end and cloud architecture, while R lacks such functionalities. Table 1.2 presents a number of useful resources and tutorials are available for implementing machine learning with R and Python.

Table 1.2 *Resources and tutorials for implementing machine learning in R and Python*

Programming language	Official documentation	Tutorial books	Online communities
Python	https://docs.python.org https://python.readthedocs .io	Géron (2019) McKinney (2012) Müller and Guido (2018) Nelson (2020)	*Python Machine Learning Tutorials Python Machine Learning*
R	https://cran.r-project.org/ manuals.html www.rdocumentation.org	James et al. (2013) Kuhn and Johnson (2013) Wickham and Grolemund (2017)	*R-bloggers stat.ethz.ch Mailing Lists*

1.3   Conclusion

The technological advancements in measurement are accompanied by machine learning. The current chapter provided an overview of common ML algorithms used in measurement. ML algorithms enable the use of complex, organic data, and contribute to two key elements of measurement: conceptualization and empirical keying. The current chapter provided recommendations and resources for using ML algorithms for measurement, emphasizing the interpretability and estimation accuracy, and describing best practices for selecting ML algorithms and tools. Recent developments in technology and measurement – many of them highlighted in the edited volume – suggest a promising potential for the future of measurement. Machine learning has a key role to play in the advancement of measurement, and we hope this chapter could help you be equipped with this powerful tool.

REFERENCES

Ahmad, H., Arif, A., Khattak, A. M., Habib, A., Asghar, M. Z., & Shah, B. (2020, January). Applying deep neural networks for predicting dark triad personality trait of online users. In *2020 International Conference on Information Networking (ICOIN)* (pp. 102–105). IEEE.

Akhtar, R., Winsborough, D., Ort, U., Johnson, A., & Chamorro-Premuzic, T. (2018). Detecting the dark side of personality using social media status updates. *Personality and Individual Differences, 132,* 90–97. https://doi.org/10.1016/j.paid.2018.05.026

Altman, N. S. (1992). An introduction to Kernel and nearest-neighbor nonparametric regression. *The American Statistician, 46*(3), 175–185. https://doi.org/10.1080/00031305.1992.10475879

Angelov, D. (2020). Top2Vec: Distributed representations of topics. *ArXiv:2008.09470 [Cs, Stat].* http://arxiv.org/abs/2008.09470

Arya, S., Mount, D. M., Netanyahu, N. S., Silverman, R., & Wu, A. Y. (1998). An optimal algorithm for approximate nearest neighbor searching fixed dimensions. *Journal of the ACM (JACM), 45*(6), 891–923. https://doi.org/10.1145/293347.293348

Batista, G., & Monard, M.-C. (2002). A study of K-nearest neighbour as an imputation method. In International Conference on Health Information Science.

Bengio, Y. (2009). *Learning deep architectures for AI.* Now Publishers Inc.

Blei, D. M., Jordan, M. I., Griffiths, T. L., & Tenenbaum, J. B. (2003). Hierarchical topic models and the nested Chinese restaurant process. *Proceedings of the 16th International Conference on Neural Information Processing Systems,* 17–24.

Bontempi, G., Birattari, M., & Bersini, H. (1999). Lazy learning for local modelling and control design. *International Journal of Control*, *72*(7–8), 643–658. https://doi.org/10.1080/002071799220830

Braun, M. T., & Kuljanin, G. (2015). Big data and the challenge of construct validity. *Industrial and Organizational Psychology: Perspectives on Science and Practice*, *8*(4), 521–527. https://doi.org/10.1017/iop.2015.77

Breiman, L. (1996). Bagging predictors. *Machine Learning*, *24*(2), 123–140.

(2001). Random forests. *Machine Learning*, *45*, 5–32. https://doi.org/10.1023/A:1010933404324

Brownlee, J. (2020, September 21). Multi-core machine learning in Python with Scikit-Learn. *Machine Learning Mastery*. https://machinelearningmastery.com/multi-core-machine-learning-in-python/

Calanna, P., Lauriola, M., Saggino, A., Tommasi, M., & Furlan, S. (2020). Using a supervised machine learning algorithm for detecting faking good in a personality self-report. *International Journal of Selection and Assessment*, *28*(2), 176–185. https://doi.org/10.1111/ijsa.12279

Cardaioli, M., Cecconello, S., Conti, M., Pajola, L., & Turrin, F. (2020). Fake news spreaders profiling through behavioural analysis. In *Working notes of CLEF 2020 – Conference and Labs of the Evaluation Forum*, Thessaloniki, Greece, September 22–25, 2020, vol. 2696 of CEUR Workshop Proceedings. CEUR-WS.org

Chaney, A., & Blei, D. (2012, May). Visualizing topic models. In *Proceedings of the International AAAI Conference on Web and Social Media* (Vol. 6, No. 1).

Chekroud, A. M., Gueorguieva, R., Krumholz, H. M., Trivedi, M. H., Krystal, J. H., & McCarthy, G. (2017). Reevaluating the efficacy and predictability of antidepressant treatments: A symptom clustering approach. *JAMA Psychiatry*, *74*(4), 370–378. https://doi.org/10.1001/jamapsychiatry.2017.0025

Chen, T., & Guestrin, C. (2016, August). Xgboost: A scalable tree boosting system. In *Proceedings of the 22nd ACM SIGKDD International Conference on Knowledge Discovery and Data Mining* (pp. 785–794).

Costa, P. T., & McCrae, R. R. (1992). Normal personality assessment in clinical practice: The NEO Personality Inventory. *Psychological Assessment*, *4*(1), 5–13. https://doi.org/10.1037/1040-3590.4.1.5

Drucker, H., Burges, C. J., Kaufman, L., Smola, A., & Vapnik, V. (1996). Support vector regression machines. *Advances in Neural Information Processing Systems*, 155–161.

Efron, B., Hastie, T., Johnstone, I., & Tibshirani, R. (2004). Least angle regression. *The Annals of Statistics*, *32*(2), 407–499. https://doi.org/10.1214/009053604000000067

Fix, E., & Hodges, J. (1951). Discriminatory analysis – nonparametric discrimination: Consistency properties. Technical Report 21-49-004,4, U.S. Air Force, School of Aviation Medicine, Randolph Field, TX.

Friedman, J. (2001). Greedy function approximation: A gradient boosting machine. *The Annals of Statistics*, *29*(5), 1189–1232. https://doi.org/10.1214/aos/1013203451

Friedman, J. H. (2002). Stochastic gradient boosting. *Computational Statistics & Data Analysis*, *38*(4), 367–378. https://doi.org/10.1016/S0167-9473(01)00065-2

Fujimoto, N. (2008). Faster matrix-vector multiplication on GeForce 8800GTX. *2008 IEEE International Symposium on Parallel and Distributed Processing*, 1–8. https://doi.org/10.1109/IPDPS.2008.4536350

Géron, A. (2019). *Hands-on machine learning with Scikit-Learn & TensorFlow: Concepts, tools, and techniques to build intelligent systems*. O'Reilly Media, Inc.

Gradus, J. L., Rosellini, A. J., Horváth-Puhó, E., Street, A. E., Galatzer-Levy, I., Jiang, T., Lash, T. L., & Sørensen, H. T. (2020). Prediction of sex-specific suicide risk using machine learning and single-payer health care registry data from Denmark. *JAMA Psychiatry*, *77*(1), 25–34. https://doi.org/10.1001/jamapsychiatry.2019.2905

Groves, R. M., Fowler Jr, F. J., Couper, M. P., Lepkowski, J. M., Singer, E., & Tourangeau, R. (2011). *Survey methodology* (Vol. 561). John Wiley & Sons.

Hansen, L. K., & Salamon, P. (1990). Neural network ensembles. *IEEE Transactions on Pattern Analysis and Machine Intelligence*, *12*(10), 993–1001.

Hassanien, A. E., Kilany, M., Houssein, E. H., & AlQaheri, H. (2018). Intelligent human emotion recognition based on elephant herding optimization tuned support vector regression. *Biomedical Signal Processing and Control*, *45*, 182–191. https://doi.org/10.1016/j.bspc.2018.05.039

Hastie, T., Tibshirani, R., & Friedman, J. (2009). *The elements of statistical learning: Data mining, inference, and prediction*. Springer Science & Business Media.

Hickman, L., Bosch, N., Ng, V., Saef, R., Tay, L., & Woo, S. E. (2022). Automated video interview personality assessments: Reliability, validity, and generalizability investigations. *Journal of Applied Psychology*, *107*(8), 1323–1351. https://doi.org/10.1037/apl0000695

Hickman, L., Song, Q. C., & Woo, S. E. (2022). Evaluating data. In K. R. Murphy (Ed.), *Data, methods and theory in the organizational sciences* (pp. 98–123). Society of Industrial and Organizational Psychology Organizational Frontiers Series. Routledge.

Hoerl, A. E., & Kennard, R. W. (1970). Ridge regression: Biased estimation for nonorthogonal problems. *Technometrics*, *12*(1), 55–67. https://doi.org/10.1080/00401706.1970.10488634

IBM Corp. (2020). *IBM SPSS statistics for Windows, version 27.0*. IBM Corp.

James, G., Witten, D., Hastie, T., & Tibshirani, R. (Eds.). (2013). *An introduction to statistical learning: With applications in R*. Springer.

Jiang, T., Gradus, J. L., & Rosellini, A. J. (2020). Supervised machine learning: A brief primer. *Behavior Therapy*, *51*(5), 675–687. https://doi.org/10.1016/j.beth.2020.05.002

Jung, Y., & Suh, Y. (2019). Mining the voice of employees: A text mining approach to identifying and analyzing job satisfaction factors from online employee reviews. *Decision Support Systems*, *123*, 113074. https://doi.org/10.1016/j.dss.2019.113074

Kenney, J. F., & Keeping, E. S. (1962). Linear regression and correlation. *Mathematics of Statistics, 1,* 252–285.

Kotsiantis, S. B. (2007). Supervised machine learning: A review of classification techniques. *Informatica (Slovenia), 31*(3), 249–268.

Kouiroukidis, N., & Evangelidis, G. (2011). The effects of dimensionality curse in high dimensional kNN search. *2011 15th Panhellenic Conference on Informatics,* 41–45. https://doi.org/10.1109/PCI.2011.45

Krajewski, R. (2020, November 26). *Python vs R: What language is better for data science projects?* Ideamotive. https://www.ideamotive.co/blog/python-vs-r-what-language-is-better-for-data-science-projects.

Kuhn, M. (2019). Parallel processing. In *The caret package.* https://topepo.github.io/caret/parallel-processing.html

Kuhn, M., & Johnson, K. (2013). *Applied predictive modeling.* Springer.

Lu, Z., Pu, H., Wang, F., Hu, Z., & Wang, L. (2017). The expressive power of neural networks: A view from the wdth. *ArXiv:1709.02540 [Cs].* http://arxiv.org/abs/1709.02540

MacQueen, J. (1967, June). Some methods for classification and analysis of multivariate observations. *Proceedings of the 5th Berkeley Symposium on Mathematical Statistics and Probability, 1*(14), 281–297.

Matusik, J. G., Heidl, R., Hollenbeck, J. R., Yu, A., Lee, H. W., & Howe, M. (2019). Wearable bluetooth sensors for capturing relational variables and temporal variability in relationships: A construct validation study. *Journal of Applied Psychology, 104*(3), 357–387. https://doi.org/10.1037/apl0000334

McKinney, W. (2012). *Python for data analysis.* O'Reilly Media.

Mitchell, T. M. (1997). *Machine learning.* McGraw-Hill.

Morgan, J. N., & Sonquist, J. A. (1963). Problems in the analysis of survey data, and a proposal. *Journal of the American Statistical Association, 58,* 415–434.

Müller, A. C., & Guido, S. (2018). *Introduction to machine learning with Python: A guide for data scientists.* O'Reilly Media.

Myles, A. J., Feudale, R. N., Liu, Y., Woody, N. A., & Brown, S. D. (2004). An introduction to decision tree modeling. *Journal of Chemometrics: A Journal of the Chemometrics Society, 18*(6), 275–285. https://doi.org/10.1002/cem.873

Nelson, D. (2020). *Data visualization in Python.* StackAbuse.

Newman, D. A. (2014). Missing data: Five practical guidelines. *Organizational Research Methods, 17*(4), 372–411. https://doi.org/10.1177/1094428114548590

Park, G., Schwartz, H. A., Eichstaedt, J. C., Kern, M. L., Kosinski, M., Stillwell, D. J., Ungar, L. H., & Seligman, M. E. P. (2015). Automatic personality assessment through social media language. *Journal of Personality and Social Psychology, 108*(6), 934–952. https://doi.org/10.1037/pspp0000020

Polyak, S. T., von Davier, A. A., & Peterschmidt, K. (2017). Computational psychometrics for the measurement of collaborative problem solving skills. *Frontiers in Psychology, 8.* https://doi.org/10.3389/fpsyg.2017.02029

Putka, D. J., Beatty, A. S., & Reeder, M. C. (2018). Modern prediction methods: New perspectives on a common problem. *Organizational Research Methods, 21*(3), 689–732. https://doi.org/10.1177/1094428117697041

Quinlan, J. R. (1986). Induction of decision trees. *Machine Learning, 1*(1), 81–106. https://doi.org/10.1007/BF00116251

(1996). Bagging, boosting, and C4.5. *Proceedings of the Thirteenth National Conference on Artificial Intelligence*, 725–730.

Roberts, M. E., Stewart, B. M., Tingley, D., Lucas, C., Leder-Luis, J., Gadarian, S. K., Albertson, B., & Rand, D. G. (2014). Structural topic models for open-ended survey responses. *American Journal of Political Science, 58*(4), 1064–1082. https://doi.org/10.1111/ajps.12103

RStudio (2020). Learn Shiny. https://shiny.rstudio.com/tutorial/

Rubin, D. B. (1976). Inference and missing data. *Biometrika, 63*(3), 581–592. https://doi.org/10.1093/biomet/63.3.581

Rudin, C. (2019). Stop explaining black box machine learning models for high stakes decisions and use interpretable models instead. *Nature Machine Intelligence, 1*(5), 206–215. https://doi.org/10.1038/s42256-019-0048-x

Salehzadeh, R. (2017). Which types of leadership styles do followers prefer? A decision tree approach. *International Journal of Educational Management, 31*(7), 865–877. https://doi.org/10.1108/IJEM-04-2016-0079

Speer, A. B. (2020). Scoring dimension-level job performance from narrative comments: Validity and generalizability when using natural language processing. *Organizational Research Methods*, 1094428120930810. https://doi.org/10.1177/1094428120930815

Steinhaus, H. (1956). Sur la division des corps matériels en parties. *Bulletin L'Académie Polonaise des Science, 1*(804), 801–804.

Tay, L., Woo, S. E., Hickman, L., & Saef, R. M. (2020). Psychometric and validity issues in machine learning approaches to personality assessment: A focus on social media text mining. *European Journal of Personality, 34*(5), 826–844. https://doi.org/10.1002/per.2290

Tibshirani, R. (1996). Regression shrinkage and selection via the lasso. *Journal of the Royal Statistical Society: Series B (Methodological), 58*(1), 267–288. https://doi.org/10.1111/j.2517-6161.1996.tb02080.x

Van der Maaten, L., & Hinton, G. (2008). Visualizing data using t-SNE. *Journal of Machine Learning Research, 9*(11). http://www.jmlr.org/papers/v9/vandermaaten08a.html

Wang, W., Hernandez, I., Newman, D. A., He, J., & Bian, J. (2016). Twitter analysis: Studying US weekly trends in work stress and emotion. *Applied Psychology, 65*(2), 355–378. https://doi.org/10.1111/apps.12065

Wickham, H., & Grolemund, G. (2017). *R for data science: Import, tidy, transform, visualize, and model data*. O'Reilly Media.

Winkielman, P., Schwarz, N., Fazendeiro, T. A., & Reber, R. (2003). The hedonic marking of processing fluency: Implications for evaluative judgment. In J. Musch & K. C. Klauer (Eds.), *The psychology of evaluation: Affective processes in cognition and emotion* (pp. 189–217). Lawrence Erlbaum Associates Publishers.

Xu, H., Zhang, N., & Zhou, L. (2020). Validity concerns in research using organic data. *Journal of Management, 46*(7), 1257–1274. https://doi.org/10.1177/0149206319862027

Youyou, W., Kosinski, M., & Stillwell, D. (2015). Computer-based personality judgments are more accurate than those made by humans. *Proceedings of the National Academy of Sciences, 112*(4), 1036–1040. https://doi.org/10.1073/pnas.1418680112

Zhang, T. (2004). Solving large scale linear prediction problems using stochastic gradient descent algorithms. *ICML 2004: Proceedings of The Twenty-first International Conference on Machine Learning* (pp. 919–926). Omnipress. https://doi.org/10.1145/1015330.1015332

Zou, H., & Hastie, T. (2005). Regularization and variable selection via the elastic net. *Journal of the Royal Statistical Society: Series B (Statistical Methodology), 67*(2), 301–320. https://doi.org/10.1111/j.1467-9868.2005.00503.x

Toward Improved Workplace Measurement with Passive Sensing Technologies
Opportunities and Challenges

Munmun De Choudhury

2.1 Introduction

The advent of pervasive technology devices has opened up new opportunities to track and measure people's *in situ* patterns of activity and affect, and obtain precise measures of a variety of attributes, characteristics, and psychological states of individuals, communities, and populations. Typical pervasive technologies pertaining to wearable, portable, or mobile computing permit continual *passive sensing* that involves the capture of data about a person without putting any extra effort in (Caceres & Friday, 2011). The concept of passive sensing comes from extensive research conducted in ubiquitous computing – some of its earliest conceptualizations have referred to this field as "context-aware computing" (Dey, 2018; Moran & Dourish, 2001). The unobtrusiveness of passive sensing makes it possible to gather data at any time, longitudinally, and with little burden on an individual's awareness, memory, or behavior. Thus, the availability of such rich and granular behavioral data from large segments of the population has the potential to advance our understanding of human behavior through unobtrusive measurement. Within an organization, the collection, accumulation, and computational modeling or analysis of such passively sensed data could benefit workers through increased awareness of their stress and productivity, as well as contribute to organizations' efforts and policies to promote worker well-being and job satisfaction, with the potential to lead to lower employee attrition and economic advantages for the organization (Lee, Kim, et al., 2019; Mathur et al., 2015; Mirjafari et al., 2019; Morshed et al., 2019; Nepal et al., 2021, 2022; Saha, Yousef, et al., 2021; Zakaria et al., 2019).

Pervasive technologies can be diverse with varied conceptualizations. This chapter concerns one of the more common forms of this technology – often termed ubiquitous technologies and may include wearable devices, Bluetooth, and smartphones, and even online tools such as social media and crowd-contributed online platforms. At the core of these technologies is the "sensor" – a device that detects and measures a property of an individual, and could be a physical (e.g., heart rate) or a virtual (e.g., online social interaction) attribute. Sensors themselves are, however, not a new phenomenon – they have existed since time immemorial. Mohr et al. (2017) rightly noted that "the Sumerians developed scales, which are essentially weight sensors, some 9,000 years ago, and we have continued to develop new sensors ever since" (p. 23). Technological advancements in the past two decades have accelerated the speed of innovation on the sensor front. In recent times, a wide variety of simple and complex sensors have been present in our mobile phones, constantly tracking our location, physical activity, social interaction and exchange, light, sound, proximate digital devices in the vicinity of the phone, and others. Along similar lines, smartwatches and wearables also contain sensors that measure and monitor activity (e.g., step count) and physiological functions (e.g., heart rate). And further, social media captures our virtual communication with our social networks, our emotional expressions, as well as our thoughts and opinions. Concretely, there are over 5.5 billion smartphone subscriptions globally (Cerwall et al., 2015), and it is estimated that there will be 25 billion Internet of Things–connected devices by 2025 (Cunningham & Whalley, 2020); while 90% of the US population uses some social media technology (Poushter et al., 2018).

Pervasive technologies, such as the ones we have described, are increasingly demonstrating a potential to better measure a variety of psychological variables both longitudinally and spanning large communities or populations, with the help of rapidly advancing computational, big analytic, and machine-learning techniques, as well as because this data can be gathered through unobtrusive means (Campbell et al., 2008; De Choudhury & Counts, 2013; Mark, Czerwinski, et al., 2016; Mirjafari et al., 2019; Purta et al., 2016; Robles-Granda et al., 2020; Saha, Reddy, et al., 2019; Shami, Yang, et al., 2014). For example, location (GPS) data can be used to track mobility traits (Pappalardo et al., 2015), smartphone usage logs have been used to assess personality (Harari et al., 2016) as well as rhythms of alertness (Abdullah et al., 2016), sensed data from smartphone (e.g., GPS-based location, accelerometer information, or microphone usage) has provided markers of sleep (e.g., bedtime or waketime, duration), social context (e.g., relationship to social contacts in the address book of the phone), mood, and stress (Harari et al., 2017; Wang et al., 2014; Zenonos et al., 2016), WiFi data has been leveraged to track sleep (Liu et al., 2015), accelerometer data collected in wearables has been used to measure physical activity (Sano et al., 2015), and social media data has been used to both quantify as well as predict mental health (De Choudhury et al., 2013). To sum up, as also noted by other scholars in recent times (D'Mello et al., 2022), passively collected sensor data from phones and wearables to social media, while still in its early stages of research, holds the promise to significantly advance measurement in a broad spectrum of areas from precision medicine and public health to how we exercise, work, and interact with each other on a daily basis.

This chapter is written against the backdrop of this emergent body of work. Starting by highlighting the limitations of conventional workplace measurement techniques, the chapter will situate the unique potential offered by capturing and analyzing data provided by a variety of social and ubiquitous technologies, ranging from smartphones and fitness watches to social media and Bluetooth-based geolocation trackers. Then I will describe existing research in this emergent field that has appropriated these technologies and their passive data for varied applications in the workplace context, such as assessing employee personality, gauging job performance, or tracking health and wellness attributes of individual workers as well as broader organizations. The chapter also dedicates significant effort to identifying and discussing the myriad challenges that would need attention and redressal in order to fully realize the benefits offered by passive sensing technologies. I will conclude with some concrete directions toward future research in this emergent area.

2.2   Limitations of Existing Workplace Measurements

Presently, the dominant method for assessing workplace-related behaviors and attributes is through the use of self-reported surveys (Smith, 2014; Wiley, 2010). These methods rely on the retrospective recollection of somewhat subjective behavioral information, and are therefore vulnerable to memory constraints of people (Golder & Macy, 2011). Consequently, these surveys often suffer from hindsight bias – that is, insights are gathered after the incidents or experiences of an individual. In fact, when researchers measure workplace behaviors in such an episodic fashion, they may further miss accounting for the context of the experience or its evolution, all of which are essential to gather a holistic understanding of behaviors. As a way to circumvent this issue, while some organizations assess workers using different methods such as peer reviews or supervisor reports, these may differ across different industries (e.g., tech, government, financial services), and self-censorship and social desirability bias may preclude an ability to gather authentic and meaningful insights. Although these methods combined with bias correcting techniques (Chittaranjan et al., 2011; Golub et al., 2000) and domain knowledge can be useful in studies of workplace behaviors, there is a need for new research into more objective, unobtrusive, and reliable methods. Importantly, manual evaluation of workers further has limitations of scaling (Groves & Peytcheva, 2008; Krumpal, 2013; Silva et al., 2007). The backdrop of the COVID-19 pandemic and the push toward remote work models may also complicate conducting such evaluations that require in-person engagement (Vaessen & Raimondo, 2020).

Recent research in studies of human behavior has recognized the value of in-the-moment data recording and acquisition approach in studies of human behavior. One prominent example centers around the proliferation of active sensing approaches, such as the use of ecological momentary assessments (EMAs) towards experience sampling (Wang et al., 2014). A variety of smartphone applications are being increasingly built to make such EMA-based data collection easier for research studies and less burdensome for participants. While this overcomes the challenges of retrospective and cross-sectional surveys, experience sampling strategies suffer from poor participant compliance, and require participants to own and use a smartphone, thus limiting data collection over longer time periods. Moreover, the underlying technical systems for surfacing EMAs are fairly complex from a technical standpoint, which necessitates highly engineered study designs (Zhang et al., 2016). As a result, researchers have to make conscious decisions to optimize for either the gathering of a large dataset, often through an intensive EMA engagement over a limited period of time that offers greater financial compensation to participants, or adopting a study design that reduces participants' response burden, such as by issuing fewer EMAs. Researchers have therefore critiqued such active sensing approaches in favor of other passive mechanisms to gather behavioral data (Froehlich et al., 2007).

Consequently, researchers have identified alternative sources of data that may be gathered unobtrusively to target questions in psychological research. Notably, Woo et al. (2020) performed a review of the literature to identify three broad classes of passive data that may be particularly valuable – social media (such as from Facebook or Twitter), internet activities (such as online searches or browsing activity), and wearable sensors (such as Fitbits or sociometric badges). To note specific examples, researchers are making use of various passive sensing technologies (Wang et al., 2014), such as through the measurement of an individual's phone usage or via behavioral measurement enabled by wearable sensors. Expectedly, as we have noted, there has been significant success in employing these popular and often commercially available sensors to study behavior, well-being, and psychological attributes (Grünerbl et al., 2015; Wang et al., 2014), stemming from their ease of data collection and because they overcome many of the limitations of self-reported data.

Passive data also offers many additional unique benefits and opportunities. By leveraging the ubiquity and widespread usage of smartphones and wearable-based passive sensors, we can obtain longitudinal and dense (or intensive) data at scale. Moreover, unlike behavioral surveys or EMAs, where responses are solicited by the research team and typically focus on gathering retrospective insights and experiences, measurement of behavior and psychological state based on passive sensing technologies can capture workplace-relevant attributes in a naturalistic setting. Such activity is real time, and happens in the course of a person's day-to-day life. Hence it is less vulnerable to not only memory bias, but also experimenter demand effects, and thus can help track various dimensions relevant to workplace assessments at a fine-grained temporal scale. Mobile and wearable sensor data are now recognized as meaningful and rich sources of information about human behavior – information that is increasingly being used to measure patterns of daily activities and human mobility (Calabrese et al., 2013; Madan et al., 2010; Yuan et al., 2013), well-being (Mariani et al., 2012), and job and academic performance (Schaule et al., 2018). It has been repeatedly shown that machine-learning models can achieve high accuracy on specific assessment tasks based on data from fairly small samples. For example, Manyika et al. (2017) estimated work load category using wearables on a sample of 20 academic participants. Importantly, passive sensing based on common tools like smartphones and social media may be less disruptive because they are often already embedded in people's routines and have broader market penetration than specialized devices employed to gather behavioral data at the workplace.

2.3   Current State of the Field

As we have mentioned, researchers have been discovering the potential of various pervasive technology devices as research tools to understand ecological contexts and behaviors of people. Some of the earliest efforts have been around reality mining (Eagle & Pentland, 2006), personal informatics (Li et al., 2010), digital phenotyping (Insel, 2017; Jain et al., 2015), and personal sensing (Klasnja et al., 2009). In recent years, these efforts have turned more comprehensive, looking at not only diverse forms of passive sensing via pervasive technologies but also aiming to assess and infer more complex constructs. In many cases, the goal was to use a type of sensing technology that is unobtrusive, portable, and able to make people comfortable to continue their typical daily activities and routines without having to carry it around or interacting with it in an active fashion. Some exemplars on this front include projects such as NetHealth (Liu et al., 2018; Purta et al., 2016), CenceMe (Miluzzo et al., 2007), StudentLife (Wang et al., 2014), CampusLife (Morshed et al., 2019; Saha et al., 2017), Tesserae (Mattingly et al., 2019), and Tiles (Mundnich et al., 2020) that share several key features. First, they have employed a suite of diverse sensors to measure attributes such as mood, mobility, technology use, and social network structure. Second, they have time-synchronized sensor data to study relationships, such as how stress covaries with events or how students' mood instability changes over a semester. In particular, the StudentLife project (Wang et al., 2014) leveraged smartphones to measure and monitor college students' daily behaviors for multiple months to assess their mental health and academic performance. I draw upon this literature to understand the landscape of the use of passive sensing technologies for the assessment of diverse workplace attributes, noting that most of these studies except the Tesserae (Mattingly et al., 2019) and Tiles projects (Mundnich et al., 2020), did not explicitly focus on the work context or organizations.

2.3.1 *Personality and Daily Activities*

It is known that personality traits can predict a worker's functioning. For instance, high conscientiousness indicates that a person is organized and responsible across situations (Anderson & Viswesvaran, 1998; Barrick & Mount, 1991), while for client-facing roles, individuals with high extraversion are assumed to be more suitable (Barrick & Mount, 1991) — probably because such individuals are more sociable. In contrast, these same studies note neuroticism, or the tendency to be less emotionally stable and being anxious, to be negatively associated with job performance. High neuroticism is also associated with low job satisfaction (Furnham & Zacherl, 1986). Lastly, openness engenders intellectual curiosity, adventuresomeness, and inquisitiveness. Enjoyment of creative and innovative work is likely dependent on this trait (Dollinger et al., 2004). In essence, differences in job performance are often attributable to within-person variances in intrinsic traits and situational factors

(Tams, 2008). Personality has also been one of the most robust constructs to forecast other organizational outcomes (Ajzen, 1987; Ones et al., 2005), including, notably, turnover outcomes (Woo et al., 2016; Zimmerman et al., 2016). Therefore, considerable research has focused on utilizing a wide range of passive sensing technologies to infer personality states within different situations. Many of these studies focused primarily on the Big Five (Barrick & Mount, 1991) and, among the various passive sensing technologies, smartphones, in particular, have been one of the most promising sources of personality-relevant assessments (Harari et al., 2020). Harari et al. (2016) characterized this landscape of personality sensing research broadly to comprise the following types of measurements: 1) behavioral measurements that capture everyday activities through sensing such as social interactions (e.g., in-person and mediated communications), 2) movement behaviors (e.g., physical activity and mobility patterns), and 3) daily life activities (e.g., activities that are mediated or not mediated by the use of technology; social interactions with a coworker via a phone's text messaging is an example of an activity mediated by technology). Although these measurements are commonplace today, given the adoption of smartphones and wearable devices, sensors in cell phones (such as GPS and Bluetooth) were employed to unobtrusively assess users' context, which were eventually used to infer personality or daily activities. Notably, the Reality Mining project (Eagle & Pentland, 2006) utilized location data and Bluetooth logs to measure social patterns in daily activities and routines, identify socially meaningful locations, and gauge organizational rhythms. Likewise, CenceMe (Miluzzo et al., 2007) used various sensors, including cameras, microphones, accelerometer, GPS, temperature, light, humidity, magnetometer, and button clicks, to integratively quantify users' activities and habits, eventually embedding these into common social networking apps to promote social interaction.

As specific examples in more recent years, the accelerometer, microphone, and light sensor in smartphones have been used to gauge people's activity levels (e.g., walking and running; Miluzzo et al., 2007), surrounding context or environment (e.g., having a conversation; Lu et al., 2009), and sleep routines (e.g., duration; Chen et al., 2013). Further, phone logs can be used to collect data about social interactions (e.g., social media app use, incoming and outgoing call logs, and text messaging behavior) (Chittaranjan et al., 2013; Schmid Mast et al., 2015). Next, Harari et al. speak of person-specific measurements that can be provided by passive sensing, specifically those that capture individual differences in thoughts and feelings. Such attributes can be invaluable in assessing personality. For instance, language information in voice data can be derived from microphones (Mehl, 2017), keystrokes can be logged by custom keyboards (Buschek et al., 2018), and linguistic markers can be extracted from screenshots of smartphones (Reeves et al., 2021), as well as gathered through analysis of social media data (Park et al., 2015). These signals have been employed in personality detection and for advancing understanding of individual differences research. Harari et al.'s final category focuses on the value provided by situational factors that can be assessed via passive sensing. The past two decades of context-aware computing research show how sensing devices can enable the logging of information about an individual's context and environment (the who, where, and when of a situation) (Abowd et al., 1998), such as by inferring locations based on GPS coordinates (recorded via a smartphone or a Bluetooth device, for instance), including even inferring the types of those locations (semantic place labels like a person who may be at home, a store, or a cafe). Such situational information may provide information on personality traits like extraversion.

Inspired by this rich body of research, scholars have argued that by combining theoretical and methodological approaches from the fields of psychology and computer science, personality measurement using passively sensed data bears the potential to advance our understanding of the behavioral and contextual aspects of personality (Harari et al., 2020). Nevertheless, alternate researchers have observed that in order to formulate effective methods for personality sensing, it is crucial to have comprehensive data that is diverse in nature, detailed in terms of behavioral observations across various situations, collected over an extended period (spanning days, weeks, or even years), and representative by including behavioral data from numerous participants across a wide range of samples (Council, 1993). Moreover, workers' behaviors are influenced by many dynamic attributes beyond personality; many scholars have, in fact, proposed theories to explain worker behaviors based on their dynamic activities (Dunn et al., 1994; Sansone et al., 2003). Passive sensing tools provide an opportunity to capture such dynamic activities to capture situational differences that account for worker performance, in addition to personality. To this end, Das Swain et al. (2019b) showed that a worker's daily activities were predictive of their job performance, with explanatory gains over what could be predicted with personality alone. Specifically, these authors harnessed logged data from smartphones, wearables, and Bluetooth beacons to computational model these daily activities at the worker level. Speaking of the particular activities that were associated with better job performance, they included batching behavior of phone use, shorter desk sessions, and longer sleep durations. These patterns were persistent even after controlling for "resilient" or "undercontrolled" personality; for instance, in predicting organizational citizenship behavior (OCB), day-level activities explained approximately 50% variance in self-reported OCB. Summatively, this indicates that predictive gains are made possible because passively modeled daily activities measure aspects of behaviors that are not accounted for by personality.

Together, this body of research shows that with passive sensing technologies, it might be now possible to capture both physical and digital/virtual activities of workers in conjunction with their personality, in order to understand and thereafter intervene to improve a variety of workplace outcomes.

2.3.2   Productivity and Job Performance

Beyond research focusing on detecting personality attributes and daily activities, passive sensing is being increasingly used to measure physiological attributes of workers, quantify productivity, and automate the evaluation of jobs, skills/expertise, wages, and even hiring decisions (Brown et al., 2014). The motivation stems from the fact that many indicators of job performance tend to establish links between a worker's ecology and their dynamic states, beyond fixed traits like personality. In fact, Dunn et al. (1994) posited a link between context (temporal, physical, social, and cultural) and workplace performance. Dunn's framework, known as Ecology of Human Performance (EHP), situates how an individual's dynamic situation and experience is central to measurement of occupational outcomes. With this approach, variabilities in job performance depend on the particular time-varying state an individual finds themselves in, above and beyond their intrinsic traits. Yet, "context" or "situation" is a broad, subjective term. Consequently, researchers have primarily adopted the daily activities of workers, obtained via passive sensors, as a proxy of context (Abowd et al., 1999; Dey, 2001). Such "context" could include passively gathered notion of activities or responses to changes in those activities (Abowd et al., 1999; Schmidt et al., 1999).

Using wearable sensor data, in particular, researchers have successfully derived physiological features, in turn, using them to estimate job performance aspects such as attentional focus (Schaule et al., 2018). As noted by Nepal et al. (2022), other works are increasingly interested in more core and long-term worker behavior constructs like productivity and examining the extent to which passive sensing technologies can help in this measurement as well as in facilitating interventions to improve it. Interest is growing in applying such approaches across organizations and industries in a generalizable manner. Crosscutting across this work is the notion of "ground truth"[1] – a source of information typically derived from self-reports on job performance inventories, that serves as the outcome of interest in computational models harnessing passively sensed data. The inventories can measure aspects like task performance, such as individual task proficiency and in-role behavior, or assess behaviors that promote the effectiveness of organizations and their members, such as interpersonal and organizational deviance and OCB. A notable example here is the Tesserae project (Mattingly et al., 2019) – the project involved over 700 information workers in investigating how passive sensing technologies can be leveraged to measure workplace performance, such as organizational citizenship behavior, as well as psychological traits and physical characteristics. Several individual studies within this project have harnessed a variety of single- and multi-sensor approaches to assess productivity and job performance. For instance, one of the studies within the Tesserae project included 554 information workers using a phone agent, beacons, and a Garmin wearable, Mirjafari et al. (2019) used unsupervised learning, specifically, *K*-means clustering on the participant responses on task performance, in-role behaviors, and OCB scores to classify them into higher and lower performers in their respective organizations. Although multiple sensors were present, the authors found that passive signals from one source alone – the Garmin wearable – was able to distinguish between performers with an area under the receiver operating characteristic curve (AUROC) of 0.72. Similarly, passively gathered activities from the smartphone agent achieved an AUROC of 0.65 in the same classification. Expectedly, combining these raised the AUROC to 0.83. This can be considered a commendable performance since AUROC typically quantifies trade-offs between the true positive rate and false positive rate of models, thus values over 70–80%, as observed in this work, are considered satisfactory and common in the published literature. Overall, this research

---

[1] Supervised machine learning problems often refer to the outcome variable as ground truth. Ground truth, practically speaking, in these cases largely implies information that can be taken as a gold standard for the outcome in question. It is important to note that ground truth may or may not indicate or capture the objective truth, and philosophical discussions about whether it does is beyond the scope of machine learning model development. For more information and connections to psychological research, refer to Tay et al. (2020).

shows how multimodality can better explain complex behaviors in the workplace.

Although not derived from passive sensors, multimodality has been explored in prior organizational measurement literature, since complementary forms of signals, when integrated, are likely to yield richer insights than any one source alone. Das Swain et al. (2019b) described how, in an effort to understand the relationship between everyday work activities and job performance, a company focusing on deriving employee analytics, known as Leesman, used self-reported individual movement data across 1,700 workplaces to understand employee performance in different corporate real-estate cultures (Barthelemy, 2019). It was found that higher movement correlated with greater satisfaction in individual tasks, as well as with creative thinking. Such observations are now being replicated and enriched through the use of passive sensing data. Returning to Das Swain et al. (2019b)'s work, the authors found confirmatory evidence that daily activities of workers explained their performance to a degree that went beyond intrinsic traits like their personality. Among other scholars, similar relationships were learned regarding social activity, gathered through wearable devices (Olguin & Pentland, 2008; Olguin et al., 2009; Olguin-Olguin, 2011). Olguin et al. (2009), in particular, reported the potential of wearable data to determine that task completion is affected by both physical activity and speech activity. Along similar lines, Montanari et al. (2017)'s work underscored the significance of fine-grained movement captured through proximate sensors in workspaces, which was able to explain the extent of diversity in those organizations. For physical movement – a type of data provided by many passive sensors – continues to be demonstrated to be highly valuable in assessing workers' task satisfaction and completion (Leesman, 2018).

Complementarily, several studies in the human–computer interaction field have leveraged passive data, in the form of web and social media data, to study employee behavior (Chancellor & Counts, 2018; De Choudhury & Counts, 2013; Hickman et al., 2019; Jhaver et al., 2019; Mark, Iqbal, et al., 2016). Some foundational work in this space investigated what motivates workers to use social media at work in the first place (Ehrlich & Shami, 2010). Formative research also situated the positives of social media use, such as Zhao and Rosson (2009)'s work which showed that social media activities were helpful in setting a "common ground" across employees, providing a level platform for interaction and social exchange. Other research reciprocated and built upon these findings. For instance, a case study at a big multinational firm noted that social technologies at the workplace were beneficial for community building as well, helping instill a sense of collective identity and empowering workers to foreground their work practices (Thom & Millen, 2012). These behaviors were interesting and present on both internal and external (to the workplace) social media sites, and persisted across different platforms' different affordances and design features (Thom & Millen, 2012; Zhang et al., 2014). Prabhakaran et al. (2012) studied power relations in email interactions of employees. Employee engagement in such mediums motivates the exploration of unstructured text, as these descriptions often offer unsolicited perspectives on work-based styles, ideas, and beliefs. Together, these studies set the stage for social media data to open up new opportunities to infer workplace productivity, performance, and related behaviors. As examples, several studies at IBM examined employee engagement by harnessing social media data (DiMicco et al., 2008; Mitra et al., n.d.; Muller et al., 2016; Shami et al., 2015). Complementary works have employed social media data to identify workers of reputation in collaborative workplace contexts (Jacovi et al., 2014) and workers' perceptions of their job roles and role ambiguities (Saha, Bayraktaroglu, et al., 2019).

To summarize, it is well recognized that an effective workplace is an environment where results can be achieved as expected by management. Physical environments affect how employees in an organization interact, perform tasks, and are led. Physical environment as an aspect of the work environment has thus directly affected the human sense and subtly changed interpersonal interactions and, thus, productivity. In many ways, the workplace environment is the most critical factor in keeping an employee satisfied in today's business world. Today's workplace is different, diverse, and constantly changing, with the environment extending beyond the conventional physical setting. The typical employer/employee relationship of old has been turned upside down. Workers are living in a growing economy and have almost limitless job opportunities. Arguably, scholars have noted that this combination of factors has created an environment where the business needs its employees more than the employees need the business (Lowe et al., 2003). The research we have described shows how notions of productivity and job performance at the workplace – aspects central to a healthy and thriving environment – may be measured with passive sensing technologies. This may open up new opportunities to design the "ideal workplace" of the 21st century, one in which a more holistic understanding of productivity and job performance is possible by taking into account workers' everyday happenings.

2.3.3   Health and Well-Being

Rich and longitudinally collected passive data has been observed to yield valuable insights into a range of health and wellness outcomes, such as employee stress, sleep, and physical activity (Quante et al., 2019; Sano et al., 2017; Smyth et al., 2018). In order to understand how batching notifications, as opposed to self-interruptions, impact work performance and stress, Mark (2015) used computational tools to examine the digital behavior of people within their email interactions. The findings of their *in situ* study confirmed as well as deviated from existing theories. They attributed the deviations to passive sensing, which could overcome the challenges imposed by survey instruments in acquiring adequate representative data of an individual's context, such as their well-being. Consequently, it is not surprising that prior work has provided methodologies to automate measuring employee affect using passive sensing technologies (De Choudhury & Counts, 2013; Hickman et al., 2019; Shami, Yang, et al., 2014). In this light, studies have reported how social media use positively correlates with workplace well-being (Hanna et al., 2017; Robertson & Kee, 2017).

More generally, mental health issues such as stress, anxiety, and affect are typical well-being dimensions studied in prior research. Per Nepal et al. (2022), most existing studies tend to ask participants to self-report such well-being attributes using psychometrically validated instruments. While some studies use responses from one-off surveys, others use experience sampling to get a fuller picture of employees' well-being over time. These ground truth scores are then used to build predictive models that employ passive data. Due to the link between stress/anxiety and heart rate (HR), many studies have also harnessed HR-based signals obtained from wrist-worn wearables that employ photoplethysmography (PPG) sensors. For example, Feng and Narayanan (2020) demonstrated how to categorize the anxiety level of nursing professionals using PPG-based HR and step counts from a Fitbit. The prediction model provided good performance over baseline overall, with an accuracy of roughly 58%, attributable to a novel pipeline for discovering behavioral consistency features from the passively sensed data. The authors' ground truth for this study was the self-reported State-Trait Anxiety Inventory median-split score. Similar to this, Jebelli et al. (2018) used a wrist wearable to monitor a participant's electrodermal activity, peripheral skin temperature, and HR through PPG signals in a study of 10 construction workers. Salivary cortisol was employed in the study as the gold standard to gauge the workers' initial stress levels. When identifying the workers' low, medium, and high stress levels, predictive models achieved an accuracy of roughly 73%.

Speaking of other mental health attributes, when Bin Morshed et al. (2019) evaluated the mood instability of 603 information workers, they discovered a negative correlation between the mood instability scores and the sleep and activity duration reported by a Garmin wearable. The authors used the self-reported positive and negative affect schedule (PANAS) to compute mood instability in the study. Similar wrist wearables were utilized by Umematsu et al. (2019) to record skin conductance, skin temperature, and acceleration from 39 employees of a Japanese corporation over the course of 30 days. Every morning, EMAs were used to collect data on stress, mood, and health. The authors then created a method for predicting the self-reported scores for the following day using the physiological data from the day before. When predicting stress, mood, and health scores, they came up with mean absolute errors (MAE) of 13.47, 14.09, and 18.51, respectively. In general, smaller MAE values are preferable, with the ideal being 0, which occurs when the observed and projected scores are exactly the same. Speech activity can account for some of the variation in predicting positive affect, according to Nadarajan et al. (2019), who employed PANAS in a different research of 50 hospital employees. Throughout their shifts, workers wore an audio badge that was specially made for them. In order to distinguish foreground speech, the authors extracted a variety of elements from the audio gathered from audio badges. To quantify both positive and negative affect from foreground activation, they next constructed a linear mixed effects model (i.e., the percentage of recording time that foreground speech is present).

Sleep constitutes another well-being attribute that has been extensively studied with passive sensing. Feng and Narayanan (2020) used PPG-based HR from Fitbit, sleep duration, sleep efficiency, and REM sleep duration features to assess the participants' sleep quality in the same study of 138 full-time nursing professionals, as mentioned before. The Pittsburgh Sleep Quality Index survey was employed in the study to get empirical data. A score below 7 was given a negative class (possible sleep disorders), and a score above 7 was given a positive class (possible sleep disorders). To find essential motifs, the authors suggested an optimization problem. The F1 score of this model was 77.47%; like AUROC, F1 quantifies the trade-off between false positives and false negatives; higher numbers are preferable, with values over 75% being excellent. Motif characteristics collected from this sensed data produced superior performance in predicting sleep quality. One Tesserae study examined the accuracy of wearable-based sleep detection by monitoring 700 information workers over the course of a year using wearables and phones due to the widespread use of this technology (Martinez et al., 2020). Martinez et al. noted that wearables might exaggerate sleep, and they suggest combining wearable data with phone usage activities (i.e., whether the phone is being used or not) to counteract this. The authors created more accurate models of self-reported sleep for information workers using the suggested method than they did utilizing either stream alone.

Focus and alertness are two more issues connected to health and well-being that have been researched utilizing passive sensing at work. For instance, Soto et al. (2021) used biometric information from an armband (such as physical activity, heart rate, skin reaction, skin temperature, and breathing) to calculate the stress, focus, and alertness of the worker. At a sizable power and automation company, 14 knowledge workers participated in the study for 8 weeks. Participants self-reported their levels of alertness, attention, and tension to provide the raw data. The researchers discovered that personalized models outperformed a generalized (or non-personalized) model, forecasting baseline improvements in the precision, recall, and accuracy score ranging from 3% improvement to up to 52% improvement.

Due to the accessibility of sensor data, personalized well-being assessments have recently drawn increased attention (Abbas et al., 2016; Andreu-Perez et al., 2015; Chawla & Davis, 2013). For instance, a different study by Soto and John (2017) discovered that individualized models to predict focus and alertness outperformed generalized models, outperforming baselines by precision, recall, and accuracy scores ranging from 3% to up to 52%. On the other hand, it is well known that well-being, along with personality, cognitive, and personality traits, can affect job performance, which in turn can have an impact on organizations more generally (Barrick & Mount, 1991; Chiaburu et al., 2011; Kamdar & Van Dyne, 2007; Tett et al., 1991; Wright & Cropanzano, 2000). Within the Tesserae study, the work of Robles-Granda et al. (2020) is noteworthy since it used a variety of sensing modalities to gauge the anxiety, sleep, and affect of the 757 information workers who were being monitored. Wearables, phone applications, Bluetooth beacons, and social media were among the sensing modalities used. When predicting affect, anxiety, and sleep quality scores, models trained on the fusion of all the variables from various sensing modalities improved the symmetric mean absolute percentage error by up to 13.9%. In a similar vein, Saha, Grover, et al. (2021) recommended contextualizing offline behaviors as gathered from passive sensors to make models better adaptable to social media signals. This is in reference to other personalized models adopting a fusion of multimodal sensing. The participants in the Tesserae study were first grouped by the scientists based on passive sensing information gleaned from their wearables, Bluetooth beacons, and smartphone applications. Then, they added variables derived from social media to predict various constructs within each cluster, improving the baseline generic model by up to 5.43% in predicting information workers' self-reported anxiety, affect, and sleep quality.

For organizations, workplace health programs are known to bear a direct or indirect relationship to health care costs, absenteeism, productivity, recruitment/retention, culture, and employee morale. As remote working blurs the line between work and life (Como et al., 2021), organizational leaders have been prioritizing employee well-being and mental health. This focus on nurturing employee well-being is recognized to be critical to developing workplace resilience. The previously highlighted research indicates the varied ways in which diverse passive sensing technologies have been employed to measure aspects of employee health and well-being. Hence, if these potentials are realized in real-world workplace contexts, it will be possible to gain a comprehensive understanding and measurement of employee well-being that expands beyond conventional physical well-being to enable building a culture of holistic well-being including physical, emotional, financial, social, career, community, and purpose.

2.3.4 Collaboration, Coordination, and Organizational Pulse

There is empirical support for the importance of coordination on worker performance from pervasive technologies (Das Swain, Reddy, et al., 2019; Eagle & Pentland, 2009; Lindberg et al., 2013). Wearables were employed by Olguin et al. (2009) to demonstrate that social contacts with peers in close proximity account for job happiness. Similar to this, it has been suggested that encouraging "spatiality," or being present with coworkers even when they are not verbally communicating, is a desirable practice for employees (Olson & Olson, 2000). Therefore, it has proven possible to determine whether groups are cooperating by looking at association logs on a campus WiFi network (Das Swain, Kwon, et al., 2020). Activity-based working (ABW) environments, a relatively new trend in office spaces that allows for flexibility of mobility and different working environments, have also been explored for collaboration and coordination (Appel-Meulenbroek et al., 2011). Through the use of wearable technology,

Brown et al. (2014) altered the spatial configuration of office spaces and examined the effect on staff interactions. Proximity-based sensing was recently employed by Montanari et al. (2017) to comprehend worker interactions in ABW environments. Although earlier research (Appel-Meulenbroek et al., 2011) warned that this design could be misused and result in a loss of productivity, they discovered that ABW flattens office hierarchies and encourages lateral collaboration. In order to develop and manage staff in a way that may be more supportive of workplace coordination, passive information contained in empirically measured day-level activities using sensors can be studied. Additionally, Meyer et al. (2016) showed how a leader's effectiveness could be operationalized as a factor of passively sensed micro-behaviors like question-asking and mimicry, and described how these behaviors are linked to a leader's ability to empathize. Collaboration and coordination among team members are considered valuable for improved workplace outcomes.

Additionally, expanding the use of passive sensing technology, including cell phones, wearables, and social media, can assist in identifying implicit types of engagement between employees that are less obvious than face-to-face or physically collocated encounters. In light of this, it has been discovered that synchronization in worker routines captures latent behaviors of coordination and, consequently, person–organization fit (Das Swain, Reddy, et al., 2019). According to these authors, workers perform better when their behavior is consistent with that of their coworkers when they spend time away from their desks. With the use of pervasive technology, this method may be extended to a worker's desktop activities and calendar schedule to determine how well coordinated or "in sync" they are with their cohort, as surmised by Das Swain, Reddy, et al. (2019). Studies on open-source software communities show that synchronization in crowd-sourced code contribution aids codebase evolution, which supports this (Lindberg et al., 2013). In general, passive sensing technologies offer a great chance to investigate social interactions using virtual interfaces that can assist in a better comprehension of coordination and collaboration.

Next, at the collective organizational level, the development and implementation of new ideas as well as the handling of unforeseen occurrences like crises, can all be impacted by corporate culture, which is understood to embody a fundamental value system (Chamberlain, 2015; O'Reilly, 1989). The effectiveness of an organization can be both indicated by and influenced by its organizational culture (Strack et al., 2014). It can have an impact on human functioning in addition to organizational outcomes. Employees tend to perform better than those in societies where they feel disposable, for instance, in organizations where they are valued (Chamberlain, 2015). Toxic or unethical attitudes can have an effect on staff morale, which can therefore lead to poor employee performance, a low retention rate, and unattractive jobs (Hofstede, 2001; Strack et al., 2014). Further, according to O'Reilly, culture plays a crucial role in fostering and sustaining the level of passion and commitment among employees (O'Reilly, 1989). Employees display higher job satisfaction when given the authority and training to develop their skills (Yilmaz & Ergun, 2008). Similar to this, businesses that promote effort and have formal reward systems have fewer cases of workplace misconduct (Vardi, 2001). Research suggests that corporate culture, rather than fundamental attributes and abilities, might explain employees' performance and productivity (Barley et al., 1988).

Earlier research has operationalized corporate culture using a variety of frameworks. According to O'Reilly III and colleagues (1991), some measure it in terms of innovation, competitiveness, decisiveness, and growth orientation. Others categorize it using two-sided scales, such as the power distance (large/small), uncertainty avoidance (strong/weak), individuality vs. collectivism, or masculinity vs. femininity (Hofstede et al., 1990). These frameworks frequently employ survey tools to gauge company culture. However, because of circumstances when employees are uncomfortable sharing their opinions or choose to have no view toward the business, survey measurements are not comprehensive (Bagheri et al., 2012; Morrison & Milliken, 2000). Furthermore, surveys may be prone to social-desirability biases even when they are administered because they are frequently under the control of the organizations (Baruch & Holtom, 2008). A lack of sincerity in responses can sometimes cause surveys, even those that are well conducted, to be biased (Baruch & Holtom, 2008). Overall, it has been claimed that traditional evaluations of corporate culture lack complexity, context, and relevance in a variety of organizational situations (Prajogo & McDermott, 2011).

In light of the above, going beyond traditional approaches to quantifying organizational culture (Cooke & Rousseau, 1988; Cooke & Szumal, 2000; Glaser et al., 1987; Hofstede et al., 1990; Quinn & Rohrbaugh, 1983), research has measured organizational culture by utilizing archived as well as employees' naturalistic experiences shared on social and online media, including emails and internal communication channels (Baruch & Holtom, 2008; Goldberg et al., 2016; Guy et al., 2016; Shami, Nichols, & Chen, 2014; Srivastava & Goldberg, 2017). For instance, the concept has been categorized using textual analysis of annual reports, which then helps to understand a firm's risk-taking behavior (Nguyen et al., 2019). Recent research has used Glassdoor to infer specific features of corporate culture, such as "goal-setting" (Moniz, 2015.) or "risk-taking behavior" since anonymous platforms like Glassdoor can create "safe spaces" for employees to share and evaluate their workplace experiences (Nguyen et al., 2019). In a similar vein, Lee and Kang (2017) discovered that "Culture and Values" has one of the largest effects on employee retention after using Glassdoor data to investigate job satisfaction. Pasch (2018) distinguished six aspects of organizational culture through language and discovered a link between how people perceive culture and how well an organization performs. The same bag-of-words study of corporate values reviews has also been linked to organizational effectiveness (Luo et al., 2016). While studies have shown that employee experiences published on sites like Glassdoor that are provided on a wide scale have the ability to quantify organizational culture, these studies only look at a small number of characteristics, and the consequences are exclusively focused on the organization. In order to fill this gap, Das Swain, Saha, et al. (2020) operationalized a measure of culture based on many characteristics combined in a domain-driven manner in terms of organizational sectors and investigated its impact on employee-centric outcomes, including job performance.

Passive and naturalistic data has been used to study other facets of organizational behavior. Employee Social Pulse is a technology that Shami, Yang, et al. (2014) presented for understanding employee thoughts and attitudes by analyzing streams of data from internal and external social media platforms. Similar to this, the successful use of dictionary-based language analysis of such streams to determine employee engagement (Golestani et al., 2018; Shami et al., 2015). Muller et al. (2016) discovered that on the interpersonal level, peers' social influence can influence an employee's engagement, and motivated peers appear to be more supportive, enthusiastic, or radiate an infectious good effect (Mitra et al., n.d.). Content endorsement via "likes" on social media has also been discovered to indicate specific features of corporate work styles through analysis of employees' social media behavior (Guy et al., 2016).

This research indicates that passive data such as that from social media may be utilized as a tool to illustrate individual- and collective-level experiences at the workplace. Scholars see significant potential that can be unlocked to improve coordination, collaboration, and cultural aspects that may influence employee behavior as workers use digital technologies, such as passive sensing tools, for a variety of purposes, including information seeking, knowledge discovery and management, expert finding, internal and external networking, and potential collaborations (Archambault & Grudin, 2012; Zhang et al., 2014).

2.4 Practical Implications

Given the immense promise we have highlighted, passive sensing technologies are being embraced by organizations to promote employees' well-being, morale, and productivity. Organizations have started using gamification, personalized advice, or even incentive schemes to motivate staff to be more active in their daily lives (Khakurel et al., 2018). Additionally, studies looking into the use of wearable devices in corporate wellness programs have reported that doing so had a favorable effect on staff members' health and well-being (Giddens et al., 2017). Thus, passive sensing technology can be applied to encourage a healthy lifestyle among the workforce as well as to monitor and evaluate the health and well-being of the workforce. Still, there are a variety of additional and novel implications that are put forth via passive sensing, which are yet to be considered in workplaces. These implications are grouped in terms of those for designing, building, and deploying worker-centric technologies as well as organization-centric tools.

2.4.1 Worker-Centric Technology Implications

Starting off, utilizing commercially available sensing technology to record typical activity states might aid in analyzing workplace performance beyond internal factors like personality. In the workplace, personas can be identified using traditional machine-learning techniques and sensor fusion (e.g., Das Swain, Saha, et al., 2019). These personas can then be used as a descriptive-analytical framework to generate new hypotheses about the connection between situational information and job performance. Beyond what can be disclosed by an individual's personality, such computationally and data-driven assessment of organizational personas can also offer a dynamic lens that highlights the relationship between routine activities and workplace functioning. Designing self-reflection tools that enable employees to continuously assess and comprehend the ambiguities in their roles and align their skill set and productivity with employer expectations can also be done using measurements of job performance obtained through computational modeling of passive sensing data. This can also aid employees in conducting ongoing evaluations of their abilities and productivity at work. Role comparisons both inside and between organizations are examples of such self-reflection tools. These can help the employees by providing more simplified information, lowering the expenses and effort associated with their job search, and improving their well-being. Additionally, discussing duties or work responsibilities involves some self-reflection. People can find the roots of their role ambiguity, workplace stress, or barriers to productivity by using passive sensing data-powered tools that help to quantify aspects of such descriptions against formal job role.

Next, physical activity and mobility have been shown to boost memory (Thomas et al., 2016), improve concentration (Budde et al., 2008), and enhance creativity (Steinberg et al., 1997). Therefore, regular activity could positively impact performance, helping workers focus better, be creative at work, relieve stress, and retain information. The level of activity and mobility during the working week is also strongly coupled with job demands. For example, a software engineer in a tech company may spend most of their working week at a workstation, while a project manager/consultant may be much more mobile. This far, such granular insights about activities have not been possible, but as the research shows, passive sensing may allow the closing of this gap. Measurements of physical activities and worker mobility can be immensely valuable from a personal improvement perspective, such as for workers, intending to optimize their work schedules as a way to achieve greater work-life balance. Novel worker-centric tools are envisioned to this end.

Additionally, it is established that self-reflection enhances well-being and job satisfaction (Di Stefano et al., 2016). Incorporating self-reflection tools with the aforementioned methods would enable automated (self) assessment of an individual's skill set, area of interest, and capacity for adapting to a given organizational role, as well as indirect assistance in estimating their productivity, well-being, and job satisfaction at both their current and potential future workplaces. An individual can evaluate their professional progress and development by tracking positions, responsibilities, and duties over time. They can also be prompted with suggestions for skill training as appropriate. These logs can serve as a diary-style data source for professional mentors and career counselors to better understand one's career trajectory, beyond the information offered in a CV, for people who desire to seek professional job-related assistance. Speaking of health and well-being in particular, innovative systems and interventions that employ passive sensing to track the likelihood of negative shifts in well-being and mood proactively may be created and deployed for workers, which can provide the right assistance to individuals in need. These can take the shape of privacy-preserving self-tracking technologies that raise people's awareness of workplace well-being issues or as interfaces that dependable caregivers, peers, and allies could use to direct timely and individualized help.

2.4.2   Organization-Centric Technology Implications

In light of the body of research we have outlined, complementary organization-centric tools that work in conjunction with worker-centric technology may be imagined. To support occupational performance, Dunn et al. (1994) note the necessity to "change" and "adapt" the situational context in their EHP framework (previously introduced). Activity is a context attribute that results from external ecosystems, such as an employee's workspace, the type of work they do, their coworkers' personalities, or even their own lifestyle (Abowd et al., 1999; Schmidt et al., 1999). Therefore, comparing organizational personas identified by passive sensing can assist personnel management teams in making modifications to behaviors, routines, and settings that can be supported for particular personalities. Passive sensing work style-related insights can offer a set of testable hypotheses for organizational study since malleability is salient to dynamic constructs like activity states. To better understand corporate culture, it could be interesting to examine workplace personas among subpopulations of organizations. It may be able to determine the core groups of individuals that succeed in particular organizations using passively collected data, as well as whether and how these groups vary across firms and how strongly performance is impacted by differences from these groups. In fact, activity-based personas can be thought of as tools for studying novel concepts of person–organization fit, such as novel multi-modal interpretations of fit that compare activity states as well as personalities within organizations. A technique like this has the ability to shed light on the dynamics of work performance among groups of people during organizational crises, turbulence, or unexpected policy changes or enforcement. Passive sensing could identify abrupt changes in activity features that correspond to high or low performance. In particular, personality changes are only gradually detected. Furthermore, context, or ecology, encompasses more than just activity. The body of work we have mentioned emphasizes examining other context variables, such as the semantics of place or social interactions.

The aforementioned research also shows how dashboards and office equipment can be created to improve the "health" or efficiency of a business. Such dashboards can discreetly and proactively evaluate various workplace structures at scale while taking into account employees' privacy concerns. The evaluations may be ongoing in real time and granular both between and within companies, industry sectors, and employer kinds. These tools can be used to discover unfavorable workplace characteristics, such as the frequently hidden reasons for employee unhappiness. In fact, many businesses already give their employees access to internal social media platforms, online discussion boards, or even email profile description spaces where they can frequently update their descriptions of their roles and areas of expertise as well as manager or peer-reviewed recommendations. By utilizing these internal statistics, businesses may decide to use these dashboards to evaluate employee behaviors and perspectives in order to make educated decisions that are worker-centric, such as job matching for open positions in internal hiring. Additionally, dashboards can be created to offer human resources and people management teams insights linked to health and wellness, which can be very beneficial for proactive assistance and well-informed decision-making in enterprises. Finally, dashboards can assist in direct initiatives to empower underrepresented groups and support them with measures that improve their welfare, such as promoting inclusive company culture and fostering a sense of belonging and intrinsic motivation among employees.

Organizations can learn about how their culture is changing over time by using passive sensing-based assessments in a continual manner. This will enable them to execute timely interventions to improve employee well-being. This can facilitate reflection on the presumptions and expectations of a work environment for both job seekers and current employees (De Choudhury & Counts, 2013; Shami, Yang, et al., 2014). After all, it is well recognized that corporate culture is related to employment desirability (Cable & Judge, 1996). Additionally, new hires and other geographically dispersed employees already make extensive use of enterprise-based social networks and collaborative knowledge bases, or "wikis," to learn about and participate in their organization's culture (Thom-Santelli et al., 2011). Given the high levels of knowledge seeking on these platforms (Albalooshi et al., 2012; Cetto et al., 2016), incorporating passively inferred organizational culture measures, like those already discussed, in them can aid teams in understanding the working environment as well as the attitudes and beliefs held by an organization. Generally speaking, the multidimensional character of workplace constructs created with passive sensors can help firms better understand the culture forming at work by asking questions like, "Does our culture encourage work-life balance? Does our company foster innovation among its employees? Or is it purely focused on productivity? Are we sufficiently praising, motivating, rewarding, and recognizing individual efforts? Do we collaborate effectively enough? Do workers love performing that?" Importantly, organizations can examine how well leadership structures model behaviors that embody the organization's ethos, how significant events (such as initial public offerings or IPOs, product releases, etc.) may impact the underlying morale, and what steps might be taken to address issues of unhealthy culture thanks to the ability to quantitatively gauge such constructs as collaboration, culture, work styles, and social behaviors.

Finally, there are repercussions for labor unions and other parties involved in the advocacy of worker rights. By combining the previously mentioned methods with participatory design and feminist approaches (Bardzell, 2010), these stakeholders can gain a more nuanced understanding of perceptions of various worker constructs, such as employee satisfaction. This will allow assessments based on large-scale (passive sensing) data to be supplemented by assessments made from workers' lived experiences. As a result, more durable and effective solutions to employee issues may be developed, such as employee-aligned incentive systems and initiatives to promote an "employee-first" culture as the key factor in organizational performance rather than a "shareholder-first" or "profit-first" culture. By seeing and appreciating the unique requirements of various individuals and groups, passive sensing in workplace evaluation can, in essence, encourage advocacy for organizational measures that aim to reduce demographic biases in workplaces (Heilman, 2012).

2.5 Challenges That Need Resolution in Future Research

The body of research we have discussed unpacks significant potential in using passively sensed data for the measurement of a range of constructs at the workplace. Despite the rich implications for workplace technology design, ranging from tools that support the worker to those that focus on facilitating decision-making at the organizational level, significant hurdles and bottlenecks remain in the practical realization of this new form of workplace measurement. In this section, I bring to the fore the major challenges that have surfaced in existing research in this emergent domain.

2.5.1   Considerations for the Passive Sensing Infrastructure

2.5.1.1   Selection, Deployment, and Shelf-Life of Sensors

The earlier description shows that there are many different ways to configure the data collection, processing, and use of a passive sensing system for assessing workplace outcomes. For example, prior studies differ in the number and type of sensors used, the location and timing of data processing, and the nature of variables being assessed or predicted. As sensors become more energy-efficient and pervasive technology makers add dedicated chips to process sensor data, it has become more practical to capture data from as many sensors as possible, for subsequent processing as needed. However, given an emphasis on technology- and data-driven approaches in this emergent field this far, currently, there exists no clear guidance on what sensors should be selected for assessing which workplace construct. Further, there is a lack of consensus on which sensors should be deployed in what study design and how. As the field matures, practical considerations will also be paramount – multimodal studies that seek to utilize a number of sensors can be difficult to deploy in the real world with varied constraints (Mattingly et al., 2019; Morshed et al., 2019; Purta et al., 2016; Saha, Reddy, et al., 2019), as they are expensive in terms of instrumentation, maintenance, and reliable functioning over extended periods of time. Moreover, unscrupulously deployed sensors to capture comprehensive measurements about a participant can introduce privacy concerns and generally overburden them (Boyd & Crawford, 2012; Rooksby et al., 2019). These issues may accrue greater complexity given differences in the culture, norms, and expectations at different organizations and workplaces. What could be parsimonious approaches or guidelines to identify what minimum number of sensors could provide the maximum coverage over a number of workplace assessments? To this end, future research can draw upon methodologies that adhere to paradigms like "small data" in (critical) data science (Boyd & Crawford, 2012; Lazer & Radford, 2017) and passive sensing (Estrin, 2014), and Occam's razor metaphor for parsimony in machine learning (Domingos, 1998).

Nevertheless, a parsimonious selection of sensors will need to go hand-in-hand with the evolution of pervasive sensing technologies. Sensing capabilities of these technologies evolve rapidly, and so do the various types of captured and logged data. As a result, the ways these technologies and their data may be used for workplace assessments will also need to adapt over time. On a related note, as more data streams are captured in studies on passive sensing, it is important to derive new features – i.e., features that can be deduced from raw sensor data, from simpler mathematical calculations to more complex behaviors – in order to facilitate downstream machine learning. These computed features should match the problem at hand, such as speech detection amongst workers in a team, an indicator of coordination. New guidance is also needed here to decide which sensors might have the greatest proclivity to derive new knowledge about new features. After all, passive data gathered from pervasive technologies is not a monolith. Neither does it exist in a vacuum. As we appropriate this data for all sorts of models to assess workplace outcomes, the question therefore is – what are we capturing, and what are we missing? How does that change over time, as technology politics, norms, users, and the broader societal contexts evolve?

2.5.1.2   *Generalizability of Sensed Data*
Most existing studies have adopted a relatively narrow focus, leveraging data gathered under specific contexts, relying on small samples, particular target populations of interest (e.g., homogeneous demographics and job roles), or controlled environments (e.g., within particular scenarios and locations). One of the most significant considerations that may limit real-world use of the passive sensing algorithms for workplace measurement is, therefore, the data gathering approach. Further, other factors can additionally limit the generalizability of findings from pervasive technologies. While an increasing number of people are adopting pervasive technologies, ranging from smartwatches to smartphones (King & Sarrafzadeh, 2018; Lee, Kim, et al., 2019), a persistent digital divide remains, which may preclude whose data may be analyzed and, thereafter, who can benefit from the computational insights from this data. The topic of the digital divide is particularly pertinent here because most passive sensing studies discussed in the previous section focus on population samples in the Western world, such as North America and Europe, and are privileged with better socioeconomic conditions. Smartphones and wearables, although increasing in the prevalence of use in the Global South (Ling & Horst, 2011), still suffer from the challenges imposed by the digital divide. Consequently, speaking of generalizability, although cross-cultural research has been emphasized by organizational psychologists (Tsui et al., 2007), current models and sensing infrastructure may not be easily adaptable to Global South contexts and evidence in this regard remains sparse. In fact, without thoughtful implementation of these infrastructures in these emerging contexts, harmful impacts may ensue. Warschauer and Ames (2010) acknowledged the ambitious and forward-looking initiative

and potential of the One Laptop per Child program in the educational sector, yet they argue that its underlying assumptions take cross-cultural generalizability at face value, which could be one of the reasons why the program did not succeed in educating vast populations in the Global South. In the context of our discussion in this chapter, a utopian vision of simply providing passive sensing technologies to diverse cultural groups will, therefore, not be sufficient for generalizability. More grounded, formative research is needed to understand barriers to the adoption and use of such pervasive technologies, and which types of tools under what context will be meaningful in the study of cross-cultural organizational behaviors.

Moreover, crosscutting across different cultures and privacy preferences and concerns may impact who uses these technologies substantially enough and in a way that suits computational analysis, extraction, and prediction of workplace attributes. For instance, some people may not truthfully report linguistic cues about their well-being, while certain others may use social media to exaggerate their experiences. As another example, smartphone usage behaviors may vary widely across individuals – studies note age-based differences – and, consequently, the kind of data that may be collected. This may hamper the generalizability and reproducibility of efforts that apply computational models trained on one subpopulation to another. Identifying and quantifying these biases will be the first step toward countering their impacts and mitigating potential risks and harms.

2.5.2   Considerations for Modeling Approaches

2.5.2.1   Representations of Ground Truth

Ground truth is central in passive sensing studies of workplaces, as it serves as the outcome on which computational and machine-learning models are trained. However, even though prior work is abundant with literature on inferring various types of psychological states of individuals from passively sensed data (Amir et al., 2017; Ciman & Wac, 2016; Coppersmith et al., 2014; Muaremi et al., 2013; Sano & Picard, 2013), in the computing field, the ground truth is often considered an unquestionable "gold standard," an issue that has recently been noted by psychology researchers as well (Tay et al., 2020). Deeper introspection of the ground truth's association with ecological factors is therefore urged. Many studies acquire ground truth *in situ* (Chan et al., 2018; Mattingly et al., 2019; Saha et al., 2017; Wang et al., 2014). While this streamlines study designs, capturing the "real" ecology of the participant, it implies the researcher(s) is/are no longer a part of those same conditions or able to undertake participatory observations on the ground truth being collected. Consequently, researchers may not have good ways to address issues like whether participants of their study tend to respond to EMA questions immediately after stressful incidents or negative experiences at the workplace, or if they provide summative self-reports of the experience from time to time. Another issue where the "distance" between the researcher and the participant can be particularly problematic is to unpack if the latter self-report their true underlying feelings or they are responding with whatever allows better impression management. Self-reports being the most typical form of ground truth, a lack of this background knowledge can diminish the value that could be derived from computational modeling of passive data, if not proven to be counter-beneficial instead.

The opacity in ground truth development in passive sensing stems from the fact that, while machine learning necessitates objective and quantifies outcomes to be assessed or predicted from data, in reality, most psychological attributes of interest in the workplace context are complex concepts and, therefore, layperson interpretations of machine-learning outcomes tend to be high-level artifacts. Even when collected *in situ* via self-reports (Chan et al., 2018), the ground truth that is collected in passive sensing studies is perhaps only an evaluative judgment of the participant's current state (Weiss, 2002). Weiss describes that "true affective states, moods, and emotions have causes and consequences distinguishable from the causes and consequences of evaluative judgments" (Weiss, 2002, p. 176). By contrast, many psychological states may also have physiological underpinnings (e.g., stress), which may not be captured adequately in self-reports (Weiss, 2002). A good example is a case where a participant is exercising and another where they are embroiled in an argument with another person. Despite both cases having many similar physiological effects, such as elevated heart rate, self-reports are likely to show a lower level of perceived stress from exercise. Perhaps this contradiction can be better reconciled using Russell (1980)'s Circumplex Model of Affect, which describes emotional response using two dimensions, arousal (or alertness) and valence (or pleasure). Self-reports tend to only capture the valence aspect of emotion, as arousal is often momentary and susceptible to the particular event/experience (Wearne et al., 2019). It is thus not surprising that in an experimental study of public speaking, Hellhammer and Schubert (2012) found that self-reported stress was correlated with the physiological state only during the stressful event, not before or after it. A similar study found that although stressors are known to impact the heart rate of participants, when their self-report of stress was sought, it was instead more correlated with their trait anxiety (Wearne et al., 2019). Having said this, we do not imply that only one representation of a specific workplace attribute is "true," nor do we conclude that various representations are mutually exclusive. What these works indicate is that the state of a participant can be interpreted differently based on the ground truth measurement approach. And since measurement approaches simply get at abstractions of ground truth, not necessarily the real truth, knowledge and recognition of these different abstractions can be important for computational models. After all, each representation can be explained by a different type of passively sensed data. Broadly speaking, we would like to encourage researchers to consider different types of gold standard for ground truth (Hovsepian et al., 2015) in order to ensure that models developed with various forms of passive sensing data are robust to multiple representations of the ground truth.

2.5.2.2   *Generalizable versus Personalized Models*
Next, concerning the prediction of social constructs, such as productivity or performance, modeling dynamic workplace variables such as well-being or affect becomes additionally challenging than stand-alone prediction approaches that use passive sensing to measure a single construct. Even though long-term longitudinal data can help alleviate some of these issues (Salganik et al., 2020), dynamic variables are impacted by a variety of situational, contextual, and personal information (Judge & Zapata, 2015; Viswesvaran & Ones, 2000) that may not always be readily captured via sensors or available due to privacy restrictions (Chiaburu et al., 2011; Wright & Cropanzano, 2000). In addition, low sample size, low sample variability, and the already-noted sample limitations may particularly paralyze machine-learning modeling approaches, most of which tend to perform well when large repositories of labeled data are available. A prevalent criticism of passive sensing, in fact, has been that the models do not adapt to new contexts and that models tend to overfit the particular sample or context, thus remaining underpowered to support translation and transferability. The emergence and rapid adoption of newer sensing technologies as well as unanticipated bottlenecks in passive data collection further complicate the situation. To this end, Mohr et al. (2017) rightly noted: "The field of [passive] sensing will likely continue to experience a tension between what is possible and what is feasible, which is related to a trade-off that occurs between small proof-of-concept studies demonstrating novelty and large studies demonstrating robustness and generalizability" (p. 42).

Consequently, modeling approaches need to adopt strategies built for and which can accommodate diverse populations spanning time frame, work context, and geography, rely on unobtrusive data collection in the varied workplace and organizational contexts, actively focus on datasets that include heterogeneous subpopulations with contrasting individual differences, and leverage signals from complementary sensors that capture a wide range of physical, behavioral, and psychological trends. Importantly, these models will have to be robust not only in terms of their performance on unseen data but also against the messiness of real-world sensor data that often includes inaccurate, incomplete, or missing entries (Mallinckrodt et al., 2003; Molenberghs et al., 2004). This is an especially salient point because no machine-learning system is 100% accurate and, thus, researchers, developers, and users in workplace contexts must come to a consensus about how much error is acceptable in particular practical settings. Benchmarking can also help create quantifiable policies on providing better explanations of the predictions/outcomes, better interpretations of the underlying functioning of the computational models, and better actionability of the inputted passively sensed data. To this end, researchers may draw upon machine-learning approaches that consider different model error representation paradigms, allowing stakeholders to easily weigh on false positives or false negatives, depending on their target optimization goal. Or perhaps they can use a metric such that a model minimizes the effect of its inaccuracy. For example, step counts provided by smartwatches may be inaccurate; however, within a particular user, those inaccuracies might be consistent or fit a pattern. Hence if the goal is to build models for behavioral measurement centering on the individual, such inaccuracies might be accounted for systematically. Future research can further explore the understanding and acceptability of error and uncertainty and how best to mitigate it in a generalizable fashion.

At the same time, models need to be personalized, where models are tailored and optimized for a particular individual (Rudovic et al., 2018). Such personalization is tackled through the use of person-centered analytical approaches where individuals are represented via patterns of their underlying characteristics, rather than a collection of population-level variables (Das Swain, Saha, et al., 2019; Howard & Hoffman, 2018; Wright & Woods, 2020). Such directions are increasingly advocated for organization science research as well (Woo et al., 2018). Aside from helping overcome between-subject variability, in agreement with Saha, Grover, et al. (2021), these approaches can be more readily usable and expressible relative to all-inclusive features, where certain features may be indeterminate, vague, or dubious. Another way to think about person-centered approaches is their ability to take into account an individual's circumstances and context. It is notable that personalized workplace assessments using passively sensed data allow us to go beyond the more common, user-profiling-like approaches to demographic information based on one's age, race, and gender, which are not only less distinguishing from a behavioral measurement perspective, but also are prone to be misused for stereotypy and discrimination at workplaces. Nonetheless, I recognize some challenges brought forth by person-centered methods. Modeling the individual and their dynamic context means additional technical overhead, which might, in turn, imply the participant has to consent to sharing data via multiple passive sensing modalities and over longer periods of time. Personalization can also be intensive in terms of statistical power and effort. One way to tackle these limitations could be to first assess the need and feasibility of building such models through pilot studies involving a small sample population. The pilot exploration can be immensely insightful in determining what level of data granularity is needed for personalization and whether and how many separate passive data streams might be needed to describe the individual's psychology and state.

Ultimately, I agree with Howard and Hoffman (2018)'s suggestion that personalized or generalized approaches are not necessarily competitive, each with its pros and cons. Instead, they are complementary in terms of methodological, statistical, and theoretical advantages. In a particular setting, one approach may be "better" for one type of outcome. Still, a nuanced understanding of the theoretical and practical goals can illuminate how each method weighs known and unknown attributes in organizational measurement. Thus, the model choice could be tempered with theory-driven strategies for technical development, carefully considering both personalization and generalizability to reasonable degrees.

2.5.2.3 *Prediction and Explanation Trade-offs*

Closely related to the previously described challenges in modeling passive sensing data is the issue of ascertaining when to optimize for predictive performance versus obtaining explanations via the computational models. Many passive sensing projects include interdisciplinary teams involving computer scientists and psychologists. Different research participants may have different goals for a project that uses passive sensing to infer workplace attributes, stemming from their disciplinary training – computer scientists tend to prioritize achieving the most accurate predictions or assessments from the passive data, while social scientists tend to be interested in the mechanisms and variable relationships that contribute to a workplace outcome. These diverging or seemingly conflicting value systems across research team members may impose novel challenges to passive sensing as to the particular methodology that needs to be adopted. For instance, recent advancements in deep learning may present better opportunities to obtain model performance not possible before. However, they lack the ability to support end users in exploring what factors or features help or hinder the performance – a piece of information that can be significant for any downstream decision. On the other hand, using traditional machine learning can help understand how specific attributes captured in the passive data contribute to the outcome of interest – thus these approaches might be better poised for explanation goals but at the cost of compromised model performance. Explanation is described as permitting an observer to determine the extent to which a particular input was determinative or influential to an output (Biran & Cotton, 2017). The prevailing recommendation is that a machine-learning model should provide an explanation in situations where a human decision-maker would be expected to do the same.

Moreover, specific modeling approaches, prioritizing prediction or explanation, may be better poised if the goal is to provide longitudinal estimates of an outcome and to capture causal relationships in the process. Predictive approaches are often employed for this purpose; however, such approaches are likely to fail since the goal is about the prediction (the what), not the explanation (the why). Yet, predictive models are used for explanation in various settings (Lundberg et al., 2020). Therefore, delineating the intended purposes of a forecasting model, which is understandably hard, can provide clues as to whether causal modeling – a set of tools that are designed to provide explanations – needs to be a part of a predictive approach. At the same time, it is important to note the following: Not every question needs to involve an explanatory model. In practice, though, when passive sensing is employed toward workplace assessments, both of the goals of prediction and explanation might be of interest; hence future work needs to consider novel machine-learning methodologies, perhaps grounded in mixed methods, to concurrently satisfy both interests.

2.5.3   *Considerations for Validation of Models Built with Passively Sensed Data*

2.5.3.1   *Construct Validity and Psychometric Issues*

Recent research in computational social science has noted that there is often limited explication of the construct validity of various psychological states of interest, beginning with clearly defining what attribute is being measured and how it is operationalized within the research (Chancellor & De Choudhury, 2020). Ernala et al. (2019) noted that the operationalizations of certain well-being states – signals that are used to train the computational models of mental health risk in workplaces – often do not measure what they purport to measure. To stakeholders in the workplace context – whether the worker themselves or their employers – currently the primary source of information around work-place attributes comprises responses gathered via validated question-naires, scales, interviews, etc. Mis-operationalizations of or opacity in the conceptualization of these constructs derived via passive sensing technologies may add complexities to the conventional assessment method as well as how the assessments are utilized in real-world appli-cations. Should they trust the assessments of these computational models at face value? What happens when the mis-operationalizations or the lack of context around ground truth development lead to contradicting assessments?

Going forward, partnership of computational researchers and organi-zational psychologists throughout the research pipeline is needed. For example, from establishing the validity of measured passive sensing behaviors, providing an appraisal of the data via qualitative coding tasks, to interpreting and situating large-scale data analysis will be needed to improve rigor and the issues of construct validity. In addition, as pre-scribed by Tay et al. (2020), as the field moves toward generalizing these findings to new technologies or new opportunities for practice, it is essential that the psychometric properties of the assessments be carefully maintained throughout the various computational modeling practices (e.g., reliability of the assessments). In these efforts, I do note that disciplinary norms of research may be a challenge. Computer science often values methodological novelty (and subsequently the new method's validity) over robustness studies that may be required for establishing generalizability, construct validity, and psychometric rigor. On the other hand, an emphasis on theory validation and theory development in social science may be more suited for establishing the validity of passive data, but in the process, it may preclude the deployment of novel sensors and novel sources of passive sensing data in workplace assessments. Navigating these issues will, therefore, also need to find ways to strike a balance between the disciplinary tensions that emphasize validity testing in different ways.

2.5.3.2   *Theoretical/Domain-Oriented Grounding*

Related to the issue just outlined lies another limitation, which is a lack of theoretical underpinning in the ways signals from pervasive technologies have been identified and computationally modeled in existing research. Most of the scales and questionnaires used for workplace assessments draw upon theoretical frameworks (Scott & Reynolds, 2010). They undergo rigorous psychometric testing and are continually adjusted as the understanding of human behavior, psychology, and organization evolves. The passive sensing technology-derived computational measurements of workers are, however, not inspired by this theory. Instead, they focus on observed behaviors, which may or may not align with theoretical models, frameworks, or guidelines in the organizational behavior literature. In the absence of supplementary and accessible details of their inner workings and groundings, how can workplace stakeholders trust these new sources of signals, adapt them to their existing practices and understandings, and thereafter act upon them?

Moreover, as also mentioned, machine-learning models often adopt a greedy data-driven approach, where all possible pieces of passive data are employed to derive all possible sets of relevant signals. Since machine-learning models are often more robust to higher dimensionality than conventional statistical approaches (e.g., regressions), the inclusion of a large number of features in an atheoretical fashion is less of a challenge. The underlying assumption of modeling passive data is often that dimensionality reduction, feature selection, or representational learning would allow overcoming the curse of dimensionality easily, providing stable results. However, in this process, machine-learning models may obfuscate the relationships between different features (or variables), which might preclude exploring the extent to which a machine-learning model represents or mimics the theoretically known or situated relationships between variables surrounding a workplace behavior or outcome. Hypothesis testing, conventionally used in psychology studies to validate theories, may also not be possible with such a machine-learning approach, limiting the practical utility of passive sensing-based workplace assessments among different stakeholders. Future research will need to find ways to strike a balance between attempts to derive a mechanistic understanding of workplace behaviors grounded in a theoretical framework, along with the abilities of machine-learning models to measure or predict variables of interest from large troves of passively gathered data. Additional considerations regarding the theoretical grounding of passive sensing assessments at the workplace may arise from the fact that such unobtrusive sensing can capture large volumes of very personal and/or sensitive information easily and rapidly; however, little guidance exists as to how such vast data should (or should not be) analyzed that is consistent with theory. Therefore, I encourage more critical investigations of computational approaches to arrive at theoretically meaningful interpretations.

2.5.3.3 Observer Effect and Efficacy in Prospective Study Designs

I note that the existing body of research relies on retrospective passive sensing data to algorithmically derive workplace assessments. For these algorithms to be usable and useful in the real world, they will have to go beyond showcasing feasibility on retrospective data to functioning accurately and reliably in prospective settings. However, multiple threads of recent research have argued as well as demonstrated how models trained on retrospective data do not necessarily translate well to the prospective setting due to issues of bias and non-representativeness (Boyd & Crawford, 2012; Lazer et al., 2014; Ruths & Pfeffer, 2014; Tufekci, 2014). Notable is the position of Olteanu et al. (2019), who noted that the validity and practical reliability of big data technologies are hampered by the complexities, idiosyncrasies, and uncertainties that surround human behavior, beyond factors that confound it.

Ruths and Pfeffer (2014) noted that studies harnessing social media data, in particular, may misrepresent or be ineffective in the real world due to people's changing behaviors. Lazer et al. (2014) similarly unpacked how the Google flu predictor algorithm that used Google search data overestimated the real-time measurement of influenza-like illnesses, despite satisfactory performance on historical data. In addition, privacy concerns may arise when retrospective data, often without participant consent, is employed in making sensitive predictions related to workplace behaviors. Fiesler and Proferes (2018) surveyed Twitter users to understand how they felt their historical data was being used for research without their knowledge or awareness, and found that the majority of respondents felt that researchers should not be able to use postings without consent. In fact, scholars fear perceptions of surveillance even when prospective research designs are adopted due to a lack of participant awareness. For example, the Facebook emotion contagion study did not seek participation consent in its experimental design, where users' social media feeds were modified prospectively (Kramer et al., 2014). The study was heavily critiqued on ethical grounds (Jouhki et al., 2016). Pertinent here is the position of Boyd and Crawford (2012), who said that conducting experiments without participant awareness and agency can perpetuate troubling perceptions of passive technologies such as "Big Brother, enabling invasions of privacy, decreased civil freedoms, and increased state and corporate control" (p. 664).

One solution to these issues that have been advocated centers around prospective research designs, where individuals are recruited with informed consent for their passively sensed data to be used in algorithms for inference of behaviors and psychological states (Kreuter et al., 2020). However, the prospective use of algorithmically derived assessments poses new challenges, which are yet to be studied and addressed. Importantly, on certain pervasive technologies such as social media, participants may self-alter their behaviors if they feel they are being "observed" – changes that would be consistent with theories of social desirability, psychological reactance, self-presentation, and reasoned action, and others (Goffman, 1959; Madden et al., 1992; Snyder, 1979; Steindl et al., 2015): As Oswald et al. (2014) noted: "Observer effect is the phenomenon that individuals might deviate from their typical behaviors, attributed to the awareness of being 'watched' or studied" (p. 57).

Currently, it is not well understood what could be systematic ways individuals adapt their use of pervasive technologies around prospective study designs. Quantifying the presence and extent of the observer effect can improve methodologies that use passively gathered data toward assessing various psychological outcomes at the workplace. In essence, a better understanding of the observer effect in the future would provide clarity to researcher expectations and support designing and developing measures to correct and account for this effect in study designs surrounding workplaces (Ruths & Pfeffer, 2014).

2.5.4   Ethical Considerations

Leveraging pervasive and ubiquitous technologies to evaluate employee behavior in the workplace has always been considered problematic (Shilton, 2009; Watkins Allen et al., 2007). Persistent monitoring may be perceived by workers to be "big brother," especially given the lack of regulations that allow or preclude what is justified (for organizational functioning) and what is excessive (Watkins Allen et al., 2007), ranging from their desktop activity to their locations. While prior studies indicate that workers appear to accept sharing personal data for research, they may be more reserved when the business interests of their employers are present. In addition, I note that although adequate deidentification of data is often touted as a solution to these matters, some forms of passively sensed data, such as those generated from GPS tracking or social media postings, can be impossible to deidentify while retaining utility downstream – GPS traces are often considered one of the most sensitive personally identifiable data; with only four spatiotemporal points, research has shown that 95% individuals can be identified (Smith et al., 2012). Without adequate means to secure the data against compromised privacy, the use of pervasive technologies for workplace assessments may erode participant trust, hampering the continued use of these tools necessarily for passive sensing study designs.

In the post-COVID-19 pandemic society, the perceptions we have discussed can be exacerbated by the irresponsible implementation of the technologies in the increasingly more prevalent and more widely advocated remote work setup, which blurs the line between workplace and home. With workers adopting different working hours in different home settings, this boundary risks being constantly compromised, and with "always on" pervasive technologies, total surveillance of the work becomes a real possibility (Allen, 2020). In this new work setting, a misstep, whether inappropriate data collection or inappropriate behavioral measurement, can not only violate the privacy of the worker but also of other occupants of their dwelling. Therefore, to operate such applications, researchers and organizations need to request not only explicit consent but also center the design of these tracking systems on the privacy of all stakeholders involved, beyond the workers themselves. In the absence of adequate and established ethical guidelines in this emergent field (Torous & Nebeker, 2017) but in agreement with contemporary writings about privacy in related spaces (Christin, 2016), I argue that to realize the potential of this research participants should be informed what the passively gathered data might reveal about them, for how long the data will be used, who will be using it, and why. End-user-friendly, transparent tools will also need to be designed to help people understand and manage their data, including the ability to define acceptable use, limit data access, delete data, or revoke consent altogether. Summarily, I envision two types of privacy models. The first one could be an approach where privacy is part of the design of the passive sensing technology or infrastructure, so that it provides the worker with more agency in controlling the type and span of data being gathered, and the worker can choose how long they feel comfortable this data being preserved, analyzed, and with what worker-centric or organizational goals in mind (Langheinrich, 2009). The second model could draw upon the theoretical concepts and approaches to differential privacy (Dwork &

Roth, 2014). Within this, the infrastructure could automatically anonymize or alter the collected data such that it retains the signals of interest but disallows reverse engineering to identify the specific worker behind the data. Some versions of such an approach are already made possible through aggregative analysis; with differential privacy approaches, they can allow more granular aggregations without compromising privacy.

Another new challenge to privacy and ethical considerations is the evolving nature of work itself, prominent in the emergence of remote and/or unstructured new work environments. Many social science theories describe the connection between social ecology and human behavior (Dunn et al., 1994; Sansone et al., 2003). In conventional organizational measurement, this ecology has largely been consistent – it comprises the workplace or the largely fixed work setting. In fact, this ecology is typically so distinctly predictable and conceptualizable for workers that researchers, over the years, have conducted a variety of studies to understand the spillover effect of home-to-work and work-to-home (Barnett, 1994; Zedeck, 1992). However, with the increasing adoption of remote work, the variability in the working environments implies it is hard to distinguish which ecology constitutes work and which constitutes home (McLaren et al., 2020). As the COVID-19 pandemic has shown, these working ecologies are further intercepted by different workers' different family setups, as well as life duties and responsibilities that took center stage during and after the pandemic. Since these individual-specific complexities of work ecology are difficult, if not impossible, to be captured by passive sensing technologies, adopting such data without additional corroboration can lead to misleading measurements, if not detrimental ones. Preventing such outcomes underscores the need for adopting person-centric approaches to infer worker experiences from the gathered data. At the same time, organizations need to request not only explicit consent but also weave privacy-preserving features into the design of their technologies.

Finally, the use of passive sensing data for workplace assessments raises questions regarding the representation of workers in digital data, particularly the implications for those who are already underrepresented and marginalized groups in the workforce – women, LGBTQ+ individuals, racial and ethnic minorities, and people with disabilities. Moreover, as mentioned in the previous section, any organizational measurement technology is of, for, and by those workers not affected by digital divide. Returning to the emergent remote work setting, technology inequities imply differential gains (and harms) among the less privileged members of the workforce. Therefore, before implementing such technologies, organizations and human resource management would need to be cognizant of who gets excluded from the data that informs their decisions and to what extent the measured behaviors are representative of the broader organizational workforce. This awareness and knowledge can also contribute to a deeper understanding of the gaps in diversity, inclusion, and equity efforts in organizations when it comes to personnel hiring and retention. Organizations will also need a way to instill trust in employing passive sensing systems toward workplace assessments, which can be achieved through a genuine recognition of the primacy of the user and instantiated by providing more agency to people to control and own their data. In addition, organizations may also consider alternative, perhaps nontechnology-mediated mechanisms to capture the experiences of those not represented in the passively sensed data. That is, this can, in turn, encourages fortifying automatically collected data with other sources of information to represent the workers in decisions equally.

Increased openness, accountability, and transparency in the data gathering and modeling approach, as well as the development of appropriate data sharing standards, will go a long way to not only advance research in this field, but also provide opportunities to replicate findings and create workplace assessment tools that are valid, reliable, and generalizable. As scholars continue to develop better guidelines and practices surrounding preserving privacy and the ethical conduct of this research, centering those practices on the worker might alleviate much of the technological and algorithmic anxiety that stems from a lack of trust.

2.6   Conclusion

Operating unobtrusive technologies to evaluate employee behavior in the workplace, whether individual or organizational, has always been considered both opportunistic and, at the same time, problematic (Shilton, 2009; Watkins Allen et al., 2007). The research described in this chapter has attempted to present a balanced view of where the benefits lie to advance organizational measurement using passive sensing data while also discussing the many challenges, ranging from the selection of the types of machine-learning models to ground truth representation, that would need to be overcome to outweigh potential risks.

Broadly, the research described here advances the vision proposed by Estrin (2014), who argued for the importance of designing approaches that can combine multiple forms of technology-facilitated and technology-mediated sensed data into a better understanding of workplaces. I believe that the use and integration of conventional (e.g., surveys and self-reports) and newer (e.g., ubiquitous and social media) technologies will enable us to better understand the factors, attributes, patterns, and changes that may reveal or unravel a variety of organizational and workplace outcomes, whether at the individual level or collective. And yet, beyond the methodological challenges we have noted, workers and worker advocates have found it concerning that organizations are now equipped to monitor large volumes of data from multiple data streams, opening up the potential for large-scale employee surveillance (Watkins Allen et al., 2007). With an increasing culture of remote work, discerning this boundary can become even more challenging, and organizations risk enforcing workers' total surveillance throughout the day (Allen, 2020). Taken together, many exciting as well as significant directions for future research in this emergent area can be envisioned.

2.6.1   *Novel Passive Sensing Technologies*

There are increasingly new forms of ubiquitous technologies that can support the passive sensing of behaviors. For instance, heart rate variability, given by wearable devices and EEG are being used together to detect anxiety and stress (Lampert, 2015). Electrodermal activity has also been used in recent studies, with high accuracy for stress detection (Liu & Du, 2018), while Internet of Things (IoT) devices are being used to continually monitor the quality of life of specific demographic groups, such as the elderly (Olmedo-Aguirre et al., 2022). Smart fabrics embedded with sensors are now allowing temporally dense measurements ranging from body temperature to levels of electrical conductivity in the skin (Castano & Flatau, 2014). There is also a technical push to develop increasingly compact devices with extended battery life so that they can sustain unobtrusive data gathering over extended periods of time. Recognizing the advantages of developing wearables with "self-repairing" characteristics that allow them to increase their service life or ensure reliable operation under varied contexts is also being explored (Li et al., 2020). Rather than connecting multiple devices that incorporate one or more sensors, the evolution of the IoT domain has also sparked interest in directly connecting individual sensors to a standardized communication scheme that allows the collection of physiological data in real-time (Wu et al., 2019).

However, as newer technologies and newer sensing paradigms make their way into the research space or in the commercial domain, their reliability needs to be thoroughly scrutinized. Relatedly, with each new ubiquitous technology, we encourage novel context-sensitive validation approaches, as well as monitoring comparative gains (or losses) against suitable gold standards. Importantly, we would like to advocate moving away from fine-grained measurements of parameters that solely capture generalized behaviors from these passive data, such as physical activity (i.e., heart rate, respiratory rate, blood pressure), instead encouraging researchers to harness the unique strength that new ubiquitous technology may offer. For instance, a new hyperlocal social media platform might be adequate for capturing local interpersonal and social interactions but not suitable for tracking sleep.

2.6.2   *Novel Measurement Approaches*

Increasingly sophisticated machine-learning and computational methods for organizational measurement from passively sensed computational data continue to emerge (Mehrotra & Musolesi, 2018). Arguably, better feature engineering and selection can help reduce the gap between sensed measurements even with the same set of sensors (Das Swain et al., 2022). As newer machine-learning techniques, such as deep neural networks, permeate the passive sensing space (Mohr et al., 2017; Plötz, 2021), newer guidelines to craft features based on domain-driven aspects of ground truth or underlying organizational/behavioral theories will be needed. At the same time, the interpretability and explainability of models need to be catered to, by encouraging researchers to articulate how the specific chosen features capture the specific organizational constructs under consideration. In addition, the objectivity of machine learning/data mining to generate inferences needs to be questioned, as newer techniques are transplanted into this space. Since unobtrusive sensing can capture large volumes of information, unfounded "fishing expedition" style data science can often yield spurious connections with the target variable (Boyd & Crawford, 2012). We discourage viewing more passive data as Maslow's golden hammer (Maslow, 1966) – a tool to solve any problem. Overengineering the "hammer" can result in finding spurious associations in the data (Boyd & Crawford, 2012; Foster et al., 2014). For example, does sensing physical behaviors actually predict stress holistically, or does it merely describe its physiological aspects? Conversely, does tracing online content explain what an individual experiences, or does it only reflect how they project themselves? Thus, similar to other works that critique yet advocate employing machine learning for health and well-being (Bone et al., 2015; Ernala et al., 2019), we encourage more critical investigations of computational models to arrive at theoretically meaningful interpretations.

2.6.3   Parsimonious Approaches to Modeling Data

Financial and personnel investments in the "big tech" space are leading to the mushroom growth of novel sensors, sensing platforms for research or commercial use, and emergence and use of social media sites/apps continue to rise. Today, researchers have a plethora of means of novel organizational measurement. However, recent research by Das Swain et al. (2022) has shown that not all sensors are the same or mutually replaceable; each sensor represents different ground truth in different ways. Consequently, many have advocated an "all-in" approach to therefore combine signals from all possible sensors practically deployable, assuming that multimodal features together can elicit new context-specific features (Saha, Grover. et al., 2021; Xu et al., 2019). That said, increasing the number of deployed passive sensors, even if not adding significantly to participant burden due to sensors' unobtrusive data gathering, presents new challenges to privacy and tracking (Boyd & Crawford, 2012; Rooksby et al., 2019). Like Das Swain et al. (2022), I therefore propose that researchers adopt a parsimonious approach while utilizing and deploying passive sensors in research studies, with the goal of maximizing collecting varied behavioral and well-being data, while minimizing intrusiveness or resource need. To this end, I am inspired by Plötz's fifth postulate, "data rule, models serve" (Plötz, 2021).

2.6.4   Novel Software Infrastructures

As the research discussed in this chapter represents, passive data harnessed from ubiquitous technologies can help make significant strides in the psychological measurement domain in general and organizational behavior area in particular. In order to improve the adoption of these approaches, data gathering, and data modeling, will have to be made more accessible to a broader disciplinary audience, including those who may not have or need the technical know-how of the internal specifics of either the sensors or the computational models. I propose that software infrastructures will need to be developed that can enable automated passive sensing of behaviors, psychological states, and well-being, combining diverse and complementary forms of sensing. These initiatives can be akin to the Aware (Ferreira et al., 2015) and SenSocial (Mehrotra et al., 2014) frameworks that allow unobtrusive tracking and archival of passive data derived from people's smartphone activity. Beyond data logging, latency and near real-time abilities to query such information will be invaluable for behavioral analysis.

Next, so far, the development and evolution of passive sensing infrastructures have primarily focused on a few utilitarian goals, such as ensuring they have autonomy, support interoperability (e.g., across different operating systems), include rapid and agile data processing, and espouse usability to end users. I note, though, in particular, that usability is typically a factor that depends on the nature and demands of this end-user population; some clients may want to optimize limited data collection over device invasiveness, or vice versa. In a workplace context, this trade-off might be more significant. On the one hand, sensing technologies requiring lesser worker attention might be less disruptive but likely to be more invasive. On the other, such tools are less likely to be widely accepted, and their autonomy and interoperability may be difficult to achieve when the worker pool is diverse. In the future, essentially, the technical developmental trend of passive sensing infrastructures will directly or indirectly impact their functionality and utility in assessing human behavior in research studies and beyond. To sum up, I suggest these attributes – autonomy, interoperability, embedded intelligence, and usability – are made a central part of the described software infrastructures so that multidisciplinary researchers and practitioners are able to benefit from the promise of passive sensing data toward nuanced and reliable organizational measurement.

REFERENCES

Abbas, A., Ali, M., Khan, M. U. S., & Khan, S. U. (2016). Personalized healthcare cloud services for disease risk assessment and wellness management using social media. *Pervasive and Mobile Computing*, *28*, 81–99.

Abdullah, S., Murnane, E. L., Matthews, M., Kay, M., Kientz, J. A., Gay, G., & Choudhury, T. (2016). Cognitive rhythms: Unobtrusive and continuous sensing of alertness using a mobile phone. In *Proceedings of the 2016 ACM international joint conference on pervasive and ubiquitous computing* (pp. 178–189).

Abowd, D., Dey, A. K., Orr, R., & Brotherton, J. (1998). Context-awareness in wearable and ubiquitous computing. *Virtual Reality*, *3*(3), 200–211.

Abowd, G. D., Dey, A. K., Brown, P. J., Davies, N., Smith, M., & Steggles, P. (1999). Towards a better understanding of context and context-awareness. In *International symposium on handheld and ubiquitous computing* (pp. 304–307).

Ajzen, I. (1987). Attitudes, traits, and actions: Dispositional prediction of behavior in personality and social psychology. In L. Berkowitz (Ed.), *Advances in experimental social psychology* (Vol. 20, pp. 1–63). Elsevier.

Albalooshi, N., Mavridis, N., & Al-Qirim, N. (2012). A survey on social networks and organization development. In *2012 international conference on collaboration technologies and systems (CTS)* (pp. 539–545).

Allen, B. (2020). *Your boss is watching you: Work-from-home boom leads to more surveillance.* https://www.npr.org/2020/05/13/854014403/your-boss-is-watching-you-work-from-home-boom-leads-to-more-surveillance

Amir, S., Coppersmith, G., Carvalho, P., Silva, M. J., & Wallace, B. C. (2017). Quantifying mental health from social media with neural user embeddings. *arXiv preprint arXiv:1705.00335.*

Anderson, G., & Viswesvaran, C. (1998). An update of the validity of personality scales in personnel selection: A meta-analysis of studies published after 1992. In *13th annual conference of the Society of Industrial and Organizational Psychology,* Dallas.

Andreu-Perez, J., Leff, D. R., Ip, H. M., & Yang, G.-Z. (2015). From wearable sensors to smart implants – toward pervasive and personalized healthcare. *IEEE Transactions on Biomedical Engineering, 62*(12), 2750–2762.

Appel-Meulenbroek, R., Groenen, P., & Janssen, I. (2011). An end-user's perspective on activity-based office concepts. *Journal of Corporate Real Estate, 13*(2), 122–135.

Archambault, A., & Grudin, J. (2012). A longitudinal study of Facebook, LinkedIn, and Twitter use. In *Proceedings of Chi 2012.* Austin, TX.

Bagheri, G., Zarei, R., & Aeen, M. N. (2012). Organizational silence (basic concepts and its development factors). *Ideal Type of Management, 1*(1), 47–58.

Bardzell, S. (2010). Feminist HCI: Taking stock and outlining an agenda for design. In *Proceedings of the SIGCHI conference on human factors in computing systems* (pp. 1301–1310).

Barley, S. R., Meyer, G. W., & Gash, D. C. (1988). Cultures of culture: Academics, practitioners and the pragmatics of normative control. *Administrative Science Quarterly, 33*(1), 24–60.

Barnett, R. C. (1994). Home-to-work spillover revisited: A study of full-time employed women in dual-earner couples. *Journal of Marriage and the Family, 56*(3), 647–656.

Barrick, M. R., & Mount, M. K. (1991). The big five personality dimensions and job performance: A meta-analysis. *Personnel Psychology, 44*(1), 1–26.

Barthelemy, C. (2019). *Workplace engagement program: A prototype for maximizing adaptation to activity-based working.* Workplace Engagement Program Report. https://capstone.extension.harvard.edu/files/capstone/files/barthelemy_hdcapstone_report.pdf

Baruch, Y., & Holtom, B. C. (2008). Survey response rate levels and trends in organizational research. *Human Relations, 61*(8), 1139–1160.

Bin Morshed, M., Saha, K., Li, R., D'Mello, S. K., De Choudhury, M., Abowd, G. D., & Plötz, T. (2019). Prediction of mood instability with passive sensing. *Proceedings of the ACM on Interactive, Mobile, Wearable and Ubiquitous Technologies, 3*(3).

Biran, O., & Cotton, C. (2017). Explanation and justification in machine learning: A survey. In *Ijcai-17 workshop on explainable ai (xai)* (Vol. 8, pp. 8–13).

Bone, D., Goodwin, M. S., Black, M. P., Lee, C.-C., Audhkhasi, K., & Narayanan, S. (2015). Applying machine learning to facilitate autism diagnostics: Pitfalls and promises. *Journal of Autism and Developmental Disorders, 45*(5), 1121–1136.

Boyd, D., & Crawford, K. (2012). Critical questions for big data: Provocations for a cultural, technological, and scholarly phenomenon. *Information, Communication & Society, 15*(5), 662–679.

Brown, C., Efstratiou, C., Leontiadis, I., Quercia, D., Mascolo, C., Scott, J., & Key, P. (2014). The architecture of innovation: Tracking face-to-face interactions with ubicomp technologies. In *Proceedings of the 2014 ACM international joint conference on pervasive and ubiquitous computing* (pp. 811–822).

Budde, H., Voelcker-Rehage, C., Pietraßyk-Kendziorra, S., Ribeiro, P., & Tidow, G. (2008). Acute co-ordinative exercise improves attentional performance in adolescents. *Neuroscience Letters, 441*(2), 219–223.

Buschek, D., Bisinger, B., & Alt, F. (2018). Researchime: A mobile keyboard application for studying free typing behaviour in the wild. In *Proceedings of the 2018 CHI conference on human factors in computing systems* (pp. 1–14).

Cable, D. M., & Judge, T. A. (1996). Person–organization fit, job choice decisions, and organizational entry. *Organizational Behavior and Human Decision Processes, 67*(3), 294–311.

Caceres, R., & Friday, A. (2011). Ubicomp systems at 20: Progress, opportunities, and challenges. *IEEE Pervasive Computing, 11*(1), 14–21.

Calabrese, F., Diao, M., Di Lorenzo, G., Ferreira Jr, J., & Ratti, C. (2013). Understanding individual mobility patterns from urban sensing data: A mobile phone trace example. *Transportation Research Part C: Emerging Technologies, 26*, 301–313.

Campbell, A. T., Eisenman, S. B., Lane, N. D., Miluzzo, E., Peterson, R. A., Lu, H., . . . Ahn, G.-S. (2008). The rise of people-centric sensing. *IEEE Internet Computing*.

Castano, L. M., & Flatau, A. B. (2014). Smart fabric sensors and e-textile technologies: A review. *Smart Materials and Structures, 23*(5), 053001.

Cerwall, P., Jonsson, P., Möller, R., Bävertoft, S., Carson, S., Godor, I., et al. (2015). *On the pulse of the networked society*. Ericsson Mobility Report. https://www.ericsson.com/en/reports-and-papers/mobility-report/reports/june-2023

Cetto, A., Klier, J., Klier, M., Richter, A., & Wiesneth, K. (2016). The blessing of giving: Knowledge sharing and knowledge seeking in enterprise social networks. In *Ecis* (p. ResearchPaper64).

Chamberlain, A. (2015). *Does company culture pay off? analyzing stock performance of 'best places to work' companies* (Tech. Rep.). Glassdoor Research Report, March 2015.

Chan, L., Swain, V. D., Kelley, C., de Barbaro, K., Abowd, G. D., & Wilcox, L. (2018). Students' experiences with ecological momentary assessment tools to report on emotional well-being. *IMWUT*.

Chancellor, S., & Counts, S. (2018). Measuring employment demand using internet search data. In *Proceedings of the 2018 CHI conference on human factors in computing systems* (p. 122).

Chancellor, S., & De Choudhury, M. (2020). Methods in predictive techniques for mental health status on social media: A critical review. *NPJ Digital Medicine, 3*(1), 1–11.

Chawla, N. V., & Davis, D. A. (2013). Bringing big data to personalized healthcare: A patient-centered framework. *Journal of General Internal Medicine, 28*(3), 660–665.

Chen, Z., Lin, M., Chen, F., Lane, N. D., Cardone, G., Wang, R., . . . Campbell, A. T. (2013). Unobtrusive sleep monitoring using smartphones. In *2013 7th international conference on pervasive computing technologies for healthcare and workshops* (pp. 145–152).

Chiaburu, D. S., Oh, I.-S., Berry, C. M., Li, N., & Gardner, R. G. (2011). The five-factor model of personality traits and organizational citizenship behaviors: A meta-analysis. *Journal of Applied Psychology, 96*(6), 1140–1166.

Chittaranjan, G., Blom, J., & Gatica-Perez, D. (2011). Who's who with big-five: Analyzing and classifying personality traits with smartphones. In *2011 15th annual international symposium on wearable computers* (pp. 29–36).

Chittaranjan, G., Blom, J., & Gatica-Perez, D. (2013). Mining large-scale smartphone data for personality studies. *Personal and Ubiquitous Computing, 17*(3), 433–450.

Christin, D. (2016). Privacy in mobile participatory sensing: Current trends and future challenges. *Journal of Systems and Software, 116*, 57–68.

Ciman, M., & Wac, K. (2016). Individuals' stress assessment using human-smartphone interaction analysis. *IEEE Transactions on Affective Computing, 9*(1), 51–65.

Como, R., Hambley, L., & Domene, J. (2021). An exploration of work-life wellness and remote work during and beyond Covid-19. *Canadian Journal of Career Development, 20*(1), 46–56.

Cooke, R. A., & Rousseau, D. M. (1988). Behavioral norms and expectations: A quantitative approach to the assessment of organizational culture. *Group & Organization Studies, 13*(3), 245–273.

Cooke, R. A., & Szumal, J. L. (2000). Using the organizational culture inventory to understand the operating cultures of organizations. In N. M. Ashkanasy, C. P. M. Wilderom, & M. F. Peterson (Eds.), *Handbook of organizational culture and climate* (Vol. 4, pp. 1032–1045). Sage.

Coppersmith, G., Harman, C., & Dredze, M. (2014). Measuring post traumatic stress disorder in Twitter. In *International AAAI conference on web and social media*.

Council, J. R. (1993). Context effects in personality research. *Current Directions in Psychological Science, 2*(2), 31–34.

Cunningham, J. A., & Whalley, J. (2020). Internet of things: Promises and complexities. In J. A. Cunningham & J. Whalley (Eds.), *The internet of things entrepreneurial ecosystems* (pp. 1–11). Springer.

Das Swain, V., Chen, V., Mishra, S., Mattingly, S. M., Abowd, G. D., & De Choudhury, M. (2022). Semantic gap in predicting mental wellbeing through passive sensing. In *CHI conference on human factors in computing systems* (pp. 1–16).

Das Swain, V., Kwon, H., Saket, B., Bin Morshed, M., Tran, K., Patel, D., ... Abowd, G. D. (2020). Leveraging wifi network logs to infer social interactions: A case study of academic performance and student behavior. *arXiv:2005.11228 [cs.HC]*.

Das Swain, V., Reddy, M. D., Nies, K. A., Tay, L., De Choudhury, M., & Abowd, G. D. (2019). Birds of a feather clock together: A study of person–organization fit through latent activity routines. *Proceedings of ACM Human-Computer Interaction* (CSCW).

Das Swain, V., Saha, K., Rajvanshy, H., Sirigiri, A., Gregg, J. M., Lin, S., ... De Choudhury, M. (2019). A multisensor person-centered approach to understand the role of daily activities in job performance with organizational personas. *Proceedings of the ACM on Interactive, Mobile, Wearable and Ubiquitous Technologies, 3*(4), 1–27.

Das Swain, V., Saha, K., Reddy, M. D., Rajvanshy, H., Abowd, G. D., & De Choudhury, M. (2020). Modeling organizational culture with workplace experiences shared on glassdoor. In *ACM CHI conference on human factors in computing systems*.

De Choudhury, M., & Counts, S. (2013). Understanding affect in the workplace via social media. In *Proceedings of the 2013 conference on computer supported cooperative work* (pp. 303–316).

De Choudhury, M., Gamon, M., Counts, S., & Horvitz, E. (2013). Predicting depression via social media. In *ICWSM*.

Dey, A. K. (2001). Understanding and using context. *Personal and Ubiquitous Computing, 5*(1), 4–7.

(2018). Context-aware computing. In J. Krumm (Ed.), *Ubiquitous computing fundamentals* (pp. 335–366). Chapman & Hall/CRC.

DiMicco, J., Millen, D. R., Geyer, W., Dugan, C., Brownholtz, B., & Muller, M. (2008). Motivations for social networking at work. In *Proceedings of the 2008 ACM conference on computer supported cooperative work* (pp. 711–720).

Di Stefano, G., Gino, F., Pisano, G. P., & Staats, B. R. (2016). Making experience count: The role of reflection in individual learning. *Harvard Business School NOM Unit Working Paper* (14-093).

Dollinger, S. J., Urban, K. K., & James, T. A. (2004). Creativity and openness: Further validation of two creative product measures. *Creativity Research Journal, 16*(1), 35–47.

Domingos, P. (1998). Occam's two razors: The sharp and the blunt. In *Kdd* (pp. 37–43).

Dunn, W., Brown, C., & McGuigan, A. (1994). The ecology of human performance: A framework for considering the effect of context. *American Journal of Occupational Therapy*, *48*(7), 595–607.

Dwork, C., & Roth, A. (2014). The algorithmic foundations of differential privacy. *Foundations and Trends® in Theoretical Computer Science*, *9*(3–4), 211–407.

D'Mello, S. K., Tay, L., & Southwell, R. (2022). Psychological measurement in the information age: Machine-learned computational models. *Current Directions in Psychological Science*, *31*(1), 76–87.

Eagle, N., & Pentland, A. (2006). Reality mining: Sensing complex social systems. *Personal and Ubiquitous Computing*, *10*(4), 255–268.

Eagle, N., & Pentland, A. S. (2009). Eigenbehaviors: Identifying structure in routine. *Behavioral Ecology and Sociobiology*, *63*(7), 1057–1066.

Ehrlich, K., & Shami, N. S. (2010). Microblogging inside and outside the workplace. In *ICWSM*.

Ernala, S. K., Birnbaum, M. L., Candan, K. A., Rizvi, A. F., Sterling, W. A., Kane, J. M., & De Choudhury, M. (2019). Methodological gaps in predicting mental health states from social media: Triangulating diagnostic signals. In *Proceedings of the 2019 CHI conference on human factors in computing systems* (pp. 1–16).

Estrin, D. (2014). Small data, where n=me. *Communications of the ACM*, *57*(4), 32–34.

Feng, T., & Narayanan, S. S. (2020). Modeling behavioral consistency in large-scale wearable recordings of human bio-behavioral signals. In *ICASSP 2020-2020 IEEE international conference on acoustics, speech and signal processing (ICASSP)* (pp. 1011–1015).

Ferreira, D., Kostakos, V., & Dey, A. K. (2015). Aware: Mobile context instrumentation framework. *Frontiers in ICT*, *2*, 6.

Fiesler, C., & Proferes, N. (2018). "Participant" perceptions of Twitter research ethics. *Social Media + Society*.

Foster, K. R., Koprowski, R., & Skufca, J. D. (2014). Machine learning, medical diagnosis, and biomedical engineering research-commentary. *Biomedical Engineering Online*, *13*(1), 94.

Froehlich, J., Chen, M. Y., Consolvo, S., Harrison, B., & Landay, J. A. (2007). Myexperience: A system for in situ tracing and capturing of user feedback on mobile phones. In *Proceedings of the 5th international conference on mobile systems, applications and services* (pp. 57–70).

Furnham, A., & Zacherl, M. (1986). Personality and job satisfaction. *Personality and Individual Differences*, *7*(4), 453–459.

Giddens, L., Leidner, D., & Gonzalez, E. (2017). The role of fitbits in corporate wellness programs: Does step count matter? In *Proceedings of the 50th Hawaii International Conference on System Sciences*.

Glaser, S. R., Zamanou, S., & Hacker, K. (1987). Measuring and interpreting organizational culture. *Management Communication Quarterly*, *1*(2), 173–198.

Goffman, E. (1959). *The presentation of self in everyday life*. University of Edinburgh Social Sciences Research Centre.

Goldberg, A., Srivastava, S. B., Manian, V. G., Monroe, W., & Potts, C. (2016). Fitting in or standing out? The tradeoffs of structural and cultural embeddedness. *American Sociological Review, 81*(6), 1190–1222.

Golder, S. A., & Macy, M. W. (2011). Diurnal and seasonal mood vary with work, sleep, and daylength across diverse cultures. *Science, 333*(6051), 1878–1881.

Golestani, A., Masli, M., Shami, N. S., Jones, J., Menon, A., & Mondal, J. (2018). Real-time prediction of employee engagement using social media and text mining. In *2018 17th IEEE international conference on machine learning and applications (ICMLA)* (pp. 1383–1387).

Golub, A., Johnson, B. D., & Labouvie, E. (2000). On correcting biases in self-reports of age at first substance use with repeated cross-section analysis. *Journal of Quantitative Criminology, 16*(1), 45–68.

Groves, R. M., & Peytcheva, E. (2008). The impact of nonresponse rates on nonresponse bias: A meta-analysis. *Public Opinion Quarterly, 72*(2), 167–189.

Grünerbl, A., Muaremi, A., Osmani, V., Bahle, G., Oehler, S., Tröster, G., ... Lukowicz, P. (2015). Smartphone-based recognition of states and state changes in bipolar disorder patients. *IEEE JBHI*.

Guy, I., Ronen, I., Zwerdling, N., Zuyev-Grabovitch, I., & Jacovi, M. (2016). What is your organization 'like'?: A study of liking activity in the enterprise. In *Proceedings of the 2016 CHI conference on human factors in computing systems*.

Hanna, B., Kee, K. F., & Robertson, B. W. (2017). Positive impacts of social media at work: Job satisfaction, job calling, and Facebook use among co-workers. In *Shs web of conferences* (Vol. 33, p. 00012).

Harari, G. M., Lane, N. D., Wang, R., Crosier, B. S., Campbell, A. T., & Gosling, S. D. (2016). Using smartphones to collect behavioral data in psychological science: Opportunities, practical considerations, and challenges. *Perspectives on Psychological Science, 11*(6), 838–854.

Harari, G. M., Müller, S. R., Aung, M. S., & Rentfrow, P. J. (2017). Smartphone sensing methods for studying behavior in everyday life. *Current Opinion in Behavioral Sciences, 18*, 83–90.

Harari, G. M., Vaid, S. S., Müller, S. R., Stachl, C., Marrero, Z., Schoedel, R., ... Gosling, S. D. (2020). Personality sensing for theory development and assessment in the digital age. *European Journal of Personality, 34*(5), 649–669.

Heilman, M. E. (2012). Gender stereotypes and workplace bias. *Research in Organizational Behavior, 32*, 113–135.

Hellhammer, J., & Schubert, M. (2012). The physiological response to trier social stress test relates to subjective measures of stress during but not before or after the test. *Psychoneuroendocrinology, 37*(1), 119–124.

Hickman, L., Saha, K., De Choudhury, M., & Tay, L. (2019). Automated tracking of components of job satisfaction via text mining of twitter data. In *Ml symposium, SIOP*.

Hofstede, G. (2001). *Culture's consequences: Comparing values, behaviors, institutions and organizations across nations*. Sage Publications.

Hofstede, G., Neuijen, B., Ohayv, D. D., & Sanders, G. (1990). Measuring organizational cultures: A qualitative and quantitative study across twenty cases. *Administrative Science Quarterly, 35*(2), 286–316.

Hovsepian, K., al'Absi, M., Ertin, E., Kamarck, T., Nakajima, M., & Kumar, S. (2015). cstress: Towards a gold standard for continuous stress assessment in the mobile environment. In *Proceedings of the 2015 ACM international joint conference on pervasive and ubiquitous computing* (pp. 493–504).

Howard, M. C., & Hoffman, M. E. (2018). Variable-centered, person-centered, and person-specific approaches: Where theory meets the method. *Organizational Research Methods, 21*(4), 846–876.

Insel, T. R. (2017). Digital phenotyping: Technology for a new science of behavior. *JAMA, 318*(13), 1215–1216.

Jacovi, M., Guy, I., Kremer-Davidson, S., Porat, S., & Aizenbud-Reshef, N. (2014). The perception of others: Inferring reputation from social media in the enterprise. In *Proceedings of the 17th ACM conference on computer supported cooperative work & social computing* (pp. 756–766).

Jain, S. H., Powers, B. W., Hawkins, J. B., & Brownstein, J. S. (2015). The digital phenotype. *Nature Biotechnology, 33*(5), 462–463.

Jebelli, H., Hwang, S., & Lee, S. (2018). EEG signal-processing framework to obtain high-quality brain waves from an off-the-shelf wearable EEG device. *Journal of Computing in Civil Engineering, 32*(1), 04017070.

Jhaver, S., Cranshaw, J., & Counts, S. (2019). Measuring professional skill development in U.S. cities using internet search queries. In *ICWSM*.

Jouhki, J., Lauk, E., Penttinen, M., Sormanen, N., & Uskali, T. (2016). Facebook's emotional contagion experiment as a challenge to research ethics. *Media and Communication, 4*(4), 75–85.

Judge, T. A., & Zapata, C. P. (2015). The person–situation debate revisited: Effect of situation strength and trait activation on the validity of the big five personality traits in predicting job performance. *Academy of Management Journal, 58*(4), 1149–1179.

Kamdar, D., & Van Dyne, L. (2007). The joint effects of personality and workplace social exchange relationships in predicting task performance and citizenship performance. *Journal of Applied Psychology, 92*(5), 1286–1298.

Khakurel, J., Melkas, H., & Porras, J. (2018). Tapping into the wearable device revolution in the work environment: A systematic review. *Information Technology & People, 31*(3).

King, C. E., & Sarrafzadeh, M. (2018). A survey of smartwatches in remote health monitoring. *Journal of Healthcare Informatics Research, 2*(1), 1–24.

Klasnja, P., Consolvo, S., McDonald, D. W., Landay, J. A., & Pratt, W. (2009). Using mobile & personal sensing technologies to support health behavior change in everyday life: Lessons learned. In *Amia annual symposium proceedings* (Vol. 2009, p. 338).

Kramer, A. D., Guillory, J. E., & Hancock, J. T. (2014). Experimental evidence of massive-scale emotional contagion through social networks. *Proceedings of the National Academy of Sciences, 111*(24), 8788– 8790.

Kreuter, F., Haas, G.-C., Keusch, F., Bähr, S., & Trappmann, M. (2020). Collecting survey and smartphone sensor data with an app: Opportunities and challenges around privacy and informed consent. *Social Science Computer Review, 38*(5), 533–549.

Krumpal, I. (2013). Determinants of social desirability bias in sensitive surveys: A literature review. *Quality & Quantity, 47*, 2025–2047.

Lampert, R. (2015). ECG signatures of psychological stress. *Journal of Electrocardiology, 48*(6), 1000–1005.

Langheinrich, M. (2009). Privacy in ubiquitous computing. In J. Krumm (Ed.), *Ubiquitous computing* (pp. 104–174). Chapman & Hall/CRC.

Lazer, D., Kennedy, R., King, G., & Vespignani, A. (2014). The parable of google flu: Traps in big data analysis. *Science, 343*(6176), 1203–1205.

Lazer, D., & Radford, J. (2017). Data ex machina: Introduction to big data. *Annual Review of Sociology, 43*, 19–39.

Lee, H., Kim, S., Couper, M. P., & Woo, Y. (2019). Experimental comparison of PC web, smartphone web, and telephone surveys in the new technology era. *Social Science Computer Review, 37*(2), 234–247.

Lee, J., & Kang, J. (2017). A study on job satisfaction factors in retention and turnover groups using dominance analysis and LDA topic modeling with employee reviews on glassdoor.com.

Lee, J., Lam, M., & Chiu, C. (2019). Clara: Design of a new system for passive sensing of depression, stress and anxiety in the workplace. In *International symposium on pervasive computing paradigms for mental health* (pp. 12–28).

Leesman. (2018). *The rise and rise of activity based working.* https://www .leesmanindex.com/The Rise and Rise of Activity Based Working Research book.pdf

Li, I., Dey, A., & Forlizzi, J. (2010). A stage-based model of personal informatics systems. In *Proceedings of the SIGCHI conference on human factors in computing systems* (pp. 557–566).

Li, S., Zhou, X., Dong, Y., & Li, J. (2020). Flexible self-repairing materials for wearable sensing applications: Elastomers and hydrogels. *Macromolecular Rapid Communications, 41*(23), 2000444.

Lindberg, A., Berente, N., Gaskin, J., Lyytinen, K., & Yoo, Y. (2013). Computational approaches for analyzing latent social structures in open source organizing. In *International conference on information systems.*

Ling, R., & Horst, H. A. (2011). *Mobile communication in the global south* (Vol. 13) (No. 3). Sage Publications.

Liu, J., Wang, Y., Chen, Y., Yang, J., Chen, X., & Cheng, J. (2015). Tracking vital signs during sleep leveraging off-the-shelf wifi. In *Proceedings of the 16th ACM international symposium on mobile ad hoc networking and computing* (pp. 267–276).

Liu, S., Hachen, D., Lizardo, O., Poellabauer, C., Striegel, A., & Milenkoviê, T. (2018). Network analysis of the nethealth data: Exploring co-evolution of individuals' social network positions and physical activities. *Applied Network Science, 3*(1), 1–26.

Liu, Y., & Du, S. (2018). Psychological stress level detection based on electrodermal activity. *Behavioural Brain Research, 341*, 50–53.

Lowe, G. S., Schellenberg, G., & Shannon, H. S. (2003). Correlates of employees' perceptions of a healthy work environment. *American Journal of Health Promotion, 17*(6), 390–399.

Lu, H., Pan, W., Lane, N. D., Choudhury, T., & Campbell, A. T. (2009). Soundsense: Scalable sound sensing for people-centric applications on mobile phones. In *Proceedings of the 7th international conference on mobile systems, applications, and services* (pp. 165–178).

Lundberg, S. M., Erion, G., Chen, H., DeGrave, A., Prutkin, J. M., Nair, B., . . . Lee, S.-I. (2020). From local explanations to global understanding with explainable AI for trees. *Nature Machine Intelligence, 2*(1), 56–67.

Luo, N., Zhou, Y., & Shon, J. (2016). Employee satisfaction and corporate performance: Mining employee reviews on glassdoor.com.

Madan, A., Moturu, S. T., Lazer, D., & Pentland, A. (2010). Social sensing: Obesity, unhealthy eating and exercise in face-to-face networks. In *Wireless health 2010* (pp. 104–110).

Madden, T. J., Ellen, P. S., & Ajzen, I. (1992). A comparison of the theory of planned behavior and the theory of reasoned action. *Personality and Social Psychology Bulletin, 18*(1), 3–9.

Mallinckrodt, C. H., Sanger, T. M., Dubé, S., DeBrota, D. J., Molenberghs, G., Carroll, R. J., . . . Tollefson, G. D. (2003). Assessing and interpreting treatment effects in longitudinal clinical trials with missing data. *Biological Psychiatry, 53*(8), 754–760.

Manyika, J., Chui, M., Miremadi, M., Bughin, J., George, K., Willmott, P., & Dewhurst, M. (2017). A future that works: AI, automation, employment, and productivity. *McKinsey Global Institute Research, Tech. Rep, 60*, 1–135.

Mariani, B., Jiménez, M. C., Vingerhoets, F. J., & Aminian, K. (2012). On-shoe wearable sensors for gait and turning assessment of patients with Parkinson's disease. *IEEE Transactions on Biomedical Engineering, 60*(1), 155–158.

Mark, G. (2015). Multitasking in the digital age. *Synthesis Lectures on Human-Centered Informatics, 8*(3), 1–113.

Mark, G., Czerwinski, M., Iqbal, S., & Johns, P. (2016). Workplace indicators of mood: Behavioral and cognitive correlates of mood among information workers. In *Proceedings of the 6th international conference on digital health* (pp. 29–36).

Mark, G., Iqbal, S. T., Czerwinski, M., Johns, P., Sano, A., & Lutchyn, Y. (2016). Email duration, batching and self-interruption: Patterns of email use on productivity and stress. In *Proceedings of the 2016 CHI conference on human factors in computing systems* (pp. 1717–1728).

Martinez, G. J., Mattingly, S. M., Young, J., Faust, L., Dey, A. K., Campbell, A. T., De Choudhury, M., Mirjafari, S., Nepal, S. K., Robles-Granda, P., Saha, K., & Striegel, A. D. (2020). Improved sleep detection through the fusion of phone agent and wearable data streams. In *Wristsense 2020*.

Maslow, A. H. (1966). *The psychology of science: A reconnaissance.* Gateway.

Mathur, A., Van den Broeck, M., Vanderhulst, G., Mashhadi, A., & Kawsar, F. (2015). Tiny habits in the giant enterprise: Understanding the dynamics of a quantified workplace. In *Proceedings of the 2015 ACM international joint conference on pervasive and ubiquitous computing* (pp. 577–588).

Mattingly, S. M., Gregg, J. M., Audia, P., Bayraktaroglu, A. E., Campbell, A. T., Chawla, N. V., ... Dey, A. K. (2019). The Tesserae project: Large-scale, longitudinal, in situ, multimodal sensing of information workers. *CHI conference on human factors in computing systems*.

McLaren, H. J., Wong, K. R., Nguyen, K. N., & Mahamadachchi, K. N. D. (2020). Covid-19 and women's triple burden: Vignettes from Sri Lanka, Malaysia, Vietnam and Australia. *Social Sciences, 9*(5), Article 87.

Mehl, M. R. (2017). The electronically activated recorder (ear): A method for the naturalistic observation of daily social behavior. *Current Directions in Psychological Science, 26*(2), 184–190.

Mehrotra, A., & Musolesi, M. (2018). Using autoencoders to automatically extract mobility features for predicting depressive states. *Proceedings of the ACM on Interactive, Mobile, Wearable and Ubiquitous Technologies, 2*(3), 127.

Mehrotra, A., Pejovic, V., & Musolesi, M. (2014). Sensocial: A middleware for integrating online social networks and mobile sensing data streams. In *Proceedings of the 15th international middleware conference* (pp. 205–216).

Meyer, B., Burtscher, M. J., Jonas, K., Feese, S., Arnrich, B., Tröster, G., & Schermuly, C. C. (2016). What good leaders actually do: Micro-level leadership behaviour, leader evaluations, and team decision quality. *European Journal of Work and Organizational Psychology, 25*(6), 773–789.

Miluzzo, E., Lane, N. D., Eisenman, S. B., & Campbell, A. T. (2007). Cenceme – injecting sensing presence into social networking applications. In *European conference on smart sensing and context* (pp. 1–28).

Mirjafari, S., Masaba, K., Grover, T., Wang, W., Audia, P., Campbell, A. T., ... Mark, G. (2019). Differentiating higher and lower job performers in the workplace using mobile sensing. *Proc. ACM IMWUT, 3*(2), Article 37.

Mitra, T., Muller, M., Shami, N. S., Golestani, A., & Masli, M. (n.d.). Spread of employee engagement in a large organizational network: A longitudinal analysis. *PACM HCI*(CSCW).

Mohr, D. C., Burns, M. N., Schueller, S. M., Clarke, G., & Klinkman, M. (2013). Behavioral intervention technologies: Evidence review and recommendations for future research in mental health. *General Hospital Psychiatry*, 35(4), 332–338.

Mohr, D. C., Zhang, M., & Schueller, S. M. (2017). Personal sensing: Understanding mental health using ubiquitous sensors and machine learning. *Annual Review of Clinical Psychology*, *13*, 23–47.

Molenberghs, G., Thijs, H., Jansen, I., Beunckens, C., Kenward, M. G., Mallinckrodt, C., & Carroll, R. J. (2004). Analyzing incomplete longitudinal clinical trial data. *Biostatistics*, *5*(3), 445–464.

Moniz, A. (2015). *Inferring employees' social media perceptions of goal-setting corporate cultures and the link to firm value*. Unpublished Working Paper.

Montanari, A., Mascolo, C., Sailer, K., & Nawaz, S. (2017). Detecting emerging activity-based working traits through wearable technology. *Proc. IMWUT*.

Moran, T. P., & Dourish, P. (2001). Introduction to this special issue on context-aware computing. *Human–Computer Interaction*, *16*(2–4), 87–95.

Morrison, E. W., & Milliken, F. J. (2000). Organizational silence: A barrier to change and development in a pluralistic world. *Academy of Management Review*, *25*(4), 706–725.

Morshed, M. B., Saha, K., Li, R., D'Mello, S. K., De Choudhury, M., Abowd, G. D., & Plötz, T. (2019). Prediction of mood instability with passive sensing. *Proceedings of the ACM on Interactive, Mobile, Wearable and Ubiquitous Technologies*, *3*(3), Article 75.

Muaremi, A., Arnrich, B., & Tröster, G. (2013). Towards measuring stress with smartphones and wearable devices during workday and sleep. *BioNanoScience*, *3*(2), 172–183.

Muller, M., Shami, N. S., Guha, S., Masli, M., Geyer, W., & Wild, A. (2016). Influences of peers, friends, and managers on employee engagement. In *Proceedings of the 19th international conference on supporting group work* (pp. 131–136).

Mundnich, K., Booth, B. M., l'Hommedieu, M., Feng, T., Girault, B., L'Hommedieu, J., ... Narayanan, S. (2020). Tiles-2018, a longitudinal physiologic and behavioral data set of hospital workers. *Scientific Data*, *7*(1), 1–26.

Nadarajan, A., Somandepalli, K., & Narayanan, S. S. (2019). Speaker agnostic foreground speech detection from audio recordings in workplace settings from wearable recorders. In *ICASSP 2019–2019 IEEE international conference on acoustics, speech and signal processing (ICASSP)* (pp. 6765–6769).

Nepal, S., Martinez, G. J., Mirjafari, S., Mattingly, S., Swain, V. D., Striegel, A., ... Campbell, A. T. (2021). Assessing the impact of commuting on workplace performance using mobile sensing. *IEEE Pervasive Computing*, *20*(4), 52–60.

Nepal, S., Martinez, G. J., Mirjafari, S., Saha, K., Swain, V. D., Xu, X., ... Campbell, A. T. (2022). A survey of passive sensing in the workplace. *arXiv preprint arXiv:2201.03074*.

Nguyen, D. D., Nguyen, L., & Sila, V. (2019). Does corporate culture affect bank risk-taking? Evidence from loan-level data. *British Journal of Management*, *30*(1), 106–133.

Olguin, D. O., & Pentland, A. S. (2008). Social sensors for automatic data collection. *AMCIS 2008 Proceedings*, 171.

Olguin, D. O., Waber, B. N., Kim, T., Mohan, A., Ara, K., & Pentland, A. (2009). Sensible organizations: Technology and methodology for automatically measuring organizational behavior. *IEEE Transactions on Systems, Man, and Cybernetics, Part B (Cybernetics)*, *39*(1), 43–55.

Olguin-Olguin, D. (2011). *Sensor-based organizational design and engineering* (Unpublished doctoral dissertation). Massachusetts Institute of Technology.

Olmedo-Aguirre, J. O., Reyes-Campos, J., Alor-Hernández, G., Machorro-Cano, I., Rodriguez-Mazahua, L., & Sánchez-Cervantes, J. L. (2022). Remote healthcare for elderly people using wearables: A review. *Biosensors*, *12*(2), 73.

Olson, G. M., & Olson, J. S. (2000). Distance matters. *Human–Computer Interaction*, *15*(2–3), 139–178.

Olteanu, A., Castillo, C., Diaz, F., & Kiciman, E. (2019). Social data: Biases, methodological pitfalls, and ethical boundaries. *Frontiers in Big Data*, *2*, 13.

Ones, D. S., Viswesvaran, C., & Dilchert, S. (2005). Personality at work: Raising awareness and correcting misconceptions. *Human Performance*, *18*(4), 389–404.

O'Reilly, C. (1989). Corporations, culture, and commitment: Motivation and social control in organizations. *California Management Review*, *31*(4), 9–25.

O'Reilly III, C. A., Chatman, J., & Caldwell, D. F. (1991). People and organizational culture: A profile comparison approach to assessing person-organization fit. *Academy of Management Journal*, *34*(3), 487–516.

Oswald, D., Sherratt, F., & Smith, S. (2014). Handling the hawthorne effect: The challenges surrounding a participant observer. *Review of Social Studies*, *1*(1), 53–73.

Pappalardo, L., Simini, F., Rinzivillo, S., Pedreschi, D., Giannotti, F., & Barabási, A.-L. (2015). Returners and explorers dichotomy in human mobility. *Nature Communications*, *6*(1), 1–8.

Park, G., Schwartz, H. A., Eichstaedt, J. C., Kern, M. L., Kosinski, M., Stillwell, D. J., . . . Seligman, M. E. (2015). Automatic personality assessment through social media language. *Journal of Personality and Social Psychology*, *108*(6), 934–952.

Pasch, S. (2018). Corporate culture and industry-fit: A text mining approach. In *IZA conference*.

Plötz, T. (2021). Applying machine learning for sensor data analysis in interactive systems: Common pitfalls of pragmatic use and ways to avoid them. *ACM Computing Surveys (CSUR)*, *54*(6), 1–25.

Poushter, J., Bishop, C., & Chwe, H. (2018). Social media use continues to rise in developing countries but plateaus across developed ones. *Pew Research Center*, *22*, 2–19.

Prabhakaran, V., Neralwala, H., Rambow, O., & Diab, M. T. (2012). Annotations for power relations on email threads. In *Lrec* (pp. 806–811).

Prajogo, D. I., & McDermott, C. M. (2011). The relationship between multi-dimensional organizational culture and performance. *International Journal of Operations & Production Management, 31*(7), 712–735.

Purta, R., Mattingly, S., Song, L., Lizardo, O., Hachen, D., Poellabauer, C., & Striegel, A. (2016). Experiences measuring sleep and physical activity patterns across a large college cohort with fitbits. In *Proceedings of the 2016 ACM international symposium on wearable computers* (pp. 28–35).

Quante, M., Wang, R., Weng, J., Kaplan, E. R., Rueschman, M., Taveras, E. M., ... Redline, S. (2019). Seasonal and weather variation of sleep and physical activity in 12–14-year-old children. *Behavioral Sleep Medicine, 17*(4), 398–410.

Quinn, R. E., & Rohrbaugh, J. (1983). A spatial model of effectiveness criteria: Towards a competing values approach to organizational analysis. *Management Science, 29*(3), 363–377.

Reeves, B., Ram, N., Robinson, T. N., Cummings, J. J., Giles, C. L., Pan, J., ... Yeykelis, L. (2021). Screenomics: A framework to capture and analyze personal life experiences and the ways that technology shapes them. *Human–Computer Interaction, 36*(2), 150–201.

Robertson, B. W., & Kee, K. F. (2017). Social media at work: The roles of job satisfaction, employment status, and Facebook use with co-workers. *Computers in Human Behavior, 70*, 191–196.

Robles-Granda, P., Lin, S., Wu, X., D'Mello, S., Martinez, G. J., Saha, K., ... Chawla, N. V. (2020). Jointly predicting job performance, personality, cognitive ability, affect, and well-being. *arXiv preprint arXiv:2006.08364*.

Rooksby, J., Morrison, A., & Murray-Rust, D. (2019). Student perspectives on digital phenotyping: The acceptability of using smartphone data to assess mental health. In *Proceedings of the 2019 CHI conference on human factors in computing systems* (p. 425).

Rudovic, O., Lee, J., Dai, M., Schuller, B., & Picard, R. W. (2018). Personalized machine learning for robot perception of affect and engagement in autism therapy. *Science Robotics, 3*(19).

Russell, J. A. (1980). A circumplex model of affect. *Journal of Personality and Social Psychology, 39*(6), 1161–1178.

Ruths, D., & Pfeffer, J. (2014). Social media for large studies of behavior. *Science, 346*(6213), 1063–1064.

Saha, K., Bayraktaroglu, A. E., Campbell, A. T., Chawla, N. V., De Choudhury, M., D'Mello, S. K., ... Yoo, D. W. (2019). Social media as a passive sensor in longitudinal studies of human behavior and wellbeing. In *Chi ext. abstracts*.

Saha, K., Chan, L., De Barbaro, K., Abowd, G. D., & De Choudhury, M. (2017). Inferring mood instability on social media by leveraging ecological momentary assessments. *Proceedings of the ACM on Interactive, Mobile, Wearable and Ubiquitous Technologies, 1*(3), 95.

Saha, K., Grover, T., Mattingly, S. M., Swain, V. D., Gupta, P., Martinez, G. J., ... De Choudhury, M. (2021). Person-centered predictions of psychological constructs with social media contextualized by multimodal sensing. *Proceedings of the ACM on Interactive, Mobile, Wearable and Ubiquitous Technologies, 5*(1), 1–32.

Saha, K., Reddy, M. D., Mattingly, S., Moskal, E., Sirigiri, A., & De Choudhury, M. (2019). Libra: On LinkedIn based role ambiguity and its relationship with wellbeing and job performance. *Proceedings of the ACM on Human-Computer Interaction, 3*(CSCW), 1–30.

Saha, K., Yousuf, A., Hickman, L., Gupta, P., Tay, L., & De Choudhury, M. (2021). A social media study on demographic differences in perceived job satisfaction. *Proceedings of the ACM on Human-Computer Interaction (CSCW)*.

Salganik, M. J., Lundberg, I., Kindel, A. T., Ahearn, C. E., Al-Ghoneim, K., Almaatouq, A., ... McLanahan, S. (2020). Measuring the predictability of life outcomes with a scientific mass collaboration. *Proceedings of the National Academy of Sciences, 117*(15), 8398–8403.

Sano, A., Johns, P., & Czerwinski, M. (2017). Designing opportune stress intervention delivery timing using multi-modal data. In *2017 seventh international conference on affective computing and intelligent interaction (ACII)* (pp. 346–353).

Sano, A., Phillips, A. J., Amy, Z. Y., McHill, A. W., Taylor, S., Jaques, N., ... Picard, R. W. (2015). Recognizing academic performance, sleep quality, stress level, and mental health using personality traits, wearable sensors and mobile phones. In *2015 IEEE 12th international conference on wearable and implantable body sensor networks (BSN)* (pp. 1–6).

Sano, A., & Picard, R. W. (2013). Stress recognition using wearable sensors and mobile phones. In *ACII*.

Sansone, C., Morf, C. C., & Panter, A. T. (2003). *The Sage handbook of methods in social psychology*. Sage.

Schaule, F., Johanssen, J. O., Bruegge, B., & Loftness, V. (2018). Employing consumer wearables to detect office workers' cognitive load for interruption management. *Proceedings of the ACM on Interactive, Mobile, Wearable and Ubiquitous Technologies, 2*(1), 1–20.

Schmid Mast, M., Gatica-Perez, D., Frauendorfer, D., Nguyen, L., & Choudhury, T. (2015). Social sensing for psychology: Automated interpersonal behavior assessment. *Current Directions in Psychological Science, 24*(2), 154–160.

Schmidt, A., Beigl, M., & Gellersen, H.-W. (1999). There is more to context than location. *Computers & Graphics, 23*(6), 893–901.

Scott, J. C., & Reynolds, D. H. (2010). *Handbook of workplace assessment* (Vol. 32). John Wiley & Sons.

Shami, N. S., Muller, M., Pal, A., Masli, M., & Geyer, W. (2015). Inferring employee engagement from social media. In *Proceedings of the 33rd annual ACM conference on human factors in computing systems* (pp. 3999–4008).

Shami, N. S., Nichols, J., & Chen, J. (2014). Social media participation and performance at work: A longitudinal study. In *Proceedings of the SIGCHI conference on human factors in computing systems* (pp. 115–118).

Shami, N. S., Yang, J., Panc, L., Dugan, C., Ratchford, T., Rasmussen, J. C., . . . Ferrar, J. (2014). Understanding employee social media chatter with enterprise social pulse. In *Proceedings of the 17th ACM conference on computer supported cooperative work & social computing.*

Shilton, K. (2009). Four billion little brothers? Privacy, mobile phones, and ubiquitous data collection. *Communications of the ACM, 52*(11).

Silva, G. E., Goodwin, J. L., Sherrill, D. L., Arnold, J. L., Bootzin, R. R., Smith, T., . . . Quan, S. F. (2007). Relationship between reported and measured sleep times: The sleep heart health study (SHHS). *Journal of Clinical Sleep Medicine, 3*(6), 622–630.

Smith, F. J. (2014). *Organizational surveys: The diagnosis and betterment of organizations through their members.* Psychology Press.

Smith, M., Szongott, C., Henne, B., & Von Voigt, G. (2012). Big data privacy issues in public social media. In *2012 6th IEEE international conference on digital ecosystems and technologies (DEST)* (pp. 1–6).

Smyth, J. M., Sliwinski, M. J., Zawadzki, M. J., Scott, S. B., Conroy, D. E., Lanza, S. T., . . . Almeida, D. M. (2018). Everyday stress response targets in the science of behavior change. *Behaviour Research and Therapy, 101*, 20–29.

Snyder, M. (1979). Self-monitoring processes. In L. Berkowitz (Ed.), *Advances in experimental social psychology* (Vol. 12, pp. 85–128). Elsevier.

Soto, C. J., & John, O. P. (2017). The next big five inventory (bfi-2): Developing and assessing a hierarchical model with 15 facets to enhance bandwidth, fidelity, and predictive power. *Journal of Personality and Social Psychology, 113*(1), 117–143.

Soto, M., Satterfield, C., Fritz, T., Murphy, G. C., Shepherd, D. C., & Kraft, N. (2021). Observing and predicting knowledge worker stress, focus and awakeness in the wild. *International Journal of Human-Computer Studies, 146*, 102560.

Srivastava, S. B., & Goldberg, A. (2017). Language as a window into culture. *California Management Review, 60*(1).

Steinberg, H., Sykes, E. A., Moss, T., Lowery, S., LeBoutillier, N., & Dewey, A. (1997). Exercise enhances creativity independently of mood. *British Journal of Sports Medicine, 31*(3), 240–245.

Steindl, C., Jonas, E., Sittenthaler, S., Traut-Mattausch, E., & Greenberg, J. (2015). Understanding psychological reactance. *Zeitschrift für Psychologie, 223*(4), 205–214.

Strack, R., Von Der Linden, C., Booker, M., & Strohmayr, A. (2014, October 6). Decoding global talent. *BCG Perspectives.*

Tams, S. (2008). Constructing self-efficacy at work: A person-centered perspective. *Personnel Review, 37*(2), 165–183.

Tay, L., Woo, S. E., Hickman, L., & Saef, R. M. (2020). Psychometric and validity issues in machine learning approaches to personality assessment:

A focus on social media text mining. *European Journal of Personality*, *34*(5), 826–844.

Tett, R. P., Jackson, D. N., & Rothstein, M. (1991). Personality measures as predictors of job performance: A meta-analytic review. *Personnel Psychology*, *44*(4), 703–742.

Thom, J., & Millen, D. R. (2012). Stuff IBMers say: Microblogs as an expression of organizational culture. In *Sixth international AAAI conference on weblogs and social media*.

Thomas, A. G., Dennis, A., Rawlings, N. B., Stagg, C. J., Matthews, L., Morris, M., ... Johansen-Berg, H. (2016). Multi-modal characterization of rapid anterior hippocampal volume increase associated with aerobic exercise. *Neuroimage*, *131*, 162–170.

Thom-Santelli, J., Millen, D. R., & Gergle, D. (2011). Organizational acculturation and social networking. In *Proceedings of the ACM 2011 conference on computer supported cooperative work* (pp. 313–316).

Torous, J., & Nebeker, C. (2017). Navigating ethics in the digital age: Introducing connected and open research ethics (core), a tool for researchers and institutional review boards. *Journal of Medical Internet Research*, *19*(2), e6793.

Tsui, A. S., Nifadkar, S. S., & Ou, A. Y. (2007). Cross-national, cross-cultural organizational behavior research: Advances, gaps, and recommendations. *Journal of Management*, *33*(3), 426–478.

Tufekci, Z. (2014). Big questions for social media big data: Representativeness, validity and other methodological pitfalls. In *Eighth international AAAI conference on weblogs and social media*.

Umematsu, T., Sano, A., Taylor, S., & Picard, R. W. (2019). Improving students' daily life stress forecasting using LSTM neural networks. In *2019 IEEE EMBS international conference on biomedical & health informatics (BHI)* (pp. 1–4).

Vaessen, J., & Raimondo, E. (2020). *Conducting evaluations in times of covid-19 (coronavirus)*. https://ieg.worldbankgroup.org/blog/conducting-evaluations-times-covid-19-coronavirus

Vardi, Y. (2001). The effects of organizational and ethical climates on misconduct at work. *Journal of Business Ethics*, *29*(4), 325–337.

Viswesvaran, C., & Ones, D. S. (2000). Perspectives on models of job performance. *International Journal of Selection and Assessment*, *8*(4), 216–226.

Wang, R., Chen, F., Chen, Z., Li, T., Harari, G., Tignor, S., ... Campbell, A. T. (2014). Studentlife: Assessing mental health, academic performance and behavioral trends of college students using smartphones. In *Proceedings of the 2014 ACM international joint conference on pervasive and ubiquitous computing* (pp. 3–14).

Warschauer, M., & Ames, M. (2010). Can one laptop per child save the world's poor? *Journal of International Affairs*, *64*(1), 33–51.

Watkins Allen, M., Coopman, S. J., Hart, J. L., & Walker, K. L. (2007). Workplace surveillance and managing privacy boundaries. *Management Communication Quarterly*, *21*(2), 172–200.

Wearne, T. A., Lucien, A., Trimmer, E. M., Logan, J. A., Rushby, J., Wilson, E., ... McDonald, S. (2019). Anxiety sensitivity moderates the subjective experience but not the physiological response to psychosocial stress. *International Journal of Psychophysiology, 141*, 76–83.

Weiss, H. M. (2002). Deconstructing job satisfaction: Separating evaluations, beliefs and affective experiences. *Human Resource Management Review, 12*(2), 173–194.

Wiley, J. (2010). *Strategic employee surveys: Evidence-based guidelines for driving organizational success.* John Wiley & Sons.

Woo, S. E., Chae, M., Jebb, A. T., & Kim, Y. (2016). A closer look at the personality-turnover relationship: Criterion expansion, dark traits, and time. *Journal of Management, 42*(2), 357–385.

Woo, S. E., Jebb, A. T., Tay, L., & Parrigon, S. (2018). Putting the "person" in the center: Review and synthesis of person-centered approaches and methods in organizational science. *Organizational Research Methods, 21*(4), 814–845.

Woo, S. E., Tay, L., Jebb, A. T., Ford, M. T., & Kern, M. L. (2020). Big data for enhancing measurement quality. In S. E. Woo, L. Tay, & R. W. Proctor (Eds.), *Big data in psychological research* (pp. 59–85). American Psychological Association.

Wright, A. G., & Woods, W. C. (2020). Personalized models of psychopathology. *Annual Review of Clinical Psychology, 16*, 49–74.

Wright, T. A., & Cropanzano, R. (2000). Psychological well-being and job satisfaction as predictors of job performance. *Journal of Occupational Health Psychology, 5*(1), 84–94.

Wu, F., Wu, T., & Yuce, M. R. (2019). Design and implementation of a wearable sensor network system for IoT-connected safety and health applications. In *2019 IEEE 5th world forum on internet of things (Wf-IoT)* (pp. 87–90).

Xu, X., Chikersal, P., Doryab, A., Villalba, D. K., Dutcher, J. M., Tumminia, M. J., ... Mankoff, J. (2019). Leveraging routine behavior and contextually-filtered features for depression detection among college students. *PACM IMWUT.*

Yilmaz, C., & Ergun, E. (2008). Organizational culture and firm effectiveness: An examination of relative effects of culture traits and the balanced culture hypothesis in an emerging economy. *Journal of World Business, 43*(3), 290–306.

Yuan, N. J., Zhang, F., Lian, D., Zheng, K., Yu, S., & Xie, X. (2013). We know how you live: Exploring the spectrum of urban lifestyles. In *Proceedings of the first ACM conference on online social networks* (pp. 3–14).

Zakaria, C., Balan, R., & Lee, Y. (2019). Stressmon: Scalable detection of perceived stress and depression using passive sensing of changes in work routines and group interactions. *Proceedings of the ACM on Human-Computer Interaction, 3*(CSCW), 1–29.

Zedeck, S. E. (1992). *Work, families, and organizations.* Jossey-Bass.

Zenonos, A., Khan, A., Kalogridis, G., Vatsikas, S., Lewis, T., & Sooriyabandara, M. (2016). Healthyoffice: Mood recognition at work using smartphones and wearable sensors. In *2016 IEEE international conference on pervasive computing and communication workshops (percom workshops)* (pp. 1–6).

Zhang, H., De Choudhury, M., & Grudin, J. (2014). Creepy but inevitable?: The evolution of social networking. In *Proceedings of the 17th ACM conference on computer supported cooperative work & social computing*.

Zhang, X., Pina, L. R., & Fogarty, J. (2016). Examining unlock journaling with diaries and reminders for in situ self-report in health and wellness. In *Proceedings of the 2016 CHI conference on human factors in computing systems* (pp. 5658–5664).

Zhao, D., & Rosson, M. B. (2009). How and why people twitter: The role that micro-blogging plays in informal communication at work. In *Proceedings of the ACM 2009 international conference on supporting group work* (pp. 243–252).

Zimmerman, R. D., Swider, B. W., Woo, S. E., & Allen, D. G. (2016). Who withdraws? Psychological individual differences and employee withdrawal behaviors. *Journal of Applied Psychology, 101*(4), 498–519.

CHAPTER 3

Information Privacy
Challenges and Opportunities for Technology and Measurement

Heng Xu and Nan Zhang

For educators and social scientists, one of the most exciting opportunities afforded by digital technologies is the ease of collecting and analyzing massive datasets that capture individual behavior and interactions in social, educational, and organizational processes. With the promise to study social and behavioral phenomena in unprecedented detail, many social scientists are attempting the methodological transition from taking measurements through surveys and experiments to extracting measurements from large amounts of data (Paxton & Griffiths, 2017). Reflecting this paradigm shift, Groves (2011) coined the term "organic data" for datasets that are organically generated (e.g., by ubiquitous sensors, on digital platforms such as social media) without an explicit research design. While some organic data are crucial for the proper functioning of the platform or device that generates them (e.g., step count for a pedometer), some other types of organic data may simply represent "data exhaust" (Harford, 2014), that is, digital trail left by human activities with no immediate use (e.g., the exact timestamp of each step sensed by the pedometer). In terms of scientific research, the use of "organic data" stands in contrast to that of "designed data," which originate from surveys or experiments that are specifically designed for research purposes.

The explosive growth of organic data collection sets the stage for innovative measurements, research designs, and practical applications. Yet, by its very nature of capturing the "digital footprints" of human activities and interactions (McFarland et al., 2016), the collection of organic data tends to raise privacy concerns for those whose personal information is being collected and analyzed. In educational settings, the collection of student data is usually governed by privacy laws and regulations such as the Family Educational Rights and Privacy Act in the USA. In organizational settings in general, privacy concerns are often pronounced when data are collected by organizations, or at least within the scope of an organization, on their employees (rather than by researchers on voluntary participants of lab experiments). For example, privacy concerns may arise when organizations collect and analyze the social media activities of their employees or prospective employees (Lee, 2018), as people's activities on social media tend to blur the boundary between professional and personal contexts (Abril et al., 2012). Similarly, employees may be concerned about their privacy when an organization uses sensory devices to track their whereabouts and calculate their "time off task" (Ravid et al., 2020), even though the collected data could be extremely useful for research studies on improving operational efficiency and workforce productivity.

The privacy concerns stemming from the collection of organic data can only be compounded when researchers or practitioners *link* the collected data with external data sources, such as administrative datasets, to reveal even more information about the individuals, for example when Twitter data are joined with voter-registration records to understand not only the expressed sentiments of an individual but also their socioeconomic status (Barberá et al., 2015). While the effective integration of (high-volume) organic data with (high-quality) administrative records is known to address many challenges in traditional research design (e.g., small sample size, nonresponse rate; Groves 2011; Ruggles 2014), the threat posed by data integration to individual privacy is also well documented in the literature. For example, in a landmark study, Sweeney (2002) demonstrated how cross-referencing an anonymized medical dataset with voter-registration records (publicly available for Cambridge, MA) revealed the medical records of William Weld, then Governor of Massachusetts.

Privacy issues arising from the collection and use of organic datasets are obviously complex, especially in educational and organizational settings, and have important legal implications (Abril et al., 2012; Peterson, 2016). Since the goal of this chapter is to provide a global perspective on the topic, we forgo a comprehensive legal treatment of the subject because the applicable laws vary considerably from country to country[1] – even from state to state in the USA (Russom et al., 2011). Instead, we refer readers to the recent law reviews (e.g., for the USA: Neace, 2019; for Australia: Koelmeyer & Josey, 2019) for the legal perspective on this topic, and focus this chapter on discussing what *researchers* need to be aware of, and

---

[1] For example, compared with US courts, European courts are known to be less preoccupied with protecting free speech when there is a trade-off to be made with privacy protection (Walker, 2012).

what precautions they need to take in terms of privacy protection, when handling the collection and analysis of organic datasets, *assuming* that the collection and analysis procedures already pass the legal compliance processes in the participating organizations. To this end, we will discuss the following three questions in order in the rest of this chapter.

From the perspective of data privacy, what types of information about an individual may be inferred from an organic dataset being collected?

From the perspective of individuals' privacy concerns, will knowledge of the organic data collection, the potential inference of personal information, and the intended use of the collected data make those individuals whose information is being collected concerned about their privacy?

Are there technical tools available to ameliorate privacy concerns while maintaining the utility of the collected organic data for research?

It is important to note that all three questions represent active research ideas in multiple disciplines, from computer science (Dwork & Roth, 2014) to psychology (Acquisti et al., 2020). In educational and organizational research, researchers are also starting to investigate issues pertinent to these questions (e.g., Alge et al., 2006; Bhave et al., 2020; Ravid et al., 2021). Nonetheless, there is still a dearth of research work that crosses disciplinary boundaries in answering these questions. Thus, we conclude the chapter with a discussion of future research topics that call for interdisciplinary collaborations in studying privacy-related phenomena in educational and employment settings.

3.1 Data Privacy Issues in Organic-Data Collection

To understand what privacy issues may arise from the collection of an organic dataset, it is important to study three questions with regard to the potential of information disclosure from the collected data. The first question is about anonymity – this is, whether (parts of) the collected data could be linked back to a specific individual. The second question is on the feasibility of data inference – that is, among the parts of collected data that may be linked back to an individual, whether additional characteristics (e.g., demographics information) about the individual could be inferred from the collected data. Finally, the third question is about the interdependency between different individuals' private information – that is, whether the data linkable to one individual could be used to infer information about other individuals (e.g., colleagues, friends). We discuss these three questions respectively as follows.

3.1.1 *Anonymity*

A common misconception with regard to the anonymity afforded by a dataset is that no record can be linked back to an individual as long as all personal identifiable information (PII; e.g., name, national ID such as social security number) is removed from the data. Research in computer science has repeatedly shown that this is not the case. In a seminal work, Sweeney (2000) found that 87% of Americans can be uniquely identified based on a combination of ZIP code, gender, and date of birth, none of which is traditionally considered as PII. Since Sweeney's finding, considerable efforts were made to assess the risk of *reidentification* from a dataset stripped of PII. The ease of such reidentification was highlighted by a series of studies that demonstrated the feasibility of identifying an individual by linking the PII-free records with news stories (Yoo et al., 2018) or publicly available databases (Gymrek et al., 2013), exploiting the uniqueness of variable values (e.g., medical diagnosis code) in a record (Loukides et al., 2010; O'Neill et al., 2016), extracting patterns distinct to each individual from complex data types such as text (Jones et al., 2007), etc. Importantly, the risk of reidentification did not stay as a concern of academic interest but instead manifested as far-reaching incidents in practice. For example, soon after AOL released a dataset consisting of anonymized logs of search queries, a reporter was able to reidentify an AOL user by linking the released dataset with a public phonebook (Barbaro et al., 2006). Similarly, not long after Netflix released the anonymized movie ratings of its users, Narayanan and Shmatikov (2008) reidentified many Netflix users in the dataset by cross-referencing the movie ratings with those posted publicly on the Internet Movie Database website. Both incidents led to lawsuits on the ground of privacy violation and resulted in eventual settlements[2] from the companies releasing the datasets.

3.1.2 *Inference*

A key distinction between organic data and the traditional, designed data, is that the former is generated from a process beyond the control of a

---

[2] AOL: Case No. 1:11-cv-01014-CMH-TRJ (ED Va. Dec. 17, 2012). Netflix: In re Netflix Privacy Litigation, Case No. 5:11-cv-00379-EJD (ND Cal. Mar. 18, 2013).

researcher. In terms of privacy, what this means is that researchers may not be fully aware of the types of private information that could be inferred from an organic dataset, raising important privacy, ethical, and legal concerns for the collection and use of such a dataset (Oswald et al., 2020). This issue is particularly pronounced when the organic dataset contains variables that are rich in contextual information – for example, geolocations, text (e.g., emails), images, audios, and videos. Consider geolocation information as an example. While it ostensibly discloses only the whereabouts of an individual at a particular point in time, existing studies showed that geolocations shared over online social networks could be used to accurately infer a variety of demographic variables including age, gender, sexual orientation, education attainment, etc. (Zhong et al., 2015). Another example is the web-browsing history of an individual. Researchers often collect such information to gauge people's interests on certain topics (e.g., political view; Comarela et al., 2018). Yet web-browsing history has been shown to accurately reveal the gender and education attainment of an individual (Hu et al., 2007; Li et al., 2017). Perhaps unsurprisingly, similar inferences can be made based on a wide variety of context-rich variables, from an individual's search query logs (Weber & Castillo, 2010) to the user name chosen by an individual for an online social network (Wood-Doughty et al., 2018), from writings (even short ones like tweets; Yo & Sasahara, 2017) to audio records (Krauss et al., 2002), etc. It is important to note that this inference issue interacts with the aforementioned anonymity issue, as the additional demographic information being inferred also makes it more likely for a record to be linked back to an individual, for example, through cross-referencing with publicly available datasets like voter registration records. Once the linkage is established, the information in the public dataset then allows the inference of even more information about the individual, compounding the threat of private-information disclosure.

3.1.3 Interconnected Privacy

The information about one individual in an organic dataset could also be used to infer the information about others because the interdependency between different characteristics of the same individual, which leads to the inference issue discussed earlier, readily applies to the characteristics of different individuals. For example, researchers have long recognized the value of organic datasets in capturing the social relationships between different individuals (Knoke & Yang, 2019). Such relationships, in turn, allow the inference of a wide variety of information for the individuals involved. For example, Wang et al. (2014) demonstrated that an individual's working relationships are the key for an accurate inference of work skills possessed by the individual, because such skills tend to be relatively homogeneous among people with close working relationships. Similarly, Dong et al. (2014) found that many demographic variables, including race, gender, and age groups, can be accurately inferred from an individual's social connections. Further, the way an individual's social connections change over time could also reveal the individual's demographic information (Dong et al., 2014). Note that the interdependency of different individuals' information extends beyond the *existence* of relationships between them, and may involve their interactions captured in the organic dataset. For example, Alsarkal et al. (2018) demonstrated how a conversation captured in a dataset, like a simple "Happy Birthday" message, could reveal the date of birth of an individual involved in the conversation.

3.2 Privacy Concerns Arising from Organic-Data Collection

Discussions in the last section clarified the many possible ways private information can be inferred from an organic dataset and linked back to an individual. While the disclosure of such information is clearly pertinent to the privacy of individual data subjects, it is important to recognize that people's need with regard to privacy is *not* about keeping all information about themselves secret, but about striking a proper balance between the need for disclosure and the need for secrecy (Acquisti et al., 2020). As such, a consensual view in the privacy research community is that whether the disclosure of certain private information is a "problem" – that is, whether such disclosure triggers people's *privacy concerns* – depends on the specific context, such as who the data subject is, why the information is disclosed, for what purpose, etc. Moreover, privacy concerns may arise for a wide variety of reasons: from the desire to keep certain information secret to the embarrassment of revealing certain activities outside the societal norm (Post, 2017), to concerns on the "Big Error" (Lazer et al., 2014; McFarland & McFarland, 2015) stemming from the hidden biases in the collected data. To understand how and why privacy concerns may arise from the collection and use of an organic dataset, it is important to examine two interrelated issues. The first is the conceptual issue of "*what is privacy.*" The second is the operational issue of how to *measure* people's privacy concerns. We discuss these two issues respectively in the rest of this section.

3.2.1 Conceptualization of Privacy

Although privacy has been extensively studied in social sciences (including philosophy, economics, psychology, law, and sociology), it is widely recognized that as a concept, privacy "is in disarray and nobody can articulate what it means" (Solove, 2006, p. 477). Scholars have proclaimed that "privacy is so muddled a concept that it is of little use" (Solove, 2007, p. 754). "Perhaps the most striking thing about the right to privacy," Thomson (1975) observes, "is that nobody seems to have any very clear idea what the right to privacy is" (p. 312). The wide scope of scholarly interests has resulted in a variety of conceptualizations of privacy, which leads Margulis (1977) to note that "theorists do not agree ... on what privacy is or on whether privacy is a behavior, attitude, process, goal, phenomenal state, or what" (p. 17).

Many efforts have been made by privacy scholars to develop a systematic understanding of privacy by integrating the different perspectives from different fields. The challenge, however, is that the conceptual picture that emerges is usually fragmented and discipline-specific (also see Smith et al., 2011 for a review). For instance, in law, perhaps the most famous conceptualization is to view "privacy as a right," first defined by Brandeis and Warren (1890) as "the right of the individual to be left alone" (p. 205). This stands in sharp contrast to the sociological view of privacy as a struggle for control between an individual and the society (Margulis 1977; Westin 1967), perhaps owing to the focus of sociology research on how the power and influence between individuals, groups, and institutions shape the collection and use of personal information in the society. Yet another conceptualization of privacy – in economics – is to define privacy as a value both in terms of its relevance to the information needed for efficient markets and its role as a piece of property (Acquisti et al., 2015). This is clearly distal to psychologists' view of privacy, which is often that of a perception or a feeling or an emotion. As Altman (1974) argues, there are many instances where no logical reason appears to exist for a person to feel that their privacy has been violated, yet that is precisely their perception. Almost all these conceptualizations have been developed (to different extents) by philosophers, who interpreted privacy as a state of "limited access or isolation" (Schoeman, 1984, p. 3), "being apart from others" (Weinstein, 1971, p. 626), etc.

The lack of conceptual clarity for privacy brings about considerable challenges not only for researchers but also for the government and organizations, making it extremely difficult for them to form coherent policies regarding data practices. For research, the National Research Council (2011) found that having ad hoc definitions each capturing a small fraction of a complex social construct, without a common understanding of what the construct really means, leads to the balkanization of a field, sparse data, or even paucity of scholarly interest. For technological development, as Lederer et al. (2004, p. 440) pointed out, "one possible reason why designing privacy-sensitive systems is so difficult is that, by refusing to render its meaning plain and knowable, privacy simply lives up to its name." For news media, "privacy" is often used as a blanket term covering everything related to the unsettling consequences of applying the latest technologies (Hao, 2018). This, in turn, confuses the general public and leads to their difficulty in making decisions related to privacy, as observed by many existing studies (Debatin et al., 2009). In sum, while copious empirical evidence has shown privacy to be multidimensional, elastic, depending upon context, and dynamic in the sense that it varies with life experience, a lack of clear, concrete, measurable, and empirically testable conceptualization of privacy is still a major challenge facing today's privacy research and practices.

3.2.2   Measurement of Privacy Concerns

Given the clear lack of consensus on what "privacy" is, there has been a movement toward the measurement of people's *privacy concerns* as the central tenet in privacy research, as noted by Smith et al. (2011). A key reason for this focus is the prevailing belief that the recent wave of privacy laws and regulations, such as the European Union's General Data Protection Regulation, is mainly driven by policymakers' understanding, acknowledgment, and respect of citizens' privacy concerns (Solove, 2021). For social scientists collecting organic datasets, asking the data subjects about their privacy concerns also appears to be a straightforward solution because, intuitively, privacy only becomes a problem when those individuals whose private information is being collected and used are *concerned* about such collection and use.

Given the practical pertinence of measuring people's privacy concerns, the literature is replete with attempts to elicit self-reported privacy concerns with survey instruments, such as the Concern for Information Privacy (CFIP) instrument developed by Smith et al. (1996). Yet accurately gauging people's privacy concerns from self-reported data is known to be a challenge. In developing the 2016 US National Privacy Research Strategy, a subcommittee of the National Science and Technology Council

(2016) notes that people's self-reported privacy concerns are often diverse, dynamic, and situation-specific, not only challenging its reliable measurement at the individual level but making it "difficult to draw general conclusions about current privacy norms or predict how these norms may develop over time" (p. 10). Specifically, self-reported privacy concerns have been criticized for suffering from two main problems, *inflation* and *uncertainty* (Xu & Zhang, 2022).

The criticism of inflation mostly arises from the frequent observation that people could express heightened privacy concerns yet refuse to take even trivial actions to protect their own privacy (Acquisti & Grossklags, 2005; Beresford et al., 2012). For this reason, researchers and practitioners often cite people's self-reported privacy concerns as inflated, exaggerating their "true" level of concerns about privacy (Wittes & Liu, 2015). The literature has also noted multiple potential causes for the inflated responses. For example, Solove (2021) contended that inflated responses are natural because the survey instruments researchers usually use to elicit people's privacy concerns (e.g., the aforementioned CFIP) do not specify the context of data collection or use in sufficient detail. As such, it is perfectly reasonable for an individual to express a high level of *general* concerns yet not be concerned about privacy in a specific context. Complementary to this point is Hong and Thong's (2013) argument that, when privacy concerns are elicited in a hypothetical manner, inflated responses should be expected because a respondent could construe "privacy concerns" as their *expectation* of others' behavior in an ideal world (e.g., whether an ideal organization *should* collect its employee's private information). In other words, there is not really any cost (or trade-off to be considered) associated with an inflated response. Providing further evidence to the inflation of self-reported responses, Marreiros et al. (2017) demonstrated that self-reported privacy concerns became inflated immediately after exposure to information about privacy (e.g., after reading a newspaper article), no matter if such exposure is positive, neutral, or negative. In other words, even those individuals who were not very concerned about the collection of their private information could report a high level of concern after hearing *something* about privacy. This challenges the fundamental feasibility of eliciting people's "true" privacy concerns through a survey questionnaire.

Besides inflation, another frequent criticism is that people are often *uncertain* about their attitudes toward privacy concerns, leading to excessive variability in their self-reported privacy concerns. Uncertainty, or a respondent's lack of an attitude in a coherent form, is a common issue for self-reported data (Bertrand & Mullainathan, 2001). What is unique for self-reported privacy concerns is that the uncertainty is not limited to respondents who are inattentive (Lelkes et al., 2012) but applies to a large part of the respondents. For example, many respondents do not seem to know the consequences of disclosing certain private information (Solove, 2021). Many others are unsure about how they feel toward privacy (Acquisti et al., 2015). Yet others are uncertain about whether the common tools for privacy protection (e.g., virtual private network, or VPN) are indeed effective (Gates, 2011). This excessive uncertainty has two pronounced consequences. One is the cue-seeking behavior it induces. That is, when survey respondents are reluctant to admit their uncertainties (e.g., for fear of being perceived as ignorant or naive; Acquisti et al., 2015), they tend to "cast around" for cues when answering survey questions about their privacy concerns (Adjerid et al., 2018). Unfortunately, such cues are rarely relevant to privacy, instead mostly concerning the design and appearance of a survey instrument (John et al., 2011) or even the physical environment surrounding the respondent when answering the question (Acquisti et al., 2015). The second consequence of excessive uncertainty is a phenomenon known as "privacy cynicism" (Hoffmann et al., 2016). That is, many people deliberately "discount risks or concerns" in order to cope with their uncertainty (Hoffmann et al., 2016). In either case, as different people respond to uncertainty in different ways (Powell & Baker, 2014), we tend to observe even more randomness in the self-reported privacy concerns.

To address the two criticisms, privacy scholars spent considerable efforts in recent years to refine the measurement of privacy concerns, in particular by carefully examining the role of *context* in the measurement process. Conceptually, Nissenbaum (2020) linked privacy concerns to a set of context-dependent situational norms. Operationally, researchers started adopting general-purpose survey instruments for measuring privacy concerns in specific contexts (e.g., Xu et al., 2012). In an educational or organizational setting, the proper contextualization of privacy-concern measurement is even more important given the empirical evidence that people's privacy concerns tend to differ considerably in workplace and personal settings (Auxier et al., 2019), and adults and adolescents tend to cope with their privacy concerns in different ways (Jia et al., 2015). To this end, researchers may benefit from a recently developed quantitative framework (Xu & Zhang, 2022) that estimates the degree of inflation and uncertainty from self-reported privacy concerns, making it possible for researchers to identify a proper contextualization and to correct both forms of bias when using self-reported privacy concerns.

3.3 Technological Solutions for Privacy Protection

In addition to the quest of understanding people's privacy concerns, privacy researchers also pursued a technical solution to the problem of privacy protection, with the goal being to maintain the utility of the organic dataset for research while eliminating the collection or inference of private information. The key rationale here is an observation that, even though an organic dataset usually consists of data about individuals, social scientists rarely use such datasets to study one individual specifically. Instead, the research goal is almost always to identify patterns or relationships that hold for a large part of the population. As research in statistics has long shown the feasibility of recovering accurate patterns from datasets that have undergone drastic changes (e.g., noise insertion) at the individual-record level (Osborne, 1991), the idea of the technical solution for privacy protection is to develop a process for *anonymizing* a dataset so as to block all potential links to the individual data subjects yet maintain the patterns and relationships that are of research interest. The existing techniques for data anonymization can be largely partitioned into two categories, *data removal* and *noise insertion*, respectively, which we discuss as follows.

3.3.1 Data Removal

Since the goal of data anonymization is to prevent any individual from being identified from the anonymized dataset, a natural idea for anonymizing a dataset is to remove the part of data that could be used to identify an individual. The data removal mechanism is rooted in this idea. Its initial implementations focused on removing variables that are obvious identifiers, such as name, address, social security number, etc. These implementations were challenged by the aforementioned discovery (Sweeney, 2000) that ZIP code, gender, and date of birth in combination can uniquely identify 87% of Americans. Following this discovery, a plethora of data removal techniques were developed to detect and rectify the issues caused by such "quasi-identifiers" (e.g., Machanavajjhala et al., 2007; Sweeney, 2002), forming the bulk of the existing literature for the data removal techniques (for a review, see Fung et al., 2010). A common idea followed by these techniques is to first identify the individuals at risk of being identified before removing the minimum necessary information to block such identifications. The removal of information could be operationalized by marking a value as missing (i.e., replacing its real value with N/A) or by reducing the precision of a value through granularity change (e.g., replacing Los Angeles with California).

A key advantage of data removal techniques is their transparency to the subsequent data analysis processes. Since most data removal techniques alter only the values in a dataset but not the structure of the dataset, a researcher who uses the dataset can readily apply any traditional statistical analysis tool over the privacy-preserved data with little change. Unfortunately, this advantage turns into a problem when researchers start integrating an anonymized dataset with other data sources. Specifically, the computer science literature has noted that, without making substantial assumptions about what the other data sources are, it is simply impossible for a data removal mechanism to block all possible links to an individual without making the data useless for research (Ganta et al., 2008). In other words, while data removal is highly attractive due to its simplicity of operation, it does not offer any rigorous anonymity guarantee that can withstand potential integration with other datasets. For this reason, there is a sharp divide between researchers and practitioners on the use of data removal mechanisms today. On the one hand, data removal remains popular in practice, frequently used or recommended by firms and government agencies for compliance with privacy laws and regulations (Article 29 Data Protection Working Party, 2014; Rocher et al., 2019). Yet, on the other hand, technical research on data removal all but ceased in the last decade, with technical researchers shifting their focus to noise insertion techniques, which we discuss next.

3.3.2   *Noise Insertion*

As discussed earlier, research in statistics, specifically calibration (Osborne, 1991), has long demonstrated the feasibility of recovering summary statistics from noise-ridden data. Leveraging this finding, earlier work on noise insertion simply anonymized a dataset by adding independent and identically distributed Gaussian noise to variable values before developing statistical techniques to recover the statistics of interest (Agrawal & Srikant, 2000). Unfortunately, this method was later found to be ineffective for privacy protection because the inherent correlation between different variables in the original dataset allows spectral methods (Bernardi & Maday, 1997) to separate the independent noise from the correlated data, thereby nullifying the anonymization achieved through noise insertion (Huang et al., 2005). This problem was solved by the development of differential privacy (Dwork et al., 2006), which guarantees that, for any individual in the dataset and any statistics of the dataset, the statistics would be indistinguishable from the same statistics of a dataset that has the individual's record removed. In other words, an individual's privacy derives from the fact that no one can learn anything new from the dataset that it cannot already learn from a dataset without the individual's data.

A key advantage of differential privacy, compared with the data removal mechanism, is that it provides a rigorous guarantee that holds *no matter* what external data sources may be available. This makes differential privacy extremely attractive in research and practice. As a result, it became the de-facto standard for the noise insertion mechanism today, and has been adopted by high-tech firms such as Apple (Tang et al., 2017) and Google (Erlingsson et al., 2014) as well as government agencies such as the US Census Bureau in its 2020 decennial Census (Abowd, 2018). To researchers who use the (anonymized) dataset, however, differential privacy presents a challenge, as the majority of implementations for differential privacy do not allow researchers access to the raw dataset, instead requiring them to interactively query the data to obtain (noisy) estimates of statistics required for research. This means that the traditional tools for statistical analysis cannot be directly applied. Instead, new tools need to be developed that take into account the way differential privacy performs noise insertion. While differentially private tools for tasks like linear regression are available (Wang, 2018), there are many other statistical analysis tools, like structural equation modeling, for which no differentially private version has been developed.

3.4 Future Research

It is clear from the earlier discussions that there is still much to be learned about the information privacy issues surrounding organic data collection and use, especially in an educational or workplace setting. While numerous inference channels have been identified, we do not yet have the full picture of what private information may be inferred from an organic dataset. The scientific community has not yet converged on a consensual definition of privacy, nor the effective means to capture people's privacy concerns. The development of technical solutions for privacy protection is also a work in progress. While all these unknowns may lead to pessimism for educational or organizational researchers wanting to take advantage of the rich knowledge afforded by organic datasets, we note that they also represent opportunities for them to contribute to the literature of information privacy, in particular to the understanding of privacy issues in educational and workplace settings. For this reason, we conclude the chapter with a discussion of future research that calls for the participation of educational and organizational researchers in the interdisciplinary efforts required to address the existing and emerging privacy challenges.

As discussed earlier, the scientific community has not formed a consensus on the definition of privacy in decades, and will unlikely converge on a consensus anytime soon. Interestingly, there are two distinct paths through which privacy researchers are attempting to address this lack of consensus. On the one hand, there are behavioral scientists who are making extensive efforts to *refine* the concepts of privacy by revealing more and more factors that affect people's perceptions or concerns of privacy (Dinev et al., 2015; Smith et al., 2011), including attention, cognition, emotion, motivation, environment, etc. On the other hand, computer scientists who develop technical solutions for privacy protection tend to treat the conceptualization of privacy as an afterthought, articulated not according to what it means to everyday people but based on what is mathematically feasible to achieve (e.g., the aforementioned different privacy guarantee). We argue that both paths could be detrimental to addressing the privacy issues *in practice*. While further refinement of privacy conceptualization could reveal factors that affect people's attitudes, beliefs, and perceptions about privacy invasions, it also risks overcomplicating the problem and producing a (somewhat defeatist) belief that everything related to privacy is fluid and must be examined on a case-by-case basis. On the other hand, oversimplifying a complex concept like privacy by rolling all of its dimensions into a singular technical definition is problematic too, as doing so may lead to a technical solution that is designed to meet everyone's need but indeed satisfies no one, causes confusions among everyday people, and make it difficult for them to make decisions with regard to the use of technical solutions (Debatin et al., 2009).

We believe that one way to address the problem of overcomplication and oversimplification in privacy research is to develop middle-range (Merton, 1968), context-contingent theories that, instead of attempting to identify the overarching features of privacy that operate in all social processes, simply aim to consolidate the empirical regularities related to privacy concerns and behavior in a specific set of similar contexts, like educational or workplace settings. A key reason behind our argument for developing context-contingent theories is the recognition that there is already ample empirical evidence suggesting the wide variation of privacy-related phenomena across contexts. For example, privacy concern and privacy-seeking behavior were found to be strongly correlated within one context (Dienlin & Trepte, 2015), virtually uncorrelated in another context (Reynolds et al., 2011), and negatively correlated in a third context (Sheehan & Hoy, 1999). As there is little evidence that an overarching theory actually exists to explain the privacy phenomena across all contexts, from a practical perspective, it may be more productive to pursue a context-contingent theory that can *approximate* what privacy means to most people in a set of specific contexts, so as to enable the development of practical solutions that can address most people's privacy concerns in these contexts. Clearly, developing context-contingency theories requires domain expertise for the corresponding contexts. Thus, we believe that the participation of educational and organizational researchers is essential for advancing our understanding of the privacy phenomena in educational and workplace settings, especially given the rapidly increasing popularity of Big Data technologies that use organic data collection and analysis to improve operational efficiency.

REFERENCES

Abowd, J. M. (2018). The U.S. Census Bureau adopts differential privacy. In *Proceedings of the 24th ACM SIGKDD International Conference on Knowledge Discovery & Data Mining* (pp. 2867–2867).

Abril, P. S., Levin, A., & Del Riego, A. (2012). Blurred boundaries: Social media privacy and the twenty-first-century employee. *American Business Law Journal, 49*(1), 63–124.

Acquisti, A., Brandimarte, L., & Loewenstein, G. (2015). Privacy and human behavior in the age of information. *Science, 347*(6221), 509–514.

(2020). Secrets and likes: The drive for privacy and the difficulty of achieving it in the digital age. *Journal of Consumer Psychology, 30*(4), 736–758.

Acquisti, A., & Grossklags, J. (2005). Privacy and rationality in individual decision making. *IEEE Security & Privacy, 3*(1), 26–33.

Adjerid, I., Peer, E., & Acquisti, A. (2018). Beyond the privacy paradox: Objective versus relative risk in privacy decision making. *MIS Quarterly, 42*(2), 465–488.

Agrawal, R., & Srikant, R. (2000). Privacy-preserving data mining. In *Proceedings of the 2000 ACM SIGMOD International Conference on Management of Data* (pp. 439–450).

Alge, B. J., Ballinger, G. A., Tangirala, S., & Oakley, J. L. (2006). Information privacy in organizations: Empowering creative and extrarole performance. *Journal of Applied Psychology, 91*(1), 221–232.

Alsarkal, Y., Zhang, N., & Xu, H. (2018). Your privacy is your friend's privacy: Examining interdependent information disclosure on online social networks. In *Proceedings of the 51st Hawaii International Conference on System Sciences* (pp. 892–901).

Altman, I. (1974). Privacy: A conceptual analysis. In D. H. Carson (Ed.), *Man-environment interactions: Evaluations and applications: Part 2* (pp. 13–28). Environmental Design Research Association.

Article 29 Data Protection Working Party. (2014). *Opinion 05/2014 on anonymisation techniques.* https://ec.europa.eu/justice/article-29/documentation/

Auxier, B., Rainie, L., Anderson, M., Perrin, A., Kumar, M., & Turner, E. (2019). *Americans and privacy: Concerned, confused and feeling lack of control over their personal information.* Pew Research Center. https://www.pewresearch.org/internet/2019/11/15/americans-and-privacy-concerned-confused-and-feeling-lack-of-control-over-their-personal-information/

Barbaro, M., Zeller, T., & Hansell, S. (2006). A face is exposed for AOL searcher no. 4417749. *New York Times.* https://www.nytimes.com/2006/08/09/technology/09aol.html

Barberá, P., Jost, J. T., Nagler, J., Tucker, J. A., & Bonneau, R. (2015). Tweeting from left to right: Is online political communication more than an echo chamber?. *Psychological Science, 26*(10), 1531–1542.

Beresford, A. R., Kübler, D., & Preibusch, S. (2012). Unwillingness to pay for privacy: A field experiment. *Economics Letters, 117*(1), 25–27.

Bernardi, C., & Maday, Y. (1997). Spectral methods. In P. G. Ciarlet & J. L. Lions (Eds.), *Handbook of numerical analysis* (Vol. 5; pp. 209–485). Elsevier.

Bertrand, M., & Mullainathan, S. (2001). Do people mean what they say? Implications for subjective survey data. *American Economic Review, 91*(2), 67–72.

Bhave, D. P., Teo, L. H., & Dalal, R. S. (2020). Privacy at work: A review and a research agenda for a contested terrain. *Journal of Management, 46*(1), 127–164.

Brandeis, L., & Warren, S. (1890). The right to privacy. *Harvard Law Review, 4*(5), 193–220.

Comarela, G., Durairajan, R., Barford, P., Christenson, D., & Crovella, M. (2018). Assessing candidate preference through web browsing history. In *Proceedings of the 24th ACM SIGKDD International Conference on Knowledge Discovery & Data Mining* (pp. 158–167).

Debatin, B., Lovejoy, J. P., Horn, A. K., & Hughes, B. N. (2009). Facebook and online privacy: Attitudes, behaviors, and unintended consequences. *Journal of Computer-Mediated Communication, 15*(1), 83–108.

Dienlin, T., & Trepte, S. (2015). Is the privacy paradox a relic of the past? An in-depth analysis of privacy attitudes and privacy behaviors. *European Journal of Social Psychology, 45*(3), 285–297.

Dinev, T., McConnell, R. A., & Smith, H. J. (2015). Informing privacy research through information systems, psychology, and behavioral economics: Thinking outside the "APCO" box. *Information Systems Research, 26*(4), 639–655.

Dong, Y., Yang, Y., Tang, J., Yang, Y., & Chawla, N. V. (2014, August). Inferring user demographics and social strategies in mobile social networks. In *Proceedings of the 20th ACM SIGKDD International Conference on Knowledge Discovery and Data Mining* (pp. 15–24).

Dwork, C., McSherry, F., Nissim, K., & Smith, A. (2006). Calibrating noise to sensitivity in private data analysis. In *Theory of cryptography conference* (pp. 265–284). Springer.

Dwork, C., & Roth, A. (2014). The algorithmic foundations of differential privacy. *Foundations and Trends in Theoretical Computer Science*, *9*(3–4), 211–407.

Erlingsson, Ú., Pihur, V., & Korolova, A. (2014). Rappor: Randomized aggregatable privacy-preserving ordinal response. In *Proceedings of the 2014 ACM SIGSAC Conference on Computer and Communications Security* (pp. 1054–1067).

Fung, B. C., Wang, K., Chen, R., & Yu, P. S. (2010). Privacy-preserving data publishing: A survey of recent developments. *ACM Computing Surveys*, *42*(4), 1–53.

Ganta, S. R., Kasiviswanathan, S. P., & Smith, A. (2008, August). Composition attacks and auxiliary information in data privacy. In *Proceedings of the 14th ACM SIGKDD International Conference on Knowledge Discovery and Data Mining* (pp. 265–273).

Gates, G. W. (2011). How uncertainty about privacy and confidentiality is hampering efforts to more effectively use administrative records in producing U.S. national statistics. *Journal of Privacy and Confidentiality*, *3*(2), 3–40.

Groves, R. M. (2011). Three eras of survey research. *Public Opinion Quarterly*, *75* (5), 861–871.

Gymrek, M., McGuire, A. L., Golan, D., Halperin, E., & Erlich, Y. (2013). Identifying personal genomes by surname inference. *Science*, *339*(6117), 321–324.

Hao, K. (2018, October 21). Establishing an AI code of ethics will be harder than people think. *MIT Technology Review*.

Harford, T. (2014). Big data: A big mistake?. *Significance*, *11*(5), 14–19.

Hoffmann, C. P., Lutz, C., & Ranzini, G. (2016). Privacy cynicism: A new approach to the privacy paradox. *Cyberpsychology: Journal of Psychosocial Research on Cyberspace*, *10*(4).

Hong, W., & Thong, J. Y. (2013). Internet privacy concerns: An integrated conceptualization and four empirical studies. *MIS Quarterly*, *37*(1), 275–298.

Hu, J., Zeng, H. J., Li, H., Niu, C., & Chen, Z. (2007). Demographic prediction based on user's browsing behavior. In *Proceedings of the 16th International Conference on World Wide Web* (pp. 151–160).

Huang, Z., Du, W., & Chen, B. (2005). Deriving private information from randomized data. In *Proceedings of the 2005 ACM SIGMOD International Conference on Management of Data* (pp. 37–48).

Jia, H., Wisniewski, P. J., Xu, H., Rosson, M. B., & Carroll, J. M. (2015). Risk-taking as a learning process for shaping teen's online information privacy behaviors. In *Proceedings of the 18th ACM Conference on Computer Supported Cooperative Work & Social Computing* (pp. 583–599).

John, L. K., Acquisti, A., & Loewenstein, G. (2011). Strangers on a plane: Context-dependent willingness to divulge sensitive information. *Journal of Consumer Research*, *37*(5), 858–873.

Jones, R., Kumar, R., Pang, B., & Tomkins, A. (2007). "I know what you did last summer" query logs and user privacy. In *Proceedings of the 16th ACM Conference on Information and Knowledge Management* (pp. 909–914).

Knoke, D., & Yang, S. (2019). *Social network analysis*. Sage Publications.

Koelmeyer, A., & Josey, N. (2019). Employment and privacy: Consent, the 'privacy act' and biometric scanners in the workplace. *LSJ: Law Society of NSW Journal*, *57*, 76–77.

Krauss, R. M., Freyberg, R., & Morsella, E. (2002). Inferring speakers' physical attributes from their voices. *Journal of Experimental Social Psychology*, *38*(6), 618–625.

Lazer, D., Kennedy, R., King, G., & Vespignani, A. (2014). The parable of Google flu: Traps in big data analysis. *Science*, *343*(6176), 1203–1205.

Lederer, S., Hong, J. I., Dey, A. K., & Landay, J. A. (2004). Personal privacy through understanding and action: Five pitfalls for designers. *Personal and Ubiquitous Computing*, *8*(6), 440–454.

Lee, D. (2018, November 27). Predictim babysitter app: Facebook and Twitter take action. *BBC News*. https://bbc.com

Lelkes, Y., Krosnick, J. A., Marx, D. M., Judd, C. M., & Park, B. (2012). Complete anonymity compromises the accuracy of self-reports. *Journal of Experimental Social Psychology*, *48*(6), 1291–1299.

Li, H., Zhu, H., & Ma, D. (2017). Demographic information inference through meta-data analysis of Wi-Fi traffic. *IEEE Transactions on Mobile Computing*, *17*(5), 1033–1047.

Loukides, G., Denny, J. C., & Malin, B. (2010). The disclosure of diagnosis codes can breach research participants' privacy. *Journal of the American Medical Informatics Association*, *17*(3), 322–327.

Machanavajjhala, A., Kifer, D., Gehrke, J., & Venkitasubramaniam, M. (2007). *l*-diversity: Privacy beyond *k*-anonymity. *ACM Transactions on Knowledge Discovery from Data (TKDD)*, *1*(1), 3–es.

Margulis, S. T. (1977). Conceptions of privacy: Current status and next steps. *Journal of Social Issues*, *33*(3), 5–21.

Marreiros, H., Tonin, M., Vlassopoulos, M., & Schraefel, M. C. (2017). "Now that you mention it": A survey experiment on information, inattention and online privacy. *Journal of Economic Behavior & Organization*, *140*, 1–17.

McFarland, A. D., Lewis, K., & Goldberg, A. (2016). Sociology in the era of big data: The ascent of forensic social science. *American Sociologist*, *47*, 12–35.

McFarland, D. A., & McFarland, H. R. (2015). Big data and the danger of being precisely inaccurate. *Big Data & Society*, July–December, 1–4.

Merton, R. K. (1968). *Social theory and social structure*. Simon & Schuster.

National Research Council. (2011). *The importance of common metrics for advancing social science theory and research: A workshop summary*. National Academies Press.

National Science and Technology Council. (2016). *National privacy research strategy.* https://www.nitrd.gov/pubs/NationalPrivacyResearchStrategy.pdf

Narayanan, A., & Shmatikov, V. (2008). Robust de-anonymization of large sparse datasets. In *Proceedings of the IEEE Symposium on Security and Privacy* (pp. 111–125). IEEE.

Neace, G. (2019). Biometric privacy: Blending employment law with the growth of technology. *UIC Law Review, 53,* 73–112.

Nissenbaum, H. (2020). *Privacy in context.* Stanford University Press.

O'Neill, L., Dexter, F., & Zhang, N. (2016). The risks to patient privacy from publishing data from clinical anesthesia studies. *Anesthesia & Analgesia, 122* (6), 2017–2027.

Osborne, C. (1991). Statistical calibration: A review. *International Statistical Review, 59*(3), 309–336.

Oswald, F. L., Behrend, T. S., Putka, D. J., & Sinar, E. (2020). Big data in industrial-organizational psychology and human resource management: Forward progress for organizational research and practice. *Annual Review of Organizational Psychology and Organizational Behavior, 7,* 505–533.

Paxton, A., & Griffiths, T. L. (2017). Finding the traces of behavioral and cognitive processes in big data and naturally occurring datasets. *Behavior Research Methods, 49*(5), 1630–1638.

Peterson, D. (2016). Edtech and student privacy: California law as a model. *Berkeley Technology Law Journal, 31*(2), 961–995.

Post, R. C. (2017). Data privacy and dignitary privacy: Google Spain, the right to be forgotten, and the construction of the public sphere. *Duke Law Journal, 67,* 981–1072.

Powell, E. E., & Baker, T. (2014). It's what you make of it: Founder identity and enacting strategic responses to adversity. *Academy of Management Journal, 57*(5), 1406–1433.

Ravid, D. M., Tomczak, D. L., White, J. C., & Behrend, T. S. (2020). EPM 20/20: A review, framework, and research agenda for electronic performance monitoring. *Journal of Management, 46*(1), 100–126.

Ravid, D. M., White, J. C., & Behrend, T. S. (2021). Implications of COVID-19 for privacy at work. *Industrial and Organizational Psychology, 14*(1–2), 194–198.

Reynolds, B., Venkatanathan, J., Gonçalves, J., & Kostakos, V. (2011, September). Sharing ephemeral information in online social networks: Privacy perceptions and behaviours. In *IFIP Conference on Human-Computer Interaction* (pp. 204–215). Springer.

Rocher, L., Hendrickx, J. M., & De Montjoye, Y. A. (2019). Estimating the success of re-identifications in incomplete datasets using generative models. *Nature Communications, 10*(1), 1–9.

Ruggles, S. (2014). Big microdata for population research. *Demography, 51*(1), 287–297.

Russom, M. B., Sloan, R. H., & Warner, R. (2011). Legal concepts meet technology: A 50-state survey of privacy laws. In *Proceedings of the*

2011 Workshop on Governance of Technology, Information, and Policies (pp. 29–37).

Schoeman, F. D. (Ed.). (1984). *Philosophical dimensions of privacy: An anthology.* Cambridge University Press.

Sheehan, K. B., & Hoy, M. G. (1999). Flaming, complaining, abstaining: How online users respond to privacy concerns. *Journal of Advertising, 28*(3), 37–51.

Smith, H. J., Dinev, T., & Xu, H. (2011). Information privacy research: An interdisciplinary review. *MIS Quarterly, 35*(4), 989–1015.

Smith, H. J., Milberg, S. J., & Burke, S. J. (1996). Information privacy: Measuring individuals' concerns about organizational practices. *MIS Quarterly, 20*(2), 167–196.

Solove, D. J. (2006). A taxonomy of privacy. *University of Pennsylvania Law Review, 154*(3), 477–560.

(2007). 'I've got nothing to hide' and other misunderstandings of privacy. *San Diego Law Review, 44*, 745–772.

(2021). The myth of the privacy paradox. *George Washington Law Review, 89*(1), 1–51.

Sweeney, L. (2000). Simple demographics often identify people uniquely. *Health (San Francisco), 671*(2000), 1–34.

(2002). *k*-anonymity: A model for protecting privacy. *International Journal of Uncertainty, Fuzziness and Knowledge-Based Systems, 10*(5), 557–570.

Tang, J., Korolova, A., Bai, X., Wang, X., & Wang, X. (2017). Privacy loss in Apple's implementation of differential privacy on MacOS 10.12. *arXiv preprint arXiv:1709.02753.*

Thomson, J. J. (1975). The right to privacy. *Philosophy & Public Affairs, 4*(4), 295–314.

Walker, R. K. (2012). The right to be forgotten. *Hastings Law Journal, 64*, 257–286.

Wang, Y. X. (2018). Revisiting differentially private linear regression: Optimal and adaptive prediction & estimation in unbounded domain. In *Proceedings of the 34th Conference on Uncertainty in Artificial Intelligence* (pp. 93–103).

Wang, Z., Li, S., Shi, H., & Zhou, G. (2014). Skill inference with personal and skill connections. In *Proceedings of COLING 2014, the 25th International Conference on Computational Linguistics: Technical papers* (pp. 520–529).

Weber, I., & Castillo, C. (2010). The demographics of web search. In *Proceedings of the 33rd International ACM SIGIR Conference on Research and Development in Information Retrieval* (pp. 523–530).

Weinstein, M. A. (1971). The uses of privacy in the good life. In J. R. Pennock & J. W. Chapman (Eds.), *Nomos XIII: Privacy* (pp. 624–692). Atherton Press.

Westin, A. F. (1967). *Privacy and freedom.* Atheneum.

Wittes, B., & Liu, J. C. (2015, May 21). *The privacy paradox: The privacy benefits of privacy threats.* Center for Technology Innovation at Brookings.

Wood-Doughty, Z., Andrews, N., Marvin, R., & Dredze, M. (2018). Predicting Twitter user demographics from names alone. In *Proceedings of the 2nd*

Workshop on Computational Modeling of People's Opinions, Personality, and Emotions in Social Media (pp. 105–111).

Xu, H., Teo, H. H., Tan, B. C., & Agarwal, R. (2012). Effects of individual self-protection, industry self-regulation, and government regulation on privacy concerns: A study of location-based services. *Information Systems Research*, *23*(4), 1342–1363.

Xu, H., & Zhang, N. (2022). From contextualizing to context-theorizing: Assessing context effects in privacy research. *Management Science*, *68*(10), 7065–7791.

Yo, T., & Sasahara, K. (2017). Inference of personal attributes from tweets using machine learning. In *2017 IEEE International Conference on Big Data* (pp. 3168–3174). IEEE.

Yoo, J. S., Thaler, A., Sweeney, L., & Zang, J. (2018). Risks to patient privacy: A re-identification of patients in Maine and Vermont statewide hospital data. *Journal of Technology and Science Education*, *2018*, 2018100901.

Zhong, Y., Yuan, N. J., Zhong, W., Zhang, F., & Xie, X. (2015). You are where you go: Inferring demographic attributes from location check-ins. In *Proceedings of the 8th ACM International Conference on Web Search and Data Mining* (pp. 295–304).

PART II

Global Perspectives on Key Methods/Topics

CHAPTER 4

Social Media Assessments around the Globe

Hanyi Min and Cristina Gonzalez

With the increasing popularity of social media, many people use social media to share and interact with others on a daily basis. Researchers have realized that people's language, behavior, and other information on social media can be used to capture constructs of interest (e.g., personality). This chapter discusses how social media platforms can be utilized for assessment. We start with a brief discussion about the definitions of social media. We then conduct a literature search based on the definition, which indicates the four most frequently studied constructs using social media information. We summarize the studies assessing these four constructs using social media. Finally, we discuss the global aspect of assessment using social media, list several future directions, and point out possible ethical concerns.

4.1 What Is Social Media?

With the increasing popularity of social media, most people can probably provide a few examples of social media (e.g., Facebook, Twitter, LinkedIn). It is, however, more difficult to provide a precise and comprehensive definition of social media (Rhee et al., 2021).

Some researchers defined social media as online platforms that facilitate interpersonal communication, networking, and connecting. Rhee and colleagues (2021) asked users to define the four major social media platforms in the United States (i.e., Facebook, Twitter, Instagram, and Snapchat). Their findings indicated that although their participants identified social interactions as one of the critical components of social media platforms, it was not necessarily the most central facet for some of the social media platforms (e.g., Twitter, Instagram, or Snapchat).

Another definition of social media by Howard and Parks (2012) focused on the production, distribution, and consumption of digital content (e.g., YouTube). Kent (2010) further pointed out that social media platforms needed to have characteristics that allow real-time interaction among users. Carr and Hayes (2015) summarized previous definitions of social media and provided a relatively comprehensive definition of social media: "Social media are Internet-based channels that allow users to opportunistically interact and selectively self-present, either in real-time or asynchronously, with both broad and narrow audiences who derive value from user-generated content and the perception of interaction with others" (p. 48).

The current chapter adopts Carr and Hayes' (2015) definition of social media. We would like to point out that this definition may need to be further refined as time goes on and new types of social media emerge, such as TikTok, Clubhouse, and virtual worlds (e.g., Meta). For instance, a key feature of Clubhouse consists of real-time virtual rooms for users to communicate with each other. The contents of the conversations are not accessible to others afterward. Regardless of this feature, Clubhouse is considered to be a social media based on the definition we have used because it allows users to interact and self-present. Other online communication platforms (e.g., Zoom, Skype) also share this real-time feature and allow a user to interact and self-present, but are less likely to be considered as social media platforms. This indicates that it is difficult to delineate clear boundaries between social media platforms and other communication technologies or platforms. We, thus, agree with Rhee and colleagues (2021) that it is beneficial to take a comparative approach to consider the similarities and dissimilarities of different social media platforms and incorporate real-world categories when researchers study social media. That is, researchers can select a few platforms that share several features or serve similar purposes and ask the respondents to compare and contrast these platforms. For instance, LinkedIn and Slack are both used for professional purposes, including work communication and job hunting. Respondents can be asked to describe the similarities and differences in their major features and functions.

4.2   Constructs Most Frequently Measured Using Social Media

Social media platforms include a variety of information and permit researchers to assess their focal construct in many different ways, such as the language used in posts, the number of posts, smile intensity of profile pictures, the number of friends, and the number of likes. To understand which constructs are most frequently studied using social media, we first entered general search terms related to social media, such as "Social Media + Measure," "Social Media + Assessment," and "Global + Social Media" between the years 2000 and 2021. The search generated 65 articles which used social media to study various topics, including personality, life satisfaction, misinformation, public/political views, tourism, and the stock market. Based on the number of studies, four groups of constructs are most frequently measured using the information on social media: personality, emotion/affect/mood, life satisfaction, and political views. Next, we summarize the studies using social media to assess these four construct groups.

4.2.1 Personality

Personality represents individuals' characteristics that account for consistent patterns of feelings, behaviors, and thoughts (Pervin et al., 2005). It has drawn a lot of research attention to predict users' personality traits using the information posted on social media. Some researchers use one source of information on social media (i.e., language, picture, or activity) to measure personality, whereas others use multiple information sources. Next, we summarize the studies based on the sources of information used for assessment.

4.2.1.1 Language

Researchers have used different approaches to measure personality from language. The first approach has human raters code (or annotate) people's personalities based on the language participants use on social media (e.g., Facebook or Twitter). For instance, Qiu and colleagues (2012 collected 142 participants' tweets over one month (the average number of tweets was 204 for each participant) and had eight undergraduate research assistants (RA) rate personality from these tweets. The authors then correlated the RA-rated personality traits with self-reported personality traits (openness: $r = 0.11$; conscientiousness: $r = 0.35$; extraversion: $r = 0.21$; agreeableness: $r = 0.43$; and neuroticism: $r = 0.74$). The correlations varied quite a bit, with neuroticism showing the strongest relationship between other-rated and self-reported personality and openness showing the weakest relationship among the five traits. There are a few potential reasons for the large variance. First, people tend to post on social media when they experience strong emotions, and they may be less likely to exhibit behaviors/words related to openness. Second, it may be easier for raters to identify neuroticism, a trait more strongly correlated with visible emotions than openness. Third, the frequency of tweeting may be a confounding factor. The authors reported that their participants have 204.07 tweets on average but with a large standard deviation (SD = 201.66). People high in neuroticism may be more likely to tweet than people high in other traits, which further provides more information for the RAs to identify neuroticism.

The second approach is applying supervised machine-learning (ML) algorithms (e.g., lasso/ridge regression) to predict personality from language. When taking this approach, researchers first obtain information from social media platforms through website scraping or archival datasets (e.g., Twitter API). Our literature review indicates that many studies using social media information to predict personality used participants from the myPersonality dataset (Kosinski et al., 2015). The myPersonality dataset has been widely used in previous studies of social media. This sample includes over six million Facebook users and information about their Facebook account and their scores on a variety of psychological measures. The majority of the sample includes US users (55%) and females (58%). The mean age is 24.15 years old (SD = 6.55). To build a machine-learning model to predict personality from language, researchers first need to obtain a training dataset in which each entry of language (e.g., Facebook posts, tweets) has a score in correspondent outcomes (e.g., one of the personality traits; also called a "label"). Then, researchers need to clean and preprocess the dataset, including removing stop words, conversing all upper case into lower case, tokenization (i.e., breaking the data into words and/or phrases), and lemmatization (e.g., "wording" and "worked" are conversed to "work"). These preprocessed words are further used as predictors in machine-learning algorithms. In supervised machine learning, the algorithms learn the association and rules between language predictors (i.e., the preprocessed words) and the outcomes (the scores or labels) and use these rules to predict personality scores on a new dataset (called a "testing dataset") (Alpaydin, 2020). More details about data preprocessing and using machine-learning techniques to analyze language data can be found in Putka and colleagues (2018), Hickman and colleagues (2020), and Guo and colleagues (2021).

Park and colleagues (2015) used a language processing model on a subset of myPersonality users (over 66,000 Facebook users). The Facebook status posts of this sample over 23 months were used as the data for analyses. The authors extracted words, phrases, and topics from the large narrative dataset, which were then used as predictors in ridge regressions. The average test–retest reliability of language-based assessments of the five personality traits over six months was 0.70 (openness: $r = 0.74$; conscientiousness: $r = 0.76$; extraversion: $r = 0.72$; agreeableness:

$r = 0.65$; and neuroticism: $r = 0.62$). Their results also demonstrated that the language-based assessments of personalities agreed with self-reported ($r = 0.39$) and other-reported ($r = 0.24$) personality. Patterns of discriminant validity across the five personality traits were similar between the language-based assessments and self-reported personalities. In another study, Schwartz and colleagues (2013) collected Facebook status updates from 74,941 volunteers (15.4 million status updates in total). The authors used ridge regression to predict personality traits from the Facebook status updates. Their predictive model achieved an average correlation of 0.35 with self-report personality across the five traits (openness: $r = 0.42$; conscientiousness: $r = 0.35$; extraversion: $r = 0.38$; agreeableness: $r = 0.31$; and neuroticism: $r = 0.31$). Thilakaratne and colleagues (2016) also used Facebook status updates to predict personality traits with the myPersonality dataset. The authors extracted the semantics of concepts and topics and used them as predictors. A support vector machine was used for prediction and achieved good performance (openness: $r = 0.37$; conscientiousness: $r = 0.34$; extraversion: $r = 0.35$; agreeableness: $r = 0.30$; and neuroticism: $r = 0.40$). In general, the relationships between ML predicted and self-reported personality scores are moderate (ranging from 0.30 to 0.42) across multiple studies, providing initial support for construct validity of ML predicted personality scores.

Extracting personality from language generally requires a relatively large amount of data and high levels of computation power, which may be difficult to obtain for researchers. Arnoux and colleagues (2017) developed a technique that achieved comparable accuracy in predicting personality using fewer tweets from an individual to address this challenge. The authors used Twitter data from 1,300 users to predict personality; their technique had an average correlation of 0.33 with self-report personality traits using 200 tweets per participant (openness: $r = 0.37$; conscientiousness: $r = 0.33$; extraversion: $r = 0.25$; agreeableness: $r = 0.29$; and neuroticism: $r = 0.42$). Their technique also achieved an acceptable correlation ($r > 0.20$) with self-reported personality traits when the authors only used 25 tweets per participant.

4.2.1.2 *Picture*

In addition to language data posted on social media, researchers have demonstrated that pictures posted on social media can also be used to predict personality traits. Celli and colleagues (2014) recruited 112 volunteers to supply their profile pictures and self-reported personality scores as a training dataset. The authors then randomly sampled 100,000 Facebook users from the myPersonality dataset and used their data as a testing dataset. The authors artificially dichotomized each personality trait into high or low (e.g., high or low in conscientiousness) and used classification algorithms to predict the dichotomous outcomes. The prediction algorithm achieved good performance with an accuracy ranging from 60.8% to 75.0% for different personality traits. Similarly, Liu and colleagues (2016) used the profile pictures of Facebook users to predict their personality traits, which were extracted from tweets. The authors applied linear regression with elastic net regularization to predict personality traits from users' profile pictures; their algorithm achieved an average correlation of 0.17. The authors pointed out that the prediction accuracy was worse than the performance of ML algorithms using text data (i.e., language information) on Facebook. However, Liu and colleagues (2016) argued that they only used one picture from each user, whereas the majority of the language-based prediction algorithms used hundreds of posts per user.

4.2.1.3   Activity

User activities on social media, such as the number of status posts or friends, can also indicate their personality traits. When social media activities are used to indicate personalities, researchers either directly correlate the activities with personality scores or use the activities to build ML models to predict personality (the same as the second approach introduced in the language section). For instance, Quercia and colleagues (2011) examined one activity of Facebook accounts, the number of contacts, and its relationship with self-reported personality traits. The authors used 172,000 Facebook users from the myPersonality dataset. The number of Facebook contacts demonstrated a significant positive relationship with extraversion ($r = 0.20$) and a significant negative relationship with neuroticism ($r= -0.07$). It did not show significant relationships with the other three personality traits.

Bachrach and colleagues (2012) used Facebook profiles of 180,000 users in the myPersonality dataset. The authors used multiple properties of Facebook accounts to predict users' personality traits. These properties included the size and density of friendship networks, the amount of uploaded and tagged photos, the number of attended events, the number of likes, and the number of group memberships. The authors analyzed these properties of Facebook accounts using regression. Extraversion was best predicted by the predictors with 33% of the variance explained, whereas agreeableness was the worst with only 1% of the variance explained. Gosling and colleagues (2011) used raters to assess similar

Facebook properties, such as the number of friends, hours spent on Facebook per week, and the number of pictures posted. They also found significant relationships between self-reported personality traits and self-reported/other-rated Facebook activities. The results were not consistent across the five personality traits or across different types of activities. In general, previous studies showed that the Facebook account activities had the strongest relationship with extraversion and did not show significant correlations with the other four traits (also see Kleanthous et al., 2016 and Kosinski et al., 2014).

4.2.1.4   *Multiple Sources of Information*

The sections above summarize the studies that have used one source of information on social media to predict users' personality traits. This section focuses on the studies predicting personality from multiple sources of information on social media platforms. Golbeck and colleagues (2011) predicted personality scores using data from 167 participants. The authors included multiple sources of information on Facebook accounts as predictors, including language, activities, and other account information (e.g., user name, birthday, relationship status). The predicted personality scores showed moderate to high correlations with self-reported personalities (openness: $r = 0.65$; conscientiousness: $r = 0.60$; extraversion: $r = 0.55$; agreeableness: $r = 0.48$; and neuroticism: $r = 0.53$).

In addition to the social media platforms widely used in the United States, Gao and colleagues (2013) used multiple sources of information extracted from a Chinese social media platform, Sina micro-blog, to predict the personality traits of 1,766 users. The predicted personality scores demonstrated moderate relationships with self-reported personalities (openness: $r = 0.38$; conscientiousness: $r = 0.41$; extraversion: $r = 0.40$; agreeableness: $r = 0.31$; and neuroticism: $r = 0.32$). Given that there are not many studies predicting personality using Chinese social media, we cannot directly compare the results of Gao and colleagues (2013) with other studies using the information on Chinese social media.

4.2.1.5   *Summary*

Our literature review showed that the majority of the studies used language and activities on social media to predict their participants' personality traits. In contrast, relatively fewer studies used pictures as the only source of information to predict personalities. In general, when multiple sources of information are used to predict personality, the correlation between predicted personality and self-reported personality outperforms those using a single source of information. In terms of the analytic method used, the studies can be categorized into two large types based on their study designs. The first approach correlates different characteristics/features on social media with self-reported personality scores (e.g., Gosling et al., 2011; Qiu et al., 2012), which is more frequently used when researchers examine the association between social media activities and personality. When this approach is used, the relationships between social media features and personality traits differ across the five personality traits. The second approach uses social media characteristics to build prediction models (e.g., Arnoux et al., 2017; Liu et al., 2016). These prediction models are used to predict personality scores, which are then correlated with self-reported personality scores. Generally, the predictive models demonstrated good performance and had weak to moderate relationships with self-reported personality scores.

4.2.2   Emotions, Mood, and Affect

Emotions, mood, and affect are three relevant but distinct constructs, although these terms are often used interchangeably in day-to-day language. Affect is a superordinate value of emotion and mood, generally considered in two independent dimensions: valence (generally *pleasant* to *unpleasant*) and activation or arousal (low to high) (Ekkekakis, 2012). An example of affect can be as general as "feeling okay" or feeling "really great." Emotions generally refer to a combination of affect, cognitive processes surrounding an event, physiological arousal to a stimulus, and subsequent behavioral reactions (De Choudhury & Counts, 2013). Emotions are directly influenced by one's surroundings and include feelings like excitement or joy.

Moods are derived from emotions and can be considered concepts used to describe these emotions, such as being bored or comforted. Moods are often showcased through the affect circumplex, due to their ability to be grouped by affective dimensions (pleasant vs. unpleasant and low arousal to high arousal). Additionally, moods can often be more specific and nuanced than general affect. For example, *bored* and *tired* are both moods that are considered to be negatively valanced and have low arousal, but constitute very distinct feelings. Thus, they offer subtle differences that researchers might wish to investigate. When deciding which construct to measure through social media data, researchers need to consider whether they are attempting to measure specific states (emotions or moods) or a broad dimension that can be used as a global domain (affect). Despite the construct differences that exist between the terms emotion, affect, and mood, these three topics are generally measured through social media data in similar fashions.

Emotions and moods have often been measured through information extracted from social media that utilizes text posts, such as Twitter and Facebook. Other work has used similar platforms but with fewer users, such as OfficeTalk, a Twitter-like microblogging tool used in corporate work environments (De Choudhury & Counts, 2013). Generally, researchers attempt to measure emotions, mood, or affect through either a categorical or dimensional model. A categorical model assumes that emotions are discrete and can be characterized through features or conditions. A typical example bases responses around Ekman's six basic emotions: anger, disgust, fear, joy, sadness, and surprise (Ekman, 1992). On the other hand, dimensional models utilize valence and arousal to classify emotions and moods to allow for more nuance. To assess these emotions, mood lexicons are established using affective rating sources such as ANEW (Affective Norms for English Words), LIWC (Linguistic Inquiry and Word Count), EARL (Emotion Annotation and Representation Language), or LiveJournal data. Kim and colleagues (2010) compared three classification models based on the categorical models of emotions (latent semantic analysis, probabilistic latent semantic analysis, and non-negative matrix factorization classifications) as well as one dimension-based estimation model based on the dimensional models of emotion. The results indicated that model performance varied across different emotions and different datasets (i.e., SemEval, ISEAR, and fairy tale). In general, the NMF-based categorical classification model performed the best in predicting fear (precision range from 0.53 to 0.70; higher the better) and joy (precision range from 0.39 to 0.80), and the dimension-based estimation model performed the best in predicting sadness (precision range from 0.34 to 0.65).

Researchers have also developed language models to classify emotions in other countries. For instance, Khan and colleagues (2021) applied machine-learning techniques to understand emotions in the Bangla language on Facebook. Their multiple classification models achieved accuracy above 50% (neural network: 50%; support vector machine: 62%). Similarly, Kirelli and Arslankaya (2020) developed language models to predict emotions using Twitter data in the Turkish language. All three predictive models in their study (i.e., naïve Bayesian, nearest neighbor, and support vector machine) achieved acceptable performance (precision: 0.75, 0.74, and 0.65, and support vector machine; F-score is

0.75, 0.74, and 0.65 for naïve Bayesian, nearest neighbor, and support vector machine).

Through similar techniques used to identify moods and emotions, some researchers have attempted to predict the likelihood of mood disorders such as depression. By utilizing sentiment analysis, researchers have attempted to see if they can accurately identify warning signs through social media data. For example, De Choudhury and colleagues (2013) utilized a multifaceted model of emotion, language, and geographical area to analyze Twitter data through a depression index and found that their model correlated with prevalence rates from the Centers for Disease Control and Prevention (r = 0.51). Researchers (e.g., Conway & O'Connor, 2016) have recognized ethical implications for assessing mental health through social media data, including privacy concerns and researcher responsibility concerns stemming from the large scale, population-level nature of the analyzed data.

These popular emotion and mood analysis methods from social media data have limitations. Despite the complexities of emotional expression, the choice of lexicon must be simplified in order to utilize machine learning or big data methods. Valence is usually confined and measured to either "positive" or "negative," although the differentiation between valences of moods can be more subtle. Some data points may involve multiple emotions, which may coexist with emotions or moods labeled to be a different valence or strength; many commonly used methods struggle to differentiate these multiple emotions, but work is being done in an attempt to distinguish them. For instance, Wang and Pal (2015) utilized a constraint optimization framework that was successful in differentiating multiple emotions in 1,800 tweets. This framework outperformed models previously utilized by 42%. Inherent population biases also exist in these datasets. Despite Twitter currently having 396.5 million users, this accounts for only 8.85% of the worldwide social media users having routine access to Twitter (Dean, 2022). Emotions are known to vary based on culture, country, and other geographical and social boundaries; this includes emotional lexicon, facial expression, categories of moods and emotions, and more (Russell, 1991). Because of these limitations, emotion researchers (e.g., De Choudhury & Counts, 2013) have suggested that social media data might be best utilized as a complement to behavioral data.

In summary, emotion, affect, and mood are frequently studied using social media data. Despite varying construct definitions, authors have often used these terms interchangeably and measured them in similar fashions. This decision can have implications for study validity; authors wishing to measure specific states (emotions or moods) versus broad dimensional affect need to keep these differences in mind. Previously, most authors in this sphere have relied on text-based posts from platforms, such as Twitter or Facebook, to assess emotion, affect, or mood, given the existence of established word affect rating sources, such as ANEW, LIWX, and EARL. Past researchers have created categorical or dimensional models that analyze emotion, affect, or mood through these established rating sources. Additionally, examples of these models have been compared for their effectiveness, with varying results depending on targeted emotion, mood, affect, or dataset (Kim et al., 2010). Thus, there is no clear best assessment technique for evaluating emotion, affect, or mood through social media data.

4.2.3 Public/Political Views

Many have investigated a thriving topic of interest through social media data: public opinion relating to political climate or public view toward political events (e.g., elections, policy). Many studies have involved event-centric opinions, such as the introduction of the "Brexit" Withdrawal Agreement, a controversial bill introduced in the United Kingdom to allow the United Kingdom to withdraw from the European Union (Agarwal et al., 2018). Such events have led to the massive influx of postings on social media that entail opinions about these specific events, which draws research attention. For instance, An and colleagues (2014) found evidence for short-term fluctuations in the quantity of climate change tweets during the aftermath of natural disaster events. Similarly, research has shown influxes of tweets about a controversial Italian election whenever news outlets reported "breaking news" surrounding a candidate (Monti et al., 2013).

To quantify support for political positions or people, some researchers have utilized metrics such as counts of fan page likes and quantity of interaction with posts (i.e., Chang et al., 2021). For example, Cameron and colleagues (2016) attempted to use the amount of Facebook friends and Twitter followers that election candidates had to indicate their level of support during national New Zealand elections. They found that these properties by themselves were not satisfactory predictors of election outcomes but that the change in Facebook support for party leaders became more significant over time.

Many researchers chose instead to utilize machine-learning methods, such as sentiment analysis, to understand public opinion through tweets (e.g., Agarwal et al., 2018; An et al., 2014; Monti et al., 2013). These machine-learning methods have allowed researchers to understand how the public feels toward certain events/political figures and feelings toward the general political climate. For instance, Min and colleagues (2021) used machine-learning techniques to extract the public's emotional reactions to "stay-at-home" and "shelter-in-place" orders during the COVID-19 pandemic using Twitter data. The authors found an increase in Twitter users' positive emotion and a decrease in negative emotion immediately after these orders were effective, indicating that Twitter users reacted positively to these orders. However, Ceron and colleagues (2014) found the issue that many popular sentiment analyses did not have the ability to understand irony or jargon in public opinion about an upcoming election. In their dataset, they noticed many instances of ironic jokes at the expense of a candidate that would have been construed as support by the algorithm. Hopkins and King (2010) attempted to resolve this by utilizing an analysis method that used more human coders when creating the training set and suggested that researchers needed to keep the tone of tweets in mind when deciding on analytic methods. Additionally, Makazhanov and colleagues (2014) found that text or sentiment analyses might require many edits to be election specific due to different topics and emotions surrounding political events. This step may add complexity to a researcher's machine-learning analysis.

In addition to utilizing social media data alone, many researchers have compared social media data to other, more traditional methods in order to validate the use of social media data. The method of collecting public opinion through polling and surveys is conventional and widely upheld (Kosicki, 2020), but there is evidence that social media analyses may be just as effective. Ceron and colleagues (2014) compared their results of the popularity of political figures from social media posts to the results from traditional surveys and found consistent correlations. Specifically, the most visible and forefront Italian leaders showed a very high popularity correlation ($r = 0.93$), whereas the correlation for lesser-known public figures was still relatively strong ($r = 0.75$). Another study used the quantity of engagement on Facebook posts of US political public figures to predict support rates for the 2016 presidential election and found that a forecasting model from the authors' data accurately predicted election results in both the electoral college and popular vote (Chang et al., 2021). The authors argued that although official polling vote shares tracked actual votes more closely than their model, these polls overestimated the support for the losing candidate in many states. In a study done by Monti and colleagues (2013), Italian political dissatisfaction with tweet sentiments had high correlations with public opinion surveys (r = 0.79). Conversely, Cameron and colleagues (2016) found significant but small effect sizes for online "support" predicting elections when compared to polling and finalized results.

In summary, public opinion on political and global events continues to draw attention from researchers that utilize social media data. These events, both local and global, have been shown to draw huge amounts of postings on social media, leading to the potential for a large dataset (An et al., 2014; Monti et al., 2013). Researchers have used a variety of metrics in order to quantify public opinions and viewpoints, such as the number of likes, friends or followers (Cameron et al., 2016), amount of interactions (Chang et al., 2021), or support estimated by machine-learning techniques. There is conflicting evidence of the effectiveness of simpler count metrics in predicting political event outcomes, but machine-learning techniques applied to social media data are shown to be equally effective as traditional polling approaches (Ceron et al., 2014).

4.2.4 *Life Satisfaction*

Life satisfaction is regarded as individuals' evaluations of their own lives. In general, the studies that have assessed life satisfaction with social media showed inconsistent correlations with the life satisfaction measured using self-report surveys. For example, Seder and Oishi (2012) found that smile intensity in first-year college students' Facebook profile photos coded by trained raters was positively correlated with students' self-reported life satisfaction in the same year (r = 0.34 and 0.38 for Study 1 and 2, respectively) and 3.5 years later (r = 0.47 and 0.57 for Study 1 and 2 respectively). Kosinski and colleagues (2013) used Facebook likes to predict life satisfaction and only found a weak relationship (r = 0.17). Collins and colleagues (2015) used the information on social media and categorized it into three types – static ego features, temporal ego features, and link features. Static ego features were the stable characteristics of a user, such as the number of friends on social media, the number of tagged photos, or the topics a user likes extracted by latent Dirichlet allocation. Temporal ego features referred to the user characters that fluctuate over time, which was operationalized as the mood swings reflected in a user's Facebook status updates. Link features were the connections between a user and other people on social media, such as the happiness (i.e., score on self-reported satisfaction with life scale) of one's friends and significant other. The researchers found that static ego features and link features demonstrated moderate to high correlations with life satisfaction and improved prediction accuracy in machine-learning predictive models. In contrast, the temporal ego features (i.e., mood swings) did not. Both Kosinski et al. (2013) and Collins et al. (2015) used volunteers recruited through the myPersonality Facebook application.

In summary, these previous studies predicted life satisfaction from different sources of information (e.g., picture, Seder & Oishi, 2012; activities, Kosinski et al., 2013; multiple sources of information, Collins et al., 2015), and found weak to moderate correlations between life satisfaction and the information on social media.

4.3   Global Aspects of Social Media Assessments

A majority of the social media platforms are accessible to people from different countries. At the same time, the demographic composition of the users of these social media platforms changes over time. This can potentially limit the generalizability of findings based on social media assessments. This section discusses a few things that researchers need to consider when assessing constructs with social media platforms.

4.3.1   Population Distribution over Time on Social Media

The distribution of different groups on social media platforms changes over time. Different groups include people of varying sex, ages, levels of education, income, or from different countries. For instance, in 2010, 52% of Twitter users were females. The majority of Twitter users (30%) in 2010 were between 26 and 34 years old (13–17: 4%, 18–25: 13%, 35–44: 27%, 45–54: 17%, older than 55: 9%) (Krum, 2010) . A report published in 2022 indicated that the proportion of male users on Twitter in 2021 has substantially increased (70.4%) compared to 2010. The age distribution of Twitter user also changed over time (13–17: 9.1%, 18–24: 21.6%, 25–34: 28.9%, 35–49: 28.2%, older than 55: 12.3%) (Iqbal, 2022).

Researchers, thus, need to be cautious when generating findings in previous studies to current situations. For example, Mittal and Goel (2012) analyzed the public's daily sentiments on Twitter and used the daily sentiments to predict stock market movements. Their results indicated that the calm and happy moods positively correlated with the closing values of the Dow Jones Industrial Index. If Mittal and Goel's (2012) study were replicated today, it is reasonable to suspect that their findings may change because Twitter users under 35 years old have increased from 47% in 2010 to 59.6% in 2021 (Norman, 2018; Vitalis, 2019), and people younger than 35 years old are less likely to invest in stocks.

4.3.2 Sample Selection and Filtering

Many social media platforms allow researchers to filter out posts or entire users when creating a dataset. For instance, researchers can filter out tweets not in English or posted by people outside the USA using Twitter API. Researchers need to decide the most appropriate data collection approach for one study based on the specific research questions. For instance, researchers have used information on social media to extract the public's opinion on certain events or political views (e.g., Min et al., 2021; Monti et al., 2013). It may be worthwhile to identify users' geographic information, especially when predicting outcomes that are only important for users at certain locations, such as election results or public attitudes toward specific policies.

Time may be another factor for researchers to consider when using social media information to predict election results. For instance, how do social media users' sentiments toward a specific candidate change over time? Does this trend differ by region/states? Thus, we recommended that researchers thoroughly consider the criteria they adopt to filter out data on social media and be transparent about their criteria when reporting results.

4.3.3 Culture Differences

When discussing cultural differences on social media, we refer to the general differences in behavior, attitude, or cognition patterns for users from different cultures. For instance, people in some cultures may openly express their negative statements, whereas those in other cultures may prefer indirect ways of expressing a negative opinion (Mandl, 2009). This may impact machine-learning models' performance or generalizability to extract emotions from language. Additionally, in cultures where women have lower status and roles, women are more likely to express less intense and less powerful emotions (e.g., anger and contempt) and express more powerless emotions (e.g., fear, sadness, shame, and guilt) (Fischer et al., 2004). This may impact the performance of machine-learning models across gender groups in different cultures.

Researchers compared social media platforms in different cultures to examine whether users on these social media platforms demonstrate different patterns (Chen & Tsoi, 2011; Gao et al., 2012; Mandl, 2009). For instance, Li and colleagues (2020) predicted politeness using English Twitter and Mandarin Weibo and found both similarities and differences in politeness expressions across the two social media platforms. Specifically, the predictors that were more highly correlated with *impoliteness* on Weibo than on Twitter included the use of all pronouns (e.g., "you"), death-related taboo, and informal language. Those more highly correlated with *politeness* on Weibo than on Twitter included future-focusing conversations, identifying with a group affiliation, and gratitude.

In another study, Gao and colleagues (2012) also compared users on two microblog platforms in Chinese and English, Sina Weibo and Twitter, and found differences in multiple dimensions. In terms of syntactic content, Sina Weibo users were less likely to use hashtags and URLs when posting microblogs compared to Twitter users. This indicates that analyzing hashtags (e.g., topic modeling for hashtags) (Romero et al., 2011) may not be appropriate on Sina. Additionally, Twitter users were twice as likely to use question marks in their posts compared to Sina Weibo users. Users on these two platforms also differed in the semantic contents of their posts. In general, users on both Sina Weibo and Twitter posted more positive posts than negative ones. For the sentiments exhibited in posts, users on Sina Weibo were 11.8% more likely to be positive than Twitter users. Moreover, the inclusion of entities (such as locations or persons) was positively correlated with sentiment for Sina Weibo users, whereas it negatively correlated with sentiment for Twitter users. Lastly, for temporal behavior, user posting behaviors also differed in these two cultures. Sina Weibo users were more active on the weekends, whereas Twitter users were more active on the weekdays.

Mandl (2009) compared two blog websites in China and Germany and found that users from these two cultures showed different patterns in their blogs as well. For instance, Chinese blogs contained more graphs than German blogs, and Chinese comments on blogs tended to be shorter than German comments. However, it is unclear whether this is a culture difference or a language difference, which is discussed in detail in the next section.

4.3.4   *Language*

When people post on social media using different languages, they may likely be from different cultures. This section focuses on the language differences caused by language lexicons, grammar rules, or word limits required by specific social media platforms (e.g., Twitter limit each tweet to be fewer than 280 characters). For instance, Gao and colleagues (2012) pointed out that the expressivity of the Chinese language might manifest as the frequent use of entities on Sina Weibo, whereas Twitter users who speak English were forced to leave out entities or use abbreviations in their microblogs. We do acknowledge that in practice, it is challenging to disentangle language differences from cultural differences.

Although many social media platforms (e.g., Twitter, Facebook) are used globally, the majority of the studies summarized in this chapter are conducted with English-speaking participants. For certain topics, such as personality, the majority of the participants were in the USA because the myPersonality dataset was used. Only a few studies have used social media information from non-English-speaking participants. For those studies, a general trend is that when researchers use language models to analyze information from social media, they develop their own predictive models/algorithms rather than using a preexisting model or algorithm. This is not surprising because different languages follow different rules and use different lexicons when expressing a single content.

Gao and colleagues (2012) used information on a Chinese microblog platform, Sina, to assess personality. Compared to other studies conducted using the information on Facebook (ranging from 0.48 to 0.65; Golbeck et al., 2011), the personality scores predicted by their predictive algorithm showed slightly weaker relationships with self-report personality (ranging from 0.31 to 0.41). There are, however, many factors that may have contributed to the relatively weaker relationship. For instance, Sina is a microblogging platform that is similar to Twitter. This type of social media platforms limits the number of words each user can put in their posts, which may have contributed to the weaker relationships (Twitter Development, n.d.). Also, similar to Twitter, the majority of the users on Sina are anonymous and do not reveal their real identity, which is different from those on Facebook. The anonymous nature of the social media platform may change what contents people post and the way they express those contents. The third explanation is that these two groups of participants use different languages and are from two completely different cultures. It is possible that some of the cultural norms make it more difficult for predictive models to predict personality from social media, which is discussed in our culture section. Given the limited number of studies conducted in Chinese social media, it is difficult for researchers to explore the potential explanation for the different strength of relationships. This is a potential research area for future researchers.

4.4 Future Directions and Ethical Considerations

With the abundance of information on social media platforms, these platforms provide great potential for assessing and studying constructs researchers are interested in. They also provide an alternative approach to assessment, which complements our traditional self- or other-report survey approach. In this section, we highlight a few potential future directions of using social media for assessment.

Social media users from different cultures may exhibit different behavior patterns, such as how they interact with friends on social media or how they express their opinions on social media. Future researchers can examine how cultural differences impact the validity and reliability of studies when they assess constructs using social media. Our culture section summarizes a few studies that have compared social media users from different cultures. There are, however, many other topics that have not been examined. For instance, researchers have used profile pictures on social media to predict personality (e.g., Celli et al., 2014; Liu et al., 2016). At the same time, social media users from different regions were found to have different preferences in choosing profile pictures (Zheng et al., 2016). Future researchers can investigate whether these cultural differences in choosing social media pictures influence the accuracy of predictive models when extracting personality traits from these social media pictures.

Additionally, future studies can be developed to disentangle language differences from cultural differences, which we acknowledge is challenging in practice. One approach that future researchers can take is to examine the behavior patterns of international users who speak English on social media (e.g., international students). For instance, Gao and colleagues (2012) found that social media users in the USA were more likely to use question marks compared to Chinese users. Suppose a study demonstrates that Chinese international students use question marks as frequently as US users on social media (e.g., Twitter or Facebook). In that case, this may indicate that the frequent use of question marks is likely to be attributed to a language difference rather than a cultural difference.

Another direction of future study is that researchers draw on construct definitions from the social sciences and combine those definitions with computation models when assessing constructs using social media platforms. Specifically, the social science literature (e.g., Batson et al., 1992) has distinguished mood, emotion, and affect. Our literature search, however, indicates that almost all researchers using social media data to analyze sentiment do not necessarily distinguish these three constructs when developing predictive models. According to the definition of these constructs, it is possible that a predictive model using a dataset over a long period of time achieves better performance in predicting mood whereas one using a dataset over a short period of time achieves better performance in predicting affect. Additionally, personality psychologists have developed multiple personality models, such as the big five model (Roccas et al., 2002) and HEXACO (Ashton & Lee, 2007). Our literature search indicates that only the big five personality model is typically assessed using social media data. Thus, one direction for future research is to assess other personality models using social media data. Future researchers, especially psychologists, can introduce definitions and theoretical models of the focal constructs when assessing those constructs with social media data, which facilitates study design and data collection.

4.4.1 Ethical Considerations

Researchers need to be aware of the potential caveats and ethical issues associated with assessment using social media data. Social media users may post content on their website without considering that their posts are accessible by a third party for research purposes (e.g., researchers). Some of the contents on social media may be distorted when they are taken out of a particular context (Golder et al., 2017). Also, other people can trace back to the individual who posted a specific context using the verbatim quote (e.g., tweets). Thus, researchers may risk participants' privacy when they share verbatim quotes in their work. We strongly recommend researchers deidentify social media posts to minimize potential negative consequences and reduce the risks to participants when sharing their study findings (Smith et al., 2012). The risk may be higher and more severe when researchers are using social media data to study sensitive constructs, such as subjective well-being, mental health, or burnout (Conway & O'Connor, 2016; McKee, 2013).

Unlike collecting data from self-report surveys, researchers frequently do not obtain informed consent from their participants when collecting data from social media. There is an ongoing debate about whether consent forms should be required to obtain social media data (e.g., Williams, 2015). Some researchers think that informed consent from the participants is not necessary because of the public nature and the anonymous nature (e.g., YouTube) of certain social media platforms (e.g., Bond et al., 2013; Mikal et al., 2016). Other researchers and users disagree and argue that informed consent should be required due to data ownership and the difficulty of deidentifying data (e.g., Chen et al., 2004; Michaelidou et al., 2016). Researchers are recommended to follow ethical guidelines (Moreno et al., 2013; Salmons & Woodfield, 2013; Townsend & Wallace, 2016) when using social media data for assessment.

4.5 Summary

In summary, social media has great promise for assessment and research purposes. Psychologists can have unique contributions to this process, given their background knowledge in the definitions and theoretical frameworks of human affect, cognition, and behavior. Researchers, however, need to develop and follow ethical guidelines to protect participants, given the novelty of assessment with social media platforms.

REFERENCES

Agarwal, A., Singh, R., & Toshniwal, D. (2018). Geospatial sentiment analysis using Twitter data for UK-EU referendum. *Journal of Information and Optimization Sciences*, *39*(1), 303–317. https://doi.org/10.1080/02522667.2017.1374735

Alpaydin, E. (2020). *Introduction to machine learning*. MIT Press.

An, X., Ganguly, A., Fang, Y., Scyphers, S. B., Hunter, A. M., & Dy, J. G. (2014). *Tracking climate change opinions from Twitter data* (Workshop on Data Science for Social Good, pp. 1–6).

Arnoux, P.-H., Xu, A., Boyette, N., Mahmud, J., Akkiraju, R., & Sinha, V. (2017). 25 tweets to know you: A new model to predict personality with social media. *Proceedings of the International AAAI Conference on Web and Social Media*, *11*, 472–475.

Ashton, M. C., & Lee, K. (2007). Empirical, theoretical, and practical advantages of the HEXACO model of personality structure. *Personality and Social Psychology Review*, *11*(2), 150–166. https://doi.org/10.1177/1088868306294907

Bachrach, Y., Kosinski, M., Graepel, T., Kohli, P., & Stillwell, D. (2012). Personality and patterns of Facebook usage. *Proceedings of the 4th Annual ACM Web Science Conference*, 24–32.

Batson, C. D., Shaw, L. L., & Oleson, K. C. (1992). Differentiating affect, mood, and emotion: Toward functionally based conceptual distinctions. In M. S. Clark (Ed.), *Emotion* (pp. 294–326). Sage Publications, Inc.

Bond, C. S., Ahmed, O. H., Hind, M., Thomas, B., & Hewitt-Taylor, J. (2013). The conceptual and practical ethical dilemmas of using health discussion board posts as research data. *Journal of Medical Internet Research*, *15*(6), e112. https://doi.org/10.2196/jmir.2435

Cameron, M. P., Barrett, P., & Stewardson, B. (2016). Can social media predict election results? Evidence from New Zealand. *Journal of Political Marketing, 15*(4), 416–432. https://doi.org/10.1080/15377857.2014.959690

Carr, C. T., & Hayes, R. A. (2015). Social media: Defining, developing, and divining. *Atlantic Journal of Communication, 23*(1), 46–65. https://doi.org/10.1080/15456870.2015.972282

Celli, F., Bruni, E., & Lepri, B. (2014). Automatic personality and interaction style recognition from Facebook profile pictures. *Proceedings of the 22nd ACM International Conference on Multimedia,* 1101–1104. https://doi.org/10.1145/2647868.2654977

Ceron, A., Curini, L., Iacus, S. M., & Porro, G. (2014). Every tweet counts? How sentiment analysis of social media can improve our knowledge of citizens' political preferences with an application to Italy and France. *New Media & Society, 16*(2), 340–358. https://doi.org/10.1177/1461444813480466

Chang, K.-C., Chiang, C.-F., & Lin, M.-J. (2021). Using Facebook data to predict the 2016 U.S. presidential election. *PLoS ONE, 16*(12), e0253560. https://doi.org/10.1371/journal.pone.0253560

Chen, L., & Tsoi, H. K. (2011). Privacy concern and trust in using social network sites: A comparison between French and Chinese users. In P. Campos, N. Graham, J. Jorge, N. Nunes, P. Palanque, & M. Winckler (Eds.), *Human-computer interaction – INTERACT 2011* (Vol. 6948, pp. 234–241). Springer. https://doi.org/10.1007/978-3-642-23765-2_16

Chen, S. L., Hall, G. J., & Johns, M. D. (2004). Research paparazzi in cyberspace: The voices of the researched. In M. D. Johns, S. L. Chen, & G. J. Hall (Eds.), *Online social research: Methods, issues, and ethics* (pp. 157–175). Peter Lang.

Collins, S., Sun, Y., Kosinski, M., Stillwell, D., & Markuzon, N. (2015). Are you satisfied with life?: Predicting satisfaction with life from Facebook. In N. Agarwal, K. Xu, & N. Osgood (Eds.), *Social computing, behavioral-cultural modeling, and prediction* (Vol. 9021, pp. 24–33). Springer International Publishing. https://doi.org/10.1007/978-3-319-16268-3_3

Conway, M., & O'Connor, D. (2016). Social media, big data, and mental health: Current advances and ethical implications. *Current Opinion in Psychology, 9,* 77–82. https://doi.org/10.1016/j.copsyc.2016.01.004

De Choudhury, M., & Counts, S. (2013). Understanding affect in the workplace via social media. *Proceedings of the 2013 Conference on Computer Supported Cooperative Work – CSCW'13,* 303. https://doi.org/10.1145/2441776.2441812

De Choudhury, M., Counts, S., & Horvitz, E. (2013). Social media as a measurement tool of depression in populations. *Proceedings of the 5th Annual ACM Web Science Conference – WebSci'13,* 47–56. https://doi.org/10.1145/2464464.2464480

Dean, B. (2022, January 5). *How many people use Twitter in 2022?* BacklinkO. https://backlinko.com/twitter-users

Ekkekakis, P. (2012). Affect, mood, and emotion. In G. Tenenbaum, R. C. Eklund, & A. Kamata (Eds.), *Measurement in sport and exercise psychology* (pp. 321–332). Human Kinetics. https://doi.org/10.5040/9781492596332.ch-028

Ekman, P. (1992). An argument for basic emotions. *Cognition and Emotion, 6*(3–4), 169–200. https://doi.org/10.1080/02699939208411068

Fischer, A. H., Rodriguez Mosquera, P. M., van Vianen, A. E. M., & Manstead, A. S. R. (2004). Gender and culture differences in emotion. *Emotion, 4*(1), 87–94. https://doi.org/10.1037/1528-3542.4.1.87

Gao, Q., Abel, F., Houben, G.-J., & Yu, Y. (2012). A comparative study of users' microblogging behavior on Sina Weibo and Twitter. In J. Masthoff, B. Mobasher, M. C. Desmarais, & R. Nkambou (Eds.), *User modeling, adaptation, and personalization* (Vol. 7379, pp. 88–101). Springer. https://doi.org/10.1007/978-3-642-31454-4_8

Gao, R., Hao, B., Bai, S., Li, L., Li, A., & Zhu, T. (2013). Improving user profile with personality traits predicted from social media content. *Proceedings of the 7th ACM Conference on Recommender Systems*, 355–358. https://doi.org/10.1145/2507157.2507219

Golbeck, J., Robles, C., Edmondson, M., & Turner, K. (2011). Predicting personality from Twitter. *2011 IEEE Third Int'l Conference on Privacy, Security, Risk and Trust and 2011 IEEE Third Int'l Conference on Social Computing*, 149–156. https://doi.org/10.1109/PASSAT/SocialCom.2011.33

Golder, S., Ahmed, S., Norman, G., & Booth, A. (2017). Attitudes toward the ethics of research using social media: A systematic review. *Journal of Medical Internet Research, 19*(6), e195. https://doi.org/10.2196/jmir.7082

Gosling, S. D., Augustine, A. A., Vazire, S., Holtzman, N., & Gaddis, S. (2011). Manifestations of personality in online social networks: Self-reported Facebook-related behaviors and observable profile information. *Cyberpsychology, Behavior, and Social Networking, 14*(9), 483–488. https://doi.org/10.1089/cyber.2010.0087

Guo, F., Gallagher, C. M., Sun, T., Tavoosi, S., & Min, H. (2021). Smarter people analytics with organizational text data: Demonstrations using classic and advanced NLP models. *Human Resource Management Journal*, 1–16. https://doi.org/10.1111/1748-8583.12426

Hickman, L., Thapa, S., Tay, L., Cao, M., & Srinivasan, P. (2022). Text preprocessing for text mining in organizational research: Review and recommendations. *Organizational Research Methods, 25*(1), 114–146. https://doi.org/10.1177/1094428120971683

Hopkins, D. J., & King, G. (2010). A method of automated nonparametric content analysis for social science. *American Journal of Political Science, 54*(1), 229–247. https://doi.org/10.1111/j.1540-5907.2009.00428.x

Howard, P. N., & Parks, M. R. (2012). Social media and political change: Capacity, constraint, and consequence. *Journal of Communication, 62*(2), 359–362.

Iqbal, M. (2022, January 11). *Twitter revenue and usage statistics (2022).* Business of Apps. https://www.businessofapps.com/data/twitter-statistics/

Kent, M. L. (2010). Directions in social media for professionals and scholars. In R. L. Heath (Ed.), *The SAGE handbook of public relations* (pp. 643–656). SAGE.

Khan, Md. S. S., Rafa, S. R., Abir, A. E. H., & Das, A. K. (2021). Sentiment analysis on Bengali Facebook comments to predict fan's emotions towards a celebrity. *Journal of Engineering Advancements, 2*(3), 118–124. https://doi.org/10.38032/jea.2021.03.001

Kim, S. M., Valitutti, A., & Calvo, R. A. (2010). Evaluation of unsupervised emotion models to textual affect recognition. *Proceedings of the NAACL HLT 2010 Workshop on Computational Approaches to Analysis and Generation of Emotion in Text, 62*–70.

Kirelli, Y., & Arslankaya, S. (2020). Sentiment analysis of shared tweets on global warming on Twitter with data mining methods: A case study on Turkish language. *Computational Intelligence and Neuroscience, 2020,* 1–9. https://doi.org/10.1155/2020/1904172

Kleanthous, S., Herodotou, C., Samaras, G., & Germanakos, P. (2016). Detecting personality traces in users' social activity. In G. Meiselwitz (Ed.), *Social computing and social media* (pp. 287–297). Springer International Publishing.

Kosicki, G. (2020). Survey methods, traditional, and public opinion polling. In J. V. d. Bulck (Ed.), *The international encyclopedia of media psychology* (pp. 1–5). John Wiley & Sons, Inc. https://doi.org/10.1002/9781119011107.iemp.0045

Kosinski, M., Bachrach, Y., Kohli, P., Stillwell, D., & Graepel, T. (2014). Manifestations of user personality in website choice and behaviour on online social networks. *Machine Learning, 95*(3), 357–380. https://doi.org/10.1007/s10994-013-5415-y

Kosinski, M., Matz, S. C., Gosling, S. D., Popov, V., & Stillwell, D. (2015). Facebook as a research tool for the social sciences: Opportunities, challenges, ethical considerations, and practical guidelines. *American Psychologist, 70*(6), 543–556. https://doi.org/10.1037/a0039210

Kosinski, M., Stillwell, D., & Graepel, T. (2013). Private traits and attributes are predictable from digital records of human behavior. *Proceedings of the National Academy of Sciences, 110*(15), 5802–5805. https://doi.org/10.1073/pnas.1218772110

Krum, R. (2010). 2010 Facebook vs. Twitter social demographics. Cool Infographics. https://coolinfographics.com/blog/2011/2/10/2010-facebook-vs-twitter-social-demographics.html

Li, M., Hickman, L., Tay, L., Ungar, L., & Guntuku, S. C. (2020). Studying politeness across cultures using English Twitter and Mandarin Weibo. *Proceedings of the ACM on Human-Computer Interaction, 4*(CSCW2), 1–15. https://doi.org/10.48550/arXiv.2008.02449

Liu, L., Preotiuc-Pietro, D., Samani, Z. R., Moghaddam, M. E., & Ungar, L. (2016, March). Analyzing personality through social media profile picture choice. *Tenth International AAAI Conference on Web and Social Media.*

Makazhanov, A., Rafiei, D., & Waqar, M. (2014). Predicting political preference of Twitter users. *Social Network Analysis and Mining, 4*(1), 193. https://doi.org/10.1007/s13278-014-0193-5

Mandl, T. (2009). Comparing Chinese and German blogs. *Proceedings of the 20th ACM Conference on Hypertext and Hypermedia – HT'09,* 299. https://doi.org/10.1145/1557914.1557964

McKee, R. (2013). Ethical issues in using social media for health and health care research. *Health Policy, 110*(2), 298–301. https://doi.org/10.1016/j.healthpol.2013.02.006

Michaelidou, N., Moraes, C., & Micevski, M. (2016). A scale for measuring consumers? Ethical perceptions of social media research. In O. Petit, D. Merunka, & O. Oullier (Eds.), *Let's get engaged! Crossing the threshold of marketing's engagement era* (pp. 97–100). Springer.

Mikal, J., Hurst, S., & Conway, M. (2016). Ethical issues in using Twitter for population-level depression monitoring: A qualitative study. *BMC Medical Ethics, 17*(1), Article 22. https://doi.org/10.1186/s12910-016-0105-5

Min, H., Peng, Y., Shoss, M., & Yang, B. (2021). Using machine learning to investigate the public's emotional responses to work from home during the COVID-19 pandemic. *Journal of Applied Psychology, 106*(2), 214–229. https://doi.org/10.1037/apl0000886

Mittal, A., & Goel, A. (2012). *Stock prediction using Twitter sentiment analysis.* Stanford University.

Monti, C., Zignani, M., Rozza, A., Arvidsson, A., Zappella, G., & Colleoni, E. (2013). Modelling political disaffection from Twitter data. *Proceedings of the Second International Workshop on Issues of Sentiment Discovery and Opinion Mining – WISDOM'13,* 1–9. https://doi.org/10.1145/2502069.2502072

Moreno, M. A., Goniu, N., Moreno, P. S., & Diekema, D. (2013). Ethics of social media research: Common concerns and practical considerations. *Cyberpsychology, Behavior, and Social Networking, 16*(9), 708–713. https://doi.org/10.1089/cyber.2012.0334

Norman, J. (2018, May 4). Young Americans still wary of investing in stocks. Gallup. https://news.gallup.com/poll/233699/young-americans-wary-investing-stocks.aspx

Park, G., Schwartz, H. A., Eichstaedt, J. C., Kern, M. L., Kosinski, M., Stillwell, D. J., Ungar, L. H., & Seligman, M. E. P. (2015). Automatic personality assessment through social media language. *Journal of Personality and Social Psychology, 108*(6), 934–952. https://doi.org/10.1037/pspp0000020

Pervin, L. A., Cervone, D., & John, O. P. (2005). Theories of personality. In L. A. Pervin, D. Cervone, & O. P. John (Ed.), *Personality: Theory and research* (pp. 365–386). Wiley.

Putka, D. J., Beatty, A. S., & Reeder, M. C. (2018). Modern prediction methods: New perspectives on a common problem. *Organizational Research Methods*, *21*(3), 689–732.

Qiu, L., Lin, H., Ramsay, J., & Yang, F. (2012). You are what you tweet: Personality expression and perception on Twitter. *Journal of Research in Personality*, *46*(6), 710–718. https://doi.org/10.1016/j.jrp.2012.08.008

Quercia, D., Kosinski, M., Stillwell, D. J., & Crowcroft, J. (2011). Our Twitter profiles, our selves: Predicting personality with twitter. *2011 IEEE Third International Conference on Social Computing*, 180–185.

Rhee, L., Bayer, J. B., Lee, D. S., & Kuru, O. (2021). Social by definition: How users define social platforms and why it matters. *Telematics and Informatics*, *59*, 101538. https://doi.org/10.1016/j.tele.2020.101538

Roccas, S., Sagiv, L., Schwartz, S. H., & Knafo, A. (2002). The big five personality factors and personal values. *Personality and Social Psychology Bulletin*, *28*(6), 789–801. https://doi.org/10.1177/0146167202289008

Romero, D. M., Meeder, B., & Kleinberg, J. (2011). Differences in the mechanics of information diffusion across topics: Idioms, political hashtags, and complex contagion on twitter. *Proceedings of the 20th International Conference on World Wide Web*, 695–704.

Russell, J. A. (1991). Culture and the categorization of emotions. *Psychological Bulletin*, *110*(3), 426–450.

Salmons, J., & Woodfield, K. (2013). Social media, social science & research ethics. *Social Media in Social Research Conference: Ethics of Social Media Research*, 1–24.

Schwartz, H. A., Eichstaedt, J. C., Kern, M. L., Dziurzynski, L., Ramones, S. M., Agrawal, M., ... & Ungar, L. H. (2013). Personality, gender, and age in the language of social media: The open-vocabulary approach. *PLoS ONE*, *8*(9), e73791. https://doi.org/10.1371/journal.pone.0073791

Seder, J. P., & Oishi, S. (2012). Intensity of smiling in Facebook photos predicts future life satisfaction. *Social Psychological and Personality Science*, *3*(4), 407–413. https://doi.org/10.1177/1948550611424968

Smith, M., Szongott, C., Henne, B., & von Voigt, G. (2012). Big data privacy issues in public social media. *2012 6th IEEE International Conference on Digital Ecosystems and Technologies (DEST)*, 1–6. https://doi.org/10.1109/DEST.2012.6227909

Thilakaratne, M., Weerasinghe, R., & Perera, S. (2016, October). Knowledge-driven approach to predict personality traits by leveraging social media data. In *2016 IEEE/WIC/ACM International Conference on Web Intelligence (WI)* (pp. 288–295). IEEE.

Townsend, L., & Wallace, C. (2016). *Social media research: A guide to ethics.* University of Aberdeen.

Twitter Development. (n.d.). *Counting characters when composing tweets.* Twitter Developer Platform. https://developer.twitter.com/en/docs/counting-characters

Vitalis, I. (2019, October 25). US demographics and the stock market. Tradimo News. https://news.tradimo.com/us-demographics-and-the-stock-market/

Wang, Y., & Pal, A. (2015, June). Detecting emotions in social media: A constrained optimization approach. *Twenty-Fourth International Joint Conference on Artificial Intelligence.*

Williams, M. (2015). Towards an ethical framework for using social media data in social research. Social Data Lab. http://socialdatalab.net/wp-content/uploads/2016/08/EthicsSM-SRA-Workshop.pdf

Zheng, W., Yuan, C.-H., Chang, W.-H., & Wu, Y.-C. J. (2016). Profile pictures on social media: Gender and regional differences. *Computers in Human Behavior, 63,* 891–898. https://doi.org/10.1016/j.chb.2016.06.041

CHAPTER 5

Game-Based Assessment around the Globe
International Differences in Privacy, Legality, and Applicant Reaction Concerns

Richard N. Landers, Vivien Lee, and Chulin Chen

The use of new technology as a means of facilitating psychometric measurement has increased dramatically over the past decades – a trend likely to continue (Tippins, 2015). The expanding array of new capabilities brought by new technologies promises myriad new affordances to job applicants and organizations alike, even as many of these promises go ultimately unfulfilled (e.g., Cubrich et al., 2021). One area of greater promise has been that of game-based assessment (GBA), for which empirical evidence has supported well-designed, thoroughly developed GBAs as a valid approach to the measurement of at least some psychometric constructs (Landers et al., 2021).

Despite this promising initial evidence, GBAs are one of the most complex employee selection methods available. The interaction between this complexity and the nation or culture where such assessments are used is unknown. Given long-standing and sometimes dramatic differences in the legal context for selection between nations (Myors et al., 2008), as well as emerging international differences related to expectations for privacy (Shen et al., 2017), this topic, therefore, emerged for the present authors as a key area of concern in relation to decision-making for both assessment vendors and developers who administer their GBAs internationally as well as for the international organizations considering adopting such tests across national borders and cultural contexts. In short, it is unclear how differences in the cultural and national environments in which GBAs are to be deployed should affect how they are developed.

To address this gap, we first provide a brief overview of games and GBAs in employee selection. Next, we present a descriptive, qualitative study examining the perspectives of both GBA vendors and organizational stakeholders on three key research questions related to 1) privacy, 2) legality, and 3) applicant reactions. Finally, we explore the implications of our findings for both vendors and organizational stakeholders more broadly.

5.1   Games and GBA in Selection

Despite growing interest and research in digital games, it remains challenging to define them clearly. The study of games occurs across many research areas, including assessment, computer science, human–computer interaction (HCI), and education (Jones, 2008). However, depending on the specific context in which games are played and discussed, the term *games* is defined differently. For example, in educational contexts, academic discussion differentiates games in general from *serious games*, which refers to games that are intentionally designed to be more than just entertainment, such as for familiarizing students with course material (Michael & Chen, 2005). In the GBA context, games have been defined as "externally structured, goal-directed type[s] of play" (Caillois, 2011; Landers et al., 2019), referring to games in which players engage in a constructed game environment, with a clear beginning and end to the player experience, with goals and rules explicitly defined and implemented by game developers that direct and control player behavior.

Most approaches to designing such games draw heavily upon interdisciplinary research and literature in areas like HCI. One of the most fundamental approaches to game design from HCI is the Mechanics-Dynamics-Aesthetics (MDA) framework (Hunicke et al., 2004). In MDA, *mechanics* refer to the program systems of a game (e.g., leaderboards, bonuses, time limit), generally conceptualized at the level of data representation and algorithm design. *Dynamics* are defined as real-time interactions between users and game mechanics over time or between mechanics over time. *Aesthetics* describe users' affective responses resulting from their exposure to and participation in dynamics. GBA designers tailor mechanics to produce ideal in-assessment dynamics, which are intended to induce positive reactions from job applicants (i.e., aesthetics) by planning for causal links between the three components.

A complementary concept of game design is *design thinking*, a human-centered method originating in the 1950s and 1960s that was later popularized by the Stanford Design School (Bjogvinsson et al., 2012). Within a design thinking approach, GBA development occurs over five overall stages (Landers et al., 2021). First, designers start by *empathizing* – gathering insights on the problem the solution wishes to solve. In GBA development, this means specifying the construct of interest and creating a shared mental model among assessment researchers, game designers, and software developers. Second, designers *define* the problem by identifying potential difficulties given user needs and external constraints; in the context of GBA, this includes concerns such as accessibility, language, and supported device types with high-quality psychometric properties and a positive experience for job applicants. Third, designers *ideate* to generate as many solutions as possible and then plan for a handful of solutions they deem best. Fourth, designers *prototype* the technology they are developing, first in analog (e.g., paper) and later in digital formats. For example, in GBA development, early prototypes are unlikely to contain sound or sophisticated graphics. Fifth, designers *test* their prototypes by soliciting feedback from users. In GBA development, this step involves testing the assessment first with development team members and later with job applicants to ensure that what is being developed meets the software's development goals as established in earlier definition stages. Importantly, the order of stages is not rigid; designers can return to earlier stages at any time to gather more or higher-quality information as necessary or repeat existing stages with small changes to fix emergent problems.

Iterative user testing is now implied during GBA development no matter what specific design framework is used. Prototypes typically undergo hundreds or thousands of revisions before one of those prototypes is ultimately deployed with authentic job candidates. In MDA, designers *tune* their product by adding, changing, and deleting game mechanics that do not help them generate desirable dynamics or achieve their aesthetic goals. On the other hand, in design thinking, designers cycle through the stages iteratively in order to redevelop and reconceptualize both the problem in hand and the created prototype until they reach a satisfying final product given the problem they defined at an earlier stage (Plattner et al., 2011; Rowe, 1986). This iteration makes GBA design and development an expensive and time-consuming process with significant risks and many unknowns.

5.1.1   *Distinguishing GBAs from Games*

GBAs are measurement tools developed either by using gamification or by gameful design to incorporate game mechanics (e.g., levels, leaderboards, points) and/or game attributes (e.g., immersion, fantasies) into traditionally nongame contexts, or by dedicated game design and development (Deterding et al., 2011; Landers & Sanchez, 2022). When viewed through the lens of selection, the application of gamification can potentially evoke a gameful experience and thereby motivate and enact targeted behavioral changes, such as increased attention and reduced performance anxiety among job applicants (Landers et al., 2018). Similarly, games also have intrinsically motivating properties that can potentially benefit assessment takers as users are typically willing to invest more time and energy in gameplay because they find games to be rewarding (Kapp et al., 2020). Although games and/or game elements admittedly form an integral part of GBAs, GBAs can be distinguished from games in that they do more than just bring fun to users. In particular, selection-based GBAs typically have two goals: providing a high-quality psychometric measurement and eliciting positive reactions from job applicants, all through the experience of a core gameplay loop (Landers & Sanchez, 2022).

Existing commercial GBA products comprise primarily stand-alone games that capture underlying psychological constructs investigated in prior literature. Common attributes of interest in the context of employee selection include cognitive ability, personality traits, emotional intelligence, problem-solving skills, and so on. Stand-alone games can come in many forms and shapes, ranging from simple computerized tasks organized in a core gameplay loop with relatively few game elements to full-on games. The key to these games is to offer players liberty in pursuing game goals while simultaneously designing the experience in a way that variance in measurable behaviors reflects constructs of interest (Landers et al., 2021); otherwise, the game may feel prescribed and mandatory, diminishing the gameful experience, and, ultimately, lose the added benefits associated with the use of GBAs (see Landers et al., 2019; Mollick & Rothbard, 2014). A popular example of selection-based GBA is the balloon analogue risk task developed by Lejuez et al. (2002). The task aims at assessing player risk-taking behavior by asking players to inflate a balloon up to the point when they think the balloon will explode across a number of trials. Each time players choose to pump the balloon, they receive a fixed amount of money as a reward. As the balloon inflates, each pump carries greater risk as players will lose all the earnings if the balloon explodes, but also a greater potential reward since the players can keep all the earnings if they cash out before the balloon explodes.

GBAs, as a form of summative assessment used by organizations for evaluating and comparing job applicants, are distinct from traditional assessments in selection in two major ways. First, from an organizational standpoint, GBAs offer vendors/organizations the opportunity to gather large amounts of information via *trace data*, which otherwise would not be possible to collect in traditional assessments. Trace data can be defined as "records of activity undertaken through an online information system" (Howison et al., 2011, p. 769). In the case of selection-based GBAs, trace data can be response times, device types (e.g., mobile vs. computer), and mouse-clicking behaviors, etc. Such data can be factored into scoring in GBA to add another information source that can help better differentiate job applicants. Second, from an applicant perspective, GBAs can improve applicant reactions to assessments (Armstrong et al., 2016). Traditional assessments are sometimes too serious and boring for applicants; in contrast, GBAs are perceived as novel and interesting. The fun experience a GBA can offer may reduce applicant test anxiety during selection (Pitoyo et al., 2019), and thus more accurately reflect job applicants' true abilities. Therefore, though both GBAs and traditional assessments aim at accurately measuring latent constructs, GBAs are unique in ways that can bring added benefits to the selection process. Organizations may even deploy GBAs with the intent to enhance perceptions of the company by job applicants, especially young college graduates, so that the company is branded and seen as interesting and on trend.

A principal goal of developing and deploying GBAs to improve the psychometric properties of preemployment assessments is frequently mentioned in the existing literature. The algorithmic, and sometimes automatic, scoring practices of GBAs offer the promise of reducing the effects of human biases stemming from practices that rely solely on human intuition as long as scoring algorithms are carefully developed to avoid replicating such biases or creating new ones (e.g., Ip, 2018; Landers & Behrend, 2023). Moreover, GBAs offer assessment researchers the potential to develop language-agnostic assessments that do not rely on the language abilities of test takers. Such assessments can eliminate language ability as a potential confound when assessing the constructs of interest. As mentioned previously, the presence and analysis of trace data can also potentially generate higher-quality data that can enhance the quality of measurement tools. Despite this promise, the majority of existing research uses samples from Western, educated, industrialized, rich, and democratic (WEIRD; Henrich et al., 2010) countries, and GBAs like other assessment types should never be automatically considered to possess cross-cultural measurement equivalence. For instance, language-agnostic GBA designs might be perceived as desirable by organizations seeking to apply assessments for use around the world that are insensitive to differences in the native languages of communities of potential applicants. In countries where the average level of education is lower or the jobs available are mainly blue-collar, this is particularly attractive. However, due to differences in prior game experience and expertise across nations and cultures, even a language-agnostic test may systematically penalize cultures that play fewer games of a similar style.

5.1.2   Core Research Questions

Despite the uncertainty regarding whether improving psychometric properties is the reason for the adoption of GBAs across nations, psychometrics remains crucial. In GBA design and development, adopting psychometric thinking as opposed to game design–only thinking aids researchers in examining the value of assessment information as well as the quality of decisions we make based on such information (Mislevy et al., 2014). More importantly, psychometrics provides metrics that improve not only assessment design but also game design by answering important questions such as what game mechanics provide more evidence of targeted behaviors and whether certain designs yield higher-quality evidence (Mislevy et al., 2014). This is particularly important because the incorporation of games and/or game elements into assessments introduces additional complexities associated with the unexpected interactions between individuals, game design elements, and assessment. Unlike the concern for psychometrics, GBA design, especially the choices of stimuli and response space, is still new and relatively unknown and may vary across national contexts and cultures.

GBAs are a relatively novel selection technique used by multinational organizations to assess and compare job applicants during the recruitment process not only in Western countries but also in other parts of the world. Bearing in mind cross-cultural differences across regions, and how that may influence GBA design, development, and deployment, we find it imperative to understand the deployment of GBAs across nations and/or cultures as we do for traditional assessments. Hence, we identified four major concerns across regions that are underdeveloped in existing GBA literature. Our first concern is privacy concerns involving the use of GBAs across countries and regions. Though advances in selection-based GBAs offer the promise of collecting larger amounts of data regarding job applicants via trace data, collecting and analyzing more data increases the demand for computing resources, data management systems (e.g., storage and protection of data), and remote internet testing. Depending on the specific design, obtaining trace data in GBAs may involve seemingly invasive procedures such as gaining permission to access local machines, introducing privacy concerns that are likely to differ across countries. Such concerns may stem from legal requirements, applicant expectations, or simply company preference. Hence, vendors and organizations are likely to have unique privacy concerns depending on where the products are being deployed. This raises our first research question: Is there meaningful variance in privacy concerns unique to GBAs across national and cultural boundaries?

Similarly, our second concern lies in the legal aspect of implementing GBAs across countries and regions. Legal systems across the world may have varying and unique requirements for deploying GBAs as a selection tool. For instance, in Europe, new assessment tools will have to be pre-approved by work councils to protect local workers. Moreover, legislation regarding data privacy, such as General Data Protection Regulation (GDPR) in Europe and the California Consumer Privacy Act, also impact local legal requirements in which GBAs are used. Given that the legal aspect of GBAs has not been well explored and that GBAs are increasingly popular across the globe, we deemed it interesting to discover whether there are drastically different legal concerns for GBAs across countries and regions. Hence, our second research question: Is there meaningful variance in legal concerns unique to GBAs across national and cultural boundaries?

Our third area of concern is job applicants' varying reactions to GBAs across countries and regions. GBAs have been repeatedly used to target candidate reactions for specific outcomes, such as employer branding, organizational attractiveness (e.g., perceived technological sophistication), and offer acceptance (Bhatia & Ryan, 2018; Bina et al., 2021). However, the cultural differences in the interpretation of novel stimuli (i.e., design) used in GBAs have not been studied thoroughly. For example, in education, it has been shown that GBA takers from different cultures have varying levels of comfort when they have to act inappropriately in-game to survive (Jackson et al., 2018), suggesting potential cultural differences in how applicants perceive and interpret novel designs. Furthermore, current studies are mostly conducted in WEIRD countries and lack the international perspectives in which GBAs should be studied. Therefore, we identified our third research question: Is there meaningful variance in applicant reactions unique to GBAs across national and cultural boundaries?

Lastly, our fourth area of concern looks at whether or not there are any other concerns unique to GBAs across national and cultural boundaries, and if there are, what are the emergent topics and themes. We will review other unique concerns raised by vendors and organizational decision-makers regarding GBAs from their personal experiences. Thus, we came up with our fourth and final question: Are there any other unique concerns about GBAs across national and cultural boundaries?

5.2 Method

5.2.1 Participants

Two populations were targeted for this qualitative study. The first consisted of developers and vendors or GBAs that operate internationally. Our search for participants started by reaching out for representatives from prominent vendors: Aon, Arctic Shores, Hirevue, Pymetrics, Revelian, and Test Partnership. We asked contacts at each of these organizations to connect us with individuals directly involved in developing, deploying, analyzing, and selling GBAs. Ultimately, seven vendor SMEs were interviewed, consisting of representation only from companies in the United States, United Kingdom, and Australia, which also reflects where our initial list of GBA vendors was located.

The second population consisted of organizational stakeholders who decided to adopt a GBA for use in employee selection internationally, whom we also identified via snowball sampling in the first sample. However, most of the individuals we approached from this population were unable to clear hurdles with their internal legal departments to speak with us. Ultimately, we were only able to interview two participants, both executives in global talent operations in two top-50 organizations within the Fortune 500. One of these two subject matter experts also had prior experience as a GBA vendor. Although both organizational stakeholders were in the United States, they managed talent assessment practices for their company on five or six continents.

5.2.2 Measures

In line with methods for descriptive qualitative studies, six questions were initially designed to guide our conversations with vendor participants and five questions for organizational stakeholders. These questions were not considered exhaustive; the team asked follow-up questions and revisited the list after each interview. The interview process was designed to obtain factual information from participants, as shown in Table 5.1.

5.2.3 Procedure and Analytic Plan

Interviews were semi-structured and descriptive in nature, which aimed to generate a comprehensive qualitative summary of important differences in GBA applications across nations and cultures. This was chosen in contrast

Table 5.1 *Initial questions for descriptive interviews*

Relevance/order	Question
Vendor questions	
Opening 1	To start, can you give us a brief overview of what GBA products you offer across international and cultural borders?
Opening 2	Can you give us a brief overview of the challenges you've faced providing GBAs across such borders?
RQ1	How have you considered applicant privacy differently across international borders for your GBA products?
RQ2	How have you considered legality differently across international borders for your GBA products?
RQ3	How have you considered anticipated applicant reactions differently across international borders for your GBA products?
RQ4	Are there any other aspects of your GBA products that you believe are unique to different countries you operate in?
Organizational stakeholder questions	
Opening	GBAs are increasingly being used to select employees in organizations like yours. Can you give us a brief overview of your experience with and understanding of GBAs?
RQ1	Do you think there are any concerns about applicant privacy when using GBAs that are unique across national borders or unique to GBAs?
RQ2	Do you think there are any concerns about the legality of GBAs that are unique across national borders or unique to GBAs?
RQ3	Do you think there are any concerns about how job applicants will react to GBAs that are unique to your country or unique to GBAs?
RQ4	Are there any other aspects of GBAs that you believe are unique to your country?

to an inductive approach, like grounded theory, which is intended to build psychological theory via the interpretive lens of the researchers. Our intent, instead, was merely to describe the variation between different countries and cultures as described by research participants. Each participant interview was scheduled for one hour via video web conference with between two and four members of the research team. All questions were asked in sequence by the lead researcher for that session, and team members asked additional follow-up questions as relevant. All interviews were recorded and transcribed.

A priori, we planned that after each interview, we would revisit the list of questions and revise as necessary. Our goal was to generate new questions from prior interviews depending on the importance/prevalence of the topic or question that we had not previously considered. Ultimately, we only added one question asked consistently of all later research participants. Specifically, during initial interviews, we noticed spontaneous and detailed mention of international variation in data collection, retention, and usage strategy. We therefore added a question on this topic as a formal follow-up question, as this emerged as an important dimension of RQ2.

After all the interviews, content analysis was conducted to understand emergent themes related to each research question. Four research members involved in some or all interview sessions independently reviewed and coded the content of the interviews. Then, research members engaged in two discussion sessions to determine emergent topics and themes. For our first discussion, each research member proposed their coded themes and topics separately for both vendor and client discussions. Emergent themes and topics were agreed upon; any disputes were resolved through discussion. For our second discussion, research members combined responses from both vendors and clients and interpreted coded categories as they pertained to research questions.

5.3   Results

As expected, we noticed relatively few concerns about the nation or culture unique to GBA versus more general concerns in the employee selection market. For example, most issues raised by SMEs related to privacy, legality, and applicant reactions were also raised by Myors et al. (2008) and Shen et al. (2017). We focus our results and discussion of those results instead on findings that revealed unique considerations in the GBA context and findings for which SMEs explicitly contrasted GBAs with other assessment types. Major themes for each RQ are summarized in Table 5.2.

5.3.1   Research Question 1: Privacy

Consistent with our motivation for the project, SMEs operating internationally were quite motivated to ensure applicant right to privacy was respected when operating within national borders where locals had such expectations. Among regions of the world served by our SMEs, Europe was generally viewed as the most concerned with privacy and applicant rights, trailed by Australia and Asia, with North America and especially the United States of much less concern. For example, one vendor SME reported that European applicants, in particular, had contacted them to exercise their right to be removed from the vendor's databases, and that

Table 5.2 *Major emergent themes*

RQ	Important findings
RQ1: Privacy	• Increased cybersecurity and cloud service security considerations due to larger quantity and variety of data obtained from GBAs • Growing data sovereignty rights in various regions around the world (e.g., the EU); applicants from these places are more likely to exercise these rights • Compliance with General Data Protection Regulation (GDPR) across countries and differences
RQ2: Legality	• General legal frameworks (e.g., GDPR, California Consumer Privacy Act, and California Privacy Rights Act) that apply to selection in general still apply to GBAs • Future legislation on the use of machine learning (ML)/AI in hiring in certain countries or regions may raise unique legal concerns • Less legal guidance on integrating ML/AI for new measurement schemes and necessary validity evidence • Default policies at the level of the most stringent legal guidelines within the markets they (vendors) serve
RQ3: Applicant reactions	• Common confusion between GBAs and other ML/AI-powered selection methods • Greater acceptance of GBAs in places where interactive mobile-based selection is already in place • No negativity towards GBAs across cultures • Greater concern regarding potential invasiveness depending on the game design • Greater concern for the lack of job relevance evidence
RQ4: Other	• Concern for explainability and transparency associated with the use of ML/AI-based prediction models • Greater importance of optimization of mobile versions of GBAs in less developed countries • (Potential) design and development of language-agnostic GBAs may minimize test-attributed differences between cultures

these requests created substantial challenges when those databases could not be queried in such a way to easily identify all locations where a particular person's data might be stored. SMEs pointed out that their privacy concerns were not necessarily unique to GBAs, but rather that certain development and administration strategies common to GBA administration heightened these concerns.

Specifically, many GBA vendors reported taking advantage of internet-based cloud services for data storage and game administration, among other purposes. This was often justified due to the high complexity of certain types of GBA data; specifically, vendors collecting trace data (e.g., data describing mouse click patterns and the timing of those patterns down to the millisecond, potentially dozens of data transfers per second per applicant; see Auer et al., 2022) generally outsourced the technical infrastructure to enable their collection, making the privacy policies of these technical partners relevant to their own privacy practices. One vendor SME, for example, described challenges with their company storing data in neither the country of the vendor nor the country of their client. SMEs expressed concern about any potential effects of data breaches of cloud servers located in those countries, as privacy violation remediation policies vary internationally, making the "correct" response difficult to identify.

5.3.2   Research Question 2: Legality

The first general legality theme we identified was that although legality is a separate concern from privacy, privacy was raised as the primary concern in relation to legality except when discussing the United States, where adverse impact was the focus as well as the generally litigious nature of that country. Because GBAs may not be obviously job-relevant, depending on the way they are designed, it was generally viewed as riskier to deploy a GBA in the United States than elsewhere in the world due to a perceived increased risk of litigation. One client SME, in charge of global talent operations for their company, described how they felt comfortable deploying novel GBAs for validation studies throughout the world but never in the United States; they believed that their organization's legal department would never approve US deployment.

The second general legality theme we identified regarded SMEs reporting unique data localization requirements unexpectedly, varying between industries and governments. Russia, China, and the European Union were all noted as particularly challenging settings for GBA administration if data were not stored within their national borders; hosting GBA trace data on cloud servers outside of those countries often appeared to be illegal for job applicants within those countries, increasing administration costs and complexity dramatically for GBA administration. Even in cases where these national guidelines are not so restrictive, GBA vendors reported that some industries or specific clients, including Chinese government offices, required this. Once again, these concerns were not described as unique to GBAs but rather made more salient by the high-volume data capture strategies employed by many GBAs.

A third legal concern that arose with several vendor SMEs was the interaction between the novelty and complexity of GBAs with requirements placed by European work councils. Closely related to trade unions, work councils negotiate with management on behalf of workers, customizing national collective bargaining agreements to local conditions for individual organizations. Work councils are therefore hyperlocal, requiring GBA vendors to essentially negotiate directly with the workforces of each organization represented by one. Because GBAs remain novel as job candidate and employee assessments, this practice places a significant administrative burden on GBA vendors to explain the merits of their GBAs not only in terms of organizational effectiveness to management but also for the benefit to front-line employees, in a way comprehensible to those front-line employees, customized to the needs and merits of each individual client organization. Relative to other assessment types, vendor SMEs reported the process of presenting their platform to work councils was easier in that GBAs appear less threatening and anxiety-provoking than other assessment types, but also more difficult in that many GBAs appear less job-relevant than other assessment types.

A fourth legal concern was regarding the pace of change in the law. SMEs noted that legal requirements surrounding data privacy continue to evolve rapidly worldwide, with new data privacy laws appearing in Australia, Europe, Malaysia, South Korea, Singapore, the Philippines, Japan, Thailand, India, and China all within the past decade, and most within the past five years. Sometimes these laws were modeled upon European Union law or even the GDPR itself, which was generally regarded to be the most mature legal approach to data privacy worldwide, but this was not universal. Because SMEs generally regarded the GDPR as the most restrictive, most reported modeling their general internal data practices on GDPR, assuming that most new major national legislation would be as restrictive or less restrictive than GDPR. However, this was again not viewed as a unique concern for GBAs but instead as amplified by common GBA data collection practices.

5.3.3 *Research Question 3: Applicant Reactions*

Although all vendors and clients reported that GBAs were generally viewed more positively than other assessment types, our analysis of applicant reactions response data also revealed larger international differences than when examining the first two research questions. First, applicants in different regions varied in their levels of GBA acceptance. SMEs commonly reported that in places where interactive mobile-based selection is already common, GBAs were seen as less novel and thus were more generally accepted. For example, one SME reported GBA roll-out in Africa, where traditional psychometric testing and interviews are also considered novel, was viewed as uncontroversial. In other places with more established national norms for employee selection practices, GBAs were more likely to be viewed as novel and nonnormative, reducing applicant acceptance and comfort. However, SMEs generally did not report any systematic negativity from applicants about GBAs across cultures so long as the job relevance of GBAs was established.

Second, applicants varied in how closely they associated GBAs with the concept of artificial intelligence (AI), which was associated with differential reactions to GBAs across regions. SMEs reported it was common to see applicants conflating GBAs with AI-based selection tools, even if AI was not actually used. For example, an SME reported that applicants in Southeast Asia were generally indifferent toward the idea of using AI in selection, which generalized to the use of GBA. The SME contrasted this with US and EU contexts in which sensitivity to the use of AI would sometimes generalize to GBA. In terms of similarities across regions, SMEs reported that across cultures, applicants for lower-complexity jobs, applicants with limited test-taking experience, and applicants in countries with weaker job application norms consistently preferred GBAs over traditional assessments.

5.3.4   Research Question 4: Other Topics

Several other topics were raised by one or more SMEs beyond our core RQs that were identified as important emergent themes. First, although the conflation of AI and GBA emerged as a problem in terms of applicant reactions, the potential to apply AI to score GBAs in a way that a greater variety of psychometric traits could be assessed was viewed as substantially positive in cultures in which lengthy application processes were nonnormative. However, because the use of AI varies in controversy between nations and cultures, the use of AI such that AI decisions could not be explained (i.e., "black box" modeling) was viewed as riskier in some parts of the world than in others.

Second, the development process for GBAs was raised by several SMEs as differing depending upon the national target markets for the GBA. Specifically, countries vary in terms of internet access modality. In some countries, especially in the Global South, most people have access to the Internet primarily through a mobile device, typically a small-screen smartphone. GBAs built primarily for desktop and laptop computers, therefore, are ill-suited for deployment in these markets. Even within the Global North, job applicants often use mobile devices to access job applications, but this is far less universal. Thus, GBA developers wishing to maximize accessibility worldwide should take a "mobile-first" design approach, designing GBAs primarily for mobile devices, supporting larger screens only as a secondary goal (Grelle & Gutierrez, 2019).

Third, both GBA vendors and GBA clients reported a major advantage of GBA was the ability to design one to be language-agnostic. It could be deployed worldwide with less need for extensive and expensive translation practices to ensure psychometric equivalence. Importantly, this is not possible for all GBAs, as some constructs assessed by GBAs may require the demonstration of language skills. However, for constructs where this is not necessary, this was viewed as a major advantage for creating a truly cross-cultural assessment.

5.4 Discussion

Although we have described the full richness of our findings, we summarize by stating that most applicant privacy and legality concerns related to the use of GBAs across countries and regions were not unique to GBAs. However, the complexities of GBA design often amplify such concerns. Additionally, applicant reactions to GBAs did differ somewhat internationally, and there were a small number of broader issues of relevance to GBA use. Issues that were unique to GBAs included legal requirements associated with data protection, storage, and retention, which were sometimes amplified by specific GBA development practices. In terms of reactions, consistent with prior research, applicant reactions to GBAs were consistently more positive than to traditional assessments (Armstrong et al., 2016), although the extent appeared to differ by region. Moreover, it was common to see job applicants, and sometimes even organizational stakeholders, confuse GBAs with AI, leading to varying levels of acceptance for GBAs that will likely fluctuate as attitudes toward AI fluctuate. Finally, additional themes that emerged unique to GBAs included the potential value of AI-based scoring methods, the differing value of mobile-first GBA design practices between the Global North and South, and the advantages of developing truly language-agnostic assessments.

We were also surprised by one concern related to this final theme that did not emerge from interview responses. Specifically, modern commercial entertainment video games are often designed to provide a personalized and unique experience for players, yet neither vendors nor clients mentioned personalization to individual players or meaningful player groups as a possible goal of GBA development. The focus instead was solely on creating gaming experiences that were both attractive and psychometrically diagnostic for all applicants regardless of nation, culture, or language. This may be in part attributable to the high cost of GBA development and even higher costs associated with engineering personalization into game design (Orji et al., 2017). If so, customization to individual cultures or nations may become more common as game development costs continue to decrease. Alternatively, this may reflect the legacy of traditional psychological measure construction practices that present differences in test-taking experience as potentially biasing and generally to be avoided. As GBA development matures, and especially as GBA measurement models improve, this perspective too may change.

5.4.1   *Limitations*

A main limitation of the current study was that despite significant effort to recruit as many participants as possible, the sample was relatively small and unbalanced, even for a descriptive qualitative study. We inferred from our discussions with potential SMEs that this was at least in part due to participant unwillingness to share proprietary information, lack of legal clearance to share organizational level information, and lack of incentives to participate. Although major differences between vendor and client responses were not observed in this study, as almost identical themes emerged from each sample, a larger client sample might lead to the discovery of more themes and topics that were not uncovered here. Particularly, we were unable to identify any international organizations that explored GBAs as a potential selection method but then rejected them, and such clients might offer a unique perspective on the weaknesses in applying GBAs across national borders and cultural contexts.

5.5   Conclusion

In sum, using a qualitative descriptive approach, this study contributed to the literature and practice of GBA design and development by outlining concerns unique to GBAs when deploying them across national and cultural borders. For practitioners, the overall news is positive. GBAs are not altogether different from existing selection methods, and the novel issues their use creates are relatively narrow in scope. However, when those differences uncovered are relevant to a particular national application context, they are critical. For example, a GBA designed for desktop computers would likely not do well if deployed in the Global South. Future practitioners and researchers should, therefore, carefully consider the implications of the intersection between GBA design practices, GBA administration strategy, national legal context, and local cultural norms in any new GBA research or deployment for employee selection.

REFERENCES

Armstrong, M. B., Ferrell, J., Collmus, A. B., & Landers, R. N. (2016). Correcting misconceptions about gamification of assessment: More than SJTs and badges. *Industrial and Organizational Psychology*, *9*(3), 671–677. https://doi.org/10.1017/iop.2016.69

Auer, E. M., Mersy, G., Marin, S., Blaik, J., & Landers, R. N. (2022). Using machine learning to model trace behavioral data from a game-based assessment. *International Journal of Selection and Assessment*, *30*(1), 82–102. https://doi.org/10.1111/ijsa.12363

Bhatia, S., & Ryan, A. M. (2018). Hiring for the win: Game-based assessment in employee selection. In J. H. Dulebohn & D. L. Stone (Eds.), *The brave new world of eHRM 2.0* (pp. 81–110). IAP Information Age Publishing.

Bina, S., Mullins, J. K., & Petter, S. (2021). Examining game-based approaches in human resources recruitment and selection: A literature review and research agenda. In *Proceedings of the 54th Hawaii International Conference on System Sciences* (pp. 1325–1334).

Bjogvinsson, E., Ehn, P., & Hillgren, P.-A. (2012). Design things and design thinking: Contemporary participatory design challenges. *Design Issues*, *28*(3), 101–116. https://doi.org/10.1162/DESI_a_00165

Caillois, R. (2011). *Man, play, and games*. University of Illinois Press.

Cubrich, M., King, R., Mracek, D., Strong, J., Hassenkamp, K., Vaughn, D., & Dudley, N. (2021). Examining the criterion-related validity evidence of LinkedIn profile elements in an applied sample. *Computers in Human Behavior*, *120*, 106742. https://doi.org/10.1016/j.chb.2021.106742

Deterding, S., Sicart, M., Nacke, L., O'Hara, K., & Dixon, D. (2011). Gamification: Using game-design elements in non-gaming contexts. In *CHI'11 extended abstracts on human factors in computing systems* (pp. 2425–2428). ACM Press.

Grelle, D. M., & Gutierrez, S. L. (2019). Developing device-equivalent and effective measures of complex thinking with an information processing framework and mobile first design principles. *Personnel Assessment and Decisions*, *5*(3). https://doi.org/10.25035/pad.2019.03.004

Henrich, J., Heine, S. J., & Norenzayan, A. (2010). The weirdest people in the world?. *The Behavioral and Brain Sciences*, *33*(2–3), 61–135. https://doi.org/10.1017/S0140525X0999152X

Howison, J., Wiggins, A., & Crowston, K. (2011). Validity issues in the use of social network analysis with digital trace data. *Journal of the Association for Information Systems, 12*(12). https://doi.org/10.17705/1jais.00282

Hunicke, R., LeBlanc, M., & Zubek, R. (2004). MDA: A formal approach to game design and game research. *Proceedings of the AAAI Workshop on Challenges in Game AI, 4*(1), 1722–1726.

Ip, C. (2018, May 4). *To find a job, play these games.* Engadget. https://www.engadget.com/2018/05/04/pymetrics-gamified-recruitment-behavioral-tests/

Jackson, G. T., Grace, L., Inglese, P., Wain, J., & Hone, R. (2018). Awkward Annie: Game-based assessment of English pragmatic skills. In A. Cheok, M. Inami, & T. Romão (Eds.), *Advances in computer entertainment technology. ACE 2017.* Lecture Notes in Computer Science, Vol. 10714. Springer. https://doi.org/10.1007/978-3-319-76270-8_54

Jones, S. E. (2008). *The meaning of video games: Gaming and textual strategies.* Routledge.

Kapp, K. M., Valtchanov, D., & Pastore, R. (2020). Enhancing motivation in workplace training with casual games: A twelve month field study of retail employees. *Educational Technology Research and Development, 68*(5), 2263–2284. https://doi.org/10.1007/s11423-020-09769-2

Landers, R. N., Armstrong, M. B., Collmus, A. B., Mujcic, S., & Blaik, J. (2021). Theory-driven game-based assessment of general cognitive ability: Design theory, measurement, prediction of performance, and test fairness. *Journal of Applied Psychology, 107*(10). https://doi.org/10.1037/apl0000954

Landers, R. N., Auer, E. M., Collmus, A. B., & Armstrong, M. B. (2018). Gamification science, its history and future: Definitions and a research agenda. *Simulation & Gaming, 49*(3), 315–337. https://doi.org/10.1177/1046878118774385

Landers, R. N., & Behrend, T. S. (2023). Auditing the AI auditors: A framework for evaluating fairness and bias in high stakes AI predictive models. *American Psychologist, 78*(1), 36–49. https://doi.org/10.1037/amp0000972

Landers, R. N., & Sanchez, D. R.(2022). Game-based, gamified, and gamefully design assessments for employee selection: Definitions, distinctions, design, and validation. *International Journal of Selection and Assessment, 30*(1), 1–13. https://doi.org/10.1111/ijsa.12376

Landers, R. N., Tondello, G. F., Kappen, D. L., Collmus, A. B., Mekler, E. D., & Nacke, L. (2019). Defining gameful experience as a psychological state caused by gameplay: Replacing the term 'gamefulness' with three distinct constructs. *International Journal of Human Computer Studies, 127*, 81–94. https://doi.org/10.1016/j.ijhcs.2018.08.003

Lejuez, C. W., Read, J. P., Kahler, C. W., Richards, J. B., Ramsey, S. E., Stuart, G. L., Strong, D. R., & Brown, R. A. (2002). Evaluation of a behavioral measure of risk taking: The balloon analogue risk task (BART). *Journal of Experimental Psychology: Applied, 8*(2), 75–84. https://doi.org/10.1037//1076-898x.8.2.75

Michael, D. R., & Chen, S. L. (2005). *Serious games: Games that educate, train, and inform.* Thomson Course Technology.

Mislevy, R. J., Oranje, A., Bauer, M. I., von Davier, A., Hao, J., Corrigan, S., Hoffman, E., DiCerbo, K., & John, M. (2014). *Psychometric considerations in game-based assessment.* GlassLab. https://www.envisionexperience.com/~/media/files/blog/glasslab- psychometrics.pdf?la=en

Mollick, E. R., & Rothbard, N. (2014). *Mandatory fun: Consent, gamification and the impact of games at work.* The Wharton School Research Paper Series. https://ssrn.com/abstract=2277103

Myors, B., Lievens, F., Schollaert, E., Van Hoye, G., Cronshaw, S. F., Mladinic, A., ... Sackett, P. R. (2008). International perspectives on the legal environment for selection. *Industrial and Organizational Psychology, 1*(2), 206–246. https://doi.org/10.1111/j.1754-9434.2008.00040.x

Orji, R., Mandryk, R. L., & Vassileva, J. (2017). Improving the efficacy of games for change using personalization models. *ACM Transactions on Computer-Human Interaction (TOCHI), 24*(5), 1–22. https://doi.org/10.1145/3119929

Pitoyo, M. D., Sumardi, S., & Asib, A. (2019). Gamification based assessment: A test anxiety reduction through game elements in Quizizz platform. *International Online Journal of Education and Teaching (IOJET), 6*(3), 456–471. http://iojet.org/index.php/IOJET/article/view/626

Plattner, H., Meinel, C., & Leifer, L. (2011). *Design thinking: Understand, improve, apply.* Springer-Verlag.

Rowe, P. (1986). *Design thinking.* The MIT Press.

Shen, W., Sackett, P. R., Lievens, F., Schollaert, E., Van Hoye, G., Steiner, D. D., ... Cook, M. (2017). Updated perspectives on the international legal environment for selection. In J. L. Farr, N. T. Tippins, W. C. Borman, D. Chan, M. D. Coovert, R. Jacobs, ... & B. Schneider (Eds.), *Handbook of employee selection* (2nd ed., pp. 659–677). Routledge. https://doi.org/10.4324/9781315690193-29

Tippins, N. T. (2015). Technology and assessment in selection. *Annual Review of Organizational Psychology and Organizational Behavior, 2*(1), 551–582. https://doi.org/10.1146/annurev-orgpsych-031413-091317

CHAPTER 6

Mobile Sensing around the Globe
Considerations for Cross-Cultural Research

*Le Vy Phan, Nick Modersitzki, Kim K. Gloystein,
and Sandrine R. Müller*

Smartphone usage around the globe accelerated throughout the 2010s. As of 2020, nearly 45% of the world's population owns a smartphone, and this percentage is expected to continue rising in the coming years (Statista, 2020). The ubiquity of mobile devices presents numerous possibilities for the use of mobile sensing. Mobile sensing methods (MSMs) make use of the multitude of sensors embedded in mobile devices and wearables to collect and process data about people's behavior and their environments (Khan et al., 2013). The ability to collect large-scale behavioral data based on people's everyday lives in a granular, continuous, and dynamic manner has inspired a wave of psychological mobile sensing research (see, e.g., Harari et al., 2016). Mobile sensing data have been used in psychological research to examine social interactions, daily activities, mobility patterns, physical activity, mood, mental health, well-being, nutrition, sleeping patterns, productivity, digital media use, and psychological situations (Harari et al., 2016; Harari, Müller, & Gosling, 2020; Mohr et al., 2017; Müller et al., 2020; Rabbi et al., 2011; Sandstrom et al., 2017; Wang et al., 2018; for detailed overviews, see Harari, Müller, et al., 2017, and Vaid & Harari, 2019). For example, sleep duration can be reliably predicted from phone recharging events, periods when the phone is stationary, and ambient silence (Lane et al., 2011). MSMs are of particular value for personality science, which involves the study of individual differences in human experiences and behavior. For example, mobile sensing data have been used to make inferences about users' personality traits (Stachl, Au, et al., 2020) or to study stable behavioral tendencies in daily life (e.g., Harari, Müller, Stachl, et al., 2020). However, most personality research using MSMs is conducted with Western, Educated, Industrialized, Rich, and Democratic (WEIRD) samples (e.g., Henrich

We thank Aaron Cohen, Namrata Goyal, Seth Margolis, and John Rauthmann for feedback on earlier versions of this manuscript.

et al., 2010a). Thus, little is known about how regional and cultural differences in mobile sensing data might influence psychological inferences drawn from diverse samples.

In this chapter, we provide an overview of psychological mobile sensing research using samples from different regions around the world. We also illustrate the conceptual underpinnings of mobile sensing research and discuss different biases that may occur when MSMs are used in cross-cultural research. We conclude with suggestions on how to mitigate these biases and promote rigorous, fair, and inclusive research in and applications of psychological mobile sensing. We note that there is also a large body of research focusing on the usage of smartphone applications for questionnaire-based ecological momentary assessment, such as experience sampling methods (e.g., Killingsworth & Gilbert, 2010; Ram et al., 2014; Stieger et al., 2015; von Stumm, 2018; Wahl et al., 2017). However, this chapter solely focuses on research using passive sensing methods.

6.1   The State of Cross-Cultural Mobile Sensing Research

To date, few studies have explicitly looked at how psychological mobile sensing research results differ between cultures or regions. Most psychological studies have focused on mobile sensing data based on one or two countries (Khwaja et al., 2019) or larger samples where regional differences were not accounted for or reported. Furthermore, most mobile sensing research is based on WEIRD samples. Figure 6.1 maps the locations of smartphone-based passive sensing studies included in the reviews on health and well-being from Cornet and Holden (2018) and on well-being from de Vries et al. (2021). An overview of the included studies and samples can be found in Table 6.1, and a detailed list can be found on this project's OSF page (https://osf.io/2wbda/). To the best of our knowledge, these are the only existing comprehensive reviews focusing on psychological applications of MSMs. Figure 6.1 shows that most sensing studies were conducted in WEIRD countries and that those studies tended to have greater sample sizes.

It has yet to be determined to what extent MSM research findings can be expected to generalize across cultures and whether assessments based on MSMs are suitable for comparative research. Cross-cultural generalizability concerns the applicability of research findings to cultural groups other than those under investigation or even to the entire human population (e.g., Deffner et al., 2021; Henrich et al., 2010b; Rad et al., 2018). Future research will show how MSMs compare to traditional psychological

Table 6.1 *Mobile sensing studies and samples by continent*

Continent	Number of studies	Sample size				
		Total	Range	M	SD	Mdn
North America[1,2]	25	1,117	7–229	44.96	64.16	18
South America	0	–	–	–	–	–
Europe[2,3,4]	32	78,712	5–26,700	2,461.09	6,730.77	22
Africa	0	–	–	–	–	–
Asia[1]	6	165	14–91	29.83	30.60	15
Oceania[3]	1	43	–	43	–	43

Note. Overview of the *k* = 60 passive sensing studies used to create Figure 6.1 grouped by continent. Multicountry studies were included once per continent. Therefore the sum of the number of studies adds up to 64.
[1][2][3][4] For details on the multicountry studies, see the list of included studies available on this project's OSF page at https://osf.io/2wbda/.

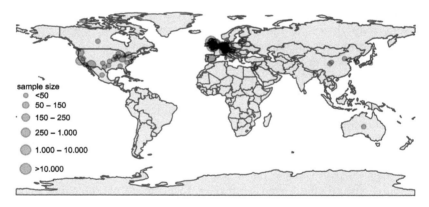

Figure 6.1   Mobile sensing study locations around the world
Note. World map depicting the locations and sample sizes of *k* = 60 passive sensing studies listed in two reviews (Cornet & Holden, 2018; de Vries et al., 2021). Studies that did not use passive sensing (*k* = 27) were excluded. Another study was removed as it provided no information on sample size. Provided information on study location was verified using the original papers. For multicountry studies that did not report the sample sizes per country, the total sample size was split evenly across the countries. This figure was created using R (R Core Team, 2021) and the tmap package (Tennekes, 2018). The data file containing a detailed description of all included studies alongside the code that was used to create this figure can be found on this project's OSF page (https://osf.io/2wbda/).

research tools (e.g., experiments or questionnaires) when it comes to producing cross-culturally robust results that illuminate human universals. However, psychological research is not just concerned with universal phenomena but also with cross-cultural variation in psychological functioning. Comparative research requires equivalent or unbiased assessments, meaning that the same constructs can be measured in the same way in each group (e.g., He & van de Vijver, 2012; van de Vijver & Tanzer, 2004). This is a prerequisite for valid interpretations of observed similarities or differences between groups (i.e., cultures; but also groups defined by other variables, such as age, gender, sexuality, disability, ethnicity, or confession). Later in this chapter (see Section 6.3), we discuss potential sources of bias in the cross-cultural application of MSMs. Importantly, such biases would not only limit the scope of insights we could gain from MSM research but could also amplify systematic discrimination and social inequalities. For example, MSMs could be used by healthcare providers to determine individualized rates and coverages of healthcare plans based on outcomes predicted from users' physical activity patterns. However, there might be systematic differences in MSM-based assessments between, for example, income groups that do not reflect actual group differences in physical activity but are due to unequal access to good network coverage and high-quality devices. Such systematic biases in data can then transfer to biases in behavioral inference and algorithmic prediction, thus leading to unfair treatment and systemic discrimination.

To the best of our knowledge, only one study from Khwaja et al. (2019) has explicitly considered the cultural context in mobile sensing research. In this study, the authors compared the performance of supervised machine learning (ML) models predicting Big Five personality traits from mobile sensing data collected from 545 participants across five countries (UK, Spain, Columbia, Peru, and Chile). To test whether algorithms trained on culturally diverse samples generalize to new countries, the authors applied a leave-one-country-out cross-validation technique. In this approach, the algorithm was trained using data from four countries, and the algorithm was then tested on data from the excluded country. This procedure was repeated five times, excluding a different country in each iteration. Additionally, the authors examined how well culture-specific models performed (i.e., training and testing a model with data from the same country). Their results indicated that using data from the same country to train and test the models (i.e., culture-specific models) significantly improved prediction accuracies for extraversion, agreeableness, and conscientiousness, while neuroticism and openness seemed to be culture-robust (i.e., the results were comparable for both approaches). Müller et al. (2021) used a similar approach to investigate whether depression can be accurately predicted from GPS data in a diverse US-based sample and in sociodemographically homogeneous subsamples. In this study, one algorithm was trained on the entire sample and then tested in homogeneous groups (e.g., women living in rural areas, or highly educated men), while another set of algorithms was trained and tested within each subsample. However, the predictive accuracies achieved in a student sample – a highly specific subculture – could not be replicated in other groups, further underscoring the need for generalizability research.

In addition to a lack of comparative mobile sensing research, few studies have utilized non-WEIRD samples. Moreover, the majority of the non-WEIRD studies we reviewed do not explicitly report sample demographics, meaning that the cultural composition of the samples could only be speculated on based on the location of the authors, description of the data collection process, and the language of the survey instruments used. For example, three studies likely used Chinese samples to examine the prediction of mood (Ma et al., 2012), emotional states (Zhang et al., 2018), and sleep quality (Bai et al., 2012) from smartphone data, but do not explicitly state so. Another recent study used a sample of Chinese university students to associate the Big Five personality traits with sensor-based daily spatial behavior obtained from telecommunication companies (Ai et al., 2019). Lee et al. (2014) likely used a Korean sample to examine correlations between smartphone addiction and daily smartphone use frequency and duration. Lastly, one study predicted loneliness from smartphone data in a sample of older adults likely based in Mexico (Sanchez et al., 2015).

To sum up, there are relatively few empirical findings that can serve as a basis to evaluate the generalizability of psychological mobile sensing research across cultural contexts (especially between WEIRD and non-WEIRD samples). Therefore, the following sections will illustrate factors that might threaten cross-cultural MSM research from a conceptual perspective. To this end, we first outline the underpinnings of MSM research. We then elaborate on potential biases that can occur in cross-cultural MSM research and conclude this chapter with strategies for bias mitigation. We note that most of the following considerations do not only apply to comparisons between cultures but also between groups defined by other variables (gender, age, etc.).

6.2 Underpinnings of Mobile Sensing Research

To illustrate the types of biases that may occur in mobile sensing data and jeopardize cross-cultural comparisons, we first must understand the conceptual underpinnings of mobile sensing research. We will focus on MSM applications for behavioral assessment (i.e., measurement of person variables; e.g., Harari et al., 2016; Harari, Müller, et al., 2017) rather than situational assessment (i.e., measurement of environment variables; e.g., Harari, Müller, & Gosling, 2020), though these are often closely linked or overlapping. For example, GPS data can be used to examine mobility behaviors or locations, and microphone data can indicate verbal behavior or social situations. Sensors are not designed to capture behaviors per se but rather to measure changes in the physical or chemical properties in their surroundings (Yan & Chakraborty, 2014). Behavioral sensing relies on the assumption that these changes are, at least on average, due to the behavior of the person in possession of the sensing device (i.e., the user); therefore, sensor data will contain rich behavioral information about a user. For example, an accelerometer measures the acceleration of a device. If a user carries the device, accelerometer data can then be used to infer whether they are walking, running, or stationary (Harari, Gosling, et al., 2017). Furthermore, unobserved behavior can be inferred from behavioral products, that is, the traces people's behaviors leave behind in their physical or digital environments (i.e., indirect measurement of person variables via measurement of environment variables). For example, light sensors measure the illuminance of surroundings but can be used to infer that a person has stepped outside or switched off the lights (together with other information). However, sensors can only capture behaviors or behavioral products associated with the physical properties they are designed to measure. For example, accelerometers are suitable for sensing physical movement, GPS data can record mobility patterns, microphones can capture social interactions, and light sensors can be used to infer sleep patterns (Harari et al., 2016; Harari, Müller, et al., 2017; Schoedel et al., 2020). This means that the availability of different types of sensors restricts the range of behaviors that can be captured.

In addition to actual sensors, metadata logs are commonly used in MSM research (Harari et al., 2016; Harari, Müller, et al., 2017). For example, phone logs record occurrences in software runs that can capture mediated behaviors (i.e., behaviors carried out through the device) such as smartphone-mediated communication (e.g., frequency and duration of calls or number of unique contacts texted) or other mediated activities (e.g., duration and frequency of phone or app usage; Harari, Müller, et al., 2017). However, logs only contain data about data (i.e., metadata) and may often have limited psychological relevance. For example, log data does not specify whether an outgoing call was made to chat with a friend, to order a pizza, or to report an issue to customer service. Furthermore, the extent to which a person's phone logs are representative of their computer-mediated behaviors depends on whether they use other devices for similar purposes (e.g., make calls from a landline or use messenger apps on a tablet or PC).

Importantly, MSM-based behavioral assessment is always *indirect* because some degree of inference is necessary to link the sensor or log data to actual behavior. Therefore, the target behavior should be considered a latent variable reflected in the data and inferred from indicators (i.e., features) through a specific computational process. For some behaviors, this can be done automatically using software already integrated into the device. For example, smartphone pedometers infer the number of steps a person has taken from data generated by sensors (mostly accelerometers, gyroscopes, and digital compasses). Certain mediated behaviors can be inferred from metadata logs with ease and near-perfect accuracy. For example, phone log data can be used to infer when a person has made a phone call. Other behavioral inferences require more complex computational processes to extract meaningful quantitative variables or *features*. This is often done using classifiers such as ML algorithms designed to compute relevant variables. For example, audio classifiers have been used to infer conversation behavior from microphone data (e.g., Harari, Müller, et al., 2017). By combining data captured by multiple sensors, more specified or contextualized behaviors can be inferred (Harari et al., 2016). Wang et al. (2014) used combined data from location sensors, microphones, and motion sensors to infer studying behavior of college students. Behavioral assessments are often aggregated across occasions or combined with other behavioral variables to create new variables representing individual *behavioral tendencies* or composite constructs. Harari, Müller, Stachl, et al. (2020) estimated individual tendencies for several communication behaviors by computing within-person averages across different time periods and using principal component analysis to create formative composite variables for texting or calling behavior.

Behavioral variables assessed using MSMs can serve as indicators of broader *latent psychological constructs* (Harari et al., 2021), such as momentary states (e.g., personality states, emotions, and momentary well-being) or stable traits (e.g., Big Five personality, cognitive abilities, and general well-being). Stachl, Au, et al. (2020) used ML techniques to predict Big Five personality domains and facets from a variety of behavioral variables inferred from smartphone data. To be inferable from mobile sensing data, a target construct needs to manifest in tangible behavioral cues that are machine-readable (i.e., that can be captured by sensors or metadata logs). As a result, target construct and behavioral cues covary, enabling the prediction of the construct from mobile sensing data. The externalization process (target construct(s) → behavioral cue) can be depicted using a Brunswikian lens model (see Figure 6.2; Phan & Rauthmann, 2021; Vinciarelli & Mohammadi, 2014). In a Brunswikian framework, the informativeness of a cue for inferences about the target construct is called its *ecological validity* (Brunswik, 1956). However, as

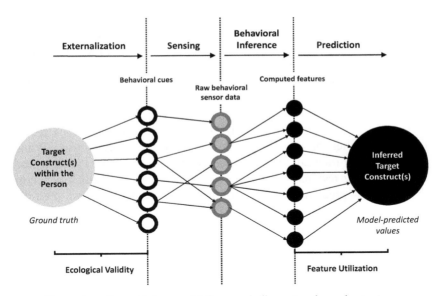

Figure 6.2   Brunswik lens model framework illustrating the underpinnings of mobile sensing

Note. Brunswikian lens model depicting the underpinnings of psychological mobile sensing. Behavioral cues relevant to one or multiple target constructs are externalized by a person. These cues are partly captured by mobile sensors. The raw sensor data is then used to compute features (i.e., behavioral variables) which, in turn, can be used to infer the target construct(s) using traditional statistical techniques or machine learning.

behavior is contextualized and determined by both the person and the situation (Rauthmann, 2016, 2021), ecological validity is not an inherent property of the cue but can vary by person, situation, and time. For example, "dancing wildly" may be an indicator of state extraversion but may be indicative of conscientiousness when executed by a professional dancer during an audition (Horstmann & Ziegler, 2020). We argue that different behaviors can also differ in how indicative of a target construct they are across different cultural contexts.

Next, behavioral cues are captured by different sensors or manifest in data logs (behavioral cues → raw behavioral sensor data; see Figure 6.2). Depending on both the nature of the target construct and the capabilities of the device, not all relevant behavioral cues externalized by a person may be machine-readable. Furthermore, several factors may affect the reliability and validity of behavioral inferences from sensor data, including the properties of the specific sensing device, how the device is being used, and the environment of the user (see Section 6.3). Assuming sensors and metadata logs have at least partially captured behavioral cues that are informative of the target construct, we now have raw sensor data that usually requires preprocessing (i.e., similar to data cleaning) and subsequent computation of features (sensor data → computed features; see Figure 6.2) for further analysis. When the goal is to infer or predict a stable construct (e.g., a personality trait), features are usually computed as behavioral summary statistics (e.g., measures of central tendencies or variability) across certain time windows (e.g., daily averages). Extracted features can then be used for traditional statistical analyses (e.g., Wang et al., 2018), or they can serve as input data for ML models.[1] Psychological mobile sensing research commonly uses supervised ML, which concerns the automatic prediction of known values of the target construct (i.e., the "ground truth" assessed using some standard criterion, e.g., self-report questionnaires) from the input data (Stachl, Pargent, et al., 2020; Tay et al., 2021). The ML algorithm selects and weights features based on training data to optimize a function that best predicts the ground truth (Lantz, 2019). The performance of the algorithm (i.e., predictive accuracy) is then evaluated using test data (known input and output; not used in

---

[1] There are studies that do not aim to predict a latent target variable or other outcome variables from mobile sensing data (and inferred behaviors but solely examine manifest behavioral patterns. Such accounts are important to describe inter- and intra-individual patterns of behavioral expression (including change and stability) and can also inform theory (i.e., explanatory account; Harari, Vaid, et al., 2020).

training).[2] If the testing yielded good results, the ML algorithm could then be applied to new data (i.e., known input data but unknown output).

In the next section, we elaborate on different types of measurement bias sources and implications for cross-cultural mobile sensing research. We focus on MSMs in the application of latent construct assessment, which may be particularly susceptible to biases since systematic errors can be introduced at each step (i.e., externalization, sensing, feature extraction, and, when applicable, prediction). Furthermore, due to the hierarchical structure of the lens model, these biases can have cascading effects: Biases in earlier steps (e.g., externalization) will affect the data generated at later steps (e.g., feature extraction). We restrict our examination of potential biases in mobile sensing to those that may occur when ML is not used (or before ML is used) to infer the target construct. Biases specific to ML applications lie outside the scope of this chapter, and readers are referred to Tay et al. (2021) for an examination of measurement bias in ML-based psychometric assessment.

6.3 Measurement Bias in Cross-Cultural Mobile Sensing Research

Measurement bias occurs when differences in observed variables cannot be fully explained by true differences in what is intended to be measured (e.g., He & van de Vijver, 2012; Oort et al., 2009; van de Vijver & Tanzer, 2004). Formally, this is a violation of measurement invariance or measurement equivalence. Measurement invariance means that the function that relates observed indicators to the latent target variable or measurement model is the same across groups (Borsboom et al., 2008; Oort et al., 2009; Putnick & Bornstein, 2016).[3] Measurement models are commonly specified using confirmatory factor analysis (CFA) or item response theory. Novel big data approaches, including many sensing studies, often use ML, which can be considered a special type of measurement model (Tay et al.,

---

[2] Very high predictive accuracies are unlikely and may be due to overfitting issues because features and ground truth come from different data sources and methods. Predictive accuracy in ML, like convergent validity in traditional psychometric assessment, is limited due to method artifacts and unique information in different data sources. It is also attenuated by measurement error and poor construct coverage. For predictive accuracies in personality computing, Wiernik et al. (2020) estimated ceilings to convergent validity at $r \approx 0.30$–0.50.

[3] Measurement invariance is typically discussed with regard to personality traits, cognitive abilities, or other broad psychological constructs. However, it is also a concern when the latent target variable is a behavior (e.g., an activity) that is not directly observed but inferred from manifest indicators or when the target construct is a formative composite variable (e.g., a behavioral tendency).

2021). Independent of the measurement model, measurement bias implies that some portion of observed variance cannot be attributed to the target construct or to random measurement error and is instead due to systematic error (i.e., nuisance factors; He & van de Vijver, 2012; van de Vijver & Tanzer, 2004). When a nuisance factor varies systematically across cultural samples, observed cross-cultural differences may not reflect true differences in the target construct. Therefore, "insight into the presence and strength of biasing effects is a prerequisite for sensible group comparisons to be made" (Borsboom, 2006, p. 178). While this chapter focuses on cross-cultural research, it is noteworthy that measurement bias may, of course, also exist regarding other sociodemographic or group-type variables (e.g., gender, age group, or education level) or dimensional attributes (e.g., latent traits or abilities; Meredith, 1993; Oort et al., 2009) that may vary within cultures.

He and van de Vijver (2012; see also van de Vijver & Tanzer, 2004) distinguished different types of biases in cross-cultural research based on the location of the systematic error source (i.e., construct level, the method level, or item level). Though this taxonomy was proposed for traditional assessment procedures (e.g., cognitive tests, questionnaires, or behavioral observation; van de Vijver & Tanzer, 2004), similar biases can be identified in cross-cultural mobile sensing research. Furthermore, these biases can occur in sensing research when passive sensing is combined with experience sampling methods or other questionnaire measures, for example, to assess the ground truth for supervised ML (Tay et al., 2021).

First, *construct bias* occurs when the definition of the target construct differs across cultures or "when not all relevant behaviors associated with the construct are present and properly sampled in each culture" (He & van de Vijver, 2012, p. 5). We argue that mobile sensing can be susceptible to this type of bias when a target construct is differentially externalized across cultures or when cross-cultural differences exist in the functional implications of relevant behaviors.

Second, *method bias* is a broad category of systematic errors rooted in research methods (He & van de Vijver, 2012; van de Vijver & Tanzer, 2004) and can be further distinguished into more specific types of bias. *Sample bias* concerns the representativeness and comparability of cultural samples. In particular, recruitment procedures and technical requirements may influence the composition of mobile sensing study samples. In the sensing process (see Figure 6.2), systematic errors may be introduced by devices and the behavior of participants (Blunck et al., 2013). *Device-type bias* results from systematic differences in the devices used by individuals in different cultural samples. Device properties and capabilities determine the types of sensing data they can provide as well as the quality of the data.

Third, *bias from user practices* can occur in cross-cultural MSM research when participants from different cultural samples vary in how they use and customize their devices. This can have a bearing on both the quantity and quality of recorded sensing data. While potential biases from device properties and user practices uniquely concern MSM-based assessment, many other biases that can occur in the application of traditional psychometric instruments do not affect MSMs. These include biases due to systematic cross-cultural differences in (a) response styles (e.g., acquiescence, extreme responding, socially desirable responding); (b) familiarity with test properties (e.g., the test/response format or the stimulus material); or (c) responses to test administration conditions (e.g., physical and social conditions, instructions, or behavior of the tester; He & van de Vijver, 2012; van de Vijver & Tanzer, 2004).

Lastly, *item bias* (or differential item functioning; see, e.g., Bauer, 2017; Borsboom, 2006) occurs when an item score covaries with cultural group membership. This can be the case when an item has been poorly translated or adapted to different cultural contexts (He & van de Vijver, 2012; van de Vijver & Tanzer, 2004). Since mobile sensing does not use items in a psychometric sense, inappropriate instrument translation and adaptation is only a concern when passive sensing is combined with traditional assessment methods (e.g., self-reports). The smallest meaningful quantitative unit in mobile sensing is a single feature extracted from the raw data. Akin to item bias, a feature can be nonequivalent across groups, for example, when it has been computed from speech or written texts in different languages (Tay et al., 2021).

In the following sections, we consider potential sources of bias in psychological MSM research (see Table 6.2 for an overview). We will discuss biases that may be caused by cross-cultural differences in (a) the target construct and its behavioral manifestations, (b) sample characteristics, (c) device properties, and (d) user practices. Furthermore, we will illustrate how (e) environmental factors may systematically affect sensing data and sensor-based behavioral inferences. We focus on bias that may occur at the construct level, in behavioral expressions, or during the sensing process (see left half of Figure 6.2). Computational biases are outside the scope of this chapter, but interested readers may refer to Tay et al. (2021) for an examination of measurement bias in ML-based psychometric assessment.

Table 6.2 *Potential biases in cross-cultural mobile sensing research*

Biases rooted in	Description and causes	Potential nuisance factors (some examples)	Illustrative example
Target construct and its behavioral manifestations	People from different cultures express different behaviors for the same level of the target construct. Behavioral manifestations of the target construct in each culture depend on cultural norms and environmental factors (e.g., opportunities and constraints).	social appropriateness or legality of certain behaviors function and cultural meaning of certain behaviors	In Country A, sidewalks are everywhere and most people walk to get from one location to another. In Country B, sidewalks are rare and when people walk, they do so mostly for exercise.
Sample characteristics	Cultural samples are not representative or not comparable. Sample compositions depend on which subpopulations were targeted by recruitment procedures and selected due to study requirements (e.g., device ownership, device-type requirements) in each culture.	demographic variables (e.g., age, gender, education) psychological variables (e.g., motivation, traits)	A freely available smartphone sensing app for Android is released. In Country A, most people use Android phones. In Country B, Android users tend to be older males with lower incomes.
Device properties	Relevant properties of software platforms or hardware vary systematically across cultural samples. Different devices may be used by participants from each cultural sample, e.g., due to regional differences in platform or device model market shares. Ambient factors that vary systematically across cultural regions (e.g., climate, geography) can also affect device performance (e.g., sensor accuracy).	platform policies processing power sensor types • sensor performance	Most participants from Country A have an X-phone which tends to undercount steps. Most participants from Country B have a Y-phone which tends to overcount steps.

User practices	Participants from different cultural samples vary systematically in how they handle and use their devices. Cross-cultural variation in user practices may be due to differences in cultural norms or environmental factors (e.g., device-related infrastructure).	• device carrying behavior (when, where, and how) • (re)charging behavior • device sharing • customized device settings	Participants from Country A tend to carry their smartphones in their pockets which allows for fairly accurate step counts. Participants from Country B tend to carry (and leave) their phones in backpacks or handbags which leads to steps being undercounted.
Environmental factors	Cultural samples live in different environments. External factors may systematically affect mobile sensing data in several ways, such as (a) by influencing participants' behavior (i.e., behavioral manifestations or user practices; see above); (b) by impairing device performance (see above) or sensing app functionality (e.g., due to poor network coverage); (c) by introducing non-behavioral variance (e.g., background noise in audio recordings); (d) by dictating how data can be collected and stored (i.e., local laws).	opportunities and constraints afforded by the environment ambient factors (e.g., climate, geography, noise) device-related infrastructure (e.g., opportunities for charging, network coverage, data cost) legal frameworks (e.g., data protection and privacy laws)	In County A, mobile data is rather inexpensive and charging stations are widely available (e.g., at bus stops and at restaurants). In Country B, mobile data is expensive and there are few opportunities for charging. Many people routinely disable mobile data to save money and battery power.

Note. Bias occurs in cross-cultural data when observed differences between cultural samples do not fully correspond to true differences in the target construct. This is the case when some nuisance factor that affects the data varies systematically across cultural samples.

6.3.1   Construct Bias and Nonequivalent Behaviors

A person's behavior depends not only on their stable traits and their current states but also on the situation and the broader environmental context in which it occurs (Rauthmann, 2021). Across cultures and regions, behavior is influenced by different presses, affordances, demands, and resources provided by the respective sociocultural and/or physical environments. Specific behaviors may be unique to certain groups (e.g., rituals) or are only possible in certain locations (e.g., taking the subway). For behaviors that can be observed across cultures, the psychological meaning may not be equivalent for several reasons. First, cross-cultural differences may exist in the normativeness or appropriateness of certain behaviors (which may additionally be age-graded or sex-dependent so that other third variables also need to be consulted). For example, littering is socially undesirable in most places, but it can be a serious violation of both cultural norms and strictly enforced local laws in some regions (van de Vijver & Tanzer, 2004). Second, the same behavior can serve different functions in different cultures. For example, in some cultures, people may mostly ride bicycles for exercise, while in other cultures, people cycle to get from A to B. Third, different behaviors can serve the same functional purpose. For example, people from some cultures may exercise by cycling or running, while people from other cultures go to the gym. Whether and why people cycle may depend on sociocultural norms but also on other environmental factors, such as the availability and affordability of other modes of transport (e.g., cars or trains) and of other means of exercise (e.g., gyms), the climate, or road safety. Similarly, how people use their smartphones (i.e., device-mediated behaviors) will vary across cultures depending on norms, but also on, for example, the availability of functionally similar alternatives (e.g., whether people also own a PC or tablet), phone plan subscriptions, and network coverage.

As a result, people from different cultures may express different behaviors reflecting the same level of the latent construct (He & van de Vijver, 2012; van de Vijver & Tanzer, 2004; Tay et al., 2021). In the lens model framework (see Figure 6.2), this means that a behavioral cue may possess high ecological validity (i.e., be a valid indicator of the target construct) in some cultures but not in others. Importantly, cross-cultural differences may not only exist in how a construct is externalized but also in the extent to which it is externalized at all. Via sensors or metadata logs, MSMs can only directly capture overt behaviors expressed in the physical or digital space – using sensors and logs, respectively – but not covert intra-psychological (e.g., perceptual, cognitive, affective, or motivational) states. Assessing the latter would require additional data sources (e.g., self-reports) or analysis (e.g., ML algorithms trained to infer mental states from behavioral data). Therefore, MSMs may be particularly susceptible to construct bias when the extent to which the target construct is externalized (i.e., expressed in observable or machine-readable behavior) varies between cultures. This may be the case, for example, when cultural norms encourage or discourage the behavioral externalization of socially evaluative traits (e.g., intelligence or ignorance; John & Robins, 1993), or when the target construct or associated behaviors are differentially stigmatized across cultures (e.g., depression; Krendl & Pescosolido, 2020). Furthermore, not all relevant behavioral cues may be appropriately sampled (or sensed) in each culture, for example, because they were identified based on previous research or by researchers from one culture. This would not only be problematic in latent construct assessment but also when determining the behaviors that constitute a formative construct. For example, typical means of smartphone-mediated communication identified in one culture (e.g., calling, texting, and certain messaging apps) may not include all relevant communication channels commonly used in another culture (e.g., other apps or browser-based clients).

6.3.2   Sample Bias

Cross-cultural comparison is valid only if the samples are representative of the target population within a given culture (e.g., Deffner et al., 2021) and comparable between cultures (e.g., He & van de Vijver, 2012). Study participant selection is based on several factors, such as (a) the reach of the recruitment campaign, (b) how the study is advertised and what incentives are offered, and (c) eligibility criteria. These factors establish a bottleneck that may inadvertently introduce sample bias. For example, when a study aims to recruit large samples from the general population by releasing and promoting a freely available smartphone application, different demographics will be targeted depending on how the app is advertised, what it promises, and what it requires. In cross-cultural research, the bottleneck created by recruitment efforts and study requirements may produce different sample compositions in different cultures. For example, participation in smartphone sensing studies requires owning a smartphone and, while smartphone usage continues to increase worldwide, there is still considerable cross-national variation. According to a 2018 survey from Pew Research Center (Silver, 2019), 95% of adult South Koreans owned a smartphone, and smartphone ownership was very common across age groups, genders, and education levels. In India, on the other hand, only 24% had a smartphone, and these were mostly young men who had completed secondary education. Furthermore, participants' devices need to meet the technical requirements of the sensing app, which means that only certain user groups (e.g., only Android users) are eligible to participate. This can lead to biased samples when the sociodemographic characteristics of users differ systematically across phone models or platforms (e.g., CivicScience; Götz et al., 2017). As device-type demographics (Blunck et al., 2013) likely also vary between cultures, the range of supported devices (e.g., Android only) can result in different sample compositions. Importantly, even seemingly matching samples (e.g., college students) may vary substantially in their demographics or in their motivation, depending on the culture they come from and how they have been recruited (He & van de Vijver, 2012; van de Vijver & Tanzer, 2004).

6.3.3   Device-Type Bias

When MSM study participants use their own device (rather than identical, calibrated ones handed out by the researchers) – as is the case in many smartphone sensing studies – their devices are also sampled. This means that assessments lack full standardization because different measurement tools (i.e., devices) are used to collect data from different people. The unique properties of different devices can have a bearing on the data and thus become potential sources of error at the person level. These aggregate to group-level biases when the distribution of different smartphone manufacturers and models varies systematically between cultural samples. This may be the case, for example, when samples are recruited from countries or regions with different phone model market shares (e.g., Counterpoint, 2021) or when device-type demographics vary across cultures (see Section 6.3.2). The devices of people sampled from different cultures may not be equipped with the same software and hardware and therefore may not provide sensing data of equal quality. Device heterogeneities exist across (a) platforms (e.g., in distribution and app store policies or in the specifications of different application programming interfaces); (b) smartphone hardware (e.g., in sensor performance, sampling rate, or processing power); and (c) software and hardware version updates (Blunck et al., 2013). Here, we focus only on biases due to variation in sensing capabilities across different devices, and we refer readers to Blunck et al. (2013) for an overview of other device heterogeneities examined from a computer science perspective. As the availability of different types of sensors dictates the types of behaviors that can be captured, devices equipped with a wider array of sensors might be able to access a broader range of behavioral expressions. Devices differ not only in the types of sensors they contain, but also in the performance of those sensors (i.e., their precision and accuracy). Precision can be seen as the psychometric reliability of a sensor. A precise sensor produces data that is mostly free from unsystematic error or noise. Sensor accuracy (i.e., trueness; akin to psychometric validity) refers to the degree to which a sensor is free from systematic error or sensor bias. For example, if a person takes exactly 100 steps at multiple occasions, a precise pedometer will show little variability in step count and the pedometer is accurate if the average indicated step count across occasions is close to 100. The performance of different sensors varies across different types of devices but also between individual devices of the same model (e.g., Chaffin et al., 2017; Kuhlmann et al., 2021; Stisen et al., 2015; Woo et al., 2020). Smartphone sensors are often poorly built and calibrated (e.g., Blunck et al., 2013; Grammenos et al., 2018; Stisen et al., 2015) because manufacturers want to reduce costs and because sensors only need to perform sufficiently well for their intended uses which do not include scientific behavioral assessment. Sensor accuracy may also change slowly over time (natural drift; e.g., Kuhlmann et al., 2021) or due to external forces, such as when the device is dropped (Stisen et al., 2015). Furthermore, environmental factors that can directly affect sensor performance may vary systematically across cultural regions. For example, motion sensor readings can be skewed in warmer climates (e.g., Kos et al., 2016) and GPS signals can be blocked by buildings or trees (e.g., Bastos & Hasegawa, 2013; Ma et al., 2020).

6.3.4 Bias from User Practices

People differ in how they use and handle their smartphones, and these individual differences in user practices are reflected in sensed data (Blunck et al., 2013). When typical user practices vary between cultures, observed cross-cultural differences (or similarities) in sensed behaviors must be interpreted with care. As far as we know, there is not a single cross-cultural investigation into different user practices, let alone a study of their implications for MSMs. Still, there is every reason to believe that cross-cultural differences exist. User practices encompass all smartphone-related behaviors that are not device-mediated activities (e.g., app usage) or communication behaviors (e.g., calling or texting). These include, for example, how often and in which contexts people have their smartphones on them, how they carry their phones, how frequently they recharge them, or whether they let other people use their phones. Needless to say, sensors can only capture behaviors that are enacted while the sensing device is on or near a person. For example, if a person leaves their phone at home when they go for a walk in the park or if it runs out of battery, it cannot count any steps. Another person who never leaves the house without their phone and never lets it run out of battery might get a higher step count, even if they have actually taken fewer steps. Furthermore, both the precision (i.e., reliability) and accuracy (i.e., validity) of the step count may not only depend on the performance of the sensors (see Section 6.3.3) but also on how the device is carried. For example, pedometers tend to be most accurate when the phone is carried in a pants pocket (e.g., Åkerberg et al., 2012; Leong & Wong, 2016), so if the phone is carried in a handbag or in the chest pocket of a jacket, the step count may be off. Across cultures, how people typically carry their phones may depend on what is in fashion (e.g., whether current devices fit into pockets on current pants), what smartphones are typically used for (e.g., whether people need their phones close at hand because they use it to pay for the subway), and others' behavior (e.g., whether phones are frequently stolen). Sensing data is also influenced by how people customize their phone settings and how they use different functions, including the functions of a sensing app used for research. For example, some people may routinely disable certain features (e.g., Bluetooth, GPS, or WiFi) or pause sensing in the app to save data and battery power (Blunck et al., 2013). Further, they might be more likely to do so when they live in regions where opportunities for charging or public WiFi hotspots are rare. Cross-cultural differences in user practices can systematically affect (a) how continuously behavioral data can be collected per person and (b) in which contexts or situations data is collected, (c) how noisy (i.e., imprecise/unreliable) the data is, and (d) how accurately (i.e., validly) behavior can be captured.

6.3.5   Bias from Environmental Factors

Environmental factors are any external factors (e.g., physical, political, legal, economic, or sociocultural) that may, directly or indirectly, affect the data collected via MSMs. In the previous sections, we have already discussed potential effects of environmental variables on people's behavior, including nonmediated and device-mediated behaviors that may be target variables or indicators in MSM-based assessment (see Section 6.3.1) as well as user practices that impact the amount and quality of recorded data (see Section 6.3.4). We have also pointed out that environmental factors can compromise sensor performance (see Section 6.3.3). Furthermore, sensors may directly record the environment, and it can be difficult to separate behavioral variance from environmental variance during feature extraction. For example, if we want to infer conversation behavior from microphone sensors, living in crowded and noisy areas can lead to an overestimation of social interactions. Beyond affecting externalization, sensing, and feature computation (see Section 6.2 and Figure 6.2), environmental variables also set the framework under which a sensing study can be conducted. For example, legal aspects dictate how data can be collected, processed, stored, and analyzed. The European Union's General Data Protection Regulation represents one of the world's strictest and most comprehensive data protection laws treating personal information protection and privacy as fundamental rights. In contrast, US data privacy laws are limited by the right to freedom of speech following a minimalistic approach. China's legal framework can be located somewhere between the EU and the USA's stance on data protection but also establishes some specificities, such as the principle of cyber-sovereignty (i.e., application of state sovereignty to cyberspace; for a detailed comparison, see Pernot-Leplay, 2020). National differences in data protection and privacy laws systematically affect the data collection process and the data itself (e.g., What type of data can be collected? How and where should data be stored?). Stricter data protection laws ensure participants' privacy, but they also make it more difficult to collect psychologically rich data containing information about why and how people show specific behaviors. For example, the content of a person's text conversations contains more psychologically meaningful information than the metadata text logs alone. Another environmental factor affecting smartphone sensing studies is mobile network coverage which can differ widely between countries (Delaporte et al., 2021). Poor network coverage can affect data quality and may result in a higher proportion of excluded data or invalid behavioral inferences.

6.4 Bias Mitigation Strategies for Mobile Sensing Research

In the previous section, we outlined possible biases in mobile sensing research and their sources (see also Table 6.2 for an overview). When data is not collected under strictly controlled laboratory conditions, but instead in people's everyday lives, it is nearly impossible to control for all potential error sources. However, there may be ways to prevent, minimize, or

---

Study planning
○ Ensure construct equivalence by defining target constructs explicitly
○ Formulate hypotheses about potential cross-cultural differences in nomological networks
○ Ensure sufficient knowledge about target constructs as well as cultural and environmental factors that might affect their manifestations (e.g., with the help of informants)
○ Operationalize constructs to be comparable across cultures (e.g., with the help of pilot studies, decentering, and convergence)
○ Define a target population that exists in each culture and is comparable across cultures
○ Capture relevant individual and demographic variables and statistically investigate differences across cultures

Study implementation
○ Ensure inclusive recruiting of representative samples via culture-specific recruiting strategies and incentives (e.g., developed with the help of informants)
○ Properly translate and adapt study information and instructions
○ Train investigators and research assistants in intercultural communication
○ Aim for consistent user practices across cultures by providing clear instructions and incentives
○ Capture and statistically control for individual differences in user practices
○ Use standardized or calibrated devices if possible, or limit functionality and sensing to what the most restrictive platforms and devices allow

---

Figure 6.3   Possible bias mitigation strategies during the planning and implementation of a cross-cultural mobile sensing study

measure and statistically account for the influence of nuisance factors. In this section, we propose mitigation strategies that could be applied to reduce biases and promote fair and methodologically sound approaches to cross-cultural mobile sensing research (see Figure 6.3 for an overview). We go through the broad stages of a generic mobile sensing study and point out mitigation strategies to consider at each stage. The strategies presented here are not exhaustive and may not be applicable to every research endeavor. Furthermore, individual projects might afford completely different approaches tailored to their specific research questions, target variables, samples, or methods.

In the planning stage, the research question is formulated, and a study is designed to address this question. First, researchers need to define the target quantity and target population and think about how each can be empirically approximated in each culture (Deffner et al., 2021; Lundberg et al., 2021).[4] To ensure construct equivalence, psychological constructs

---

[4] In an optimal scenario, researchers would be able to a priori formulate a formalized generative causal modeling framework to determine what inferences can be drawn concerning generalizability (Deffner et al., 2021). However, given the complexity of models and the great number of

should be explicitly defined, and testable statements should be formulated about potential cross-cultural differences in nomological networks (van de Vijver & Tanzer, 2004). This requires a sufficient knowledge of not only the construct itself but also cultural and environmental factors that might affect associated behavioral manifestations. For formative behavioral constructs (e.g., exercising), equivalence can be accomplished by carefully considering which behaviors may constitute the construct in each culture. Informants can provide expertise in local culture and regional distinctions (He & van de Vijver, 2012; van de Vijver & Tanzer, 2004). Next, researchers should consider how constructs can be operationalized to be comparable across cultures. This could be partially accomplished by deductive, rational reasoning but is best empirically investigated through pilot studies. There are two general approaches to the empirical development of cross-culturally comparable instruments: (a) simultaneous development in multiple cultures to find common indicators (i.e., decentering); or (b) independent development within cultures and subsequent administration of all instruments in all cultures (i.e., convergence; He & van de Vijver, 2012). In mobile sensing, decentering could mean collecting data from several cultures and identifying features that can be computed and constitute ecologically valid indicators of the target construct in every culture. Convergence might involve independently identifying and assessing construct-relevant behaviors using MSMs tailored to each culture, possibly using different sensor types and computing different features. In subsequent cross-cultural studies, all of these culture-specific MSMs would then be used together. The convergence approach is considerably more arduous but allows for the examination of both universal and culture-specific aspects. However, it might not be possible to collect the same type of data in each culture, for example, due to heterogeneities in the sensing capabilities of devices (see Section 6.3.3) or local data protection laws (see Section 6.3.5). Pilot studies should also include convergent measures of the target construct (e.g., questionnaires for which measurement invariance has already been demonstrated) as well as behavioral self-reports or observer reports. If behavioral ratings show differential associations with the target construct, they can be excluded from further investigations to avoid measurement bias (Tay et al., 2021). Lastly, researchers should clearly define a target population that exists in each culture and is

---

variables in mobile sensing studies as well as a presumably greater focus on description and prediction (rather than explanation; see Harari, Vaid, et al., 2020, and Yarkoni & Westfall, 2017 for a detailed distinction), such an approach would not be feasible.

comparable across cultures. Depending on whether researchers are mostly interested in cross-cultural similarities or differences, a diverse or homogenous subpopulation should be targeted (Boehnke et al., 2011; He & van de Vijver, 2012). In smartphone sensing studies, researchers need to ensure that the target population is sufficiently represented among smartphone users in each culture and that smartphone ownership is not correlated with any variables (e.g., income) that may compromise sample comparability. If this is not the case, researchers may be forced to (a) define a narrower target population, which would reduce the within-culture generalizability of the findings, (b) exclude cultural groups in which the target population cannot be representatively sampled, or (c) attempt to statistically account for all potential covariates. In any case, researchers should ensure that relevant demographic variables and other theoretically relevant individual differences are assessed. Even when these variables are not intended to be included in the main analyses, they can be used to examine the comparability of cultural samples or to perform robustness checks. Furthermore, to mitigate possible biases from device-type demographics, researchers should determine the devices and operating systems typically used by the target population in each culture and create or select an inclusive sensing app, keeping in mind that "the range of supported devices should be as wide as possible, and at least reflect the targeted user groups in a representative manner" (Blunck et al., 2013, p. 1091).

The next stage concerns the implementation of the study, including the sampling and data collection processes. Participants are ideally selected from each culture such that the sample is representative of the predefined target population. Since sampling from the target population completely at random is rarely possible, researchers should attempt to make their recruitment efforts as inclusive as possible. Reaching certain demographics may require culture-specific recruiting strategies and incentives. For example, German senior citizens could be contacted via senior centers and nursing homes, whereas in China, it might be more effective to contact younger family members since intergenerational cohabitation is common. Local informants or collaborators can provide valuable information about how the target populations can be best approached. In addition, they can assist with properly translating and adapting study information and instructions. Researchers should ensure that participants are trained on each function and setting, are provided with examples and exercises where needed, and are encouraged to ask questions to assure that they fully understand the instructions. Investigators or research assistants who are in direct contact with participants should abide by standardized protocols and should optimally be trained in intercultural communication. To reduce biases from user practices, participants should also be clearly instructed on how to use the device during the data collection period (charging their phone regularly, always carrying it with them, etc.). If compliance with instruction is measurable, it can be explicitly incentivized. User practices cannot be fully standardized across cultural samples (e.g., participants cannot be obliged to carry their phones in their pockets). However, in some cases, it may be possible to assess individual differences in such practices through self-reports or estimates from sensor data for inclusion as categorical variables in analyses (e.g., in robustness checks). Biases from device properties can be mitigated by limiting functionality and sensing to what the more restrictive platforms and the less capable devices allow (Blunck et al., 2013). Researchers can also try to assess the performance of relevant sensors (for a validation approach, see Kayhan et al., 2018) or use archival data to account for differences between devices (Kos et al., 2016). Optimally, participants receive devices with identical, calibrated sensors, or the sensors embedded in their own devices can be auto-calibrated in the field (e.g., Altini et al., 2014; Sailhan et al., 2017). Lastly, because sensing software is rarely fully developed before data collection, researchers should expect that different software versions are needed to accommodate new requirements (to refine data collection, make use of previously unused sensors, etc.) or to debug. It is important to note that any software changes should be meticulously documented. Datasets from different versions can still be merged and used if they are adjusted accordingly based on documented changes (Blunck et al., 2013).

In the final, data-analytical stage, features are computed from raw sensor data and used for further analyses. As we have focused explicitly on biases that can occur at earlier stages and would already exist in raw sensor data, we will not go into significant detail here. Instead, we refer the reader to the relevant literature. Tay et al. (2021) proposed examining feature computing bias by correlating behavioral features from sensor data with behavioral observer rating. Differential associations between observer-rated behaviors and extracted features between cultures would indicate bias, and affected features should be excluded from further analyses. However, it should be kept in mind that observer rating can also harbor different biases and should be, thus, interpreted with caution.

The appropriate data-analytical approach depends on the study goal; conventional statistical approaches should be chosen to describe the data and make statistical inferences, while ML might be better suited to maximize prediction (Breiman, 2001; Yarkoni & Westfall, 2017). When features computed from sensing data are treated as test items and analyzed with traditional descriptive and inferential statistical approaches, a wide range of modeling techniques are available to examine measurement invariance (differential item functioning analysis to detect item bias, multi-group CFAs, modeling subject and context variables, etc.; van de Vijver & Tanzer, 2004). We refer the reader to the rich literature on measurement invariance testing (for overviews on the topic see, e.g., Tay et al., 2015; Teresi, 2006; van de Vijver & Leung, 2021). However, traditional statistical methods may often not be suitable for mobile sensing data, for example, when there are large numbers of features but relatively few observations (i.e., participants; Orrù et al., 2020). For mitigation strategies concerning measurement bias in ML-based assessment, we refer the reader to Tay et al. (2021).

Lastly, from a meta-scientific perspective, it is important that researchers explicitly specify and report their targeted populations, contexts, and behavioral variables and indicate the degree of representativeness of their tested samples, situations (or situational variables), and behaviors (see "Constraints on Generalizability" statements; Simons et al., 2017). This practice would facilitate cumulative science, enabling other researchers to conduct direct replications and more targeted investigations of boundary conditions (Simons et al., 2017). From a cumulative science perspective, it would also be beneficial if mobile sensing researchers from computer science adopt some psychological reporting standards regarding, for example, sample description, materials, and descriptive statistics (e.g., Müller et al., in press provided a checklist of methodological information to report for GPS research).

6.4.1   Limitations of Bias Mitigation Strategies

The proposed mitigation strategies can minimize biases in cross-cultural mobile sensing research. However, in many cases, they might be challenging to implement. As mentioned before, biases in mobile sensing research can have cascading effects. This implies that biases must be circumvented or accounted for at each iterative stage of the research process to avoid their subsequent propagation. We recognize that this is time-consuming, labor-intensive, and cumbersome, and often not feasible. We also realize that many mobile sensing studies are not designed from scratch but use existing data. These studies need to work with the data they have but should be aware of, and also openly discuss, possible data heterogeneities and biases. Furthermore, mitigating biases often involves excluding participants (e.g., in distribution-based sample matching), measurement intervals, behavioral cues, or extracted features. While sequential exclusion may enhance comparability, there is a trade-off with validity. Specifically, limiting the representativeness of the sample and measurement contexts poses a threat to external validity. Excluding behavioral cues or computed features might lead to poor target construct coverage, affecting both content and construct validity.

One potential avenue to circumvent the issue of equivalence is to abandon its necessity in the first place. To do this, we need to refocus the aim of our research to generalize within cultures instead of between cultures. As such, nested analyses (such as multilevel models) can allow for teasing apart the effects and relationships that only hold within a specific culture compared to those that generalize across the cultures included in the model.

6.5 Conclusion

Mobile sensing can be used to assess people's real-life behaviors objectively, unobtrusively, and with high temporal resolutions. It might be especially suited for cross-cultural research since it does not use verbal items that need to be adapted into different languages – and inappropriate instrument translation or insufficient adaptation to different cultural contexts are the roots of many biases that can jeopardize cross-cultural comparisons. Furthermore, as smartphone ownership continues to increase worldwide, smartphone sensing research might be able to sample subpopulations that would not typically participate in psychological research, thus promoting more diverse and inclusive research. However, to date, only very few cross-cultural mobile sensing studies have been conducted, and multicountry studies often fail to acknowledge or examine possible cross-cultural differences. In this chapter, we illustrated different biases that can occur when conducting cross-cultural mobile sensing studies and proposed mitigation strategies to minimize these biases. We believe that more and especially rigorous comparative research is needed to establish and refine MSMs for cross-cultural psychology. Therefore, we encourage cross-cultural researchers to make use of mobile sensing approaches, which may prove to be an invaluable addition to their methodological toolkit.

REFERENCES

Ai, P., Liu, Y., & Zhao, X. (2019). Big Five personality traits predict daily spatial behavior: Evidence from smartphone data. *Personality and Individual Differences, 147,* 285–291. https://doi.org/10.1016/j.paid.2019.04.027

Åkerberg, A., Lindén, M., & Folke, M. (2012). How accurate are pedometer cell phone applications? *Procedia Technology, 5,* 787–792. https://doi.org/10.1016/j.protcy.2012.09.087

Altini, M., Vullers, R., Van Hoof, C., van Dort, M., & Amft, O. (2014, March). Self-calibration of walking speed estimations using smartphone sensors. In *2014 IEEE International Conference on Pervasive Computing and Communication Workshops (PERCOM WORKSHOPS)* (pp. 10–18). IEEE. https://doi.org/10.1109/PerComW.2014.6815158

Bai, Y., Xu, B., Ma, Y., Sun, G., & Zhao, Y. (2012). Will you have a good sleep tonight? Sleep quality prediction with mobile phone. In I. Balasingham (Ed.), *Proceedings of the 7th International Conference on Body Area Networks* (pp. 124–130). Institute for Computer Sciences, Social-Informatics and Telecommunications Engineering. https://doi.org/10.4108/icst.bodynets.2012.250091

Bastos, A. S., & Hasegawa, H. (2013). Behavior of GPS signal interruption probability under tree canopies in different forest conditions. *European Journal of Remote Sensing, 46*(1), 613–622. https://doi.org/10.5721/eujrs20134636

Bauer, D. J. (2017). A more general model for testing measurement invariance and differential item functioning. *Psychological Methods, 22*(3), 507–526. https://doi.org/10.1037/met0000077

Blunck, H., Bouvin, N. O., Franke, T., Grønbæk, K., Kjaergaard, M. B., Lukowicz, P., & Wüstenberg, M. (2013). On heterogeneity in mobile sensing applications aiming at representative data collection. In F. Mattern (Ed.), *Proceedings of the 2013 ACM Conference on Pervasive and Ubiquitous Computing Adjunct Publication* (pp. 1087–1098). Association for Computing Machinery. https://doi.org/10.1145/2494091.2499576

Boehnke, K., Lietz, P., Schreier, M., & Wilhelm, A. (2011). Sampling: The selection of cases for culturally comparative psychological research. In D. Matsumoto & F. J. R. van de Vijver (Eds.), *Cross-cultural research methods in psychology* (pp. 101–129). Cambridge University Press.

Borsboom, D. (2006). When does measurement invariance matter? *Medical Care, 44*(11), S176–S181. https://doi.org/10.1097/01.mlr.0000245143.08679.cc

Borsboom, D., Romeijn, J. W., & Wicherts, J. M. (2008). Measurement invariance versus selection invariance: Is fair selection possible? *Psychological Methods, 13*(2), 75–98. https://doi.org/10.1037/1082-989X.13.2.75

Breiman, L. (2001). Statistical modeling: The two cultures (with comments and a rejoinder by the author). *Statistical Science, 16*(3), 199–231. https://doi.org/10.1214/ss/1009213726

Brunswik, E. (1956). *Perception and the representative design of psychological experiments* (2nd ed.). University of California Press.

Chaffin, D., Heidl, R., Hollenbeck, J. R., Howe, M., Yu, A., Voorhees, C., & Calantone, R. (2017). The promise and perils of wearable sensors in organizational research. *Organizational Research Methods, 20*(1), 3–31. https://doi.org/10.1177/1094428115617004

Cornet, V. P., & Holden, R. J. (2018). Systematic review of smartphone-based passive sensing for health and wellbeing. *Journal of Biomedical Informatics, 77*, 120–132. https://doi.org/10.1016/j.jbi.2017.12.008

Counterpoint. (2021, September 13). *Top 5 smartphone model share for 8 countries.* https://www.counterpointresearch.com/top-5-smartphone-model-share-8-countries/

de Vries, L. P., Baselmans, B. M., & Bartels, M. (2021). Smartphone-based ecological momentary assessment of well-being: A systematic review and recommendations for future studies. *Journal of Happiness Studies, 22*(5), 2361–2408. https://doi.org/10.1007/s10902-020-00324-7

Deffner, D., Rohrer, J. M., & McElreath, R. (2021). *A causal framework for cross-cultural generalizability.* PsyArXiv. https://doi.org/10.31234/osf.io/fqukp

Delaporte, A., Bahia, K., Carboni, I., Cruz, G., Jeffrie, N., Sibthorpe, C., Suardi, S., & Groenestege, M. T. (2021). *The state of mobile internet connectivity 2021.* GSM Association. https://www.gsma.com/r/wp-content/uploads/2021/09/The-State-of-Mobile-Internet-Connectivity-Report-2021.pdf

Götz, F. M., Stieger, S., & Reips, U. D. (2017). Users of the main smartphone operating systems (iOS, Android) differ only little in personality. *PLoS ONE, 12*(5), e0176921. https://doi.org/10.1371/journal.pone.0176921

Grammenos, A., Mascolo, C., & Crowcroft, J. (2018). You are sensing, but are you biased? *Proceedings of the ACM on Interactive, Mobile, Wearable and Ubiquitous Technologies, 2*(1), 1–26. https://doi.org/10.1145/3191743

Harari, G. M., Gosling, S. D., Wang, R., Chen, F., Chen, Z., & Campbell, A. T. (2017). Patterns of behavior change in students over an academic term: A preliminary study of activity and sociability behaviors using smartphone sensing methods. *Computers in Human Behavior, 67*, 129–138. https://doi.org/10.1016/j.chb.2016.10.027

Harari, G. M., Lane, N. D., Wang, R., Crosier, B. S., Campbell, A. T., & Gosling, S. D. (2016). Using smartphones to collect behavioral data in psychological science. *Perspectives on Psychological Science, 11*(6), 838–854. https://doi.org/10.1177/1745691616650285

Harari, G. M., Müller, S. R., Aung, M. S. H., & Rentfrow, P. J. (2017). Smartphone sensing methods for studying behavior in everyday life. *Current Opinion in Behavioral Sciences, 18*, 83–90. https://doi.org/10.1016/j.cobeha.2017.07.018

Harari, G. M., Müller, S. R., & Gosling, S. D. (2020). Naturalistic assessment of situations using mobile sensing methods. In J. F. Rauthmann, R. A. Sherman, & D. C. Funder (Eds.), *The Oxford handbook of psychological situations* (pp. 299–311). Oxford University Press.

Harari, G. M., Müller, S. R., Stachl, C., Wang, R., Wang, W., Bühner, M., Rentfrow, P. J., Campbell, A. T., & Gosling, S. D. (2020). Sensing sociability: Individual differences in young adults' conversation, calling, texting, and app use behaviors in daily life. *Journal of Personality and Social Psychology*, *119*(1), 204–228. https://doi.org/10.1037/pspp0000245

Harari, G. M., Stachl, C., Müller, S. R., & Gosling, S. D. (2021). Mobile sensing for studying personality dynamics in daily life. In J. F. Rauthmann (Ed.), *The handbook of personality dynamics and processes* (pp. 763–790). Academic Press. https://doi.org/10.1016/B978-0-12-813995-0.00029-7

Harari, G. M., Vaid, S. S., Müller, S. R., Stachl, C., Marrero, Z., Schoedel, R., Bühner, M., & Gosling, S. D. (2020). Personality sensing for theory development and assessment in the digital age. *European Journal of Personality*, *34*(5), 649–669. https://doi.org/10.1002/per.2273

He, J., & van de Vijver, F. (2012). Bias and equivalence in cross-cultural research. *Online Readings in Psychology and Culture*, *2*(2), 1–19. https://doi.org/10.9707/2307-0919.1111

Henrich, J., Heine, S. J., & Norenzayan, A. (2010a). Beyond weird: Towards a broad-based behavioral science. *Behavioral and Brain Sciences*, *33*(2–3), 111–135. https://doi.org/10.1017/s0140525x10000725

(2010b). The weirdest people in the world? *Behavioral and Brain Sciences*, *33*(2–3), 61–83. https://doi.org/10.1017/S0140525X0999152X

Horstmann, K. T., & Ziegler, M. (2020). Assessing personality states: What to consider when constructing personality state measures. *European Journal of Personality*, *34*(6), 1037–1059. https://doi.org/10.1002/per.2266

John, O. P., & Robins, R. W. (1993). Determinants of interjudge agreement on personality traits: The Big Five domains, observability, evaluativeness, and the unique perspective of the self. *Journal of Personality*, *61*(4), 521–551. https://doi.org/10.1111/j.1467-6494.1993.tb00781.x

Kayhan, V. O., Chen, Z., French, K. A., Allen, T. D., Salomon, K., & Watkins, A. (2018). How honest are the signals? A protocol for validating wearable sensors. *Behavior Research Methods*, *50*(1), 57–83. https://doi.org/10.3758/s13428-017-1005-4

Khan, W. Z., Xiang, Y., Aalsalem, M. Y., & Arshad, Q. (2013). Mobile phone sensing systems: A survey. *IEEE Communications Surveys & Tutorials*, *15*(1), 402–427. https://doi.org/10.1109/SURV.2012.031412.00077

Khwaja, M., Vaid, S. S., Zannone, S., Harari, G. M., Faisal, A. A., & Matic, A. (2019). Modeling personality vs. modeling personalidad: In-the-wild mobile data analysis in five countries suggests cultural impact on personality models. *Proceedings of the ACM on Interactive, Mobile, Wearable and Ubiquitous Technologies*, *3*(3), 1–24. https://doi.org/10.1145/3351246

Killingsworth, M. A., & Gilbert, D. T. (2010). A wandering mind is an unhappy mind. *Science*, *330*(6006), 932–932. https://doi.org/10.1126/science.1192439

Kos, A., Tomažič, S., & Umek, A. (2016). Evaluation of smartphone inertial sensor performance for cross-platform mobile applications. *Sensors*, *16*(4), 1–15. https://doi.org/10.3390/s16040477

Krendl, A. C., & Pescosolido, B. A. (2020). Countries and cultural differences in the stigma of mental illness: The East–West divide. *Journal of Cross-Cultural Psychology*, *51*(2), 149–167. https://doi.org/10.1177/0022022119901297

Kuhlmann, T., Garaizar, P., & Reips, U.-D. (2021). Smartphone sensor accuracy varies from device to device in mobile research: The case of spatial orientation. *Behavior Research Methods*, *53*(1), 22–33. https://doi.org/10.3758/s13428-020-01404-5

Lane, N. D., Mohammod, M., Lin, M., Yang, X., Lu, H., Ali, S., ... & Campbell, A. (2011, May). Bewell: A smartphone application to monitor, model and promote wellbeing. In *5th International ICST Conference on Pervasive Computing Technologies for Healthcare* (pp. 23–26).

Lantz, B. (2019). *Machine learning with R: Expert techniques for predictive modeling* (3rd ed.). Packt Publishing.

Lee, H., Ahn, H., Choi, S., & Choi, W. (2014). The SAMS: Smartphone addiction management system and verification. *Journal of Medical Systems*, *38*(1), 1–10. https://doi.org/10.1007/s10916-013-0001-1

Leong, J. Y., & Wong, J. E. (2016). Accuracy of three Android-based pedometer applications in laboratory and free-living settings. *Journal of Sports Sciences*, *35*(1), 14–21. https://doi.org/10.1080/02640414.2016.1154592

Lundberg, I., Johnson, R., & Stewart, B. M. (2021). What is your estimand? Defining the target quantity connects statistical evidence to theory. *American Sociological Review*, *86*(3), 532–565. https://doi.org/10.1177/00031224211004187

Ma, L., Zhang, C., Wang, Y., Peng, G., Chen, C., Zhao, J., & Wang, J. (2020). Estimating urban road GPS environment friendliness with bus trajectories: A city-scale approach. *Sensors*, *20*(6), 1580. https://doi.org/10.3390/s20061580

Ma, Y., Xu, B., Bai, Y., Sun, G., & Zhu, R. (2012). Daily mood assessment based on mobile phone sensing. In G.-Z. Yang (Ed.), *2012 Ninth International Conference on Wearable and Implantable Body Sensor Networks* (pp. 142–147). Institute of Electrical and Electronics Engineers. https://doi.org/10.1109/bsn.2012.3

Meredith, W. (1993). Measurement invariance, factor analysis and factorial invariance. *Psychometrika*, *58*(4), 525–543. https://doi.org/10.1007/BF02294825

Mohr, D. C., Zhang, M., & Schueller, S. M. (2017). Personal sensing: Understanding mental health using ubiquitous sensors and machine learning. *Annual Review of Clinical Psychology*, *13*(1), 23–47. https://doi.org/10.1146/annurev-clinpsy-032816-044949

Müller, S. R., Bayer, J. B., Ross, M. Q., Mount, J., Stachl, C., Harari, G. M., Chang, Y.-J., & Le, H. T. K. (2022). Analyzing GPS Data for Psychological Research: A Tutorial. *Advances in Methods and Practices in Psychological Science*, *5*(2). https://doi.org/10.1177/25152459221082680

Müller, S. R., Chen, X. L., Peters, H., Chaintreau, A., & Matz, S. C. (2021). Depression predictions from GPS-based mobility do not generalize well to large demographically heterogeneous samples. *Scientific Reports, 11*, 1–10. https://doi.org/10.1038/s41598-021-93087-x

Müller, S. R., Peters, H., Matz, S. C., Wang, W., & Harari, G. M. (2020). Investigating the relationships between mobility behaviours and indicators of subjective well-being using smartphone-based experience sampling and GPS tracking. *European Journal of Personality, 34*(5), 714–732. https://doi.org/10.1002%2Fper.2262

Oort, F. J., Visser, M. R., & Sprangers, M. A. (2009). Formal definitions of measurement bias and explanation bias clarify measurement and conceptual perspectives on response shift. *Journal of Clinical Epidemiology, 62*(11), 1126–1137. https://doi.org/10.1016/j.jclinepi.2009.03.013

Orrù, G., Monaro, M., Conversano, C., Gemignani, A., & Sartori, G. (2020). Machine learning in psychometrics and psychological research. *Frontiers in Psychology, 10*, 1–10. https://doi.org/10.3389/fpsyg.2019.02970

Pernot-Leplay, E. (2020). China's approach on data privacy law: A third way between the US and the EU? *Penn State Journal of Law & International Affairs, 8*(1), 49–117. https://elibrary.law.psu.edu/jlia/vol8/iss1/6

Phan, L. V., & Rauthmann, J. F. (2021). Personality computing: New frontiers in personality assessment. *Social and Personality Psychology Compass, 15*(7), 1–17. https://doi.org/10.1111/spc3.12624

Putnick, D. L., & Bornstein, M. H. (2016). Measurement invariance conventions and reporting: The state of the art and future directions for psychological research. *Developmental Review, 41*, 71–90. https://doi.org/10.1016/j.dr.2016.06.004

Rabbi, M., Ali, S., Choudhury, T., & Berke, E. (2011, September 17–21). Passive and in-situ assessment of mental and physical well-being using mobile sensors. In J. Landay & Y. Shi (Chairs), *How healthy?* [Symposium]. Proceedings of the 13th International Conference on Ubiquitous Computing, Beijing, China. https://doi.org/10.1145/2030112.2030164

Rad, M. S., Martingano, A. J., & Ginges, J. (2018). Toward a psychology of homo sapiens: Making psychological science more representative of the human population. *Proceedings of the National Academy of Sciences, 115*(45), 11401–11405. https://doi.org/10.1073/pnas.1721165115

Ram, N., Conroy, D. E., Pincus, A. L., Lorek, A., Rebar, A., Roche, M. J., Coccia, M., Morack, J., Feldman, J., & Gerstorf, D. (2014). Examining the interplay of processes across multiple time-scales: Illustration with the intraindividual study of affect, health, and interpersonal behavior (iSAHIB). *Research in Human Development, 11*(2), 142–160. https://doi.org/10.1080/15427609.2014.906739

Rauthmann, J. F. (2016). Motivational factors in the perception of psychological situation characteristics. *Social and Personality Psychology Compass, 10*(2), 92–108. https://doi.org/10.1111/spc3.12239

(2021). Capturing interactions, correlations, fits, and transactions: A person-environment relations model. In J. F. Rauthmann (Ed.), *The handbook of personality dynamics and processes* (pp. 427–522). Academic Press. https://doi .org/10.1016/b978-0-12-813995-0.00018-2

R Core Team. (2021). *R: A language and environment for statistical computing.* R Foundation for Statistical Computing. https://www.R-project.org/

Sailhan, F., Issarny, V., & Tavares-Nascimiento, O. (2017, October). Opportunistic multiparty calibration for robust participatory sensing. In *2017 IEEE 14th International Conference on Mobile Ad Hoc and Sensor Systems (MASS)* (pp. 435–443). IEEE. https://doi.org/10.1109/MASS.2017.56

Sanchez, W., Martinez, A., Campos, W., Estrada, H., & Pelechano, V. (2015). Inferring loneliness levels in older adults from smartphones. *Journal of Ambient Intelligence and Smart Environments, 7*(1), 85–98. https://doi.org/ 10.3233/ais-140297

Sandstrom, G. M., Lathia, N., Mascolo, C., & Rentfrow, P. J. (2017). Putting mood in context: Using smartphones to examine how people feel in different locations. *Journal of Research in Personality, 69,* 96–101. https://doi.org/10 .1016/j.jrp.2016.06.004

Schoedel, R., Pargent, F., Au, Q., Völkel, S. T., Schuwerk, T., Bühner, M., & Stachl, C. (2020). To challenge the morning lark and the night owl: Using smartphone sensing data to investigate day–night behaviour patterns. *European Journal of Personality, 34*(5), 733–752. https://doi.org/10.1002/ per.2258

Silver, L. (2019, February 5). *Smartphone ownership is growing rapidly around the world, but not always equally.* Pew Research Center. https://www .pewresearch.org/global/2019/02/05/smartphone-ownership-is-growing-rap idly-around-the-world-but-not-always-equally/

Simons, D. J., Shoda, Y., & Lindsay, D. S. (2017). Constraints on Generality (COG): A proposed addition to all empirical papers. *Perspectives on Psychological Science, 12*(6), 1123–1128. https://doi.org/10.1177/ 1745691617708630

Stachl, C., Au, Q., Schoedel, R., Gosling, S. D., Harari, G. M., Buschek, D., Völkel, S. T., Schuwerk, T., Oldemeier, M., Ullmann, T., Hussmann, H., Bischl, B., & Bühner, M. (2020). Predicting personality from patterns of behavior collected with smartphones. *Proceedings of the National Academy of Sciences of the United States of America, 117*(30), 17680–17687. https://doi .org/10.1073/pnas.1920484117

Stachl, C., Pargent, F., Hilbert, S., Harari, G. M., Schoedel, R., Vaid, S., Gosling, S. D., & Bühner, M. (2020). Personality research and assessment in the era of machine learning. *European Journal of Personality, 34*(5), 613–631. https://doi.org/10.1002/per.2257

Statista. (2020, August 20). *Number of smartphone users from 2016 to 2021.* https:// www.statista.com/statistics/330695/number-of-smartphone-users-worldwide/

Stieger, S., Götz, F. M., & Gehrig, F. (2015). Soccer results affect subjective well-being, but only briefly: A smartphone study during the 2014 FIFA World Cup. *Frontiers in Psychology, 6.* https://doi.org/10.3389/fpsyg.2015.00497

Stisen, A., Blunck, H., Bhattacharya, S., Prentow, T. S., Kjærgaard, M. B., Dey, A., Sonne, T., & Jensen, M. M. (2015). Smart devices are different: Assessing and mitigating mobile sensing heterogeneities for activity recognition. In *Proceedings of the 13th ACM Conference on Embedded Networked Sensor Systems* (pp. 127–140). Association for Computing Machinery. https://doi.org/10.1145/2809695.2809718

Tay, L., Meade, A. W., & Cao, M. (2015). An overview and practical guide to IRT measurement equivalence analysis. *Organizational Research Methods*, *18*(1), 3–46. https://doi.org/10.1177/1094428114553062

Tay, L., Woo, S. E., Hickman, L., Booth, B. M., & D'Mello, S. (2021). *A conceptual framework for investigating and mitigating Machine Learning Measurement Bias (MLMB) in psychological assessment*. PsyArXiv. https://doi.org/10.31234/osf.io/mjph3

Tennekes, M. (2018). Tmap: Thematic maps in R. *Journal of Statistical Software*, *84*(6), 1–39. https://doi.org/10.18637/jss.v084.i06

Teresi, J. A. (2006). Overview of quantitative measurement methods: Equivalence, invariance, and differential item functioning in health applications. *Medical Care*, *44*(11), S39–S49. https://doi.org/10.1097/01.mlr .0000245452.48613.45

Vaid, S., & Harari, G. M. (2019). Smartphones in personal informatics: A framework for self-tracking research with mobile sensing. In H. Baumeister & C. Montag (Eds.), *Digital phenotyping and mobile sensing* (pp. 65–92). Springer. https://doi.org/10.1007/978-3-030-31620-4_5

van de Vijver, F., & Leung, K. (2021). *Methods and data analysis for cross-cultural research* (2nd ed.). Cambridge University Press.

van de Vijver, F., & Tanzer, N. K. (2004). Bias and equivalence in cross-cultural assessment: An overview. *European Review of Applied Psychology*, *54*(2), 119–135. https://doi.org/10.1016/j.erap.2003.12.004

Vinciarelli, A., & Mohammadi, G. (2014). A survey of personality computing. *IEEE Transactions on Affective Computing*, *5*(3), 273–291. https://doi.org/10 .1109/TAFFC.2014.2330816

von Stumm, S. (2018). Feeling low, thinking slow? Associations between situational cues, mood and cognitive function. *Cognition and Emotion*, *32*(8), 1545–1558. https://doi.org/10.1080/02699931.2017.1420632

Wahl, D. R., Villinger, K., König, L. M., Ziesemer, K., Schupp, H. T., & Renner, B. (2017). Healthy food choices are happy food choices: Evidence from a real life sample using smartphone based assessments. *Scientific Reports*, *7*(1), 17069. https://doi.org/10.1038/s41598-017-17262-9

Wang, R., Chen, F., Chen, Z., Li, T., Harari, G., Tignor, S., Zhou, X., Ben-Zeev, D., &. Campbell, A. T. (2014, September 13–17). StudentLife: Assessing mental health, academic performance and behavioral trends of college students using smartphones. In A. J. Brush (Ed.), *Proceedings of the 2014 ACM International Joint Conference on Pervasive and Ubiquitous Computing* (pp. 3–14). Association for Computing Machinery. https://doi .org/10.1145/2632048.2632054

Wang, W., Harari, G. M., Wang, R., Müller, S. R., Mirjafari, S., Masaba, K., & Campbell, A. T. (2018). Sensing behavioral change over time: Using within-person variability features from mobile sensing to predict personality traits. *Proceedings of the ACM on Interactive, Mobile, Wearable and Ubiquitous Technologies, 2*(3), 1–21. https://doi.org/10.1145/3264951

Wiernik, B. M., Ones, D. S., Marlin, B. M., Giordano, C., Dilchert, S., Mercado, B. K., Stanek, K. C., Birkland, A., Wang, Y., Ellis, B., Yazar, Y., Kostal, J. W., Kumar, S., Hnat, T., Ertin, E., Sano, A., Ganesan, D. K., Choudhoury, T., & Al'Absi, M. (2020). Using mobile sensors to study personality dynamics. *European Journal of Psychological Assessment, 36*(6), 1–13. https://doi.org/10.1027/1015-5759/a000576

Woo, S. E., Tay, L., Jebb, A. T., Ford, M. T., & Kern, M. L. (2020). Big data for enhancing measurement quality. In S. E. Woo, L. Tay, & R. W. Proctor (Eds.), *Big data in psychological research* (pp. 59–85). American Psychological Association. https://doi.org/10.1037/0000193-004

Yan, Z., & Chakraborty, D. (2014). *Semantics in mobile sensing.* Morgan & Claypool. https://doi.org/10.2200/S00577ED1V01Y201404WBE008

Yarkoni, T., & Westfall, J. (2017). Choosing prediction over explanation in psychology: Lessons from machine learning. *Perspectives on Psychological Science, 12*(6), 1100–1122. https://doi.org/10.1177/1745691617693393

Zhang, X., Li, W., Chen, X., & Lu, S. (2018). MoodExplorer: Towards compound emotion detection via smartphone sensing. *Proceedings of the ACM on Interactive, Mobile, Wearable and Ubiquitous Technologies, 1*(4), 1–30. https://doi.org/10.1145/3161414

PART III

Regional Focus

CHAPTER 7

Technology and Measurement in Asia

Q. Chelsea Song, Hyun Joo Shin, Nakul Upadhya, and Timothy Teo

The technology and measurement applications in Asia offer important and unique insights. Asia has the largest number of smartphone, internet, and digital assessment users (e.g., Johnson, 2021), and thus activities in Asia represent a substantial proportion of technology and measurement applications around the globe. Compared to the rest of the globe, technological measurement applications in Asia have forged a unique path, due to its distinctive research and development, regional restrictions, and cultural influences. Asia is also a very diverse place and applications in Asia exhibit regional differences. To better understand the forementioned characteristics, the current chapter reviews technology and measurement in Asia. Specifically, the first half of the chapter (Part 1) summarizes current applications and research in Asia, as well as related regulations and legal environments. The second half of the chapter (Part 2) compares the existing applications in Asia with the rest of the world, discusses factors influencing the applications in Asia, and highlights potential developmental areas for Asia.

PART 1. CURRENT TECHNOLOGICAL APPLICATIONS IN ASIA

7.1 Common Types of Technology and Measurement Applications in Asia

In Asia, common technologies used for psychological measurement include smartphones, wearable devices, social media, computerized adaptive testing, and game-based assessments. These technologies, as well as their key areas of application, are summarized in Table 7.1 and then discussed.

Table 7.1 *Types of technology used for measurement in Asia and corresponding constructs*

Technology	Construct	Example data	Example studies
Smartphones	- Stress - Depression - Knowledge	- Physiological signals - Mobile-application-based assessment	[Japan] Kido et al. (2016) [South Korea] Yang et al. (2017) [Taiwan] Hung et al. (2016) [Hong Kong] Zhang et al. (2012) [Iran] Yarahmadzehi and Goodarzi (2020)
Wearable devices	Stress	- Physiological signals	[Turkey] Can et al. (2019) [Japan] Ishio and Abe (2017)
Social media	- Subjective well-being - Knowledge	- Tweets - Blog posts - CAT assessment scores	[China] Qi et al. (2015) [China] Li et al. (2020) [Taiwan] Tseng (2016)
Computerized adaptive testing			[Taiwan] Lee et al. (2018)
Game-based assessment	- Knowledge & skills - Cognitive ability - Personality	- Game-based assessment scores - Interaction log-in simulation environments - Game-based assessment scores - Interaction log-in simulation environments	[Taiwan] Hou (2015) [Indonesia] Risnani and Adita (2018) [Taiwan] Shih et al. (2019) [Philippines] Dumdumaya and Rodrigo (2018) [Philippines] Dumdumaya et al. (2018) [Philippines] Palaoag et al. (2015)

7.1.1 Smartphones

Smartphones are ubiquitous, sensor-rich, and computationally powerful devices. They offer internet access, camera and microphone, and operating systems that support numerous digital applications. These features allow us to conduct mobile assessments, administer online surveys, and collect in-the-moment behaviors through texts, audios, and videos (e.g., Harari et al., 2016; Hung et al., 2016; Yang et al., 2017; Yarahmadzehi & Goodarzi, 2020).

Some noteworthy examples of smartphone use in Asia involve the measurement of stress and depression. Smartphones' hardwares offer new ways of measuring stress and depression. For example, researchers in Japan captured heart rate variability (HRV) data using smartphone cameras to measure users' mental stress levels (Kido et al., 2016). HRV is a key indicator of mental stress levels, which were traditionally measured using special devices with limited accessibility (e.g., electrocardiogram, photo-plethysmogram). Instead, the researchers used smartphone cameras – a widely accessible device – to capture blood vessel activities in the fingertip (that were pressed against the camera) and to measure HRV and stress. Compared to conventional methods, smartphones enabled readily available and momentary measurement of stress with a comparable level of accuracy. Similarly, South Korean scientists developed the smartphone diagnostic unit (SDU), a biosensor attachment to a smartphone, to measure the stress level of users in real time (Yang et al., 2017). The SDU detects stress-level biomarkers in saliva (e.g., cortisol and C-reactive protein) and analyzes them using a smartphone application. The smartphone-based stress measurement demonstrated similar accuracy as conventional methods (e.g., the ELISA kit). With its lightweight and low-cost features, it offers possibilities for more effective and scalable stress measurement management in the future.

In addition to the smartphone's hardware characteristic, its powerful software capabilities and internet connectivity is also key to stress and depression measurement and intervention. Researchers in Taiwan developed a smartphone application, iHope, to perform daily ecological momentary assessment (EMA) of depression, anxiety, and sleep that contributes to integrated depression management (Hung et al., 2016). In a validation study, the participants were asked to log their depression and anxiety twice a day, along with sleep and other stress-related information. This information was uploaded and analyzed in a cloud server in real time, providing momentary assessment and feedback to aid depression management. Given the limited mental health literacy and resources in Taiwan and many Asian societies, the smartphone-based EMA can be an important, accessible tool for depression screening and self-monitoring (Li et al., 2014). Furthermore, Hong Kong researchers used a combination of a smartphone application and pulsometer for continuous stress monitoring (Zhang et al., 2012). A smartphone application, "deStress," collects HRV from a wearable biosensor. When the application detects high stress levels, it provides the user with respiration-based biofeedback to alleviate the stress level, providing systematic stress monitoring and intervention. The combined application of smartphone and wearable sensors was able to effectively measure and alleviate stress instantaneously, contributing to reduced mental health risks.

Smartphones are also used to administer formative online assessments in classrooms, contributing to classroom learning. One such mobile assessment was used in Iran to provide learning feedback and help students improve their vocabulary attainment. Over 10 assessment-and-feedback cycles, the mobile assessment was found to promote a greater improvement in vocabulary attainment (an average 64.65-point increase in vocabulary assessment score) compared to the traditional paper-and-pencil assessment (an average 50.85-point increase in vocabulary assessment score; Yarahmadzehi & Goodarzi, 2020). Compared to the traditional paper-and-pencil assessments, formative mobile assessments were better equipped to tailor to the student's needs and more effectively facilitate learning.

7.1.2   Wearable Sensors

Wearable sensors, such as fitness trackers and smartwatches, are portable devices that are becoming more and more prevalent in our daily lives. They share similar advantages as smartphones; however, compared to smartphones, wearable sensors are especially capable of measuring physiological signals (e.g., heartbeat, blood pressure). Thus, in Asia, wearable sensors are commonly adopted to measure stress and other emotional states.

Researchers in Turkey developed an automatic stress detection system to measure stress using physiological signals (e.g., heart activities and skin conductance) captured by wearable devices (Can et al., 2019). The device classifies an individual's stress state into three levels (low, medium, high), and evaluation results showed that the device yielded a high average classification accuracy of 88%, comparable to the accuracy of traditional methods (e.g., electroencephalography). The application is compatible with various wearable sensors, such as Samsung Gear S and S2 and

Empatica E4 smartwatches, offering a flexible and real-time measure of stress that contributes to stress monitoring and management. Japanese researchers used a wristband-type wearable device to measure and monitor the affective well-being of elders in an aging and depopulating village (Ishio & Abe, 2017). The wearable device collected HRV data and assessed the users' physiological stress levels and affective states continuously throughout the day. The device helped identify several key sources of positive and negative affective well-being and enabled effective interventions to improve the affective well-being of the elderly villagers.

7.1.3 Social Media

Social media are online platforms where people can connect with one another and share emotions and thoughts (Boyd & Ellison, 2007). These platforms, which include Facebook, Twitter, Reddit, LinkedIn, and YouTube, have become an inseparable part of modern life, with billions of people in the Asia-Pacific region using at least one social media (Tankovska, 2021). Every day, social media generates myriad data that comes in various forms. These include texts, images, videos, network connections (e.g., followers and followers), and number of likes. Among them, text data is most used in Asia, especially to measure group-level subjective well-being and emotion.

A number of studies from China used text data from Weibo, a Chinese Twitter-like platform with about 500 million active daily users, to measure subjective well-being and emotion (e.g., Li et al., 2020; Qi et al., 2015). As an example, Weibo posts were used to explore the impacts of COVID-19 on mental health. The researchers collected Weibo posts one week before, and one week after the official declaration of COVID-19 and conducted sentiment analysis to measure emotion, sensitivity to social risks, and life satisfaction of the social media users. Findings suggested that, compared to before COVID-19 was declared, in the week after the declaration, the users' negative emotions and sensitivity to social risks increased, while positive emotions and life satisfaction decreased. Such social media-based measurement allows users to track real-time trends in public sentiments and study their antecedents and consequences.

7.1.4 Computerized Adaptive Testing

Computerized adaptive testing (CAT) is a computer-administered measurement tool designed to measure examinees' knowledge level. CAT administers test items based on the examinee's performance on prior items, enabling an adaptive, efficient, and accurate measure of knowledge levels (Chang, 2015; Chang et al., 2021). Around the globe, CAT has been widely used in language proficiency testing, such as the TOEFL, GRE, and GMAT tests (Rudner, 2010). In Asia, in addition to language proficiency, CAT is often used in education settings to assess and foster learning (Lee et al., 2018; Tseng, 2016).

Researchers in Taiwan used CAT to test English-as-foreign-language (EFL) high school students' vocabulary knowledge and compared the performance of CAT with traditional paper-and-pencil tests (Tseng, 2016). Compared to paper-and-pencil tests, CAT measured examinees' vocabulary knowledge with similar accuracy, but with about one-third of the test-taking time. CAT was shown to be an efficient and accurate alternative to paper-and-pencil tests. Another group of researchers in Taiwan developed a dynamic CAT program that assesses learning progress and provides tailored feedback to students to foster learning (Lee et al., 2018). The CAT program incorporates inputs from both students and teachers to deliver individualized assessments to students. A comparison with conventional paper-and-pencil tests showed that CAT was more effective in classifying examinees' knowledge level and could do so more efficiently.

7.1.5   Game-Based Assessment

Game-based assessments (GBAs) are digital tools that utilize interactive virtual scenarios to measure an individual's knowledge, skills, personality, and other characteristics. In these assessments, individuals are placed in a virtual scenario and are asked to complete a series of tasks, accompanied by feedback from the computer program. The user often learns how to complete the task through trial and error (Prensky, 2001). The user's activities in the virtual simulation environment (e.g., game scores, number of trials, use of hints) are then used to estimate various individual characteristics.

In Asia, GBAs are used to measure students' knowledge and skills in educational settings. Researchers in Indonesia developed an educational GBA for measuring scientific knowledge (e.g., knowledge on biology) and found support for content and construct validity of the assessment (Risnani & Adita, 2018). Moreover, the GBA received positive user responses from students, suggesting that it is an engaging and valid alternative to the conventional paper-and-pencil tests. Similarly, researchers in Taiwan used a role-playing simulation game to measure students' learning flow (i.e., an individual's mental state when they are fully immersed in an activity) and reflective behavioral patterns by analyzing the task log files. Compared to traditional learning assessment and self-report questionnaires, the GBA provided more accurate and detailed information on learning processes (Hou, 2015).

In addition to knowledge and skills, GBAs are also used to measure cognitive ability. Researchers from Taiwan developed an apple shooting game to measure students' mathematical ability (Shih et al., 2019). In the game, students are instructed to calculate the number of steps needed to accurately shoot an apple, where performance on the task relies on mathematical ability (e.g., addition and subtraction for how many steps to move the arrow). The game provides feedback to students, for example, on whether they successfully shot the apple. Some students might succeed in one trial, and others might need multiple trials. Their activities are recorded in a log file and used to measure their mathematical ability.

GBAs are also used to measure persistence. In the Philippines, researchers measured individuals' persistence using behavioral markers identified from interaction logs of a learning-by-teaching system (Dumdumaya et al., 2018; Dumdumaya & Rodrigo, 2018; Palaoag et al., 2015). Behavior markers that were critical indicators of persistence included time spent working on tasks despite challenges and failures, frequency of attempts to solve challenging, failed or uncompleted tasks, and time spent reviewing additional resources after a failure.

Further, studies in Asia have found that GBA and learning tools can enhance students' motivation in learning (e.g., mathematics; Hung et al., 2019). GBAs are engaging and can be tailored to the students' own learning pace and style, and are effective both as an assessment and a learning tool.

As a brief summary, five main types of technology – smartphones, wearable devices, social media, computerized adaptive testing, and game-based assessment – are currently used in Asia to measure stress, emotion, and subjective well-being, as well as knowledge, skills, abilities, and personalities. There are some common patterns among these applications. Stress measurement generally relies on physiological signals (e.g., HRV) and is often measured using smartphone and wearable sensors that can capture and analyze the signals. Emotion and subjective well-being tend to be reflected in semantic expressions and behavioral patterns, and are often measured using social media and smartphones. Knowledge, skills, and ability assessment rely on the interaction between the user and the application; thus, they are often measured using smartphone-based assessments, CAT, and GBA that can solicit responses from the users and adapt to or interact with the user inputs.

As we will discuss in more detail in the rest of the chapter, the technological applications in Asia are shaped by research focuses, technology regulations, and cultural influences. Due to the current research focuses in Asia, the use of smartphones, wearable sensors, and social media has mainly focused on measuring mental health and subjective well-being, but has not yet been extended to measuring other complex cognitive and attitudinal constructs such as personality and interpersonal relations. Social media applications (e.g., Weibo) are further influenced by technology regulations that impact the content and its distribution. Compared to other parts of the world, there also have been many applications of CAT and GBA to facilitate education in Asia, potentially due to the region's general emphasis on education and knowledge attainment. In the following sections, we discuss in detail the research, technology-related regulations, and cultural factors that influence technological measurement applications in Asia.

7.2   Legal Issues Related to Measurement in Asia

The growth of technological measurement applications in Asia has also promoted developments in legislation. Legislation around data and technology in Asia primarily regulates two stages of the data collection pipeline. The first type of legislation centers around controlling digital activities and supervising what citizens and organizations can do online. The second type of legislation focuses on defining the privacy rights of consumers and citizens and regulating data access by third parties such as governments or companies. These developments in legislation closely reflect the advancement in technological measurement application in Asia.

7.2.1   Digital Activities

A large portion of legislation on digital content and activity in Asia focuses on promoting self-regulation. Self-regulation encourages organizations to self-moderate their platforms: Organizations hold liability if consumers or other organizations make complaints, but otherwise, they are generally not actively monitored or enforced by regulatory agencies. One example of this type of regulation is the Malaysian Communications and Multimedia Content Code (or the Code; Azmi, 2004). This is a set of guidelines, standards, and procedures centered around the dissemination of content based on the Communications and Multimedia Act of 1998. Organizations that comply with the Code receive a number of benefits, including defense against prosecution and legal action in court. Similarly, China adopted the "Public Pledge on Self-discipline for China's Internet Industry" in 2002 (aka the Pledge; Weber & Jia, 2007). The Pledge is very similar to the Code in Malaysia and focuses on moderating the channels and type of content disseminated.

7.2.2 Data Privacy and Security

Privacy legislation in Asia primarily focuses on obtaining consent from users, implementing data security measures, and creating an institution to enforce the legislation. One such example is Malaysia's Personal Data Protection Act (PDPA) of 2010. This act prohibits users from processing personal data without the consent of the subject. The PDPA also states that consent must be recorded and be properly kept by the users (Hamzah et al., 2019). Like Malaysia, Singapore also has legislation around data protection, termed the PDPA (Personal Data Protection Commission, 2021). The Singaporean PDPA was established in 2012 and aimed to regulate the flow of data among organizations. This piece of legislation created the Personal Data Protection Commission, a government entity that serves as Singapore's main authority in matters relating to personal data protection. Similarly, the Philippines' 2012 Data Privacy Act also established an enforcement agency (the National Privacy Commission) and regulations around collecting, recording, processing, and deleting data (National Privacy Commission, 2016).

South Korea has the 2011 Personal Information Protection Act (PIPA), which sets requirements on data protections, mandating that any information given must be protected via technical, administrative, and physical measures (e.g., limiting access to data related to passwords or pin numbers). The PIPA places the burden of proof on the users processing the data, and not on regulatory agencies. In Japan, the Act on the Protection of Personal Information (Personal Information Protection Commission, 2021) requires organizations that aim to use data to enact security measures and create ways to process complaints about data use.

The inception of the General Data Protection Regulation (GDPR) by the European Union in 2016 fostered more countries in Asia to propose and pass legislation to safeguard data security and privacy. Some of the new developments are overhauls of existing data rules that were outdated or were too general, while many are filling the void of data and technology regulations. In general, these legislations provide protection toward data usage through technological, administrative, and physical measures. They also require consent from subjects, especially for medical and personal data, to guard data privacy. One such example is Thailand's 2019 PDPA, which draws heavily from the regulations set forth by the European Union's GDPR, and includes strong consent requirements for data collection, the right to request deletion of data, and the right to object to data processing (Greenleaf & Suriyawongkul, 2019). The PDPA also established a Personal Data Protection Commission in charge of enforcing the regulations outlined in the PDPA (Greenleaf & Suriyawongkul, 2019). Another example of privacy legislation inspired by the GDPR is the 2019 Indian Personal Data Protection Bill (Singh & Ruj, 2020). This bill aims to bring about a comprehensive overhaul to India's current data protection regime, covering mechanisms for the protection of personal data, including prescribing compliance requirements for all forms of personal data, broadening the rights given to individuals, and introducing a central data protection regulator. The Bill is currently being studied by the Indian Parliament (Singh & Ruj, 2020).

China is also undergoing major changes in privacy regulations. Due to its authoritarian press system, privacy in China was not well protected in the traditional media age, and even less so in the new media arenas (e.g., social media; Wu et al., 2011). Additionally, privacy appeals are judged and protected under the right of reputation based on the General Principles of The Civil Law of The People's Republic of China established in 1988, which many believe is unable to keep pace with the growth of the Internet (Wu et al., 2011). However, China has recently taken steps to improve data privacy and protection by introducing the 2020 Personal Information Protection Law Draft, which lays down privacy regulations comparable to other countries in Asia (Qi et al., 2021). This is an ongoing trend, and more legislation and amendments are expected to be passed in the near future to adapt to the growing use of technology and measurement in Asia and synchronize with the global understanding of data management.

7.2.3   Biometric Privacy

In addition to the general regulations on data usage, extra protections are placed on biometric data. In India, primary concerns on data privacy emerged predominantly around the government's biometric identity project, Aadhaar. Aadhaar is currently the world's largest biometric identity database with 1.2 billion subscribers in 2018, and multiple industries – including public-sector oil marketing companies and banks – are using Aadhaar information for verification services (Singh, 2019). Critics of this system oppose the development and use of the database, citing that it may lead to mass surveillance and fairness issues as rural areas have disproportionately limited access to the benefits provided by this system (Singh, 2019). As a response, in 2019, India limited the Aadhaar data for state welfare programs and not private usage (Ministry of Law and Justice, 2019). South Korea also has a similar biometric database called the Korean Biobank Network that contains human biospecimens and data (Kim et al., 2018). Access to this system is regulated by two major acts: The Bioethics and Safety Act of 2005 (BSA) and the PIPA. The BSA mandates that written consent must be obtained from the biospecimen donor, and that the donor must be informed of the list of individuals and institutions with potential access to the data. The PIPA mandates that additional consent is needed if a biospecimen donor's data is shared across borders. A special committee (the Distributive Review Committee) reviews and approves the usage of the biobank data (Kim et al., 2018).

PART 2. MOVING FORWARD: TECHNOLOGY ACCEPTANCE AND FUTURE DEVELOPMENTS IN ASIA

To better understand the current technology and measurement applications in Asia, we compared them with other parts of the globe and reviewed potential factors that could influence the development and acceptance of technological applications in Asia. A summary of potential development areas can be found in Table 7.2.

7.3   Potential Developmental Areas

There are exciting potentials for technology and measurement developments in Asia through (1) extension of current technological applications, (2) exploration of new technologies, and (3) exploration of new application areas.

7.3.1   *Extension of Current Technological Applications*

One technology that has a lot of potential to grow in Asia is smartphones, due to their ability to triangulate behavioral data (e.g., social interactions,

Table 7.2 *Future developments in Asia*

Technology	Measurement
Smartphones	- Cognitive, affective, and attitudinal states
Social media	- Personality
	- Interpersonal relationships
Wearable sensors	- Psychological disorders
	- Group collaboration and problem-solving
	- Team formation
	- Communication
	- Co-influence of individual and group behaviors
Public network cameras	- Human behaviors
	- Emotions
	- Cognitive state
	- Personality traits
Internet behavior	- Stress and emotion

daily activities, mobility patterns) and self-reported survey data to capture a holistic account of one's psychological states (Harari et al., 2016). Although smartphone-based measurements are largely focused on stress and depression in Asia, in other parts of the globe smartphones are used to measure many other cognitive, affective, and attitudinal states (for reviews, see Harari et al., 2016; Miller, 2012). For instance, smartphones are used to measure daily variations in emotional states (Sandstrom et al., 2016), interpersonal behaviors (Schmid Mast et al., 2015), and social networks (Kobayashi et al., 2015). With over 2 billion active smartphone users in Asia (Tankovska, 2021), the expansion of smartphone-based measurement could have a widespread impact on our understanding of human psychology and behavior, as well as important practical implications for Asia.

In Asia, applications of wearable devices apart from stress assessment have not been explored thoroughly. Many wearable devices are equipped to capture location and behavioral data (e.g., proximity, time spent in a conversation, emotional states before, during, and after an interaction), and can synchronize the information among multiple devices (Gravina et al., 2017). These capabilities can be leveraged to measure interpersonal dynamics like communication, collaboration, and team forming (e.g., Alshamsi et al., 2015; Fournet & Barrat, 2014; Kozlowski et al., 2016; Zhang et al., 2018). For example, proximity and behavioral data (e.g., sit or stand in close distance) from wearable devices could be used to measure relationships and interactions among coworkers; and recent studies found support for convergent, discriminant, and criterion-related validity of such measures (Matusik et al., 2019).

Social media, whose main measurement application in Asia is focused on emotion and subjective well-being, could also provide network connection and user activity data to assess personality traits and interpersonal relationships. For instance, researchers used text posts, profile photos, video blogging, and momentary behavioral traces to capture broad dimensions of personality traits (e.g., Akhtar et al., 2018; Biel & Gatica-Perez, 2013), and used communication patterns and network structures to measure interpersonal relationships (Gilbert & Karahalios, 2009; Manago et al., 2012; Vaterlaus et al., 2016).

7.3.2   Exploration of New Technologies

Beyond the main technological tools already used, Asia has much space to explore other promising technologies, such as internet activities and public network cameras. Internet behaviors (e.g., search history, page views, time spent on web pages) could be used to measure subjective well-being and emotion (e.g., Ayers et al., 2013), and public network cameras could be used to assess emotions and social interactions (e.g., Cocca et al., 2016; Hernandez et al., 2012).

The recent COVID-19 pandemic significantly accelerated the use of public network cameras in Asia, where countries like China and South Korea applied them to identify and manage infections. Even before the pandemic, Chinese cities already had sophisticated security camera infrastructure with facial recognition functions installed for public safety purposes. The pandemic has led the government to repurpose the existing surveillance system by combining it with thermal imaging to identify individuals with high temperatures (Chen et al., 2020). South Korea also utilized facial recognition and thermal imaging to identify potential virus carriers. The South Korean government further paired this data with credit card purchase data to create a spatiotemporal map to assist contact tracing. These measures greatly helped reduce the spread of the virus, resulting in South Korea having one of the world's lowest infection and death rates (Sonn & Lee, 2020). In addition to pandemic control, public network cameras are also widely used in Asia to reduce theft and crime. For example, Vaak, a Japanese startup, developed an artificial intelligence software that hunts for potential shoplifters using security camera records that identify potentially suspicious body language, including fidgeting and restlessness. The software analyzes security camera footage and alerts staff about potential thieves via a smartphone application (Belova, 2020).

Along with their use in surveillance, public network cameras have tremendous potential in measuring psychological states. Researchers in India utilized public network cameras in universities to identify students with anxiety and depression (Sinha et al., 2020). The system used facial recognition to analyze the emotions of students as they walked past the cameras, and those exhibiting alerting degrees of negative emotions (e.g., sadness, disgust, and anger) were referred to mental health counselors. Further, there are a number of other areas where public network cameras have the potential to improve psychological measurement. While thermal imaging was effectively used for COVID-19 contact tracing, given that body temperature change is one of the physiological responses to intense emotion (Wioleta, 2013), the same technology can also be used to identify an individual's emotions. While body language was used to identify shoplifting behavior, the same metric can be utilized to track emotional changes (Metallinou et al., 2011). Given sufficient attention to data privacy, adapting public network cameras to measure and study the psychological state of people can tremendously benefit Asian societies.

7.3.3 Exploration of New Areas of Applications

In Asia, while many technological measurement applications focus on education (e.g., formative knowledge assessment) and the improvement of subjective well-being and mental health (e.g., stress monitoring and management), there are very limited applications related to the work setting. Comparatively, in other regions of the globe (e.g., North America, Europe), advanced technologies are increasingly used for work-related applications, including resume screening (Sinha et al., 2021), automated video interviews (Hickman et al., 2022), and performance appraisal (Speer, 2021; for reviews, see Oswald et al., 2020; Song et al., 2020). There is much potential in Asia for using technology to improve assessment for work-related applications. For one, much knowledge and experience obtained from educational and mental health applications in Asia could be applied to the workplace. Knowledge and skills assessments used in classrooms could provide valuable information in designing assessments for personnel selection and training, and ecological monitoring of emotion and attitudes could help inform employee job satisfaction and team collaboration dynamic. In fact, Asia already has many beneficial conditions for adapting work-related applications. As an example, Asia has one of the most users in job-related social media and databases such as LinkedIn (more than 200 million users; Apollo Technical, 2021); the rich data and platforms could be used to develop, test, and implement potential applications. With globalization and rapid changes in jobs and the workplace, technology applications in measurement for work-related applications are an important next step for Asia.

7.4   Understanding Technological Applications in Asia

Beyond research advancements, certain technological applications in Asia are influenced by two main factors: restrictions around technologies, such as restrictions on social media, and cultural factors surrounding technology acceptance.

7.4.1   *Restrictions on Certain Technologies*

As mentioned earlier, digital activities such as traditional media and press are restricted in many parts of Asia. Research has found that in the regions with relatively strong restrictions (e.g., China, Malaysia, Singapore), individuals relied on social media more heavily for personal and political expressions, whereas in regions with fewer restrictions (e.g., Hong Kong, South Korea, Taiwan), the expression toward political topics was more balanced between social media and the press (Lin et al., 2011; Skoric et al., 2016). The restrictions advanced the use of social media platforms as new channels for personal, especially political, expressions. In recent years, social media facilitated a number of social movements in some parts of Asia; however, because of these movements, regulators have moved on to impose stronger restrictions on social media (e.g., Indonesia, Malaysia, Singapore, Thailand; Laungaramsri, 2016; Weiss, 2014). Whether it promotes or hinders social media expression, the regulations on digital activities substantially influence social media usage in Asia.

7.4.2   *Broader Factor: Technology Acceptance in Asia*

The development of technological measurement in Asia is also related to an individual's acceptance of technologies, which could be explained using the technology acceptance model (TAM), a theoretical model that has largely been supported by studies in Asia (e.g., Cho et al., 2020, China; Faqih, 2016, Jordan; Khlaisang et al., 2019, Thailand; Mei, 2019, China; Abbasi et al., 2015, Pakistan; Teo et al., 2011, Turkey; Teo & Noyes,

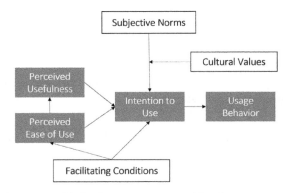

Figure 7.1   Technology acceptance model and its extensions
Note. Based on Davis (1989), Schepers and Wetzels (2007), Venkatesh and Davis
(1996, 2000).

2014, Singapore; Teo et al., 2015, Singapore; Teo, 2016, Thailand; Teo et al., 2019, China). As shown in Figure 7.1 (gray boxes), TAM describes how motivational factors affect attitude toward and actual usage of technology (Davis, 1989; Schepers & Wetzels, 2007; Venkatesh & Davis, 1996, 2000).

Recent cross-cultural studies suggested extensions to the theory, highlighting the effect of subjective norms and cultural values, as well as facilitating conditions (e.g., technological and infrastructure support) on the acceptance and use of technologies in measurement (see Figure 7.1, white boxes). Importantly, recent research suggests that the key to technological acceptance in Asia may lie in subjective norms and improved facilitating conditions.

Social and subjective norms influence people's perceived usefulness of, and intention to use technology (Basak et al., 2015, Turkey; Teo & Huang, 2019, China; Lee et al., 2015, South Korea and Ireland; Teo et al., 2007, Singapore). That is, if an influential person, for instance, a teacher, supervisor, coworker, or peer, promotes the use of technology, the individuals are more likely to perceive the technology to be useful and are more likely to use it. Cultural dimensions further moderate this influence of social norms on technological acceptance. At the group level, individuals in Asia tend to have high uncertainty avoidance and power distance (Hofstede, 2001, 2011). Cross-cultural studies consistently found that individuals with high uncertainty avoidance and power distance tend to follow social norms to decide whether to use new technologies (Abbas & Mesch, 2015, Israel; Huang et al., 2019, China [compared to Spain]; Lee et al., 2015, South Korea [compared to Ireland]; Tarhini et al., 2016, Lebanon [compared to England]). This effect was also found for other cultural dimensions, but conclusions were mixed (e.g., Teo, 2011). These findings suggest that social norms might be a key to the development and use of technology for measurement in Asia.

Another important factor is facilitating conditions (i.e., objective factors that the individuals believe make it easy to implement certain technology; e.g., Venkatesh et al., 2003). Supportive facilitating conditions tend to improve the perceived ease of use and contribute to increased technology acceptance and use (Mei et al., 2018, China; Mohammad-Salehi et al., 2020, Iran; Sangeeta & Tandon, 2020, India). However, recent studies showed that many regions in Asia lack key resources, including policy, infrastructure, and trained personnel support, hindering the use of technology in measurement (Tarhini et al., 2016, Lebanon; Teo et al., 2007, Singapore; Teo et al., 2016, Singapore). The lack of resources, which is partially related to the economic differences across regions, further fosters the difference in technological measurement applications across Asia. Indeed, in our literature review, the majority of applications took place in regions with relatively high gross domestic product (GDP), such as China and Japan, and many regions with low GDP were not represented in the literature. With continuous economic development and advancement in technology (e.g., faster internet, cheaper computer) allowing easier access to technology, it is our hope that the gap across regions will narrow and the technological application and acceptance in Asia increase overall.

7.5 Conclusion

Many promising technology and measurement applications are currently taking place in Asia. Five main types of technology – smartphones, wearable sensors, social media, computerized adaptive tests, game-based assessment – are used in Asia to measure stress, subjective well-being, mental health, knowledge, skills, and personality. These developments in technological applications are accompanied by continuously evolving regulations to guide and safeguard the collection and use of data. Moving forward, there are many exciting new potentials for technology and measurement in Asia, including applying the current technological applications to measure psychological and behavioral constructs, exploring new technologies such as internet data and public network cameras, and using technological measurement to improve work-related applications.

Developments in technological measurement in Asia are influenced by legislative policies on digital activities and data privacy, as well as technological acceptance, cultural factors, and facilitating conditions. Advancements in these areas could further advance technological measurement applications in Asia.

REFERENCES

Abbas, R., & Mesch, G. S. (2015). Cultural values and Facebook use among Palestinian youth in Israel. *Computers in Human Behavior, 48*, 644–653. https://doi.org/10.1016/j.chb.2015.02.031

Abbasi, M. S., Tarhini, A., Hassouna, M., & Shah, F. (2015). Social, organizational, demography and individuals' technology acceptance behaviour: A conceptual model. *European Scientific Journal, 11*(9), 48–76. https://eujournal.org/index.php/esj/article/view/5279

Akhtar, R., Winsborough, D., Ort, U., Johnson, A., & Chamorro-Premuzic, T. (2018). Detecting the dark side of personality using social media status updates. *Personality and Individual Differences, 132*, 90–97. https://doi.org/10.1016/j.paid.2018.05.026

Alshamsi, A., Pianesi, F., Lepri, B., Pentland, A., & Rahwan, I. (2015). Beyond contagion: Reality mining reveals complex patterns of social influence. *PLoS ONE, 10*(8), e0135740. https://doi.org/10.1371/journal.pone.0135740

Apollo Technical. (2021). *LinkedIn users by country and statistics (2021)*. https://www.apollotechnical.com/linkedin-users-by-country/

Ayers, J. W., Althouse, B. M., Allem, J. P., Rosenquist, J. N., & Ford, D. E. (2013). Seasonality in seeking mental health information on Google. *American Journal of Preventive Medicine, 44*(5), 520–525. https://doi.org/10.1371/journal.pone.0061373

Azmi, I. M. (2004). Content regulation in Malaysia: Unleashing missiles on dangerous web sites. In *The 18th BILETA Conference: Controlling Information in the Online Environment*, https://www.bileta.org.uk/wp-content/uploads/Content-Regulation-in-Malaysia-Unleashing-Missiles-on-Dangerous-Websites.pdf

Basak, E., Gumussoy, C. A., & Calisir, F. (2015). Examining the factors affecting PDA acceptance among physicians: An extended technology acceptance model. *Journal of Healthcare Engineering, 6*(3), 399–418. https://doi.org/10.1260/2040-2295.6.3.399

Belova, L. (2020). Experience of artificial intelligence implementation in Japan. In *E3S Web of Conferences* (Vol. 159, p. 04035). EDP Sciences. https://doi.org/10.1051/e3sconf/202015904035

Biel, J. I., Tsiminaki, V., Dines, J., & Gatica-Perez, D. (2013, December). Hi YouTube! Personality impressions and verbal content in social video. In Proceedings of the 15th ACM on International Conference on Multimodal Interaction (pp. 119–126).

Boyd, D. M., & Ellison, N. B. (2007). Social network sites: Definition, history, and scholarship. *Journal of Computer-Mediated Communication*, *13*(1), 210–230. https://doi.org/10.1111/j.1083-6101.2007.00393.x

Can, Y. S., Chalabianloo, N., Ekiz, D., & Ersoy, C. (2019). Continuous stress detection using wearable sensors in real life: Algorithmic programming contest case study. *Sensors*, *19*(8), 1849. https://doi.org/10.3390/s19081849

Chang, H. H. (2015). Psychometrics behind computerized adaptive testing. *Psychometrika*, *80*(1), 1–20. https://doi.org/10.1007/s11336-014-9401-5

Chang, H. H., Wang, C., & Zhang, S. (2021). Statistical applications in educational measurement. *Annual Review of Statistics and Its Application*, *8*, 439–461. https://doi.org/10.1146/annurev-statistics-042720-104044

Chen, B., Marvin, S., & While, A. (2020). Containing COVID-19 in China: AI and the robotic restructuring of future cities. *Dialogues in Human Geography*, *10*(2), 238–241. https://doi.org/10.1177/2043820620934267

Cho, H., Chi, C., & Chiu, W. (2020). Understanding sustained usage of health and fitness apps: Incorporating the technology acceptance model with the investment model. *Technology in Society*, *63*, 101429. https://doi.org/10.1016/j.techsoc.2020.101429

Cocca, P., Marciano, F., & Alberti, M. (2016). Video surveillance systems to enhance occupational safety: A case study. *Safety Science*, *84*, 140–148. https://doi.org/10.1016/j.ssci.2015.12.005

Davis, F. D. (1989). Perceived usefulness, perceived ease of use, and user acceptance of information technology. *MIS Quarterly*, *13*(3), 319–340. https://doi.org/10.2307/249008

Dumdumaya, C. E., Banawan, M. P., & Rodrigo, Ma. M. T. (2018). Identifying students' persistence profiles in problem solving task. In *Adjunct publication of the 26th Conference on User Modeling, Adaptation and Personalization* (pp. 281–286). https://doi.org/10.1145/3213586.3225237

Dumdumaya, C., & Rodrigo, M. M. (2018). Predicting task persistence within a learning-by-teaching environment. In *Proceedings of the 26th International Conference on Computers in Education* (pp. 1–10).

Faqih, K. M. S. (2016). An empirical analysis of factors predicting the behavioral intention to adopt internet shopping technology among non-shoppers in a developing country context: Does gender matter? *Journal of Retailing and Consumer Services*, *30*, 140–164. https://doi.org/10.1016/j.jretconser.2016.01.016

Fournet, J., & Barrat, A. (2014). Contact patterns among high school students. *PLoS ONE*, *9*(9), e107878. https://doi.org/10.1371/journal.pone.0107878

Gilbert, E., & Karahalios, K. (2009, April). Predicting tie strength with social media. In Proceedings of the SIGCHI Conference on Human Factors in Computing Systems (pp. 211–220). https://doi.org/10.1145/1518701.1518736

Gravina, R., Alinia, P., Ghasemzadeh, H., & Fortino, G. (2017). Multi-sensor fusion in body sensor networks: State-of-the-art and research challenges. *Information Fusion*, *35*, 68–80. https://doi.org/10.1016/j.inffus.2016.09.005

Greenleaf, G., & Suriyawongkul, A. (2019). Thailand – Asia's strong new data protection law. *Privacy Laws & Business*, 161. https://doi.org/10.2139/ssrn .3502671

Hamzah, M. A., Ahmad, A. R., Hussin, N., & Ibrahim, Z. (2019). Personal data privacy protection: A review on Malaysia's cyber security policies. *International Journal of Academic Research in Business and Social Sciences*, 8(12). https://doi.org/10.6007/ijarbss/v8-i12/5251

Harari, G. M., Lane, N. D., Wang, R., Crosier, B. S., Campbell, A. T., & Gosling, S. D. (2016). Using smartphones to collect behavioral data in psychological science: Opportunities, practical considerations, and challenges. *Perspectives on Psychological Science*, 11(6), 838–854. https://doi.org/ 10.1177/1745691616650285

Hernandez, J., Hoque, M., Drevo, W., & Picard, R. W. (2012, September). Mood meter: Counting smiles in the wild. In *Proceedings of the 2012 ACM Conference on Ubiquitous Computing* (pp. 301–310).

Hickman, L., Bosch, N., Ng, V., Saef, R., Tay, L., & Woo, S. E. (2022). Automated video interview personality assessments: Reliability, validity, and generalizability investigations. *Journal of Applied Psychology*, 107(8), 1323–1351. https://doi.org/10.1037/apl0000695

Hofstede, G. (2001). *Culture's consequences: Comparing values, behaviors, institutions and organizations across nations*. Sage.

    (2011). Dimensionalizing cultures: The Hofstede model in context. *Online Readings in Psychology and Culture*, 2(1), 1–26. https://doi.org/10.9707/ 2307-0919.1014

Hou, H.-T. (2015). Integrating cluster and sequential analysis to explore learners' flow and behavioral patterns in a simulation game with situated-learning context for science courses: A video-based process exploration. *Computers in Human Behavior*, 48, 424–435. https://doi.org/10.1016/j.chb.2015.02.010

Huang, F., Teo, T., Sánchez-Prieto, J. C., García-Peñalvo, F. J., & Olmos-Miguelánez, S. (2019). Cultural values and technology adoption: A model comparison with university teachers from China and Spain. *Computers & Education*, 133, 69–81. https://doi.org/10.1016/j.compedu.2019.01.012

Hung, C.-Y., Sun, J. C.-Y., & Liu, J.-Y. (2019). Effects of flipped classrooms integrated with MOOCs and game-based learning on the learning motivation and outcomes of students from different backgrounds. *Interactive Learning Environments*, 27(8), 1028–1046. https://doi.org/10.1080/ 10494820.2018.1481103

Hung, S., Li, M. S., Chen, Y. L., Chiang, J. H., Chen, Y. Y., & Hung, G. C. L. (2016). Smartphone-based ecological momentary assessment for Chinese patients with depression: An exploratory study in Taiwan. *Asian Journal of Psychiatry*, 23, 131–136. https://doi.org/10.1016/j.ajp.2016.08.003

Ishio, J., & Abe, N. (2017). Measuring affective well-being by the combination of the day reconstruction method and a wearable device: Case study of an aging and depopulating community in Japan. *Augmented Human Research*, 2(1), 1–19. https://doi.org/10.1007/s41133-017-0006-2

Johnson, J. (2021). *Number of online users worldwide 2020, by region*. Statistica, https://www.statista.com/statistics/249562/number-of-worldwide-internet-users-by-region/

Khlaisang, J., Teo, T., & Huang, F. (2019). Acceptance of a flipped smart application for learning: A study among Thai university students. *Interactive Learning Environments*, *29*(5), 772–789. https://doi.org/10.1080/10494820.2019.1612447

Kido, S., Hashizume, A., Baba, T., & Matsui, T. (2016). Development and evaluation of a smartphone application for self-estimation of daily mental stress level. *International Journal of Affective Engineering*, *15*(2), 183–187. https://doi.org/10.5057/ijae.IJAE-D-15-00029

Kim, H., Kim, S. Y., & Joly, Y. (2018). South Korea: In the midst of a privacy reform centered on data sharing. *Human Genetics*, *137*(8), 627–635. https://doi.org/10.1007/s00439-018-1920-1

Kobayashi, T., Boase, J., Suzuki, T., & Suzuki, T. (2015). Emerging from the cocoon? Revisiting the tele-cocooning hypothesis in the smartphone era. *Journal of Computer-Mediated Communication*, *20*(3), 330–345. https://doi.org/10.1111/jcc4.12116

Kozlowski, S. W. J., Chao, G. T., Chang, C.-H. (D.), & Fernandez, R. (2016). Using big data to advance the science of team effectiveness. In S. Tonidandel, E. B. King, & J. M. Cortina (Eds.), *Big data at work: The data science revolution and organizational psychology* (pp. 272–309). Routledge/Taylor & Francis Group.

Laungaramsri, P. (2016). Mass surveillance and the militarization of cyberspace in post-coup Thailand. *Austrian Journal of South-East Asian Studies*, *9*(2), 195–214. https://doi.org/10.14764/10.ASEAS-2016.2-2

Lee, C., Wang, M., Wang, C., Teytaud, O., Liu, J., Lin, S., & Hung, P. (2018). PSO-based fuzzy markup language for student learning performance evaluation and educational application. *IEEE Transactions on Fuzzy Systems*, *26*(5), 2618–2633. https://doi.org/10.1109/TFUZZ.2018.2810814

Lee, H., Chung, N., & Jung, T. (2015). Examining the cultural differences in acceptance of mobile augmented reality: Comparison of South Korea and Ireland. In I. Tussyadiah & A. Inversini (Eds.), *Information and communication technologies in tourism 2015* (pp. 477–491). Springer International Publishing.

Li, H., Zhang, T., Chi, H., Chen, Y., Li, Y., & Wang, J. (2014). Mobile health in China: Current status and future development. *Asian Journal of Psychiatry*, *10*, 101–104. https://doi.org/10.1016/j.ajp.2014.06.003

Li, S., Wang, Y., Xue, J., Zhao, N., & Zhu, T. (2020). The impact of COVID-19 epidemic declaration on psychological consequences: A study on active Weibo users. *International Journal of Environmental Research and Public Health*, *17*(6), 2032. https://doi.org/10.3390/ijerph17062032

Lin, Y. R., Bagrow, J. P., & Lazer, D. (2011, July). More voices than ever? Quantifying media bias in networks. In *Fifth International AAAI Conference on Weblogs and Social Media*.

Manago, A. M., Taylor, T., & Greenfield, P. M. (2012). Me and my 400 friends: The anatomy of college students' Facebook networks, their communication patterns, and well-being. *Developmental Psychology, 48*(2), 369–380. https://doi.org/10.1037/a0026338

Matusik, J. G., Heidl, R., Hollenbeck, J. R., Yu, A., Lee, H. W., & Howe, M. (2019). Wearable bluetooth sensors for capturing relational variables and temporal variability in relationships: A construct validation study. *Journal of Applied Psychology, 104*(3), 357–387. https://doi.org/10.1037/apl0000334

Mei, B. (2019). Preparing preservice EFL teachers for CALL normalisation: A technology acceptance perspective. *System, 83*, 13–24. https://doi.org/10.1016/j.system.2019.02.011

Mei, B., Brown, G. T., & Teo, T. (2018). Toward an understanding of preservice English as a foreign language teachers' acceptance of computer-assisted language learning 2.0 in the People's Republic of China. *Journal of Educational Computing Research, 56*(1), 74–104. https://journals.sagepub.com/doi/10.1177/0735633117700144

Metallinou, A., Katsamanis, A., Wang, Y., & Narayanan, S. (2011, May). Tracking changes in continuous emotion states using body language and prosodic cues. In *2011 IEEE International Conference on Acoustics, Speech and Signal Processing (ICASSP)* (pp. 2288–2291). IEEE. https://doi.org/10.1109/ICASSP.2011.5946939

Miller, G. (2012). The smartphone psychology manifesto. *Perspectives on Psychological Science, 7*(3), 221–237. https://doi.org/10.1177/1745691612441215

Ministry of Law and Justice. (2019). The Aadhaar and other laws (Amendment) Act, 2019. https://uidai.gov.in/images/news/Amendment_Act_2019.pdf

Mohammad-Salehi, B., Vaez-Dalili, M., & Heidari Tabrizi, H. (2021). Investigating factors that influence EFL teachers' adoption of Web 2.0 technologies: Evidence from applying the UTAUT and TPACK. *TESL-EJ, 25*(1), n1.

National Privacy Commission. (2016, July 19). *Republic Act 10173 – Data Privacy Act of 2012.* https://www.privacy.gov.ph/data-privacy-act/

Oswald, F. L., Behrend, T. S., Putka, D. J., & Sinar, E. (2020). Big data in industrial-organizational psychology and human resource management: Forward progress for organizational research and practice. *Annual Review of Organizational Psychology and Organizational Behavior, 7*, 505–533. https://doi.org/10.1146/annurev-orgpsych-032117-104553

Palaoag, T. D., Rodrigo, M. M. T., & Andres, J. M. L. (2015). An exploratory study of student persistence and its relationship with achievement while using a game-based learning environment. In *Proceedings of the 23rd International Conference on Computers in Education.* Asia-Pacific Society for Computers in Education.

Personal Data Projection Commission. (2021). *Personal Data Protection Commission overview.* https://www.pdpc.gov.sg/Overview-of-PDPA/The-Legislation/Personal-Data-Protection-Act

Personal Information Protection Commission. (2021). *Act on the Protection of Personal Information*. https://www.japaneselawtranslation.go.jp/en/laws/view/4241/en

Prensky, M. (2001). Fun, play and games: What makes games engaging. *Digital Game-Based Learning, 5*(1), 5–31. https://doi.org/10.1145/950566.950567

Qi, G., Li, Q., & Abernethy, D. (2021). *China releases personal information protection law*. https://www.natlawreview.com/article/china-releases-draft-personal-information-protection-law

Qi, J., Fu, X., & Zhu, G. (2015). Subjective well-being measurement based on Chinese grassroots blog text sentiment analysis. *Information & Management, 52*(7), 859–869. https://doi.org/10.1016/j.im.2015.06.002

Risnani, L. Y., & Adita, A. (2018). Development of digital education game as an alternative assessment instruments in science learning for junior high school. In *Proceedings of the 5th Asia Pacific Education Conference (AECON 2018)* (pp. 77–83). https://doi.org/10.2991/aecon-18.2018.17

Rudner, L. M. (2010). Implementing the graduate management admission test computerized adaptive test. In W. J. van der Linden & C. W. Glas (Eds.), *Elements of adaptive testing* (pp. 151–165). Springer.

Sandström, J., Swanepoel, D. W., Carel Myburgh, H., & Laurent, C. (2016). Smartphone threshold audiometry in underserved primary health-care contexts. *International Journal of Audiology, 55*(4), 232–238. https://doi.org/10.3109/14992027.2015.1124294

Sangeeta, & Tandon, U. (2020). Factors influencing adoption of online teaching by school teachers: A study during COVID-19 pandemic. *Journal of Public Affairs, 21*(4), e2503. https://doi.org/10.1002/pa.2503

Schepers, J., & Wetzels, M. (2007). A meta-analysis of the technology acceptance model: Investigating subjective norm and moderation effects. *Information & Management, 44*(1), 90–103. https://doi.org/10.1016/j.im.2006.10.007

Schmid Mast, M., Gatica-Perez, D., Frauendorfer, D., Nguyen, L., & Choudhury, T. (2015). Social sensing for psychology: Automated interpersonal behavior assessment. *Current Directions in Psychological Science, 24*(2), 154–160. https://doi.org/10.1177/0963721414560811

Shih, S.-C., Kuo, B.-C., & Lee, S.-J. (2019). An online game-based computational estimation assessment combining cognitive diagnostic model and strategy analysis. *Educational Psychology, 39*(10), 1255–1277. https://doi.org/10.1080/01443410.2018.1501468

Singh, P. (2019). Aadhaar and data privacy: Biometric identification and anxieties of recognition in India. *Information, Communication & Society, 24*(3), 1–16. https://doi.org/10.1080/1369118X.2019.1668459

Singh, R. G., & Ruj, S. (2020). *A technical look at the Indian Personal Data Protection Bill*. arXiv preprint arXiv:2005.13812.

Sinha, A. K., Amir Khusru Akhtar, M., & Kumar, A. (2021). Resume screening using natural language processing and machine learning: A systematic review. *Machine Learning and Information Processing: Proceedings of ICMLIP 2020*, 207–214.

Sinha, S., Mishra, S. K., & Bilgaiyan, S. (2020). Emotion analysis to provide counseling to students fighting from depression and anxiety by using CCTV surveillance. In D. Swain, P. Pattnaik, & P. Gupta (Eds.), *Machine learning and information processing* (pp. 81–94). Springer. https://doi.org/10.1007/978-981-15-1884-3_8

Skoric, M. M., Zhu, Q., Goh, D., & Pang, N. (2016). Social media and citizen engagement: A meta-analytic review. *New Media & Society*, *18*(9), 1817–1839. https://doi.org/10.1177/1461444815616221

Song, Q. C., Liu, M. Q., Tang, C., & Long, L. (2020). Applying principles of big data to the workplace and talent analytics. In S. E. Woo, L. Tay, & R. W. Proctor (Eds.), *Big data in psychological research* (pp. 319–344). APA Books.

Sonn, J. W., & Lee, J. K. (2020). The smart city as time-space cartographer in COVID-19 control: The South Korean strategy and democratic control of surveillance technology. *Eurasian Geography and Economics*, *61*(4–5), 482–492. https://doi.org/10.1080/15387216.2020.1768423

Speer, A. B. (2021). Scoring dimension-level job performance from narrative comments: Validity and generalizability when using natural language processing. *Organizational Research Methods*, *24*(3), 572–594. https://doi.org/10.1177/1094428120930815

Tankovska, H. (2021). *Distribution of worldwide social media users in 2020, by region*. Statista. https://www.statista.com/statistics/454772/number-social-media-user-worldwide-region/

Tarhini, A., Teo, T., & Tarhini, T. (2016). A cross-cultural validity of the E-learning Acceptance Measure (ElAM) in Lebanon and England: A confirmatory factor analysis. *Education and Information Technologies*, *21*(5), 1269–1282. https://doi.org/10.1007/s10639-015-9381-9

Teo, T. (2011). Factors influencing teachers' intention to use technology: Model development and test. *Computers & Education*, *57*(4), 2432–2440. https://doi.org/10.1016/j.compedu.2011.06.008

(2016). Modelling Facebook usage among university students in Thailand: The role of emotional attachment in an extended technology acceptance model. *Interactive Learning Environments*, *24*(4), 745–757. https://doi.org/10.1080/10494820.2014.917110

Teo, T., Fan, X., & Du, J. (2015). Technology acceptance among pre-service teachers: Does gender matter? *Australasian Journal of Educational Technology*, *31*(3), Article 3. https://doi.org/10.14742/ajet.1672

Teo, T., Faruk Ursavaş, Ö., & Bahçekapili, E. (2011). Efficiency of the technology acceptance model to explain pre-service teachers' intention to use technology: A Turkish study. *Campus-Wide Information Systems*, *28*(2), 93–101. https://doi.org/10.1108/10650741111117798

Teo, T., & Huang, F. (2019). Investigating the influence of individually espoused cultural values on teachers' intentions to use educational technologies in Chinese universities. *Interactive Learning Environments*, *27*(5–6), 813–829. https://doi.org/10.1080/10494820.2018.1489856

Teo, T., Lee, C. B., & Chai, C. S. (2007). Understanding pre-service teachers' computer attitudes: Applying and extending the technology acceptance model. *Journal of Computer Assisted Learning, 24*(2), 128–143. https://doi.org/10.1111/j.1365-2729.2007.00247.x

Teo, T., & Noyes, J. (2014). Explaining the intention to use technology among pre-service teachers: A multi-group analysis of the Unified Theory of Acceptance and Use of Technology. *Interactive Learning Environments, 22*(1), 51–66. https://doi.org/10.1080/10494820.2011.641674

Teo, T., Zhou, M., Fan, A. C. W., & Huang, F. (2019). Factors that influence university students' intention to use Moodle: A study in Macau. *Educational Technology Research and Development, 67*(3), 749–766. https://doi.org/10.1007/s11423-019-09650-x

Teo, T., Zhou, M., & Noyes, J. (2016). Teachers and technology: Development of an extended theory of planned behavior. *Educational Technology Research and Development, 64*(6), 1033–1052. https://doi.org/10.1007/s11423-016-9446-5

Tseng, W.-T. (2016). Measuring English vocabulary size via computerized adaptive testing. *Computers & Education, 97*, 69–85. https://doi.org/10.1016/j.compedu.2016.02.018

Vaterlaus, J. M., Barnett, K., Roche, C., & Young, J. A. (2016). "Snapchat is more personal": An exploratory study on Snapchat behaviors and young adult interpersonal relationships. *Computers in Human Behavior, 62*, 594–601. https://doi.org/10.1016/j.chb.2016.04.029

Venkatesh, V., & Davis, F. D. (1996). A model of the antecedents of perceived ease of use: Development and test. *Decision Sciences, 27*(3), 451–481.

(2000). A theoretical extension of the technology acceptance model: Four longitudinal field studies. *Management Science, 46*(2), 186–204. https://doi.org/10.1287/mnsc.46.2.186.11926

Venkatesh, V., Morris, M. G., Davis, G. B., & Davis, F. D. (2003). User acceptance of information technology: Toward a unified view. *Management Information Systems Quarterly, 27*(3), 425–478. https://doi.org/10.2307/30036540

Weber, I., & Jia, L. (2007). Internet and self-regulation in China: The cultural logic of controlled commodification. *Media, Culture & Society, 29*(5). https://doi.org/10.1177/0163443707080536

Weiss, M. L. (2014). New media, new activism: Trends and trajectories in Malaysia, Singapore and Indonesia. *International Development Planning Review, 36*(1), 91–109. https://doi.org/10.3828/idpr.2014.6

Wioleta, S. (2013, June). Using physiological signals for emotion recognition. In *2013 6th International Conference on Human System Interactions (HSI)* (pp. 556–561). IEEE. https://doi.org/10.1109/HSI.2013.6577880

Wu, Y., Lau, T., Atkin, D. J., & Lin, C. A. (2011). A comparative study of online privacy regulations in the US and China. *Telecommunications Policy, 35*(7), 603–616. https://doi.org/10.1016/j.telpol.2011.05.002

Yang, J.-S., Shin, J., Choi, S., & Jung, H.-I. (2017). Smartphone diagnostics unit (SDU) for the assessment of human stress and inflammation level assisted by biomarker ink, fountain pen, and origami holder for strip biosensor. *Sensors and Actuators B: Chemical, 241*, 80–84. https://doi.org/10.1016/j.snb.2016.10.052

Yarahmadzehi, N., & Goodarzi, M. (2020). Investigating the role of formative mobile based assessment in vocabulary learning of pre-intermediate EFL learners in comparison with paper based assessment. *Turkish Online Journal of Distance Education, 21*(1), 181–196. https://doi.org/10.17718/tojde.690390

Zhang, J., Tang, H., Chen, D., & Zhang, Q. (2012). deStress: Mobile and remote stress monitoring, alleviation, and management platform. In *2012 IEEE Global Communications Conference (GLOBECOM)* (pp. 2036–2041). https://doi.org/10.1109/GLOCOM.2012.6503415

Zhang, Y., Olenick, J., Chang, C. H., Kozlowski, S. W., & Hung, H. (2018). TeamSense: Assessing personal affect and group cohesion in small teams through dyadic interaction and behavior analysis with wearable sensors. *Proceedings of the ACM on Interactive, Mobile, Wearable and Ubiquitous Technologies, 2*(3), 1–22.

CHAPTER 8

Technology-Enabled Measurement in Singapore

David Chan

Technological innovations and technology applications in areas such as social media, online communication, digital transactions, artificial intelligence, and big data analytics have transformed the way that governments and businesses operate and deliver their services. This, in turn, has significantly affected and will continue to affect people's lives, livelihoods, way of life, and quality of life. The historic changes in terms of size, speed, and scope of these technological effects translate into significant practical impacts on well-being and functioning at multiple levels, including the individual, dyad, group, organization, and society.

In management, psychology, and various disciplines in the social sciences, much has been spoken and written on how technological transformation and the related rapidly evolving changes have led to both novel adaptability demands and new aspirational goals and opportunities for individuals, groups, and societies (e.g., Benner & Waldfogel, 2023; Hanelt et al., 2020). In contrast, less attention has been given to the emerging issues in research, policy, and practice concerning the use of technology-enabled measurement of the psychological constructs and processes involved in the various causal effects, temporal dynamics, or other types of changes on how people think, feel, and act in the "new normal" of a digital and data society. Moreover, these and other issues of technology-enabled measurement are increasingly complex. The need to examine them has become more urgent as societies continue to function amid the protracted COVID-19 crisis as well as anticipate and navigate postpandemic realities.

When used appropriately, technology can help researchers and practitioners better measure various constructs and phenomena of interest and hence better understand, predict, and influence them to address social and behavioral issues. The purpose of this chapter is to share and discuss the key issues and experiences in Singapore associated with digital transformation and data society, which show both challenges and

239

opportunities in technology-enabled measurement which are probably applicable elsewhere in other cities and countries, albeit manifested differently. The overall aim is to contribute to integrating advances in technology, measurement principles, and insights from the social and behavioral sciences. To do this, I will use Singapore's digitization transformation journey toward being a Smart Nation as an example and a point of departure to discuss the importance of explicitly addressing research, policy, and practice in technology-enabled measurement of psychological constructs and processes.

This chapter is organized as follows. I will begin by providing an overview of Singapore's context of technological innovations, capabilities, and national strategies. This will be followed by a nontechnical discussion on how the production, collection, analysis, interpretation, and use of various types of data are related to important conceptual and methodological issues in psychological measurement. These discussions will focus on the crucial notion of "changes over time." Throughout the chapter, I will illustrate how we can better integrate technology-enabled solutions and psychological measurement to examine real-world issues and enhance the well-being of individuals and society. I will end by highlighting how the psychology of working together matters in understanding and practicing effective collaboration.

For the purpose of this chapter, I will construe technology-enabled measurement issues in terms of "the 3 C's" – *contexts*, *changes*, and *collaborations*. Explicating these three sets of issues provides a roadmap for understanding Singapore's digital transformation and guiding its ongoing journey towards a Smart Nation and data society. Many of these issues were also salient and critical in making sense of how Singapore has been dealing with the COVID-19 crisis (for an account of the psychology of Singapore's response to COVID-19, see Chan, 2020), such as understanding the impact of technology use on public trust amid the pandemic challenges (Chan, 2021).

8.1   Contexts

The current issues of technology-enabled measurement in many cities and countries are located within the contexts of their ongoing digital transformation and transition to a data society. These societal transformations around the globe range from widespread use of technology amid rapid urbanization to systematic "whole-of-society" efforts to build smart cities. Historically, the transformation may be traced back to the Digital

Revolution (also known as the Third Industrial Revolution; see Rifkin, 2011) that began in the late 1900s with the advent of information technology, which subsequently became more advanced and widely adopted as new technologies developed. These included supercomputers, computer chips, and semiconductor wafers, as well as the extensive use of personal computers, the Internet, mobile telephone, and computing-related communication technologies in the production and communication processes. These technological advances and the practical adoption of their applications for businesses and government services were central in the emergence of the knowledge-based, high-tech economies around the world where automation in manufacturing, efficiency in service delivery, and global connectivity are expected norms, evaluation standards, and competitive advantages.

The ubiquitous use of information technology has continued to influence every aspect of life and daily functioning for several decades now. However, it is only in the past decade that an exponential increase in the pace and intensity of the digital transformation has gone beyond quantitative differences in magnitude to qualitative differences in impact and implication. Much has been written to describe the nature of these recent changes, often referred to as the *Fourth Industrial Revolution* (also known as Industry 4.0). This phrase was first used by the team of scientists developing a high-tech strategy for the German government, who released their final report in 2011 at the Hannover Fair discussing the revolutionization of global value chains. It was subsequently made popular by Klaus Schwab, who introduced it to a wider audience in an article published in the American magazine *Foreign Affairs* (Schwab, 2015) and further popularized in the book he subsequently published on the topic (Schwab, 2016).

We can better appreciate the advances and applications of technology-enabled measurement in the ongoing digital transformation in the Fourth Industrial Revolution, including their accompanying challenges and opportunities, when we examine the various issues in the contexts in which they occur. Scientists and practitioners are better prepared and can contribute more significantly when they understand the contexts of the issues that matter to people and the different stakeholders, as well as how the different parts of the contextual systems are interdependent and interrelate. Adequate contextual knowledge, which is distinct from the technical knowledge and proficiency on how technology-enabled measurement works, involves knowing specifically how technological innovations and applications in diverse areas have transformed the way that governments, businesses, organizations, and individuals operate and deliver their services in a manner that has significantly affected people's lives and living and practically impacted their well-being and functioning as they live, work, learn and play not only as individuals but also in their interactions with others at the level of the dyad, group, organization, and society.

The critical contextual issues relevant to technology-enabled measurement revolve around what I call in this chapter "the three I's" of the future economy and society, namely, *industries, innovation,* and *individuals.*

8.1.1   Industries

Much has been written on how the future of industries is closely tied to technological advances in many areas and their applications in finance, commerce, security, healthcare, urban planning, and other domains. These megatrends in technology are in areas including social media, mobile internet, wearables, 3D printing, cloud computing, Internet of Things (IoT), robotics, autonomous vehicles, machine learning and other types of artificial intelligence, renewable energy and sustainable resource management, and blockchain technology. In the past decade, like many other world cities, Singapore has reacted or embraced the technological advances in these areas in ways that have brought about major transformations in manufacturing, finance, healthcare, and other key industrial sectors. The nature and pace of change, made more complex and rapid as technologies combine and multiply their impact, directly affect the economic capabilities of a city or country and the lives of its inhabitants. The future economy depends on how we respond to these technological changes and what and how we decide on the technology-related industries to develop as our economic growth engines.

The contextual issues associated with industries are essential because we need to understand how the relevant technology has helped or hindered the various sectors and businesses, similarly or differently. More specifically, measurement specialists should have at least an adequate and up-to-date basic knowledge of the megatrends in technological disruptions that are shaping industries and the nature and extent of the substantive impact on the future economy and society. This will facilitate identifying, understanding, and pre-empting the consequences or implications for the type of constructs or phenomena of interest to be measured, analyzed, and interpreted. For example, constructs and processes of adaptability (e.g., Chan, 2014a), resilience (e.g., Fletcher & Sarkar, 2013), and trust (e.g., Mayer et al., 1995) at multiple levels of analysis (e.g., individual, team, organization, industry), including their cross-levels and joint effects (Chan, 1998a; Kozlowski & Klein, 2000; Rousseau, 1985), are critical in many of the major changes that different industries are undergoing that substantively impact the nature of work. Depending on the specific industries and technologies, the changing nature of work includes, to varying extent, how jobs are designed and work is organized, what tasks are to be accomplished and competencies are required, how workers and teams interact, and how supervision is carried out and performance is evaluated. Measurement specialists will need to make adequate linkages between the substantive issues in the specific industry contexts and the ways we conceptualize, operationalize, and collect/analyze data on adaptability and resilience constructs that are consistent with the novel demands due to the rapid changes in the nature of work. I will elaborate on these measurement implications in the next section that examines issues of change.

8.1.2 *Innovation*

In addition to adaptability and resilience, innovation and its associated constructs such as creativity and openness are critical concepts and capabilities for cities and countries to survive and thrive amid technological disruptions. In this regard, the central issue for technology-enabled measurement is how to integrate technology and measurement to examine and enhance innovation. The demands for innovation are occurring in the context of the ongoing digital revolution, characterized by rapid advances and expansive applications in digital technologies that transform the way we live, learn, work, and play.

It is important to understand the context of innovation for a city or country, including its capabilities and climate for innovation and how they relate to the city goals and country strategies. In the case of the city-state of Singapore, there is a national focus on innovation with whole-of-government and whole-of-nation efforts to develop innovation-driven industrial clusters in specific areas to help drive the country's economy. One of the foundations spanning these clusters is Singapore's strategic vision to become a Smart Nation – a world-class city-state with a leading economy and society powered by digital innovation and technology-enabled solutions to meet its citizens' changing needs and aspirations. Although there is no sole definition of what a "Smart Nation" or "Smart City" is, the term has been commonly used by governments and city planners in the past two decades to refer to a city/country as a data society that has been digitally transformed by applying technology systematically and extensively to produce smart urban solutions to improve the lives of its people. In a Smart Nation or Smart City, these urban solutions are not isolated piecemeal responses but holistically integrated infrastructures and services that enable more efficient functioning and ways of life that will enhance the quality of life of its inhabitants. Smart urban solutions are data-driven and technology-enabled. They typically involve transportation systems that enable more people to move around more efficiently, buildings and other infrastructures that are energy-efficient and sustainable, health services that enhance the registration, diagnosis and treatment of patients, and government services that make it easier for people to find information and influence decision-making processes in the city or country. The smart solutions optimize the flow of people, data, things, and energy by making active use of mobile connectivity, real-time data, open data, artificial intelligence, cloud services, and the IoT, which refers to the network of software, sensors, and other physical objects that allows things to be connected to the Internet and each other.

Singapore has identified and implemented several key strategic national projects, which are enablers for the country's Smart Nation drive. For example, the project CODEX (Core Operations, Development Environment, and eXchange) develops a national digital platform that enables the government to deliver better digital services to the public faster and more cost-efficiently as well as allow the public and private sectors to work together better to develop user-centric services for the public. This involves various major initiatives such as building a government data architecture for common data standards and formats across different government ICT systems that were designed and operated independently to allow better data sharing across agencies and shifting less sensitive government data to commercial cloud computing provided by leading private sector capabilities. This addresses the problems of economies of scale, interoperability, and agility brought about by the previous silo approach where public agencies were each building their systems to meet their respective requirements. Another project is building hardware and software to enhance digital payments. As a part of the national initiative to encourage cashless payment to speed up transactions, the adoption of digital payment has been accelerated by the COVID-19 pandemic due to the increase in online purchases and digital transactions.

Singapore's efforts to catalyze economic growth and drive innovation amid the digital transformation are a means to enhance the well-being of its people. A fundamental goal of the Singapore Government in envisioning the Smart Nation is to develop a fair, just, and inclusive society where all segments of the population and society are able to harness digital infocomm technologies (e.g., mobile connectivity, sensor technologies, high-speed networks, IoT, and big data analytics) and benefit from them.

Innovation at work is about doing things differently and better such that it contributes directly to individual, organizational, and sectoral productivity. There is a need to innovate and adapt to the rapidly changing nature of jobs, work processes, and industries brought about by technological disruptions to function more effectively. This requires teams and organizations to innovate, which depends on individual innovation of the employee and the employer. The climate for innovation in Singapore provides many opportunities for measurement specialists and social scientists to contribute to evidence-based policy and practice as adequate conceptualization and measurement of innovation-relevant constructs at multiple levels of analysis will become more important. Examples of these constructs include creativity, pattern recognition, openness to experience, risk-taking, learning goal orientation, competitive advantage, adoption of innovation, and person–environment fit.

8.1.3   Individuals

The third "I" is about *individuals*, which is the ultimate focus of Singapore's transformation efforts for industries to adapt to changes and adopt innovation. This people-centric effort is evident in the case of Singapore, where national and societal efforts are explicated in terms of what the future economy means for the people and the kind of society that the people want. The national and collective narrative is that the adoption of technology and innovation is the enabler for harnessing benefits for individuals and hence a means to people-centric ends. What should ultimately matter are individuals' well-being, competence, and functioning, and the kinds of job and nature of work that they can expect and will experience. Integral to this narrative is the belief that people-centric policies and interventions that put individuals at the core will survive and thrive. This is mediated by positivity such as optimism, hope, efficacy beliefs, resilience, trust, morale, sense of belonging, group identity, and performance. This belief is consistent with the social and behavioral sciences research in diverse areas such as motivation, learning, work engagement, job performance, team functioning, organizational commitment, leadership, social capital, psychological capital, adaptability, and subjective well-being.

Given the people-centric focus on individuals in the context of techno-logical advances, digital transformation, and data society, researchers and practitioners in the data sciences need to understand how technology-enabled measurement can contribute to established ways of operationaliz-ing and assessing constructs/processes relating to people's cognition, affect, and behavior. For example, in the study of social capital (Coleman, 1988; Putnam, 1995), wearables and visual analytics allow the collection of big data that can provide spatial-temporal information on people's social interactions in a naturalistic setting. When adequately operationalized, analyzed, and interpreted, this technology-enabled measurement can com-plement the traditional survey and observational methods for assessing focal constructs such as the bonding and bridging facets of social capital and processes of interest such as the development of social networks (e.g., Stone, 2003).

8.1.4   Connecting Industries, Innovation, Individuals

The substantive issues of the three critical "I's" I have described are interrelated. Industries and innovation affect each other. Technological and digital transformations in industries and innovation should be people-centric to focus on what it means for individuals and understood within the context of the issues people care about. Conversely, individuals will influence industries and innovation since how people think, feel and act will lead to attitudes, preferences, judgment, choices, and decisions that in turn affect individual and collective actions that directly impact industries and innovation.

In Singapore, these linkages manifest themselves in specific key ques-tions that have dominated policy deliberations and public debates. These questions involve multiple constructs and interconstruct relationships, with added challenges and opportunities of assessment and validation due to the use of technology-enabled measurement. A clear example concerns the various questions on industry, innovation, and individual (people-centric) issues related to the implications of the local–foreigner composition of the population in Singapore and its changes. Will a new growth industry create good jobs for Singaporeans? Do we have the Singaporean core comple-mented by suitable foreigners with the relevant skills to work in the industry and sustain it? Compared to previous years, the past two decades in Singapore have seen a large and continuous inflow of foreigners due to globalization and the Singapore Government's increased efforts to attract foreign investments and build a world-class city. However, in recent years, the problems of an overreliance on the foreigner workforce in Singapore have not only become more politically sensitive but also more complex. Having economic engines that are critically dependent on a large foreigner workforce is likely to create many unintended negative consequences related to social, sustainability, and security issues. As a result, the Singapore Government has publicly made a political commitment to calibrate the inflow of foreigners while explicitly emphasizing to citizens that it is existential for the small country without natural resources to remain open, attractive, and welcoming to foreigners to come to Singapore to live, work, learn, and play. Political assurance and public engagement are complex and difficult. It is not easy for the Singapore Government to say what it means and mean what it says. If Singaporean workers do not have the relevant skills, should Singapore still invest in the new growth industry now, or should it wait for some time, but can it afford to wait? Is Singapore's strategy, and the timeline required, to develop the skills of the Singaporean workforce well aligned with the nature and pace of industry and technological changes as well as the time sensitivity of innovation and its adoption? If not, what does this mean for the people's way of life and quality of life? These important policy issues and sociopolitical questions involve constructs, interconstruct relationships, and processes (e.g., nature and rate of change in population composition profile, access to amenities, crowd movements, urban mobility, social interactions in naturalistic settings, local–foreigner social integration, skill acquisition, adoption of innovation) that can be assessed and examined using technology-enabled measurement (e.g., wearables, visual analytics, digital transactions) to complement traditional modes of data and measurement in the social sciences (e.g., surveys, interviews, focus group discussions).

It is important to understand the complexity of the relationships linking industries, innovation, and individuals. This explains why in recent years, the Singapore Government has increasingly invested much more effort to consult diverse stakeholders and involve experts from different disciplines and industries in various ways, in both the design stages during policy formulation and the execution stages during policy implementation. The "balancing" act amid tensions and consequences between the seemingly opposing goals of a cosmopolitan city and a cohesive country raises difficult sociopolitical issues for the government and people but also important research and practical questions. Some examples are questions concerning how to conceptualize and measure relevant constructs and processes in phenomena such as a conflict between desirable but apparently contrary goals, paradoxical mindsets in policymaking, social resilience and individual adaptation to changes, regulatory goal focus to prevent negatives and promote positives, and those involving changes and consequences of public trust, psychological capital, social capital, intergroup relations, and social cohesion (for discussion on these issues in the Singapore context, see Chan, 2015a, 2017).

The relevance of the above constructs and processes is evident in Singapore's journey to become a Smart Nation. The relevance is also clear in the ways that Singapore has responded to the COVID-19 crisis, including Singapore's policymaking and public reactions in the implementation of crisis management measures and the tension and balance between lives and livelihood when faced with decisions to lock down to protect public health and reopening to ensure economic, social, and psychological well-being. For example, at the beginning of the COVID-19 pandemic, digital contact tracing tools and solutions were swiftly conceptualized and implemented by the Singapore Government to ringfence the virus spread and help understand the virus transmission so that fewer people will be infected and the healthcare system will not be overloaded. The mandatory and widespread adoption of digital contact tracing directly impacted businesses and industries both positively (e.g., allowing continued operations instead of imposing closures and lockdowns) and negatively (e.g., need for additional resources to implement data management measures). At the same time, the innovative use of the technology-enabled solutions and the data collected raised issues of individual privacy, treatment of data, and public trust (for details, see Chan, 2020). The nature of these technology-based effects and their implications will depend on how countries and cities handle the substantive issues and developments in their contextual situations concerning industries, innovation, and individuals.

The desire to embrace technology alone does not make a city or nation smart. To harness the benefits of technology requires an additional set of contextual factors, which jointly constitute the ecosystem to support the development of substantive issues of industries, innovation, and individuals. I characterize this important supporting ecosystem in terms of another three I's namely, *infrastructure*, *institutions*, and *implementation*.

8.1.5   Infrastructure

In many Asian cities, infrastructure development often lags behind rapid urbanization leading to interrelated and complex problems in housing, waste management, pollution, transport, and delivery of public services. Infrastructure development, especially in physical and virtual connectivity, is one of the foundations of a technologically advanced city that can continuously attract foreign investments and global talent for its industries and innovation and provide a people-centric and highly livable place for the individual city dwellers. Singapore stands out among Asian cities in its accomplishments and continuous efforts to build the infrastructure to support the future economy and data society. This includes both the physical space, such as transport connectivity, integrated amenities, and the virtual space, such as efficient e-government services for meeting business and social needs. An example of integrated infrastructure is the comprehensive national project on the Smart Nation Sensor Platform, which uses various sensors, other IoT devices, and data to create smart solutions and build a smart, secure, green, sustainable, and livable city. This project is an anchor initiative that integrates infrastructure and a common technical architecture to create pervasive connectivity for everyone, everything, and everywhere so that individuals, businesses, and public agencies can leverage on technology to improve lives. For example, some housing estates in Singapore have deployed smart meters, connected to a wireless sensor network, that transmit real-time data on water usage and water leaks via a mobile app. This technology-based solution allows households to detect water leaks early and develop water-saving habits. Another example is the widespread deployment of sensors on lampposts to collect data on air quality, rainfall, and footfall to improve urban planning, such as making decisions on amenities and designing safer footpaths and roads for pedestrians.

In my scientific advisory work to Singapore's government agencies and contributions to policy deliberations and public discourse, I often reiterate the importance of three guiding principles when developing Singapore's infrastructure, which may also be relevant to other cities. These principles could help promote positive outcomes and prevent negative consequences as city planners design and implement technology-based assessments.

First, planners should design and develop every infrastructure beyond its primary intended function. Whether it is an amenity in a walkway, a transport node, or an e-government service, every infrastructure item is part of a larger system with the potential to affect other parts of the system or even another system, either positively or negatively. A good guide is always to see how an infrastructure item can have multiple effects, and therefore serve multipurpose or interfacing functions as well as prevent unintended negative consequences. An example is in urban mobility planning, where road transport infrastructure items can be better designed for intensive, multiple, integrated, and mixed use to enhance connectivity and interfaces between transport and other urban systems. In land-scarce Singapore, it is possible to enhance vibrancy and quality of life in high-density living by utilizing the land beneath road flyovers and viaducts for small commercial enterprises (e.g., coffee shops, convenience stores, eateries) and social spaces (training rooms, therapeutic gardens). The planning parameters will be guided by strategic selection of areas, deployment of sensors and wireless networks, and design of new typologies with consideration for privacy, noise, physical and digital connectivity, and volume of activities within the neighborhood. Allocating commercial and social spaces beneath flyovers and viaducts, which are currently underutilized land due to the necessity of installing road infrastructure items, could help to activate street life and build community distinctiveness and identity.

The second principle is that planners, developers, and users should enhance flexibility and adaptability in land use to integrate economic and social goals. With Singapore's advances in digital connectivity and wireless networks, high-rise buildings and building clusters could accommodate a wide range of land use (e.g., residential, childcare, elderly care, small businesses, light industries) with multiple and compatible functions to meet the changing economic and social needs of different segments of the population. Although this requires a policy and mindset shift from the current highly zoned land use to more flexible land-use zoning plans to integrate economic and social goals, the change is not as radical as it may appear. Singapore's past 50 years of success in infrastructure development happened because urban planning and design were driven not only by the need to support economic activities but also the mission to improve people's quality of life, characteristic of both a cohesive country and a global city. Many trade-offs in land-use situations are real and urgent. However, much more can be accomplished when the approach focuses on what economic and social goals have in common and how their differences can, in fact, complement each other. For example, in the past decade, there has been increasing recognition among leaders and citizens in Singapore that it is a false dichotomy to have to choose between the cosmopolitan vibrancy of a global city and the national solidarity of a cohesive country. Global city goals and national country goals are not mutually exclusive, and they need not be inherently contradictory opposites. Moreover, they can be mutually reinforcing and contribute to Singapore's larger goal of being a "city-in-a-country."

In this regard, I have developed and advocated applying the constructs of "home-in-community" and "paradoxical policymaking" as building blocks of a city-in-a-country and unifying concepts for policy deliberations and public discussions (Chan, 2015b, 2015c). As explained in Section 8.2 on "Changes," technology-enabled measurement offers exciting opportunities and potential to assess these constructs and their antecedents, correlations, and consequents in novel and valid ways. When done adequately, it will, in turn, enhance the accuracy of the inferences we can make from the vast volume, high velocity, and disparate variety of big data available and accessible in Singapore's ongoing digital transformation to a data society.

The third principle is to incorporate social and behavioral insights in urban solutions, and Smart Nation advances. This requires knowing the scientific evidence on how people think, feel, and behave when they interact with things, data, and other people in different environments. Using this evidence-based approach, one should apply the research adequately to design and implement land use, urban management, and the use of smart devices and big data to lead to enhancements to people's quality of life. Increasingly, city planners around the globe are recognizing the importance of incorporating insights from the social and behavioral sciences, in combination with expertise in architecture and design, to understand, predict, and influence how people behave in their urban environment and interact with the various urban systems. Social and behavioral insights on people's attitudes and behaviors as they interact with technology (e.g., public trust in the use of individual-level data, adoption of new technology) will be critical for the effective use of technology-based assessments to contribute positively toward a digital and data society.

8.1.6 Institutions

An important part of the ecosystem is the variety of institutions working in tandem to provide sustained and sustainable support for the transformation efforts to a digital economy and data society. Institutions such as universities and other institutes of higher learning, research institutes, national research councils, research funding agencies, industry associations, consortiums, and foundations not only offer financial and physical resources but also provide structures and processes that jointly enable and facilitate the progression pathways from ideation to implementation.

Singapore has made huge national investments through various institutions to promote research, innovation, and enterprise, which are fundamental strategies and capabilities to drive the transformation of the country into a knowledge-based economy and data society. Led by the Singapore Government and leaders across the academic, public, private, and people sectors, these national-level institutions adopt a whole-of-society approach to enhance translational research in areas of national strategic interests and encourage industrial sectors and businesses to pivot and transform amid technological advancements and the digital revolution.

At the highest level, the national efforts are strategized and driven by the Research, Innovation and Enterprise Council (RIEC). This national council is chaired by the Singapore Prime Minister and comprises cabinet ministers and distinguished local and foreign members from the business, science, and technology communities, signaling the importance of and political commitment to the national R&D agenda. Set up in 2006, the RIEC has its roots in Singapore's national R&D journey that started three decades ago when the country established the National Science and Technology Board in 1991 (which was restructured a decade later as the Agency for Science, Technology and Research or A*STAR) and launched its first five-year National Technology Plan in the same year. The plan, known as the National Technology Plan 1995 (for the period 1991–1995), aimed to develop high-technology activities to move the country up the economic value chain and build a strong base of scientists, engineers, and technologists to help drive economic and enterprise transformation. These plans would be refreshed every five years to position Singapore as an innovation-driven and knowledge-based economy. This resulted in the subsequent Science and Technology Plan for 2000, 2005, and 2010. In 2010, Singapore's R&D strategy was expanded to span research, innovation, and enterprise (RIE), which led to the RIE2015 and RIE2020 plans that included translation, commercialization, and innovation strategies to tap in to the growing pipeline of promising research outputs and support enterprises. Responding to the rapidly evolving global and technology landscape, the RIE plans have also evolved to include White Space funding for unanticipated needs and opportunities. This has enabled Singapore to respond nimbly to new priorities and to seed capabilities in then-new technology areas that subsequently turned out to be critical such as cybersecurity and food.

In 2021, building on the achievements and progress of the past two RIE plans, Singapore launched its RIE2025 plan with a budget of SGD25 billion over the 2021–2025 period. The plan was formulated in anticipation of and in preparation for the future challenges from rapid technological advancements, accelerating digitalization, evolving global trade flows, increasing emphasis on climate change and sustainability, and the multifaceted disruptions due to the COVID-19 pandemic. RIE2025 is organized along four strategic domains (Manufacturing, Trade and Connectivity; Human Health and Potential; Urban Solutions and Sustainability; and Smart Nation and Digital Economy). Investments support these domains to build a robust base of capabilities and peaks of international excellence in academic research, develop the RIE workforce by nurturing a vital research and innovation talent pipeline, and accelerate enterprise innovation.

In the past decade, as Singapore invested heavily in science and technology for its economic and social development, it has become increasingly evident that more attention and investment is needed in tandem for social sciences and humanities research in order to address various urgent and complex social issues such as aging, social mobility, and quality of life. Singapore universities have a good share of top researchers and scholars in the various disciplines in the social sciences and humanities, but there has not been a similar level of national strategic investment in these disciplines in the way that science and technology has received. Thus, in 2016, Singapore set up the Social Science Research Council (SSRC), which is a national-level institution to provide strategic and concerted direction to support and strengthen the social science and humanities research ecosystem in ways that will benefit the social and economic development of Singapore and the Asian region. Comprising policymakers and prominent social science and humanities academics, the SSRC develops capabilities and nurtures human capital through funding research projects, awarding research fellowships, and forming partnerships in the research ecosystem.

Singapore has invested a lot in promoting rigorous and relevant research across the various disciplines in its national strategic efforts to generate solutions to current problems and responses to anticipated future challenges. The research ecosystem will continue to evolve for the future economy and society. Three strategic principles will be increasingly important to guide efforts to integrate the roles of various institutions such as the universities and funding agencies.

The first guiding principle is to promote cross-disciplinary and translational research that produces effective real-world applications. Our knowledge is organized into distinct disciplines and professions, but real-world problems and solutions are not similarly compartmentalized. Research should improve people's lives and practice should be evidence-based.

To make a meaningful and practical impact in society, universities and research institutes may need to revisit some of their strategic research areas, personnel selection practices, and incentive systems. Funding agencies may need to revise some grant policies. A change may also be needed for many researchers and professionals. A silo mentality that sets up barriers between disciplines or between science and practice needs to be broken. The support for cross-disciplinary and translational research must lead to constructive actions, not just pay lip service.

The second guiding principle is to enrich the experiences for students and workers by improving the fit between what they do and what they want and are able to do. There are various ways to optimize their match with the courses or nature of work. For example, consider an individual's competence and choices when making selection and assignment decisions, redesign work processes where practical, and provide a learning environment that helps individuals develop their abilities and interests and acquire relevant knowledge and skills. These people-centric approaches can enable individuals to translate their aptitude and passion into effective actions to function adaptively, resulting in increased economic and social well-being.

The third guiding principle is to revise and integrate education models and workforce development programs to mutually reinforce preemployment training and continuous education and training. Close collaboration between educational institutes and industries should become the norm rather than the exception. Examples include meaningful student internships, industry-based degree programs, and integrating continuous employee education in career development.

8.1.7   Implementation

One of the open secrets of the success of well-intended strategies and well-designed policies, or ingredients for their failure, is the effectiveness in their implementation. The Singapore Public Service is well known for its efficiency in delivering public services. However, in the rapidly changing environment of the digital transformation, economic and social strategies and their associated initiatives must be implemented effectively rather than consistently deterministically as prescribed by fixed rules. In my advisory work, I have emphasized three approaches to help government policies and the public, private, and people sectors function more adaptively.

First, there is a continuous need to review land use and related urban policies. With technological advances as well as the revision of training models and the increasing adoption of flexi-hours, flexi-workplace, and flexi-work (accelerated by the adaptation to the COVID-19 pandemic), the land-use needs for educational institutes and industries such as manufacturing and logistics may change quite drastically. Zoning policies for land use may need to be more flexible to make provisions for mixed use and time-related use. For example, if a building or a piece of land is earmarked for a particular long-term use but is left vacant for some long period due to delayed implementation, then perhaps the default is to allow it for a variety of other uses in the interim rather than increasing the opportunity cost and having to justify the nonusage.

Second, there is urgency in ensuring an effective transformation of the Singapore Public Service into a future-ready organization. This involves developing adaptive organizational structures and work processes as well as an organizational culture of public officers with adaptive attitudes, behaviors, and mindsets. The adaptability, which ensures that policies and work operations are meeting public needs, has to be rooted in the values of integrity, service, and excellence. A future-ready public service is a people-centric organization with leaders who prioritize the well-being of both its employees and the public.

Third, there is a need to refine structures and processes and develop norms to ensure intentions for whole-of-government and whole-of-society approaches are effectively implemented. This involves identifying and addressing the barriers to information sharing and collaboration. Examples of barriers could include bureaucratic procedures, work processes, decision-making authority, incentive system, fear of errors, organizational cynicism, and conflicting needs of the agencies, sectors, or stakeholders involved. Fortuitously, the COVID-19 pandemic has provided the impetus for accelerated implementation of some of the ongoing whole-of-government and whole-of-society initiatives, and it has naturally and rapidly removed resistance and overcome obstacles. Examples include adopting digital payment for purchases and teleconferencing in education, work, and healthcare, which has substantial and substantive effects on learning, flexi-work, and telemedicine.

In summary, to understand the contexts of technology-enabled measurement, it is important to appreciate how a country or city addresses the substantive issues of industries, innovation, and individuals, as well as the supporting ecosystem involving infrastructure, institutions, and implementation. In the case of Singapore, which is a small city-state with existential reason to survive and aspirational motivation to thrive, the country would be well advised to examine these different I's and integrate them for the development of its future economy and society. More generally, to advance our science and practice of technology-enabled measurement and make positive contributions, it is important for us to understand the technological innovations and capabilities, the country's relevant national strategies and the city's planning parameters, as well as how the different stakeholders are interdependent and these effects are interrelated.

8.2   Changes

In psychology and various disciplines in the social sciences, much has been spoken and written about how technological transformation and the related rapidly evolving changes have led to both novel adaptability demands and new aspirational goals and opportunities for individuals, groups, and societies (e.g., Chan, 2000a, 2000b, 2014a). In contrast, less attention has been given to the emerging issues in research, policy, and practice concerning the use of technology-enabled measurement of the social-psychological constructs and processes involved in the various causal effects, temporal dynamics, or other types of changes on how people think, feel, and act in the "new normal" of a digital and data society. Using Singapore as an example and by examining the conceptualization and assessment of changes over time as well as the importance of various constructs and processes, this section highlights some of the key issues and several areas that require more attention and effort to advance technology-enabled measurement. Many of these areas involve the need for measurement specialists to acquire a better understanding and examine the nature of technology-enabled tools, data, and analytical techniques. Specifically, we need to explicate and address the questions involving how technology-enabled approaches produce, collect, analyze, interpret, and use various types of data and relate them to important conceptual and methodological issues in social and psychological measurement.

8.2.1   Varieties of Tools, Data, and Analytics

The basic goal of technology-enabled measurement is to gain insights from the large volume of available or accessible data, which are often disparate and dynamic, to discover some phenomena and understand them better to make predictions, recommendations, or decisions that affect people's lives in important ways. The data may come from areas such as social media, online communication, digital transactions, spatial-temporal information, artificial intelligence, and big data analytics. In the past one or two decades, it has been increasingly evident how technological innovations and applications in these areas have transformed the way that governments, businesses, organizations, and individuals operate and deliver their services.

Currently, there is no consensus on a classification or any widely adopted typology of the different types of technology-enabled tools, data, and analytics. This is not necessarily a limitation, given that an application or a context of use may involve practically any combination of the varieties of tools, data, and analytics. To make substantive contributions, measurement specialists will need to be at least familiar with and have a working knowledge of the various types of technology-enabled tools, data, and analytics in these megatrends, including both the commonalities and differences across them.

The concept of using data as inputs to make evidence-based decisions is, of course, not new. Formally or informally, leaders, researchers, and practitioners have always been generating, collecting, and using empirical data on people's attitudes and behaviors to provide information and derive insights on customers' preferences, employee perceptions, and public opinions to make business, organizational, and political decisions. Until about two decades ago, the most common type of such data was probably the self-report data obtained from respondents through structured surveys. For many decades, self-report data collected using the survey method have been the staple for measurement specialists through the research process, from conceptualization and measurement of constructs (e.g., defining the conceptual content and writing survey items to represent it) to data collection, analysis, and interpretation. When adequately conducted and collected, the survey method and self-report data have been shown to be useful in providing theoretical insights and practical implications. They constitute a large part of the empirical base for measurement science and practice. In addition, there is nothing inherently problematic with self-report data, and many of the criticisms are often overstated (Chan, 2009).

However, there are situations where the survey method and its self-report data are not suitable such as in contexts where the likelihood for social desirability responding is high, accurate memory expected of the responses to survey items is difficult, and valid operationalization of the study constructs or processes is conceptually not possible or practically not feasible. Conversely, in the past one to two decades, the ubiquitous and routine use of technology such as posting of texts, images, and videos on social media, performing a large variety of digital transactions via the Internet, and providing geospatial-temporal and state-based (e.g., physiology) information through the use of personal mobile devices (e.g., mobile phones, wearables) for public transport, exercise, and other location-specific activities (e.g., visits to parks, malls, or offices) has been producing a vast amount of naturally occurring data. Most of such data, often referred to as big data, not only do not have the above limitations (e.g., social desirability and memory errors) but also provide a large amount of new and rich data that potentially could provide reliable and valid measurement of the intended constructs or generate new knowledge or insights on various phenomena of interest (Chan, 2009; Qiu et al., 2018).

"Big data" naturally brings to mind a large dataset containing a huge number of data points that are not readily analyzed by traditional analytical techniques. Somewhat unfortunately, the label tends to highlight the *volume* (i.e., "big") of the data at the expense of the other two "V" characteristics, namely *velocity* and *variety*. Although volume per se does pose challenges, many of these are technical issues such as storage and speed of processing and not problems of complexity. Moreover, many technical problems have been solved with the rapid technological advances pertaining to computational size and power. In contrast, the two characteristics, velocity and variety, both of which are related to the foundational and multifaceted notion of changes, raise many complex issues for science and practice, but they have not been given the attention that they need. Let us take a closer look at the complexity and challenges of these two characteristics, which involve issues of integration and interpretation.

Variety of data refers to the diversity of data sources and formats. A range of variety can be present even within what seems to be a single area of disruptive technology. Take the area of social media, for example, where news and information have driven accelerated rates of change in all domains of life by shortening the time for communication to instantaneous and expanding dissemination to reach a global audience, through the power of virality where users reshare to their social network the content posted by other users. The variety of social media data includes different formats such as texts, images, and videos shared to virtual communities in different social networks and discussion forums such as community blogs, Facebook, Twitter, LinkedIn, Reddit, Quora, Instagram, Snapchat, and YouTube. The variety of data formats and sources raises important measurement issues such as confounds and problems of integration and interpretation due to format-construct or source-construct distinctions, scaling and comparability of the multiple indicators of a construct, and the appropriateness and feasibility of reflective versus formative models in construing the relationships linking measures and constructs.

The velocity characteristic of big data is often summarized as accelerated rates of change, described as a rapid increase, often exponentially, in the amount of data and magnitude of change over time. The virality of social media posts is a clear example of how the change in data can increase at an accelerated pace when people respond with comments each time individuals reshare a post to multiple individuals in their social networks. Central to the velocity characteristic is the notion of the rapid magnitude of change, which refers to the increasing volume of data, but it is often associated with increasing complexity due to increased and increasing volume and variety. Consider the example of cloud computing, which uses shared computer resources (hardware and software) to deliver services over the Internet or Intranet instead of locally using dedicated computing resources. Cloud computing enables users (companies and individuals) to access on-demand computer processing on a pay-for-use basis via their computers and mobile devices. The growth of this disruptive technology has the characteristic of data velocity as it becomes easy and agile for companies and individuals to scale up the services they wish to access, which means increasing not only data volume but also data variety in a shorter time. Examples of data velocity and how velocity is practically tied to increases in data volume and variety can be similarly observed in other areas of ongoing technological disruption such as wearables, IoT, and applications of artificial intelligence.

In short, data velocity is about the rapid and accelerated rates of change but also much more. It has been useful to characterize big data in terms of volume, velocity, and variety. However, it is important to understand how these three Vs interrelate or are interdependent in practice and conceptually what linkages are possible, given their implications for our science and practice of technology-enabled measurement in general and treatment of big data in particular. Less commonly, a fourth V, veracity, is also used to describe big data to refer to its trustworthiness in terms of its quality, defined broadly. Unlike the first three Vs, which are descriptive characteristics of the nature of big data, veracity is more about the inferential assessment of data quality such as reliability, validity, and other psychometric properties, which measurement of any type of data should be concerned with. Hence, it is more appropriate to examine data quality separately instead of adding veracity as a fourth descriptive characteristic of big data.

To advance technology-enabled measurement, it is important to understand the constructs and processes representing the phenomena of interest as well as the three Vs of big data in terms of the multifaceted notion of changes. This involves explicating the interrelationships connecting data volume, velocity, and variety as well as integrating and interpreting their linkages with the focal constructs and processes, especially in the context of changes over time.

8.2.2   Conceptualizing and Assessing Changes over Time

Most fundamentally, it is important to conceptualize and assess the different facets of changes over time explicated by Chan (1998a). For example, any observed changes over time need to be decomposed into random fluctuations versus systematic changes in the focal variable. When systematic change over time exists, the trajectory of a variable may have time-varying correlates and the trajectory may affect or be affected by the trajectories of other variables, such that we need multivariate models that specify and test relationships linking changes in different focal variables. Finally, there may be between-group differences in one or more of the various facets of changes over time. These groups may be observed groupings such as gender and culture groups or unobserved (or latent) groupings distinguishable by distinct characteristics of changes over time (Chan, 1998a; Wang & Chan, 2011).

Understanding the above complexities and the various facets of change over time, in terms of both the conceptual and methodological consider-ations, is necessary in order to make adequate substantive inferences from the assessment of changes over time. Big data researchers can use well-established advanced statistical models such as structural equation model-ing and latent growth modeling to address the complexities involved in a variety of these changes and uncover the dynamics of social and psycho-logical processes (for an example on how to integrate these statistical models, see Chan, 1998a).

It is also important to consider changes over time in the context of multilevel longitudinal analyses. Big data share a similar structure with traditional data in social and psychological research, which is one where the data are often longitudinal and hierarchical because they reflect the temporal and multilevel nature of the substantive phenomenon under study (Chan, 1998a, 1998b, 2010, 2013, 2014b). This provides excellent opportunities to study the interaction between individuals, organizations, and environments. However, current big data research mainly focuses on cross-sectional studies at the individual level. For example, studies have used big data to examine how individuals' temporal orientations are associated with their personality and well-being (Park et al., 2017) and how political orientation affects subjective well-being (Wojcik et al., 2015). A limited number of studies performed longitudinal analysis to examine the change of psychological processes. For instance, Golder and Macy (2011) revealed individual-level diurnal and seasonal mood rhythms using millions of tweets across 84 countries. Using data from Facebook users across US states, Liu et al. (2018) examined the main effects of societal-level cultural tightness–looseness and its interaction effects with individuals' social network density on impression management in terms of online emotional expression.

The use of big data should be maximized to explicate and test cross-level interactions and inter-individual differences in intra-individual changes over time (Chan, 1998a, 2005, 2013). For example, big data about employees are hierarchical because each employee belongs to a team within a company. To understand how the mood of employees affects their company's performance, a multilevel longitudinal analysis could be performed. Furthermore, there could be changes over time in an inherently cross-level construct such as person–group fit, which is a composite construct involving two levels (Chan, 2005).

Finally, it is possible to combine assessment of construct dimensionality and assessment of construct dynamics to examine changes in construct dimensionality over time. Chan (2005) explained the different approaches and techniques and provided examples for conceptualizing and assessing changes in construct dimensionality over time.

8.3 Collaborations

Earlier in this chapter, when discussing the contextual issues of industries, innovation and individuals and how these three I's could be supported by a contextual ecosystem involving another three I's (infrastructure, institutions, and implementation), I briefly described Singapore's collaboration efforts in terms of its whole-of-government and whole-of-society approaches. I also described how institutions such as the SSRC develop research talent across disciplines and encourage them to work together to generate theoretical insights and address practical problems in an interdisciplinary way, such as integrating perspectives across the computational, social, and behavioral sciences. I will end the chapter with this final section on how working together matters in collaborations involving technology-enabled measurement. I will discuss several key issues in terms of multi-disciplinarity and mindsets.

8.3.1 *Multidisciplinarity*

Similar to other countries, the technical experts working on technology-enabled measurement and big data analytics in Singapore are mainly scientists and engineers in computer sciences and computing technologies. Many are experts in data sciences with the relevant technical knowledge, skills, and experience in data mining to achieve the intended goals, such as analyzing sentiments, predicting crowd movements, tracking patterns of activities and interactions, and identifying user characteristics and their preferences and behaviors. To achieve these goals in the respective substantive areas, the computer-based data science experts approach measurement using advances in computing technologies and tools such as mobile connectivity, personal biometric systems, natural language processing, machine learning, and wearables and sensors designed to capture a variety of information such as position, proximity, movement, image, temperature, sound, pressure, and radiation. They conduct analyses using relatively recent techniques such as text analysis, visual analytics, agent-based modeling, network analysis, information propagation analysis, geospatial modeling, and various types of data mining and modeling analyses involving text, image, audio, video, or spatial-temporal information. They also aid scientific communication to users and the public by presenting findings in more readily interpretable and relatable ways using computer-based data visualization tools and dashboards. These modes of presentation translate multilevel, multidimensional, and malleable data in dynamic ways that more closely mirror the nature of the constructs, interconstruct relationships, and processes, thereby aiding understanding. This advantage is not simply cosmetic, and it goes beyond effective communication. The dynamic system presentation approach also allows us to ask "what if" questions by conducting sensitivity and impact analysis to examine how changes in some parameters (quantitative or qualitative changes in constructs and relationships) may affect others. This has direct practical value for scenario-based planning and implications for recommendations on interventions.

When used appropriately, the abovementioned technology-enabled measurement and analyses are not only necessary or well suited (due to the nature of the data source, format, volume, velocity, or variety) but also have the potential to discover knowledge and produce insights in ways that are not possible by relying solely on traditional modes of measurement/data (e.g., survey self-report data) and conventional statistical analyses (e.g., general linear models). However, exclusive reliance on these computing technologies, tools, and techniques is not sufficient for accurate inferences from data with regard to measurement, analysis, and interpretations. Accuracy of inferences refers to the quality and scientific defensibility of the data-driven conclusions arrived at from a purportedly adequate evidence-based approach. It is the basis for predictive power, explanatory value, and intervention efficacy. Hence, in technology-enabled measurement, it is critical to assess the adequacy of a study's design, construct definition and operationalization, data collection, data analytical techniques, and interpretation of findings using well-established scientific measurement concepts such as sampling, reliability, and validity.

Experts from the fields of computing technologies and measurement sciences have knowledge, skills, and experience that complement each other, and they should also work with experts in the relevant content areas such as researchers in the social and behavioral sciences who are familiar with the literature on the constructs and processes of the substantive phenomena of interest. While computing scientists and engineers have important technical knowledge and experience in dealing with data mining, measurement specialists and social-behavioral scientists have important roles to play in various research functions involving sensing, detection, and interventions, which collectively may be called dynamic modeling and impact analysis. This involves the application of measurement expertise and content area knowledge to help identify, understand, predict, and influence the emergent patterns and dynamic modeling of the huge volume, rapid velocity, and diverse variety of the data.

The contribution of measurement specialists and social-behavioral scientists should substantively complement the contribution of the computing scientists and engineers instead of serving as a supplementary role by offering ad hoc advice and expertise in psychometric skills or content knowledge in the substantive phenomena under study. To make substantive complementary contributions, measurement specialists and social-behavioral scientists should acquire a basic working knowledge of the technical concepts and issues associated with the advances in computing data sciences, particularly those related to the availability of big data. This working knowledge will also help social-behavioral scientists to advance their research interests by enhancing their conceptualization and assessment of study constructs and processes (for specific examples on applying big data analytics to organizational psychology research, see Tonidandel et al., 2016).

The implication here is that close collaboration involving experts from multiple disciplines working together is required for technology-enabled measurement to effectively progress toward its intended goals of discovering knowledge, producing insights, and generating solutions to problems. Singapore is a good example of dedicated efforts to enhance multidisciplinary collaboration. In the last two decades, the country's research climate and ecosystem involving technology-enabled measurement have increasingly focused more on effective collaboration across multiple disciplines. Over the years, all the six Singapore universities have been aligning themselves with the country's national strategic priorities, such as those identified by the RIEC. The universities have been moving away from disciplinary silos and enhancing interdisciplinary collaboration as they formulate strategic focus areas in their research, education, and training and evolve their structures, processes, curricula, incentives, and talent selection and development. When managing curiosity-driven or thematic research grants, the RIEC, the SSRC, and various national-level public sector agencies have also been actively encouraging multidisciplinary research such as those that integrate advances in computational technologies and insights from the social and behavioral sciences. There are also other ongoing institutional efforts in Singapore to bridge the computational sciences and the social-behavioral sciences. For example, the A*STAR has begun (in 2021) implementing a new horizontal technology program to address Singapore's national challenges by integrating research expertise from the social-behavioral sciences and the multidisciplinary capabilities that cut across the various A*STAR institutes.

8.3.2 Mindsets

Finally, in a collaboration involving technology-enabled measurement, there is a whole set of important issues concerning mindsets that is seldom explicitly examined or even publicly mentioned. These mindset issues concern assumptions, attitudes, and behaviors regarding approaches to working together across disciplines as well as more generally across different stakeholders. Given the scale, complexity, and multidimensionality of the issues involved in any given problem associated with technology-enabled measurement, many different stakeholders such as policymakers, professionals, businesses and other industry actors, NGOs, the public, and relevant experts from multiple different disciplines have to work together to address the issues and cocreate solutions to the problem. The effectiveness and validity of technology-enabled measurement and, therefore, research quality, outcomes, and utility can be impacted in important ways by how and how well the different experts or stakeholders in the research process work together.

Working together effectively is not easy, and it does not come naturally even if everyone involved is able and willing to help. In this chapter, I have emphasized that when decisions and actions are driven by the end goal of a high-quality and scientifically defensible technology-enabled measurement, it is possible to cocreate solutions to research problems. However, it will take more than just having clear, common goals and good intentions to yield sound research processes and successful research outcomes. As Singapore or any city and country strives to survive and thrive in the digital transformation and emerge stronger as a data society through adequate technology-enabled measurement and rigorous and relevant data sciences, how do we translate the theoretical possibility of working together effectively to a practical plausibility? This is my focus in the final section of this chapter.

8.3.3 Biases and Speaking Up

When working together, stakeholder actions with the best of intentions may lead to unintended negative consequences because everyone is susceptible to human cognitive biases. As shown in the vast amount of research in cognitive and social psychology, one of the most common biases is the human tendency to seek out, interpret, and remember information that confirms one's own existing beliefs or actions. This confirmatory bias is maladaptive when different stakeholders are working together in the collaboration process, whether directed toward research coworkers or those who are providers of the data or users of the research findings. For example, at a multidisciplinary expert team meeting, an expert who starts off believing that a fellow team member from another discipline wants to do only the minimal and what that member has expertise in will dismiss the genuine concerns brought up and disagree with the proposals without an objective discussion on the pros and cons. Similarly, if a decision-maker who is a potential data source provider has a preconceived belief that a principal investigator is exaggerating the research needs, then the decision-maker is more likely to doubt the information provided by all members of the research team and see the team's requests as unreasonable.

Confirmatory bias gets more severe if the dynamics in the team working together encourage groupthink (Janis, 1982), where members of a highly cohesive group withhold dissenting views to go along with

majority opinion due to pressures to conform or maintain social har-
mony, or if the authority structure leads to members keeping quiet or
expressing only views that they think those in power want to hear. This
happens most often in teams that value consensus and cohesion, or when
there is strong pressure to agree with the leader or the more senior team
members. The consequences are not just bad decisions made but also
misplaced confidence in decisions purportedly supported by the group.
That is why it is important to develop a climate of trust and openness
when working together so that everyone can honestly speak up and
genuinely contribute.

The conducive climate of trust and openness for working together takes
time to evolve, which is often longer than the time period that those in
need can wait. That means it is also critical for individual researchers or
stakeholders to have the character, in addition to the competence, for
advancing research integrity and quality when working together in the
collaboration. They need moral courage to speak up for what they believe
is right and the practical skills to surface alternative views constructively
and effectively. Speaking up courageously and constructively and a climate
that values truth and tact are mutually reinforcing. Therefore, it is critical
to develop a work climate that is conducive for a genuine exchange of
ideas. It is also important to form work teams comprising a mix of team
members with a sufficiently heterogeneous background in the team
because high within-team homogeneity may over-emphasize consensus
and cohesion to the extent that is creates conformity and complacency.

8.3.4   Seeing Things from Another's Perspective

One of the most critical aspects of working together is learning to see
things from another's perspective. This requires constant reminder (to self
and to others) and proactive effort because it is human tendency to only
see things from our own viewpoint rather than from another's perspective.
Even when everyone is presented with the same facts, they can have
different meanings when seen from different perspectives. The perspective
each person adopts influences what is considered central or peripheral,
obvious or obscure, and even present or absent, just like the view of our
living room and the things in it can look very different depending on
where we stand. If we do not understand a person's perspective (the person
may be an expert from another discipline or a stakeholder in the collaboration process), what is very meaningful and sensible to them may look
absurd to us. However, if we are going through the same situation or share

similar experiences as the person, we may behave just like the person did and think it is perfectly normal or the right thing to do.

Research in the social and behavioral sciences has shown that we do not see things as they are. We see things as we are and how we are affected by the events or situations. We make interpretations according to our beliefs and past experiences about ourselves and others. We give meanings to things in the context of the circumstances we live or find ourselves in. Moreover, once we have adopted a perspective, it is difficult to suspend or change it. It is even harder to take another's perspective that is different from ours. This is mainly due to the human tendency of confirmatory bias I have described. We see what we expect to see. We seek out and interpret information in a way that will likely confirm our perspective.

If we can see things differently, from another person's perspective, we can have fewer strong disagreements and more constructive responses to contentious issues when working together in the collaboration. At the minimum, we will be more careful in what we say or do in a difficult situation to avoid escalating the negatives. On many complex technology-enabled measurement issues such as an expert's readiness or resistance to using a data type for measuring a construct, can we suspend or get outside our own perspective and try to see things from another's perspective? If we can, and when we do so, we may find our own perspective not as valid as we thought, or at least it is not the only valid one. Of course, we may still hold on to our perspective for good reasons, but we are now able to address the differences better because we understand the other perspective.

In sum, working together in the problem-solving or collaboration process is not just about contributing our expertise/resources and expressing our perspectives. If we learn to see things from another's perspective and apply it adequately, we are more likely to prevent misunderstandings, enable constructive conversations, and achieve win-win solutions among the different collaborators or stakeholders. Most importantly, it will then ultimately benefit the research processes and outcomes that the collaboration was intended for.

In Singapore as well as other cities and countries, many task forces, committees, multiagency teams, cross-sector or community partnerships, and cross-functional teams involving multiple different experts and stakeholders have been formed, and necessarily so, to achieve objectives that involve technology-enabled measurement. This has been occurring for some time in recent years amid a digital transformation and became more urgent as societies use technology to combat the COVID-19 crisis, tackle its multidimensional problems, and deal with postpandemic realities. For these collective group efforts to translate into intended positive outcomes, researchers and all individuals need to pay attention to issues of biases, speaking up, and perspective-taking when they work together in the problem-solving or collaboration process. In short, whether we are a measurement specialist, a computer scientist, or a social-behavioral science expert, we need to have the humility to recognize that we as an individual expert alone do not have all the critical information and hence answers, and we need to have the ability and willingness to learn from others. All team members need to recognize their inter-dependence and work together to collaborate effectively. As researchers or educators training our students to be independent and competent researchers, we need to appreciate the importance of humility and learning orientation so that we can be effectively involved in collaboration, which has become a necessary process in advancing technology-enabled measurement.

To conclude, I hope that this chapter has given readers some food for thought on how focusing on contexts, changes, and collaborations can provide us a roadmap, or at least a heuristic or a springboard, to contribute to technology-enabled measurement and make a positive difference to science and practice in the ongoing digital revolution and transformation to a data society.

REFERENCES

Benner, M. J., & Waldfogel, J. (2023). Changing the channel: Digitization and the rise of "middle tail" strategies. *Strategic Management Journal*, *44*(1), 264–287. https://doi.org/10.1002/smj.3130

Chan, D. (1998a). The conceptualization and analysis of change over time: An integrative approach incorporating longitudinal means and covariance structures analysis (LMACS) and multiple indicator latent growth modeling (MLGM). *Organizational Research Methods*, *1*(4), 421–483. https://doi.org/10.1177/109442819814004

(1998b). Functional relations among constructs in the same content domain at different levels of analysis: A typology of composition models. *Journal of Applied Psychology*, *83*(2), 234–246. https://doi.org/10.1037/0021-9010.83.2.234

(2000a). Conceptual and empirical gaps in research on individual adaptation at work. In C. L. Cooper & I. Robertson (Eds.), *International review of industrial and organizational psychology* (Vol. 15, pp. 143–164). Wiley.

(2000b). Understanding adaptation to changes in the work environment: Integrating individual difference and learning perspectives. In G. R. Ferris (Ed.), *Research in personnel and human resources management* (Vol. 18, pp. 1–42). JAI Press.

(2005). Current directions in personnel selection. *Current Directions in Psychological Science, 14*(4), 220–223. https://doi.org/10.1111/j.0963-7214 .2005.00368.x

(2009). So why ask me? – Are self-report data really that bad? In C. E. Lance & R. J. Vandenberg (Eds.), *Statistical and methodological myths and urban legends: Received doctrine, verity, and fable in the organizational and social sciences* (pp. 311–338). Routledge.

(2010). Advances in analytical strategies. In S. Zedeck (Ed.), *APA handbook of industrial and organizational psychology* (Vol. 1, pp. 85–113). American Psychological Association.

(2013). Advances in modeling dimensionality and dynamics of job performance. In K. J. Ford, J. Hollenbeck, & A. M. Ryan (Eds.), *The psychology of work* (pp. 211–228). American Psychological Association.

(2014a). *Individual adaptability to changes at work: New directions in research.* Routledge.

(2014b). Time and methodological choices. In A. J. Shipp & Y. Fried (Eds.), *Time and work (Vol. 2): How time impacts groups, organizations, and methodological choices* (pp. 146–176). Psychology Press.

(2015a). *People matter.* World Scientific Publishing.

(2015b). Approaches to emergent group differences. In M. Mathew, C. Gee, & W. F. Chiang (Eds.), *Singapore perspectives 2014* (pp. 41–50). World Scientific Publishing.

(2015c). Understanding and assessing social issues in Singapore. In D. Chan (Ed.), *50 years of social issues in Singapore* (pp. 293–322). World Scientific Publishing.

(2017). *Psychological capital.* World Scientific Publishing.

(2020). *Combating a crisis: The psychology of Singapore's response to COVID-19.* World Scientific Publishing.

(2021). The psychology of trust amid COVID-19 challenges. *SID Directors Bulletin, 2021*(2), 6–13. https://ink.library.smu.edu.sg/soss_research/3390

Coleman, J. S. (1988). Social capital in the creation of human capital. *The American Journal of Sociology, 94*, 95–120.

Fletcher, D., & Sarkar, M. (2013). A review of psychological resilience. *European Psychologist, 18*(1), 12–23. https://doi.org/10.1027/1016-9040/a0001124

Golder, S. A., & Macy, M. W. (2011). Diurnal and seasonal mood vary with work, sleep, and daylength across diverse cultures. *Science, 333*(6051), 1878–1881. https://doi.org/10.1126/science.1202775

Hanelt, A., Bohnsack, R., Marz, A., & Marante, C. (2020). A systematic review of the literature on digital transformation: Insights and implications for strategy and organizational change. *Journal of Management Studies, 58*(5), 1159–1197. https://doi.org/10.1111/joms.12639

Janis, I. L. (1982). *Groupthink* (2nd ed.). Houghton Mifflin.

Kozlowski, S. W. J., & Klein, K. J. (2000). A multilevel approach to theory and research in organizations: Contextual, temporal, and emergent processes.

In K. J. Klein & S. W. J. Kozlowski (Eds.), *Multilevel theory, research, and methods in organizations* (pp. 3–90). Jossey-Bass.

Liu, P., Chan, D., Tov, W., & Tong, V. (2018). Effects of cultural tightness-looseness and social network density on expression of positive and negative emotions: A large-scale study of impression management by Facebook users. *Personality and Social Psychology Bulletin*, 44(11), 1567–1581. https://doi .org/10.1177/0146167218770999

Mayer, R. C., David, J. H., & Schoorman, F. D. (1995). An integrative model of organizational trust. *Academy of Management Review*, 20(3), 709–734. https://doi.org/10.2307/258792

Park, G., Schwartz, H. A., Sap, M., Kern, M. L., Weingarten, E., Eichstaedt, J. C., . . . Seligman, M. E. P. (2017). Living in the past, present, and future: Measuring temporal orientation with language. *Journal of Personality*, 85(2), 270–280. https://doi.org/10.1111/jopy.12239

Putnam, R. D. (1995). Tuning in, tuning out: The strange disappearance of social capital in America. *Political Science and Politics*, 28(4), 664–683. http://www .jstor.org/stable/420517

Qiu, L., Chan, S. H.-m., & Chan, D. (2018). Big data in social and psychological science: Theoretical and methodological issues. *Journal of Computational Social Science*, 1(1), 59–66. https://doi.org/10.1007/s42001-017-0013-6

Rifkin, J. (2011). *The third industrial revolution: How lateral power is transforming energy, the economy, and the world*. Palgrave Macmillan.

Rousseau, D. M. (1985). Issues of level in organizational research: Multi-level and cro-level perspectives. In B. M. Staw & L. Cummings (Eds.), *Research in organizational behavior* (pp. 1–7). JAI Press.

Schwab, K. (2015, December 12). *The fourth industrial revolution: What it means and how to respond*. Foreign Affairs. https://www.foreignaffairs.com/world/ fourth-industrial-revolution

(2016). *The fourth industrial revolution*. World Economic Forum.

Stone, W. (2003). Bonding, bridging and linking with social capital. *Stronger Families Learning Exchange Bulletin*, 4(1), 13–16.

Tonidandel, S., King, E. B., & Cortina, J. M. (2016). *Big data at work: The data science revolution and organizational psychology*. Routledge.

Wang, M., & Chan, D. (2011). Mixture latent Markov modeling: Identifying and predicting unobserved heterogeneity in longitudinal qualitative status change. *Organizational Research Methods*, 14(3), 411–431. https://doi.org/10 .1177/1094428109357107

Wojcik, S. P., Hovasapian, A., Graham, J., Motyl, M., & Ditto, P. (2015). Conservatives report, but liberals display, greater happiness. *Science*, 347 (6227), 1243–1246. https://doi.org/10.1126/science.1260817

CHAPTER 9

A European Perspective on Psychometric Measurement Technology

Nigel Guenole, Cicek Svensson, Bart Wille, Kristina Aloyan, and Peter Saville

There have been at least two major technology-driven revolutions in applied psychological measurement in industry that have occurred in living memory. The first involved the shift from paper-based to remote computer-based testing, following the wide-scale availability of the Internet. During this, the first notable wave of technological influence on testing, the field witnessed considerable advances in psychometric models for measuring latent traits. These are now routinely implemented in large-scale computerized adaptive testing programs. Computer-based testing was available prior to the Internet, of course, but the development of the Internet certainly encouraged this testing approach. This first technological revolution in testing generated considerable concern. There was worry that the constructs assessed across paper-based and internet-based testing methods would not be equivalent, and there was concern that unproctored remote testing would lead to higher levels of cheating.

By and large, these concerns were assuaged with the passing of time. Measurement equivalence analyses of the psychometric test data showed that tests functioned similarly between offline and online formats (Mead & Drasgow, 1993), albeit practitioners often make caveats about some screen formats being inappropriate for some assessments (e.g., spatial reasoning on small screens). Concerns about construct equivalence have also lessened as standardized screen display formats for mobile devices have emerged. Despite the fact that fraudulent activity does occur in certification licensing programs, some research revealed that concerns about cheating in remote testing might be overemphasized, as people on the whole do not cheat on psychological assessments (e.g., Nye et al., 2008). Internet-based testing even spurred innovative approaches to remotely proctor test-taking sessions, so long as privacy legislation can be successfully navigated. Some of these solutions involve detecting screen capture attempts, copy and paste prevention, periodic snapshots of the test taker for identification matching, detectors that identify when more than one person appears in the camera lens, and video recording of the testing sessions. On the whole, the industry rose to the challenge of making psychological measurements with internet technology, and numerous sets of best practice guidelines now exist (e.g., Lievens, 2006).

The second revolution is one we are in the midst of currently. It is driven by algorithmic scoring of newly available "Big Data" sources, such as unstructured text, chatbot conversations, social media content, sensor data from mobile and other Internet of Things (IoT) devices, and even the process data gathered from game-based testing experiences, to name but a few examples. There is as much, perhaps more, concern about the impact of this new technology on measurement as there was during the time that internet testing was becoming common. Concerns center on outcomes such as reliability, validity, privacy, and fairness. This time around, however, there is a fundamental difference in the application of technology to psychological measurement. Namely, applied psychologists and technologists are developing psychological measurement approaches that harness data that are unstructured (as opposed to structured) and that oftentimes were not originally intended for psychological measurement.

The unstructured data present a challenge because our most well-tested psychometric models from classical test theory, factor analysis, and item response theory are for structured data. The secondary usage of data, in turn, creates privacy concerns. For instance, new assessment methods have seen social media content scraped and scored, log data created by players of serious games collected by stealth and analyzed for psychological meaning, and the sensor data from wearable and mobile devices scored to infer standing on psychological traits. We do not expect it would be too contentious to say that technology has not impacted the traditional psychological constructs we hope to measure; perhaps with the exception that temporal perspectives on traditional constructs are now more commonly discussed. Instead, the impact of technology has been on how measurements are made and how they are reported.

Much has already been written about both waves of technological influence on measurement in regard to how measurements are made and reported. Writings include recent edited volumes by Dragsow (2015), Scott et al. (2017), and Tippins and Adler (2011); special issues with commentaries on the topic of measurement and technology from Morelli et al. (2017); guidelines from relevant testing bodies such as the International Test Commission (2005); a multitude of guidelines from commercial firms; and even a journal devoted to technology and testing issues, the *Journal of Technology and Testing*. These writings, for the most part, reveal advancements in testing technology and their adoption are an international affair, but with heavy North American influence. This chapter, therefore, will instead provide a European perspective on the state of technology for psychological measurement among applied practitioners. Recognizing that the technology advancements themselves are international in nature, we will examine aspects of technology and measurement that can be considered uniquely *European*. That is, we report here on a survey examining the attitudes of European practitioners working in talent acquisition and development, and the attitudes of European workers experiencing these assessment methods during this second wave of technological innovation in measurement.

We apply an industrial-organizational psychology lens, examining attitudes to technology developments in prehire situations for talent acquisition (candidate attraction, recruiting, and selection) and posthire situations for talent development (measuring work attitudes including employee engagement, citizenship behavior, counterproductivity and turnover intentions; skill acquisition at work; and learning and development). We report on the practitioner perspectives in these areas regarding a) the current use of technology for psychological measurement in Europe, b) the adoption of emerging applications of technology in Europe, and c) the acceptance of technology for psychological measurement in Europe. It is worth noting that the data we analyzed was collected from January to April 2021, when the world had acclimatized to new ways of working. We expect that any changes in perceptions of technology for assessment that are attributable to COVID-19 are likely to be reflected in responses.

9.1 Method

We used a survey of talent management practitioners in Europe who are using measurement technologies in talent management. We define measurement technology broadly to include common methods people use to take psychological measurements. There are many ways to categorize the measurement technologies that we might have followed, and often, the edges between where one method finishes and another begins are blurred. For instance, questionnaires are a measurement technology frequently administered as part of an assessment center, while assessment centers are a measurement technology in their own right that might include questionnaires. To some degree, boundaries between assessment methods are arbitrary, but there are still distinctions made in practitioners' minds.

In this research, we survey our participants about nine different categories of measurement technology based on our experience in industry. The measurement technologies we ask about are *interviews*, *questionnaires*, *assessment and development centers*, *situational judgment tests (SJTs)*, *game-based assessment (GBA)*, *text parsing*, for instance, on resumés and cover letters, *scoring of digital footprints including social media*, and *IoT technology* such as smartphones.

9.2 Participants

The survey we report was a convenience survey that was distributed among the personal networks of the authorship team and was also promoted on the LinkedIn professional networking website to The Psychometrics Forum as well as to the European Network of Selection Researchers. We received 229 responses overall, of which 182 were from Europe. Given the convenience sampling methodology, unsurprisingly, the survey was not balanced across European countries and can certainly not be considered a random sample. The largest number of respondents came from where the authors had strong networks – the United Kingdom, Belgium, and Sweden, and also Serbia. The exact breakdown was as follows. Belgium (9%), Croatia (2%), Denmark (1%), Finland (1%), France (3%), Germany (3%), Greece (2%), Hungary (1%), Italy (4%), Netherlands (2%), Northern Ireland (1%), Poland (1%), Romania (4%), Serbia (10%), Spain (6%), Sweden (10%), Switzerland (6%), Turkey (1%), and the UK & Ireland (34%).

Given that the sample is a convenience sample, we do not undertake inferential statistical analyses. Instead, we report descriptive statistics on the prevalence of different forms of measurement technology and beliefs about their use. Importantly, for each method, we asked a screener question that first asked whether a particular method was used, which was asked of all participants. A final question that was also asked of all participants was on whether privacy legislation such as General Data Protection Regulation (GDPR) had impacted their decision to use or not use a particular technology. Questions about specific measurement technologies, however, were only asked of those who answered yes to the question about whether they use the method.

The chapter sections that follow first provide a high-level overview of existing measurement technology research in each area, followed by a discussion of survey results from practitioners who use these assessment methods in Europe. Some of the questions about the assessment methods were common across different assessment methods, while some were unique. The common questions related to topics that are relevant for all measurement methods, principally reliability, validity, adverse impact, candidate experience, and level of seniority at which methods are deployed. Other questions are specific to specific methods, such as the format of the scenario presentation for a situational judgment test, or whether emotions are assessed in automated video interviewing. For each measurement method, we first present the common questions across methods, followed by results for more specific follow-up questions. Before we proceed, it is worth discussing interpretations of common psychometric terms.

9.3 Interpretations of Common Psychometric Terms

9.3.1 Interpretations of Reliability

Different forms of reliability are appropriate for different psychometric applications. Internal consistency reliability might be appropriate when gauging whether a set of items is sufficiently homogenous to warrant interpretation of a score as a measure of a construct. In contrast, test-retest reliability might be appropriate for testing the stability of a construct over measurement occasions. Notwithstanding that different reliability forms are important for different applications, test–retest reliability is appropriate for many, if not most, applications in prehire recruitment and selection and posthire applications in talent management. This is because we tend to measure constructs or knowledge that are relatively stable over time frames relevant to organizational applications, at least in the absence of intervention. For that reason, when we ask practitioners about their perceptions of the reliability of different assessment methods, we refer to test–retest reliability. In terms of reliability benchmarks, we used labels of very reliable (close to 0.80, or higher), somewhat reliable (close to 0.70), and unreliable (close to 0.60, or lower).

9.3.2 Interpretations of Validity

A similar case can be made that different forms of validity matter for different applications as was made for reliability. For example, in the context of validity, content validity might be appropriate when assessing the suitability of a measure as an indication of a candidate's domain knowledge, while face validity might be appropriate when gauging whether candidates are likely to have a favorable reaction to an assessment process in a hiring situation. While there are forms of validity with less and more relevance to different applications, predictive validity for job performance is important to many, if not most, applications of assessment in organizations. Therefore, when we referred to validity in our survey, we were explicit in referring to predictive validity. In terms of predictive validity benchmarks, when we asked practitioners about their views on the validity of different measurement methods, we used labels of very predictive (close to 0.30 or higher), somewhat predictive (close to 0.20), and not predictive (close to 0.10 or lower).

9.3.3   *Interpretations of Adverse Impact*

Reliability and validity have been the overriding concerns when evaluating the appropriateness of different selection methods for some time. However, alongside these two critical criteria are others that are commonly considered equally important, and one of these is adverse impact. Adverse impact occurs when the selection rates for a protected group are lower than those of a majority group. Typically, a threshold of $^4/_5$ is used, with adverse impact indicated if a protected group is selected at less than $^4/_5$ of the rate at which a majority group is selected due to the use of a selection tool. Because the $^4/_5$ threshold can be triggered in a sample due to random fluctuation when the threshold is not reached in a population, the $^4/_5$ rule is typically supplemented with a statistical test such as the Z-test for independent proportions, which is equivalent to the chi-test test for independence in a 2 × 2 contingency table. The Z-test is also known as the 2-standard deviation (SD) rule because an absolute value of approximately 2 (1.96) indicates significance at the 0.05 level (Collins & Morris, 2008). While many organizations that do large-volume recruitment undertake adverse impact analyses, general beliefs about the adverse impact of different methods might preclude their use in others. It is therefore essential to assess the attitudes of users regarding the adverse impact of different methods. We asked candidates whether they believed measurement methods would lead to the following adverse impact levels, small (close to Cohen's d of 0.20 or lower), medium (close to Cohen's d of 0.50), or high adverse impact (close to Cohen's d of 0.80 or higher).

9.3.4   *Interpretations of Candidate Experience*

In recent times our conversations with users of measurement technology have taken an interesting turn. Reliability and validity evidence, once the supreme criteria against which the appropriateness of an assessment was judged, are now joined by conversations about the candidate experience. Examples of the sorts of comments that have been made are that "questionnaires are 20th-century technology, but we need to provide 21st-century experiences" and "the candidate experience is just as important as the prediction of posthire performance." The reasons are many but broadly center around the value of managing brand perceptions that can be created around strong candidate experiences. In a competitive hiring marketplace, strong employer brands attract higher-quality talent. Firms also want to reject certain candidates but still have them as consumers of their products, apply next time a suitable opportunity arises, and recommend the organization to colleagues and friends. Given that there is at least an apocryphal association between newer assessment methods such as GBA and candidate experience, we surveyed users of each assessment method on the views of the candidate experience of each method. We used a Likert scale for this survey question that ranged from 1 representing a very positive candidate experience to a 5 representing a very negative candidate experience.

9.4 The Method versus Construct Distinction

We asked about the measurement characteristics for all methods in general rather than in relation to specific constructs. For measurement technologies that are not intended to assess a particular construct, such as SJTs and perhaps GBA, this distinction is not as relevant. People regularly talk of reliability and validity with respect to the method in general because these technologies measure heterogeneous content as opposed to homogenous content. However, for technologies that assess constructs, the reliability and validity of the measure can vary markedly depending, for instance, on whether a cognitive or a noncognitive construct is assessed.

On the one hand, a general perception of these features of measurement methods might be argued to lack the finer-grained interpretation of assessing perceptions of methods crossed with constructs. On the other hand, other features of measurement technologies impact reliability and validity, such as how carefully the items that are included are chosen, how many items are included in an assessment, and the assessment conditions under which the assessment takes place. We did not separate out the impact of any such features. A reason in favor of this approach is that our experience is that, among practitioners, generalized attitudes toward measurement methods are common. Perhaps most importantly, the generalized attitudes approach has the advantage of being consistent with the notion that this chapter is about measurement technologies – each of our question sets refers to the properties of a measurement technology overall. For researchers who are interested in the granular differences in reliability and validity perceptions when the same method is used to assess different constructs, we refer the reader to Hausknecht et al. (2004).

9.5   Chapter Structure

We have chosen to present our results according to the measurement method or technology instead of other possible ways. Other ways might have included presenting the challenge that the assessment methodology resolved, such as recruitment or learning and development. However, our data collection strategy was to survey users of different measurement technologies about their attitudes and beliefs about a method. We did not ask questions of people about measurement technologies they indicated they did not use. This means that responses to questions about different measurement technologies are not always based on the same samples. Instead, they are based on different subsamples of users. However, our rationale is that we are writing a chapter on measurement technologies used in Europe, and therefore, organizing the results according to the different measurement technologies is appropriate. In the question that is specific to each method (e.g., whether video, animation, or text was used for SJTs), proportions need not add to 100 because respondents could choose one, some, or all of the responses.

9.5.1   Prevalence of Assessment Methods in Europe

We asked all practitioners first about their use of each category of assessment methodology. For this question, the sample of respondents answering about each measurement technology was the same and can be compared. The prevalence rates for each of the nine measurement technologies were as follows: interviews (87%), questionnaires (78%), assessment and development centers (51%), SJTs (29%), GBA (15%), IoT technology (2%), text parsing (5%), digital footprint scoring (5%), and chatbots (3%). We show the comparison in Figure 9.1. These results reveal that despite the considerable excitement about these methods and the marketing power of many of the emerging measurement technology vendors, among sample participants in this survey, traction in organizations is limited. Instead, the dominant assessment methodologies used by organizations in our sample are those we know well, interviews, questionnaires, and assessment and

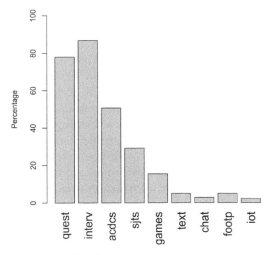

Figure 9.1   Prevalence of different measurement methods used by European
survey respondents

Note. N = 182. quest = questionnaires; interv = interviews; acdcs = assessment and development
centers; games = GBA; text = text parsing, e.g., resumés; chat = chatbots; footp = digital footprint
scraping; iot = IoT assessment technology.

development centers. Of the "newer" methodologies being used, we see
SJTs and games featuring most prominently.

The reason for the low adoption rate of these newer technologies is
impossible to discern from our survey. Reasons may include the relative
lack of maturity in the scientific evidence for the measurement capabilities
of these technologies, or perhaps concerns in relation to these measurement methodologies regarding fairness or perhaps privacy, a topic we
return to shortly. One thing we note is that our experience is that there
is no shortage of firms offering products and services that use technologies
like text parsing, IoT, and digital footprint scraping for talent management. We now turn to thoroughly exploring attitudes toward specific
assessment methods. In the following sections, results only represent the
opinions of users of each technology. Across-methodology comparisons are
not advised because different participants used different technologies.

9.6   Privacy Concerns with Measurement Technologies

A key feature that separates traditional methods of measurement, such as
questionnaires and interviews, from emerging technologies is the nature

of the data that they analyze. In traditional approaches to measurement, best practice suggests that information is limited to that identified by job analysis as relevant to the job. Moreover, in typical situations, it is analyzed with the examinee's awareness. That is, the information was provided with the intention that it would be assessed. With newer assessment methods, the best practice is still that a job analysis determines the relevance of the information to the assessment process, but the relevance or otherwise of the information a scoring algorithm might use is not so clear-cut. Take social media profile information presented on Facebook or Twitter. Personal information here may or may not be relevant for the prediction of job performance, but studies indicate that some employers do look at this information (Levinson, 2010). In most cases, such information will not have been generated by the individual with the awareness that it would be psychologically assessed. Even where the individual does know that they are being assessed, in some approaches like stealth assessment in GBA, the individual does not know what exactly is being assessed. The growing emphasis on privacy globally is shown by the GDPR, which specifies how personal data can be processed, which came into force in 2016.

With this background as context, it would be useful to know the extent to which privacy concerns impacted decisions regarding the appropriateness (or inappropriateness) of different measurement technologies. To get at this question, we asked participants whether privacy concerns had impacted their decisions about whether to use specific assessment methodologies. This question, like the question on the prevalence of different methods, was asked of all participants in the survey. The results are presented in Figure 9.2. We see that, overall, concerns with privacy do not appear to be a determining feature with respect to usage or nonusage of measurement technologies. The highest percentage of the sample indicating they did not use a measurement technique for reasons related to privacy was just 16%. However, this was for scoring digital footprints and social media, which is one of the emerging measurement methods that have hallmark characteristics that prompt concern, that is, data with potentially only fringe relevance to job performance and using data that were not generated by individuals with the express purpose of psychological assessment as part of a job application. In fact, the top five measurement methods that practitioners indicated not using due to privacy concerns were newer assessment technologies involving nontraditional data sources that people generate without full awareness of how these data will be used. These technologies include digital footprint scoring (16%), IoT

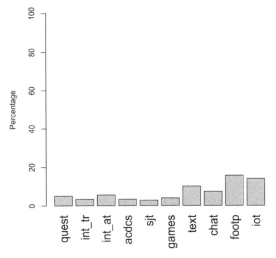

Figure 9.2   Privacy concerns with measurement technologies
Note. N=182. quest = questionnaires; int_trad = traditional interviews; interv_aut = automated interviews; acdcs = assessment and development centers; games = GBA; text = text parsing, e.g. resumés; chat = chatbots; footp = digital footprint scraping; iot = IoT assessment technology.

technology (14%), resumé parsing (10%), and automated interviewing (6%). Overall, concerns about privacy do exist with respect to assessment methodology, but there appear to be other factors at play governing their use or nonuse.

9.7   Interviews

Interviews involve assessment of candidates' potential work performance based on their responses to questions from a future employer or manager. Interviews are one of the most popular methods in personnel selection (McDaniel et al., 1994; Ryan & Ployhart, 2014). They are popular because they permit contact with candidates, which allows observing a candidate's interpersonal behavior, such as communication style, as well as probing technical skills. They also allow examination of credentials identified in other selection methods (e.g., CVs, reference letters). The observation of interpersonal behavior seems a particularly attractive aspect of interviews. A recent survey showed that competency-based interviews were one of the most used selection methods across surveyed organizations in the UK (CIPD, 2020). Existing meta-analyses also show that, among various possible selection methods, interviews are perceived very favorably by candidates (Anderson et al., 2010; Hausknecht et al., 2004).

Interviews can be unstructured, semistructured or structured, face-to-face or digital, synchronous and asynchronous. In structured interviews, the process is highly standardized, meaning that interviewers follow a predefined set of questions and procedures for all candidates applying for the job (Chamorro-Premuzic & Furnham, 2010; Dipboye, 1994). Such standard-ization allows interviewers to use ratings or scales to compare candidates. In contrast, unstructured interviews do not follow the same structure, and the questions may vary greatly from one candidate to another. Unstructured interviews are often guided by interviewers' judgments on what would be the best way to lead the interview process. Semistructured interviews assume some predefined structure and questions but at the same time give an opportunity to vary the interview process between candidates. The typology of structured/unstructured interviews is broadly used in the organizational literature. However, there is great variation in the ways that structured interviews are defined and measured in existing research (Macan, 2009).

There have been numerous reviews on the topic of employment inter-view validity, including by Arvey and Campion (1982), Harris (1989), Judge et al. (2000), Levashina and Campion (2007), Moscoso (2000), and Posthuma et al. (2002). While unstructured interviews offer greater flex-ibility for interviewers and interviewees, structured interviews are generally considered to be more reliable and valid (Levashina et al., 2014; McDaniel et al., 1994). Salgado and Moscoso (2002) examined what is typically measured by conventional interviews (i.e., those that primarily focus on applicants' credentials, descriptive information of experience, and self-evaluative questions) and behavioral interviews (i.e., those that focus on job-related behaviors and experiences). Behavioral interviews were related to social skills, job knowledge, and experience, as well as situational judgment. Conventional interviews were related to the Big Five personality traits, social skills, job experience, and general mental ability.

Another meta-analysis by Roth and Huffcutt (2013) examined the relationship between employment interviews and cognitive ability. Specifically, they reanalyzed the results of earlier work by Berry et al. (2007) and reported a corrected correlation of 0.42 between employment interviews and cognitive ability, while Berry et al.'s (2007) meta-analysis reported a corrected correlation of 0.27. In another meta-analysis of criterion-related validity of employment interviews Huffcutt et al. (2013) estimated the mean-corrected validity for unstructured interviews was 0.20 and for highly structured interviews to be 0.70. Employment interviews have also been scrutinized regarding applicant faking (Law et al., 2016; Levashina & Campion, 2007; Melchers et al., 2020). Melchers et al. (2020) highlighted that there is limited evidence on the effects of faking as well as ways that such faking can be detected.

While selection interviews can be conducted in live face-to-face format, rapid technological developments offer innovative ways for interviewing candidates. This includes synchronous video interviews (SVIs) and asynchronous or automated video interviews (AVIs), and use of artificial intelligence (AI) (Woods et al., 2020). SVIs assume that candidates interact with the interviewer online in real time. AVIs can be conducted at any time without the presence of an interviewer. In AVIs, candidates generally receive instructions on how to complete the interview and how to record their answers to the interview questions. Due to their asynchronous nature, AVIs may be more cost and labor effective for organizations and help to screen a larger pool of applicants (Lukacik et al., 2020; Suen et al., 2019). However, evidence on AVIs' reliability and validity as a selection method is limited (Hickman, Saef, et al., 2021).

There is also growing interest in machine-learning algorithms to assess applicants' characteristics (verbal and nonverbal behaviors) from employment interviews (Naim et al., 2015). For example, Hickman, Bosch, et al. (2021) developed machine-learning algorithms to predict the Big Five personality traits (both interviewees' self-ratings and interviewers' ratings) from video interviews. The findings showed that interviewers' ratings of candidate personality could be predicted more accurately with language-based algorithms than self-reports on personality. In summary, while the forms and ways of conducting employment interviews change and develop, reflecting the advancements in business and selection practices, interviews remain popular among organizations and practitioners.

9.7.1 European Trends with Interviews

Interviews are the most frequently used measurement technology we surveyed about, with 87% of respondents indicating their organizations use the method. Participants are relatively accurate in their perception of the prevalence of interviews, with 99% reporting they are widely or very widely used. The most frequent domains in which interviews are used are depicted in the upper panel of Figure 9.3. This highlights that they are most commonly used for recruitment (89%), followed by career management (50%), performance management (37%), learning and development (34%), culture interventions (21%), and finally, restructuring (21%). The

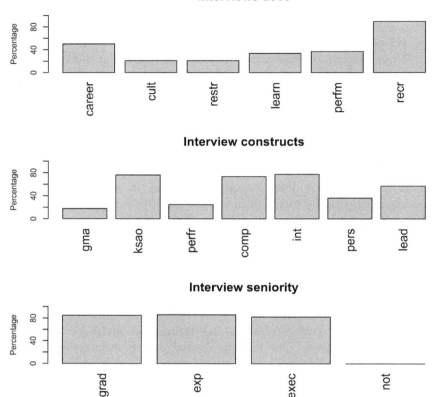

Figure 9.3 **Interviews**

Upper panel. Use of interviews in common assessment contexts
Note. N = 158. career = career development; cult = organizational culture; restr = restructuring;
learn = learning and development; perfm = performance management; recr = recruitment.

Middle panel. Constructs measured with interviews
Note. N = 158. gma = general mental ability; ksaos = general job knowledge; perfr = job
performance; comp = competencies; int = motives, values and interests; pers = personality;
lead = leadership potential.

Lower panel. Use of interviews at different levels of seniority
Note. N = 158. grad = graduate; exp = experienced hire; exec = executive; not = not used for selection.

most common constructs assessed with interviews are depicted in
Figure 9.3 (middle panel). Interviews are most frequently used to assess
motivation and interests (77%), followed by technical competencies
(knowledge, skills, abilities and other characteristics, or KSAOs) (76%),
behavioral competencies (73%), leadership potential (57%), personality

(36%), performance management (25%), and general mental ability (18%). Interviews are used extensively across seniority levels as a measurement technology, as indicated in the lower panel of Figure 9.3. Users reported using them at the graduate (85%), experienced (86%), and executive hiring (82%) levels, suggesting usage is consistent across levels. The candidate experience of interviews was rated as very positive or somewhat positive by 70% of respondents.

Among our respondents, the majority, 62%, considered interviews somewhat reliable, and 33% considered the assessments unreliable. The majority, 70%, considered interviews somewhat predictive, 16% considered interviews very predictive, and 13% believed they were not very predictive of performance. With respect to adverse impact, the majority, 50%, believed interviews led to moderate adverse impact against protected groups, 17% believed they led to large adverse impact, and 32% believed they led to small levels of adverse impact. Traditional and face-to-face interviews are both quite common, with 81% and 72% using each type of interview, respectively. By a long way, the most common form of interview was synchronized interviewing. Only 13% of respondents that indicated they used interviews reported using asynchronous interviews, compared to 90% that reported using synchronized interviews. It is most common to use semistructured interviews, with 70% of interview users reporting this format, compared to 56% using fully structured and only 14% using unstructured formats. We asked what was scored in interviews. Results revealed that responses to the questions themselves were scored by 79%, body language was scored by 30%, candidate expressions were scored by 29%, intonation was scored by 24%, and text transcripts were evaluated by just 13% of the sample. By a long way, human ratings were the most common scoring approach, with 71% of the sample reporting doing so. Human qualitative evaluations were reported by 42% of the sample, and algorithmic approaches for quantitative and qualitative evaluations were reported by 2% and 6% of the sample.

9.8 Questionnaires

Questionnaires are among the most pervasive technology approaches for psychological assessment, and with good reason. More than a century of research has shown that they can be used to measure the constructs that are relevant to talent management, such as ability, personality, and interests, in a reliable and valid way. In fact, part of the challenge facing new technological approaches to measurement lies in measuring psychological

attributes to reliability and validity standards that were originally established using questionnaires. It is not unreasonable to say that as far as the
traditional criteria of reliability and validity go, no other measurement
comes close to standardized questionnaires. They can be used to assess
right versus wrong scored maximum performance cognitive constructs and
rating scale based on typical performance noncognitive constructs that
predict the performance outcomes we care about most in organizational
settings, such as task performance (e.g., quality, quantity, timeliness of
work outputs) and contextual performance (e.g., citizenship behavior,
counterproductivity). All the while, questionnaires demonstrate construct
validity, meaning well-designed questionnaire-based measures of psychological constructs assess what we claim they assess, which is critically
important for feedback. Despite the flexibility of questionnaires, they are
not without criticism. The two strongest criticisms of questionnaires,
adverse impact and faking, carry the most weight when questionnaires
are used to measure two of the most frequently assessed constructs in
industrial psychology, cognitive ability and personality.

9.8.1   *European Trends with Questionnaires*

Standardized questionnaires are the second most frequently used measurement technology, with 78% of respondents indicating their organizations
use the method. Participants are relatively accurate in their perception of
the prevalence of interviews, with 89% reporting they are widely or very
widely used. The most frequent domains in which questionnaires are used
are listed in the upper panel of Figure 9.4. This highlights that they are
most frequently used for recruitment (90%), followed by career management (57%), learning and development (53%), performance management
(43%), culture interventions (41%), and finally, restructuring (20%).
Questionnaires are most frequently used to assess personality (95%),
motivation and interests (81%), general mental ability (80%), leadership
potential (62%), behavioral competencies (58%), technical KSAOs (47%),
and performance (28%) (see Figure 9.4, middle panel). Questionnaires are
used extensively across seniority levels as a measurement technology. Users
reported using them at the graduate (84%), experienced (83%), and
executive hiring (71%) levels, indicating there is a mild drop-off in the
use of standardized questionnaires at the most senior levels of hiring. These
results are illustrated in the lower panel of Figure 9.4.

   The reliability of questionnaires is viewed relatively favorably by our
sample. A total of 46% believed they were very reliable, 51% believed they

Questionnaire uses

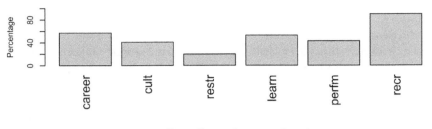

Questionnaire constructs

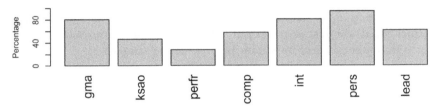

Questionnaire seniority

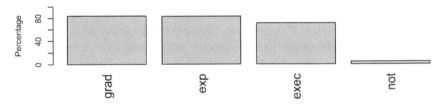

Figure 9.4   **Questionnaires**

Upper panel. Use of questionnaires in common assessment contexts
Note. N = 142. career = career development; cult = organizational culture; restr = restructuring; learn = learning and development; perfm = performance management; recr = recruitment.

Middle panel. Constructs measured with questionnaires
Note. N = 142. gma = general mental ability; ksaos = general job knowledge; perfr = job performance; comp = competencies; int = motives, values, and interests; pers = personality; lead = leadership potential.

Lower panel. Use of questionnaires at different levels of seniority
Note. N = 142. grad = graduate; exp = experienced hire; exec = executive; not = not used for selection.

were somewhat reliable, and just 3% believed they were unreliable. The pattern was similar for predictive validity, where 47% said questionnaires were very valid, 51% said they were somewhat valid, and 2% said that questionnaires were not valid. Most of the respondents who reported using questionnaires, 45%, reported that they had low adverse impact, with 31% indicating moderate adverse impact and 9% indicating high adverse impact. There were 15% who reported being unsure. The candidate experience for questionnaires was rated as very good or good by 77% of the sample. Just over half, 52%, of the sample reported using adaptive questionnaires.

The most common administrative approach was to use unproctored questionnaires, which 59% of the sample reported doing. Remote supervision (e.g., via camera technology) was reported by 25% of the sample, and in-person supervision was used by 23% of the sample. The most common administrative method was for desktop computing, reported by 71% of the sample, followed by mobile-enabled assessment by 48% and paper-based administration for just 14%. Appropriate norms were considered important or very important by 76% of the sample.

9.9   Assessment and Development Centers

Assessment and development centers (ACDCs) are one of the popular and long-established assessment methods in human resource management (Thornton & Gibbons, 2009). An assessment center (AC) involves a comprehensive evaluation of candidates applying for the job, while a development center (DC) involves the same evaluation in a posthire situation for applications like succession and leadership development. Typically, ACDCs include different elements (presentations, interviews, simulation exercises, etc.) with the aim to observe and examine candidates' behaviors and performance across situations. These behaviors and performance are usually evaluated by multiple assessors who are trained to evaluate participants by following a standardized assessment process (Lievens, 2009; Thornton & Gibbons, 2009). Applicants are commonly invited to take part in an assessment day during which they complete a series of individual or group-based tasks and exercises observed by the company assessors. According to the International Task Force on Assessment Center Guidelines (2015) (hereinafter The Guidelines, 2015), ACs must include clearly defined behavioral constructs related to the job with a clear link to the assessment center elements. Candidate behaviors in the ACDCs can then be classified based on these behavioral constructs. The Guidelines (2015) also underscore the importance of simulation exercises as the key vehicle for ACDC assessment because they provide opportunities for candidates to display behavioral responses to various work-related situations.

ACDCs are valued by organizations because they provide a rounded view of applicants (Thornton & Rupp, 2006). From the applicants' perspective, ACDCs are perceived as a more face-valid method compared to cognitive ability tests (Macan et al., 1994). At the same time, ACs can be very time, cost and labor consuming and challenging to manage over time (Robertson & Smith, 2001). Due to their complexity, ACs also require thorough design and development to ensure the quality and reliability of assessment process. ACDCs have been extensively researched on the topic of their validity. While the criterion-related validity of dimension ratings is well established (e.g., Arthur et al., 2003; Meriac et al., 2008), there have been many debates concerning the construct-related validity of ACs. In his review paper, Lance stated that "ACs measure candidate behavior as it relates to the exercises that are constructed and not the dimensions that are defined for assessors to rate candidate behavior" (Lance, 2008, p. 92). It is rare for psychometric analysis to show more evidence for dimensions than for task performance in assessment centers (for an exception, see Guenole et al., 2013).

The widespread use of technology has also affected the design and implementation of ACDCs. For instance, effective integration of software may facilitate and automatize some internal processes (scheduling, briefing, etc.). ACDCs can also be delivered virtually through various technological solutions and cover a wider pool of potential applicants (Howland et al., 2015). Additionally, virtual ACs may increase efficiency and speed of assessment since candidates are not required to change locations, and the data can be collected and analyzed with technology. This may be particularly valuable to organizations in light of the recent COVID-19 pandemic and limited opportunities for travel and in-person assessments of candidates. However, while there are apparent benefits associated with virtual ACs in personnel selection, a point of concern is the impact of increased automatization on interpersonal interactions and subsequent applicants' reactions. This is an issue that requires further research evidence to back up current industry practices.

9.9.1 European Trends with ACDCs

ACDCs are the third most frequently used measurement technology with 51% of respondents indicating their organizations use the method. Participants slightly overestimated the prevalence of ACDCs, with 63% reporting they are widely used. The most frequent domains in which ACDCs are used are listed in the upper panel of Figure 9.5. This highlights

ACDC uses

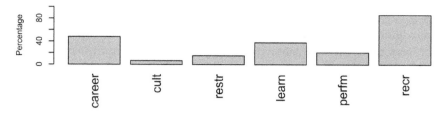

ACDC constructs

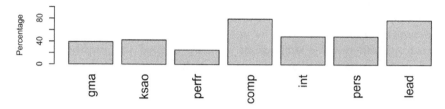

ACDC seniority

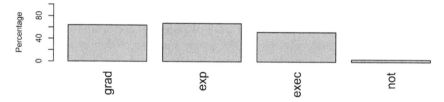

Figure 9.5 **ACDCs**

Upper panel. Use of ACDCs in common assessment contexts
Note. N = 92. career = career development; cult = organizational culture; restr = restructuring; learn = learning and development; perfm = performance management; recr = recruitment.

Middle panel. Constructs measured with ACDCs
Note. N = 92. gma = general mental ability; ksaos = general job knowledge; perfr = job performance; comp = competencies; int = motives, values, and interests; pers = personality; lead = leadership potential.

Lower panel. Use of ACDCs at different levels of seniority
Note. N = 92. grad = graduate; exp = experienced hire; exec = executive; not = not used for selection.

that they are most frequently used for recruitment (86%), followed by career management (48%), learning and development (38%), performance management (21%), restructuring (15%), culture interventions (7%). ACDCs are most frequently used to assess behavioral competencies

(79%), leadership potential (77%), motives and interests (49%), personality (49%), behavioral competencies (42%), general mental ability (39%), and performance (25%) (see Figure 9.5, middle panel). ACDCs are used reasonably frequently across levels, with just under two-thirds reporting using these in hiring graduates (64%), a similar figure to experienced hires (67%). There was noticeably less use of ACDCs for executive hiring, with just over half of ACDC users applying the method to this form of hiring (52%). These results are illustrated in the lower panel of Figure 9.5.

The retest reliability of ACDCs is perceived as favorable, with 32% indicating they produce very reliable data, 65% indicating they produce somewhat reliable data, and 4% indicating ACDCs produce unreliable data. Their predictive validity is seen very favorably by our sample, with 54% indicating scores are very predictive of performance and 46% indicating ACDC scores are somewhat predictive. Most users, 41%, believed ACDCs led to low adverse impact, while 29% believed the adverse impact was moderate, 11% believed it was high, and 19% were unsure. The most common format was still in person, 77%, followed by supervised remote ACDCs, 47%, and ACDCs that were remote with unsupervised elements, 13%. The candidate experience of ACDCs was reported as very positive or somewhat positive by 93% of users.

9.10 Situational Judgment

Situational judgment tests (SJTs) are a measurement methodology that can be used to assess a variety of job-related knowledge, skills, and abilities (Lievens et al., 2005; Lievens & Sackett, 2007; McDaniel Cabrera & Nguyen, 2001; Motowidlo et al., 1990; Weekley et al., 2015; Weekley & Jones, 1999). They are usually comprised of a stimulus describing a challenging managerial scenario and require a response of the test taker. The stimulus format can take different presentation forms. Most commonly, text is used, but it is also common to see animations and video because of the impact this has on candidate experiences and research suggesting these formats lead to lower adverse impact (Chan & Schmitt, 1997). The response formats are typically rating scales and rankings or partial rankings. However, it is also possible for the candidate to write a text response, or today record a video or audio response. When candidates are told to indicate what would be most effective, scores tend to correlate more with cognitive abilities, and when asked to indicate what they would do, they tend to correlate more with noncognitive constructs like personality (McDaniel et al., 2001). Because the responses have been, in the past, primarily rankings and ratings, SJTs are considered low-fidelity simulations. Sackett and Lievens (2008) considered SJTs samples of work behavior rather than signs of future performance because they are highly contextualized representations of on-the-job situations.

SJTs are a relatively popular measurement method for hiring and for development due to their high face validity, moderate criterion-related validity, and low adverse impact against protected demographic groups (Chan & Schmitt, 1997; Whetzel et al., 2008). SJTs are best considered measures of generalized knowledge, skills, and abilities. As indicated by their often low internal consistency reliabilities (Catano et al., 2012; Kasten & Freund, 2016), they are a poor option for measuring psychological constructs, at least when considering the reliability and convergent and discriminant validity achievable by traditional psychometric standards with questionnaires (Guenole et al., 2015, 2017; Lievens, 2017). Recent attention in SJT design has turned to how to gamify the candidate experience through the use of candidate immersion approaches (e.g., multimedia technology) and giving the candidate control (e.g. choosing the order in which the assessment is completed) (Landers et al., 2020) and introducing branching into the designs of SJTs (Reddock et al., 2020).

9.10.1   European Trends with SJTs

SJTs are the fourth most frequently used measurement technology, with 29% of respondents indicating their organizations use the method. Participants slightly overestimated the prevalence of SJTs, with 40% reporting they are widely or very widely used. The most frequent domains in which questionnaires are used are illustrated in the upper panel of Figure 9.6. This highlights that they are most frequently used for recruitment (79%), followed by learning and development (36%), career management (30%), culture interventions (13%), performance management (11%), and restructuring (6%). SJTs are most frequently used to assess behavioral competencies (62%), KSAOs (45%), motives and interests (43%), leadership potential (43%), general mental ability (32%), personality (30%), and performance (19%) (see Figure 9.6, middle panel). SJTs are perceived by users as most applicable for graduate hiring (75%) and experienced hires (72%). One-quarter of SJT users indicated using SJTs for executive hiring (25%), 72% for experienced hiring, and 76% for graduate hiring. SJT use across seniority levels is shown in the lower panel of Figure 9.6. The candidate experience of SJTs was considered very positive or somewhat positive by 78% of users.

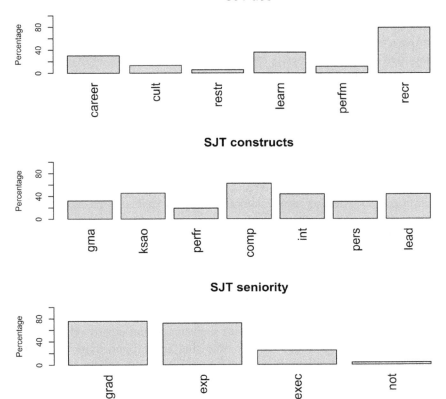

Figure 9.6 **Situational judgment**
Upper panel. Use of SJTs in common assessment contexts
Note. N = 53. career = career development; cult = organizational culture; restr = restructuring; learn = learning and development; perfm = performance management; recr = recruitment.
Middle panel. Constructs measured with SJTs
Note. N = 53. gma = general mental ability; ksaos = general job knowledge; perfr = job performance; comp = competencies; int = motives, values, and interests; pers = personality; lead = leadership potential.
Lower panel. Use of SJTs at different levels of seniority
Note. N = 53. grad = graduate; exp = experienced hire; exec = executive; not = not used for selection.

Perceptions of the retest reliability of SJTs were relatively positive, with 21% believing they were very reliable, 66% reporting they were somewhat reliable, and 13% reporting that they are unreliable. Similarly, the perceptions of predictive validity were positive, with 31% reporting SJTs were very predictive, 63% reporting they were somewhat predictive, and just 6% reporting they were not predictive of performance. Only 9% reported that SJTs produced large adverse impact, 63% reported moderate adverse impact, and 63% reported low adverse impact. Most respondents, 82%, reported using text vignettes for SJT scenarios, 30% used animations, and 20% used video footage. In terms of response formats, 85% used multiple-choice or ratings and ranking options, 25% allowed text responses, and small proportions reported allowing video or audio responses (6% and 8%, respectively). One-quarter reported using branching in their SJTs.

9.11 Game-Based Assessment

Game-based assessment (GBA) and related concepts refer to an emerging approach to assessing psychological attributes that aim to increase the engagement of test takers. GBA has been referred to by several names, including serious games and gamification (Georgiou et al., 2019). According to Fetzer et al. (2017), however, gamification refers to the inclusion of gaming elements – such as interactive problem-solving, sensory stimuli, and the use of technology, to name a few examples – in nongame situations, while GBA refers to utilizing game elements to create a game that will not be strictly used for fun. If the definitions of these two subelements of the games assessment literature sound closely related, it is unsurprising. In fact, the authors note that there is no hard boundary between where gamification ends and games-based assessment begins.

Fetzer et al. (2017) propose that the primary objective of GBA is to increase the engagement of examinees in an assessment process. Later in their chapter, they discuss a second objective of GBA as being to offer incremental validity in the prediction of job performance, implying that evidence suggests games indeed offer incremental validity over other measures such as traditional general mental ability tests and Big Five personality questionnaires. However, the evidence to date that this potential has been fulfilled is limited. In a more recent paper, Melchers and Basch (2021) mention being able to find only a single paper that provided evidence of GBA scores predicting job performance. The resolution of the apparent discrepancy appears to be in the broader interpretation of the notion of GBA by Fetzer et al. (2017). These authors consider simulations, such as situational judgment tests and assessment centers, as GBAs.

In this section, we take a narrower view of GBA as involving game elements absent in traditional assessments, such as specific goals for the game and ongoing feedback delivered via technology. From this perspective, the view of Melchers and Basch (2021) appears correct. The evidence of the predictive validity of such games is limited. Very few GBAs appear in the published literature demonstrating reliability, construct validity, or predictive validity. One point to recognize in this debate is that GBA is a methodology rather than a construct, so what we would hope to see is evidence of reliability and validity for the constructs we know well, such as cognitive ability and personality, but measured with GBA (e.g., Georgiou et al., 2019; Landers et al., 2022).

The challenge for the field of GBA designers is that often games are back-fitted in the sense that there is little or no empirical evidence of the reliability and validity for a given game, and scoring protocols are rarely available either. The article by Melchers and Basch (2021) is an excellent case in point. These authors reported that, unfortunately, no evidence on reliability or validity was available and that it was not possible to discuss the scoring algorithm with any degree of clarity.

9.11.1   European Trends with Games

GBA is the fifth most frequently used measurement technology, with 15% of respondents indicating their organizations use the method. Participants overestimated the prevalence of GBAs, with 29% reporting they are widely used. The most frequent domains in which GBAs are used are illustrated in the upper panel of Figure 9.7. This highlights that they are most frequently used for recruitment (79%), career management (39%), learning and development (36%), performance management (11%), culture and engagement (7%), and restructuring (7%). GBA is most frequently used to assess general mental ability (79%), personality (46%), behavioral competencies (32%), interests and motivations (32%), leadership potential (29%), KSAOs (18%), and performance (11%) (see Figure 9.7, middle panel). While general mental ability (GMA) technology is used for hiring at all levels, there is a marked drop-off in the perception of the appropriateness of this form of assessment from graduate to executive hiring. In total, 89% of users reported using GBA for graduate hiring, 54% reported using assessments for experienced hires, and 21% reported using GBAs for executive hires. This is shown in the lower panel of Figure 9.7. Norms were considered important or very important by 78% of the sample.

Perceptions of the test–retest reliability of GBAs were favorable, with 25% indicating that such assessments were very reliable, 61% indicating they were somewhat reliable, and 7% indicating they were unreliable. Perceptions of the predictive validity of GBAs were also favorable, with

Game uses

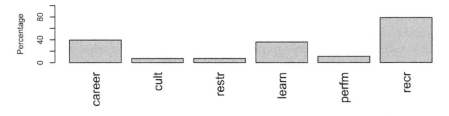

Game constructs

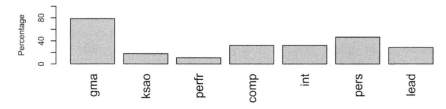

Game seniority

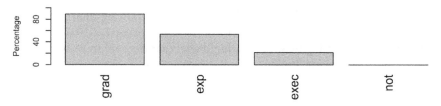

Figure 9.7 **Game-based assessment**
Upper panel. Use of GBA in common assessment contexts
Note. N = 28. career = career development; cult = organizational culture; restr = restructuring; learn = learning and development; perfm = performance management; recr = recruitment.

Middle panel. Constructs measured with GBA
Note. N = 28. gma = general mental ability; ksaos = general job knowledge; perfr = job performance; comp = competencies; int = motives, values, and interests; pers = personality; lead = leadership potential.

Lower panel. Use of GBA at different levels of seniority
Note. N = 28. grad = graduate; exp = experienced hire; exec = executive; not = not used for selection.

36% believing they are very predictive, 46% believing they are somewhat predictive, and just 8% believing they are not predictive. With respect to adverse impact, 11% reported that GBAs produce large adverse impact, 29% reported moderate adverse impact, and 46% reported no adverse impact. The most common type of GBA was specifically designed games for assessment purposes, 89%, while gamified assessments were slightly less common, 39%. Just under half, 46%, of the sample reported that candidates knew what they were being assessed against compared to 25% that did not know, and 29% reported candidates were sometimes aware.

9.12   Emerging Technology

9.12.1   Social Media and Digital Footprints

Individuals' online activity on social media channels, such as LinkedIn, Twitter, Facebook, and Snapchat, creates digital footprints which can be used by employers in personnel selection. Recruiters and hiring managers report checking online activity as an additional source of information regarding applicants' characteristics and behaviors (e.g., Van Iddekinge et al., 2016). While the use of digital footprints appears a popular practice to guide hiring decisions, there are many unanswered questions related to applicants' reactions to such screening, the legality of such practices, as well as validity of this method in employee selection context (Becton et al., 2019; Woods et al., 2020). Because social media sites may contain both job-relevant and nonrelevant information that may be indicative of different demographic backgrounds, there is also a question regarding adverse impact resulting from selection decisions based on social media profiles (Van Iddekinge et al., 2016; Wade et al., 2020; Woods et al., 2020). Industry seems to be ahead of academic research on the topic of digital footprints and the use of social media, with evidence from academic research just getting underway. For instance, Roth et al. (2016) present a research agenda regarding the use of social media for hiring. They outline the need to explore the underlying processes for social media judgments, questions related to constructs and validity of social media assessments, adverse impact and group differences (e.g., based on age, gender, ethnicity), as well as questions related to applicants' reactions.

9.12.1.1   European Trends with Digital Footprints
Just nine respondents indicated they used social media scraping for assessment. Of those, five reported using the technology in recruitment, two in performance management, two in culture and engagement, and one in each of learning and development and restructuring. Only two participants believed the approach was widely or very widely used. The most common application was the measurement of leadership potential and competency

management with three responses; personality, interests, and KSAOs with two respondents; and GMA and performance, each with a single respondent indicating they used the approach for measuring these constructs. Of the nine respondents using digital footprint scoring, three reported using it for graduate hiring, three reported using it for experienced hires, and two reported using it for executive hiring. Because numbers were so small in this category, we do not report attitudes about reliability, validity, and adverse impact.

9.12.2 *Chatbots*

Assessment solutions can also include chatbots, which are virtual agents capable of communicating with job applicants at various stages of the selection process. Chatbots are exceptionally versatile. They can be used to conduct initial screening interviews, answer applicants' inquiries, give updates regarding selection stages, and they can also be integrated as part of other assessment tools. Other routine tasks, such as interview scheduling, can also be performed by chatbots, speeding up the selection process (Nawaz & Gomes, 2020). Given the increased focus on hiring and retaining the best talent in organizations, chatbots may be helpful in screening large pools of potential candidates and reducing the screening pressure from hiring managers. Additionally, they may help to avoid interviewer biases at screening stages since chatbots use automatic and standardized procedures. However, although chatbots can be an attractive tool to aid selection processes, there is very little scientific evidence that explores their relevance or effectiveness in the context of hiring decisions, nor on applicants' attitudes to this method. The gradual shift toward AI-based selection currently observed in the industry needs to be supported by sound research that would enable effective integration of chatbots in future HR practices.

9.12.2.1 *European Trends with Chatbots*
Just five respondents reported using chatbots for assessment. Two people reported using chatbots in recruitment, one in career management and one in the area of culture and engagement. One indicated that none of the areas we asked about described their chatbot application, and no other information is available on what they did do with chatbots. One respondent indicated that chatbots were used for assessment in many areas, including performance assessment, competency assessment, motives and interests assessment, and assessment of leadership potential. One respondent indicated they used chatbots to assess GMA only. One indicated they

used chatbots to assess motives and interests only. One indicated they used chatbots to assess personality. With respect to seniority levels where chatbots are applied, three indicated using chatbots with graduate hires, two with experienced hires, and one with executive hires. Because numbers were so small in this category we do not report attitudes about reliability, validity, and adverse impact.

9.12.3   Resumé Parsing

Traditionally, resumés were screened by recruiters to assess the key information about candidates; the AI solutions now offer resumé parsing – automatic extraction, analysis, and storage of relevant information from resumés in an organized manner. Given a large number of resumés that hiring managers may generally go through (and not to mention different styles and formats of resumés submitted by applicants), resumé parsing is an efficient solution for analyzing and structuring information based on specific algorithms for future use by managers. It also may reduce the time spent on initial candidate screening and, as a result, reduce hiring costs in organizations. Like other emerging AI-based solutions in human resources (e.g., chatbots), resumé parsing method has not been extensively covered in organizational research. Here, academic literature lags behind companies that set the trend on using the parsing method as part of their AI-based solutions.

9.12.3.1   European Trends with Text Parsing

Just 10 people reported using text parsing for psychological assessment in their organizations. Of these respondents, five reported using parsing in a recruitment context; three in career management; two in learning and development; two in performance management; and one in culture and engagement. In terms of what gets measured with parsing, technical KSAOs are reported as being measured by five respondents, behavioral competencies by five respondents, performance was reported by two respondents, personality was reported by two respondents, and in each case, a single respondent reported measuring GMA, motives and interests, and leadership potential with parsing. The small number of respondents that reported using parsing indicated they used it across all levels of seniority. Three indicated using parsing for graduate hires, three indicated using it for experienced hires, and two reported using the approach for executive hires. Because numbers were so small in this category, we do not report attitudes about reliability, validity, and adverse impact.

9.12.4   Internet of Things

The term Internet of Things (IoT) has become increasingly popular in the light of technological advancements, including AI and Big Data, and it describes the interconnection between physical objects and devices through digital networks to exchange data. Nowadays, physical devices (smartphones, tablets, virtual assistants, etc.) can gather and share large amounts of information about individuals, and integration of these devices into selection processes may significantly enhance existing human resource practices. With increasing reliance on "smart" objects used for communication, work, and everyday life, human resources specialists are now exploring and testing IoT-based methods to interact with applicants, and further digitalize recruitment and selection processes. While there is a proliferation of IoT devices organizations are rapidly adopting, there are many unexplored questions from both practical and research perspectives. For instance, the issue of when it is appropriate to use such data, how it should be stored, and what permissions are required remain unagreed, let alone psychometric considerations of reliability and validity. The amounts of data that may be generated through smart devices also require different approaches toward data analytics and data processing. "Smart" devices may be vulnerable to various risks (for example, hacking) and misuse of information. To date, there is very limited evidence from organizational research concerning the application of IoT for employee selection.

9.12.4.1   European Trends with IoT

Just five respondents indicated that they used IoT technology for assessment in talent management. Of these, the approach was used in recruitment, career management, culture and engagement, and performance management. In terms of what was measured with IoT technology, the few respondents who reported using this technology reported using it across a wide variety of areas, including GMA, technical competencies, behavioral competencies, interests and motives, personality and leadership potential, even performance.

9.13   Conclusion

The level of technological innovation has never been as high as today and will probably even be higher tomorrow. Without a doubt, many of these evolutions (think Big Data, Virtual Reality, etc.) carry huge potential for business applications, and the field of HR and personnel assessment, in particular, are currently discovering several of the opportunities that they have to offer. From our survey among assessment professionals across Europe, it appears that this adoption process is still happening at a relatively modest pace, especially as regards the newer technologies. Nevertheless, "HR Tech" is gaining momentum, and we generally expect to see a growing number of applications being used in different areas of the talent management process, including assessment. It is a great time to be involved in HR, and assessment in particular.

New technologies come with new opportunities, but of course they also come with new challenges. However, we prefer to frame this positively instead of pointing at the "dangers" and "threats" associated with the (early) adoption of technology. What we are seeing is that the challenges that present themselves – many of them inevitably related to reliability and validity – require intense collaboration between practitioners and scientists. Let us not be the practitioner who thinks that science is too slow for these types of applications or that scientific concepts (such as reliability and validity) have become obsolete in this era of fast technological evolutions. On the other hand, let us also not be the overly conservative scientist who can only see the "validity threats," fostered by an almost trait-like reluctance to explore potentially disrupting trends.

There are few – if any – scientists who have the resources (or know-how) to develop innovative technologies that can be readily applied in real-life assessment settings outside the lab. Similarly, it may be too unrealistic to expect practitioners to patiently and diligently wade through all phases of the scientific validation process. Again, rather than seeing this as a problem, we should stress the opportunities here. For scientists, this represents a great chance to (finally) do research that has real and direct "applied value." For practitioners, teaming up with scientists will boost product quality (and offer competitive advantage directly and indirectly) in a business world where evidence-based practice becomes increasingly important.

REFERENCES

Anderson, N., Salgado, J. F., & Hülsheger, U. R. (2010). Applicant reactions in selection: Comprehensive meta-analysis into reaction generalization versus situational specificity. *International Journal of Selection and Assessment, 18*(3), 291–304. https://doi.org/10.1111/j.1468-2389.2010.00512.x

Arthur, W., Day, E. A., McNelly, T. L., & Edens, P. S. (2003). A meta-analysis of the criterion-related validity of assessment center dimensions. *Personnel*

Psychology, *56*(1), 125–153. https://doi.org/10.1111/j.1744-6570.2003 .tb00146.x

Arvey, R. D., & Campion, J. E. (1982). The employment interview: A summary and review of recent research. *Personnel Psychology*, *35*(2), 281–322. https:// doi.org/10.1111/j.1744-6570.1982.tb02197.x

Becton, J. B., Walker, J. H., Gilstrap, J. B., & Schwager, P. H. (2019, June 13). Social media snooping on job applicants: The effects of unprofessional social media information on recruiter perceptions. *Personnel Review*, *48*(5), 1261–1280. https://doi.org/10.1108/PR-09-2017-0278

Berry, C. M., Sackett, P. R., & Landers, R. N. (2007). Revisiting interview–cognitive ability relationships: Attending to specific range restriction mechanisms in meta-analysis. *Personnel Psychology*, *60*(4), 837–874. https://doi .org/10.1111/j.1744-6570.2007.00093.x

Catano, V. M., Brochu, A., & Lamerson, C. D. (2012). Assessing the reliability of situational judgment tests used in high-stakes situations. *International Journal of Selection and Assessment*, *20*(3), 333–346. https://doi.org/10 .1111/j.1468-2389.2012.00604.x

Chamorro-Premuzic, T., & Furnham, A. (2010). *The psychology of personnel selection*. Cambridge University Press. https://doi.org/10.1017/ CBO9780511819308

Chan, D., & Schmitt, N. (1997). Video-based versus paper-and-pencil method of assessment in situational judgment tests: Subgroup differences in test performance and face validity perceptions. *Journal of Applied Psychology*, *82*(1), 143–159. https://doi.org/10.1037/0021-9010.82.1.143

CIPD. (2020). *Resourcing and talent planning survey 2020*. https://www.cipd.org/ globalassets/media/knowledge/knowledge-hub/reports/resourcing-and-tal ent-planning-2020_tcm18-85530.pdf

Collins, M. W., & Morris, S. B. (2008). Testing for adverse impact when sample size is small. *The Journal of Applied Psychology*, *93*(2), 463–471. https://doi .org/10.1037/0021-9010.93.2.463

Dipboye, R. L. (1994). Structured and unstructured selection interviews: Beyond the job-fit model. *Research in Personnel and Human Resources Management*, *12*, 79–123. https://www.academia.edu/download/44957092/ STRUCTURED_AND_UNSTRUCTURED_SELECTION_ IN20160421-2666-opzc8p.pdf

Drasgow, F. (2015). *Technology and testing: Improving educational and psychological measurement*. Routledge.

Fetzer, M., McNamara, J., & Geimer, J. L. (2017). Gamification, serious games and personnel selection. In H. W. Goldstein, E. D. Pulakos, C. Semedo, & J. Passmore (Eds.), *The Wiley Blackwell handbook of the psychology of recruitment, selection and employee retention* (pp. 293–309). Wiley.

Georgiou, K., Gouras, A., & Nikolaou, I. (2019). Gamification in employee selection: The development of a gamified assessment. *International Journal of Selection and Assessment*, *27*(2), 91–103. https://doi.org/10.1111/ijsa.12240

Guenole, N., Chernyshenko, O. S., Stark, S., Cockerill, T., & Drasgow, F. (2013). More than a mirage: A large-scale assessment centre with more dimension variance than exercise variance. *Journal of Occupational and Organizational Psychology*, *86*(1), 5–21. https://doi.org/10.1111/j.2044-8325.2012.02063.x

Guenole, N., Chernyshenko, O., Stark, S., & Drasgow, F. (2015). Are predictions based on situational judgement tests precise enough for feedback in leadership development? *European Journal of Work and Organizational Psychology*, *24*(3), 433–443. https://doi.org/10.1080/1359432X.2014.926890

Guenole, N., Chernyshenko, O. S., & Weekly, J. (2017). On designing construct driven situational judgment tests: Some preliminary recommendations. *International Journal of Testing*, *17*(3), 234–252. https://doi.org/10.1080/15305058.2017.1297817

Harris, M. M. (1989). Reconsidering the employment interview: A review of recent literature and suggestions for future research. *Personnel Psychology*, *42*(4), 691–726. https://doi.org/10.1111/j.1744-6570.1989.tb00673.x

Hausknecht, J. P., Day, D. V., & Thomas, S. C. (2004). Applicant reactions to selection procedures: An updated model and meta-analysis. *Personnel Psychology*, *57*(3), 639–683. https://doi.org/10.1111/j.1744-6570.2004.00003.x

Hickman, L., Bosch, N., Ng, V., Saef, R., Tay, L., & Woo, S. E. (2021). Automated video interview personality assessments: Reliability, validity, and generalizability investigations. *Journal of Applied Psychology*, *107*(8), 1323–1351. https://doi.org/10.1037/apl0000695

Hickman, L., Saef, R., Ng, V., Woo, S. E., Tay, L., & Bosch, N. (2021). Developing and evaluating language-based machine learning algorithms for inferring applicant personality in video interviews. *Human Resource Management Journal*. https://doi.org/10.1111/1748-8583.12356

Howland, A. C., Rembisz, R., Wang-Jones, T. S., Heise, S. R., & Brown, S. (2015). Developing a virtual assessment center. *Consulting Psychology Journal: Practice and Research*, *67*(2), 110–126. https://doi.org/10.1037/cpb0000034

Huffcutt, A. I., Culbertson, S. S., & Weyhrauch, W. S. (2013). Employment interview reliability: New meta-analytic estimates by structure and format. *International Journal of Selection and Assessment*, *21*(3), 264–276. https://doi.org/10.1111/ijsa.12036

International Taskforce on Assessment Center Guidelines. (2015). Guidelines and ethical considerations for assessment center operations. *Journal of Management*, *41*(4), 1244–1273. https://doi.org/10.1177/0149206314567780

International Test Commission. (2005). *ITC guidelines on computer-based and internet delivered testing*, version 1.0. https://www.intestcom.org/files/guideline_computer_based_testing.pdf

Judge, T. A., Cable, D. M., & Higgins, C. A. (2000). The employment interview: A review of recent research and recommendations for future research. *Human Resource Management Review, 10*(4), 383–406. https://doi.org/10 .1016/S1053-4822(00)00033-4

Kasten, N., & Freund, P. A. (2016). A meta-analytical multilevel reliability generalization of situational judgment tests (SJTs). *European Journal of Psychological Assessment: Official Organ of the European Association of Psychological Assessment, 32*(3), 230–240. https://doi.org/10.1027/1015-5759/a000250

Lance, C. E. (2008). Why assessment centers do not work the way they are supposed to. *Industrial and Organizational Psychology, 1*(1), 84–97. https:// doi.org/10.1111/j.1754-9434.2007.00017.x

Landers, R. N., Armstrong, M. B., Collmus, A. B., Mujcic, S., & Blaik, J. (2022). Theory-driven game-based assessment of general cognitive ability: Design theory, measurement, prediction of performance, and test fairness. *Journal of Applied Psychology, 107*(10), 1655–1677. https://doi.org/10.1037/ apl0000954

Landers, R. N., Auer, E. M., & Abraham, J. (2020). Gamifying a situational judgment test with immersion and control game elements: Effects on applicant reactions and construct validity. *Journal of Managerial Psychology, 35*(4), 225–239. https://doi.org/10.1108/JMP-10-2018-0446

Law, S. J., Bourdage, J., & O'Neill, T. A. (2016). To fake or not to fake: Antecedents to interview faking, warning instructions, and its impact on applicant reactions. *Frontiers in Psychology, 7*, Article 1771. https://doi.org/ 10.3389/fpsyg.2016.01771

Levashina, J., & Campion, M. A. (2007). Measuring faking in the employment interview: Development and validation of an interview faking behavior scale. *Journal of Applied Psychology, 92*(6), 1638–1656. https://doi.org/10.1037/ 0021-9010.92.6.1638

Levashina, J., Hartwell, C. J., Morgeson, F. P., & Campion, M. A. (2014). The structured employment interview: Narrative and quantitative review of the research literature. *Personnel Psychology, 67*(1), 241–293. https://doi.org/10 .1111/peps.12052

Levinson, M. (2010). *Social networking ever more critical to job search success*. CIO. https://www.cio.com/article/280120/careers-staffing-social-networking-ever-more-critical-to-job-search-success.html

Lievens, F. (2006). The ITC guidelines on computer-based and internet-delivered testing: Where do we go from here? *International Journal of Testing, 6*(2), 189–194. https://doi.org/10.1207/s15327574ijt0602_7

    (2009). Assessment centres: A tale about dimensions, exercises, and dancing bears. *European Journal of Work and Organizational Psychology, 18*(1), 102–121. https://doi.org/10.1080/13594320802058997

    (2017). Construct-driven SJTs: Toward an agenda for future research. *International Journal of Testing, 17*(3), 269–276. https://doi.org/10.1080/ 15305058.2017.1309857

Lievens, F., Buyse, T., & Sackett, P. R. (2005). The operational validity of a video-based situational judgment test for medical college admissions: Illustrating the importance of matching predictor and criterion construct domains. *Journal of Applied Psychology, 90*(3), 442–452. https://doi.org/10.1037/0021-9010.90.3.442

Lievens, F., & Sackett, P. R. (2007). Situational judgment tests in high-stakes settings: Issues and strategies with generating alternate forms. *Journal of Applied Psychology, 92*(4), 1043–1055. https://doi.org/10.1037/0021-9010.92.4.1043

Lukacik, E.-R., Bourdage, J. S., & Roulin, N. (2020). Into the void: A conceptual model and research agenda for the design and use of asynchronous video interviews. *Human Resource Management Review, 32*(1), Article 100789. https://doi.org/10.1016/j.hrmr.2020.100789

Macan, T. (2009). The employment interview: A review of current studies and directions for future research. *Human Resource Management Review, 19*(3), 203–218. https://doi.org/10.1016/j.hrmr.2009.03.006

Macan, T. H., Avedon, M. J., Paese, M., & Smith, D. E. (1994). The effects of applicants' reactions to cognitive ability tests and an assessment center. *Personnel Psychology, 47*(4), 715–738. https://doi.org/10.1111/j.1744-6570.1994.tb01573.x

McDaniel, M. A., Morgeson, F. P., Finnegan, E. B., Campion, M. A., & Braverman, E. P. (2001). Use of situational judgment tests to predict job performance: A clarification of the literature. *Journal of Applied Psychology, 86*(4), 730–740. https://doi.org/10.1037/0021-9010.86.4.730

McDaniel, M. A., Whetzel, D. L., Schmidt, F. L., & Maurer, S. D. (1994). The validity of employment interviews: A comprehensive review and meta-analysis. *Journal of Applied Psychology, 79*(4), 599–616. https://doi.org/10.1037/0021-9010.79.4.599

McDaniel Cabrera, M. A., & Nguyen, N. T. (2001). Situational judgment tests: A review of practice and constructs assessed. *International Journal of Selection and Assessment, 9*(1–2), 103–113. https://doi.org/10.1111/1468-2389.00167

Mead, A. D., & Drasgow, F. (1993). Equivalence of computerized and paper-and-pencil cognitive ability tests: A meta-analysis. *Psychological Bulletin, 114*(3), 449–458. https://doi.org/10.1037/0033-2909.114.3.449

Melchers, K. G., & Basch, J. M. (2021). Fair play? Sex-, age-, and job-related correlates of performance in a computer-based simulation game. *International Journal of Selection and Assessment, 30*(1), 48–61. https://doi.org/10.1111/ijsa.12337

Melchers, K. G., Roulin, N., & Buehl, A.-K. (2020). A review of applicant faking in selection interviews. *International Journal of Selection and Assessment, 28*(2), 123–142. https://doi.org/10.1111/ijsa.12280

Meriac, J. P., Hoffman, B. J., Woehr, D. J., & Fleisher, M. S. (2008). Further evidence for the validity of assessment center dimensions: A meta-analysis of the incremental criterion-related validity of dimension ratings. *Journal of*

Applied Psychology, 93(5), 1042–1052. https://doi.org/10.1037/0021-9010.93.5.1042

Morelli, N., Potosky, D., Arthur, W., Jr, & Tippins, N. (2017). A call for conceptual models of technology in I-O psychology: An example from technology-based talent assessment. *Industrial and Organizational Psychology, 10*(4), 634–653. https://doi.org/10.1017/iop.2017.70

Moscoso, S. (2000). Selection interview: A review of validity evidence, adverse impact and applicant reactions. *International Journal of Selection and Assessment, 8*(4), 237–247. https://doi.org/10.1111/1468-2389.00153

Motowidlo, S. J., Dunnette, M. D., & Carter, G. W. (1990). An alternative selection procedure: The low-fidelity simulation. *Journal of Applied Psychology, 75*(6), 640–647. https://doi.org/10.1037/0021-9010.75.6.640

Naim, I., Tanveer, M. I., Gildea, D., & Hoque, M. (2015). *Automated analysis and prediction of job interview performance.* http://arxiv.org/abs/1504.03425

Nawaz, N., & Gomes, A. M. (2020). Artificial intelligence chatbots are new recruiters. *International Journal of Advanced Computer Science and Applications, 10*(9). https://doi.org/10.2139/ssrn.3521915

Nye, C. D., Do, B.-R., Drasgow, F., & Fine, S. (2008). Two-step testing in employee selection: Is score inflation a problem? *International Journal of Selection and Assessment, 16*(2), 112–120. https://doi.org/10.1111/j.1468-2389.2008.00416.x

Posthuma, R. A., Morgeson, F. P., & Campion, M. A. (2002). Beyond employment interview validity: A comprehensive narrative review of recent research and trends over time. *Personnel Psychology, 55*(1), 1–81. https://doi.org/10.1111/j.1744-6570.2002.tb00103.x

Reddock, C. M., Auer, E. M., & Landers, R. N. (2020). A theory of branched situational judgment tests and their applicant reactions. *Journal of Managerial Psychology, 35*(4), 255–270. https://doi.org/10.1108/JMP-10-2018-0434

Robertson, I. T., & Smith, M. (2001). Personnel selection. *Journal of Occupational and Organizational Psychology, 74*(4), 441–472. https://doi.org/10.1348/096317901167479

Roth, P. L., Bobko, P., Van Iddekinge, C. H., & Thatcher, J. B. (2016). Social media in employee-selection-related decisions: A research agenda for uncharted territory. *Journal of Management, 42*(1), 269–298. https://doi.org/10.1177/0149206313503018

Roth, P. L., & Huffcutt, A. I. (2013). A meta-analysis of interviews and cognitive ability. *Journal of Personnel Psychology, 12*(4), 157–169. https://doi.org/10.1027/1866-5888/a000091

Ryan, A. M., & Ployhart, R. E. (2014). A century of selection. *Annual Review of Psychology, 65*, 693–717. https://doi.org/10.1146/annurev-psych-010213-115134

Sackett, P. R., & Lievens, F. (2008). Personnel selection. *Annual Review of Psychology, 59*, 419–450. https://doi.org/10.1146/annurev.psych.59.103006.093716

Salgado, J. F., & Moscoso, S. (2002). Comprehensive meta-analysis of the construct validity of the employment interview. *European Journal of Work and Organizational Psychology*, *11*(3), 299–324. https://doi.org/10.1080/13594320244000184

Scott, J. C., Bartram, D., & Reynolds, D. H. (2017). *Next generation technology-enhanced assessment: Global perspectives on occupational and workplace testing.* Cambridge University Press.

Suen, H.-Y., Chen, M. Y.-C., & Lu, S.-H. (2019). Does the use of synchrony and artificial intelligence in video interviews affect interview ratings and applicant attitudes? *Computers in Human Behavior*, *98*, 93–101. https://doi.org/10.1016/j.chb.2019.04.012

Thornton, G. C., & Gibbons, A. M. (2009). Validity of assessment centers for personnel selection. *Human Resource Management Review*, *19*(3), 169–187. https://doi.org/10.1016/j.hrmr.2009.02.002

Thornton, G. C., III, & Rupp, D. E. (2006). *Assessment centers in human resource management: Strategies for prediction, diagnosis, and development.* Lawrence Erlbaum Associates.

Tippins, N. T., & Adler, S. (2011). *Technology-enhanced assessment of talent.* Jossey-Bass.

Van Iddekinge, C. H., Lanivich, S. E., Roth, P. L., & Junco, E. (2016). Social media for selection? Validity and adverse impact potential of a Facebook-based assessment. *Journal of Management*, *42*(7), 1811–1835. https://doi.org/10.1177/0149206313515524

Wade, J. T., Roth, P. L., Thatcher, J. B., & Dinger, M. (2020). Social media and selection: Political issue similarity, liking, and the moderating effect of social media platform. *The Mississippi Quarterly*, *44*(3), 1301–1357. https://doi.org/10.25300/misq/2020/14119

Weekley, J. A., Hawkes, B., Guenole, N., & Ployhart, R. E. (2015). Low-fidelity simulations. *Annual Review of Organizational Psychology and Organizational Behavior*, *2*(1), 295–322. https://doi.org/10.1146/annurev-orgpsych-032414-111304

Weekley, J. A., & Jones, C. (1999). Further studies of situational tests. *Personnel Psychology*, *52*(3), 679–700. https://doi.org/10.1111/j.1744-6570.1999.tb00176.x

Whetzel, D. L., McDaniel, M. A., & Nguyen, N. T. (2008). Subgroup differences in situational judgment test performance: A meta-analysis. *Human Performance*, *21*(3), 291–309. https://doi.org/10.1080/08959280802137820

Woods, S. A., Ahmed, S., Nikolaou, I., Costa, A. C., & Anderson, N. R. (2020). Personnel selection in the digital age: A review of validity and applicant reactions, and future research challenges. *European Journal of Work and Organizational Psychology*, *29*(1), 64–77. https://doi.org/10.1080/1359432X.2019.1681401

CHAPTER 10

Testing and Measurement in North America with a Focus on Transformation

Liberty Munson

To stay relevant, transformation is necessary regardless of industry, and one might say it is long overdue in the assessment and measurement industry. As the growth of the cloud makes computing and technology more prevalent in our daily lives and substantially increases computing power (Anderson, 2017; International Data Corporation, 2020; MIT Technology Review, 2020, 2021), the assessment and measurement industry has been slow to act on the opportunities that both bring. A quick internet search reveals all the ways that the cloud is enabling digital transformations across many industries (e.g., https://cloudblogs.microsoft.com/industry-blog/digital-transformation/), yet we do not see the same transformations happening in our industry.

Looking around us, we can see that the cloud is fundamentally changing the way we interact with the world as organizations start to leverage this increased computing power to fuel artificial intelligence (AI) solutions that are becoming increasingly common in the technologies we use every day (Faggella, 2020; Goddard, 2020; Saeed, 2020); AI is embedded in our devices, our homes, our cars, our cities, and more. This interweaving of our lives and technology is changing expectations that people have about the world and, by extension, assessments.

However, we have a long history in which we have relied heavily on structured responses, such as multiple-choice questions, on assessments because these types of questions are easy to score, making the assessment process repeatable, objective, and scalable. Although those types of assessments are artificial, low-fidelity evaluations of skills, we have a difficult time letting go of that history and exploring what is possible with technology because it will require rethinking the psychometric paradigms and practices that we have used with much success in the past. But if the opt-out of testing movement (University of California, 2020) has taught us anything, this modality for assessing skills is becoming outdated and is often perceived as biased, unfair, and lacking in credibility. We need to reimagine what assessment and our psychometric models could be in a world where assessing performance is becoming a more realistic option in the evaluation of knowledge, skills, and abilities and in a world where technology is creating opportunities to think differently about the questions we ask, how we ask them, and how we evaluate the responses.

We are only starting to recognize the promise that technology will allow us to truly innovate in assessment design and delivery in a meaningful way. Yes, small steps have been taken, but our industry has been slow to adopt anything that is truly different or that challenges the status quo, and that is likely to be to our detriment. We need to think big, and even if we cannot implement those big ideas, by thinking big, we can leap toward innovation in ways that fundamentally change how we approach assessment.

Advances in technology and computing power are an opportunity for us to challenge the status quo; they will allow us to innovate and assess skills in more authentic ways that will give us better insight into someone's knowledge, skills, and abilities. The question we should be asking and attempting to answer is: "How can assessment developers leverage the power of the cloud and technology to measure skills more accurately and create higher fidelity in the assessment process?"

It is with this framework in mind that I am approaching the discussion of testing and measurement in North America. When possible, I will include a discussion of the innovation that could be enabled by technology and how it might address or mitigate some of the challenges that I describe. I will also share some thoughts on how we could leverage technology to think differently about all aspects of assessment from design to development to delivery regardless of geography. My goal is to spark ideas that may lead to truly innovative solutions to assessment challenges. By no means am I suggesting that the challenges described in this chapter, nor the opportunities enabled by technology, are unique to North America; in fact, in most cases, the same challenges are being faced all over the world in varying degrees and the same opportunities exist, but I will highlight what is of importance when it comes to measurement and assessment in North America.

But, to further set the stage, I will start by sharing some background on the Microsoft Certification Program because doing so will provide additional context on the perspective I bring to this conversation.

10.1   Overview of Microsoft's Certification Program and Exams

All Microsoft Certification exams are computer-based and are delivered through testing centers or online proctoring. They are available around the world and can be taken at any time.

Microsoft was the first certification program of any significant size to embrace online proctoring. We have also led the certification industry in adding a wider variety of item types to our exams, moving beyond multiple-choice questions to include more interactive item types that allow us to measure higher-level skills. The item types include build list, hot area, active screen, drag-drop, and performance elements (i.e., labs) that increase the fidelity of the assessment process, and quite honestly, the face validity of our exams.

Through our listening channels (e.g., program surveys, blogs, exam comments), we have data that suggests that many of our certification candidates prefer to demonstrate their skills through performance; as a result, we have committed to having labs as part of the evaluation process for all of our role-based certifications. To that end, each certification will contain at least one exam that contains at least one lab with up to 15 tasks that must be completed in Azure, Microsoft 365, or Dynamics 365. In order to complete those tasks, examinees connect to the technology through the exam interface, ensuring a seamless assessment experience, but in a way that allows them to complete the tasks in the technology itself, not through a simulated environment. This requires a significant amount of integration across platforms, bandwidth, and computing power that is only possible with the advances in technology that we have seen over the past five years.

Because Microsoft certification exams are based on rapidly changing cloud-based technologies, this introduces measurement challenges of its own. While this article is not focused on the measurement challenges of keeping assessments up to date in a rapidly changing environment (it is worth noting that even outside IT, knowledge domains are doubling more rapidly than ever before, often within a few months or years, so this affects all assessments to some extent), I would be remiss in not pointing out that constantly updating and refreshing our certification exams was one of the impetuses for my interest in leveraging technology to find innovative solutions to ensure that our measurement processes are valid, reliable, and fair over time. Ensuring equivalence across examinees when the content domain changes every few months, monthly, or even weekly is only possible with creative solutions that are enabled by technology.

These are the experiences that set the framework for what follows. Let us now turn to some of the key issues and challenges surrounding testing and measurement in North America.

10.2 Privacy Laws and Regulations

Privacy has long tentacles into the way we think about the delivery of assessments. Some of you may be familiar with the General Data Protection Regulation (GDPR) (GDPR EU, 2021), Europe's overarching privacy mandate protecting personal information. "Personal information" includes but may not be limited to examinee name, address, email address, payment card information, and, possibly, test scores. In some instances, personal data can extend beyond the test to include tracked user interactions with websites, marketing materials, sales, etc. (Association for Test Publishers (ATP), 2019). The GDPR places overall responsibility for protecting personal information on the "Data Controller," or the person or organization that collects and/or uses the data. What you may be less familiar with is that California recently enacted the California Consumer Privacy Act (CCPA; CCPA, 2018) that is similar in many ways to the GDPR. Although a testing program may comply with the GDPR, it may have additional obligations under the CCPA (e.g., the CCPA gives individuals the right to prevent companies from selling their private information). Even more recently, California passed Proposition 24, enacting the California Privacy Rights Act of 2020 (CPRA; Californians for Consumer Privacy, 2021). This act expands the privacy protections under the CCPA and went into effect on January 1, 2023. Other US states (most recently, amendments to the Nevada Privacy of Information Collected on the Internet from Consumers Act became effective [October 1, 2021], setting out new requirements for the collection of covered information by websites) are considering or have enacted similar laws (Rippy, 2021) as California leads the way. The different approaches to privacy state by state are creating a complex matrix of requirements that testing programs need to understand and implement appropriately (ATP, 2021). More concerning, however, is that with each new iteration of these privacy laws, the open nature of the wording could be interpreted to mean that elements of the assessment experience, such as test scores and results, are "personal information" that is protected under the law, subject to the same stringent requirements of protection to which more tradition personally identifiable information (e.g., social security number) is held.

Beyond the USA, Canada is adding more privacy regulations as well (Office of the Privacy Commissioner of Canada, 2019). These regulations define the rights and protections for how businesses may use personal information and what it is and to what extent automation can be used, and in what ways. Mexico, on the other hand, has not had any significant legislation related to privacy since enacting the Federal Law on Protection of Personal Data Held by Private Parties in 2010 with clarifications made in 2011 (DLA Piper, 2021); in 2017, a law protecting the public sector went into effect (Recio, 2017).

Understanding privacy laws is important because each jurisdiction in which an assessment is delivered (or through which the data may flow) may have different requirements related to data flows, databases where the data may be stored, how it is collected and processed, and so on. Further, the collection, use, and processing of personal information must be clearly communicated to the examinee and, in most instances, some sort of acknowledgment is required. The nuances and interpretations of these rules and regulations and how they impact assessment and measurement are still being understood, but a few implications are of immediate concern. For example, in most of these regulations, the data controller must give the customer the option to be "forgotten." This means that organizations must remove all traces of that individual from all their databases, including those of subcontractors and partners. Depending on the complexity of the organization's databases and their partner/subcontractor ecosystem, this is no small undertaking. For example, for someone to be "forgotten" at Microsoft, we must remove them not only from all of Microsoft's databases (they may have X-box, Hotmail, or Live accounts, certifications, and so on), we also have to remove them for all of our partners' databases if they are doing business on Microsoft's behalf. For certification exams, this includes our exam delivery providers. Some assessment organizations have other partners that are involved in the delivery of exams that may have information about that customer, such as online proctoring providers, lab hosters, support agencies, etc. As the data controller, it's Microsoft's responsibility to ensure that the individual has been forgotten across our ecosystem.

An interesting nuance that is often overlooked is that being forgotten also means that you must expunge the individual's testing history, including any certifications, licenses, or other credentials they have earned. This is not something many people realize when they make this request, so communicating what being forgotten means is critical because if they change their minds later, by definition, about being forgotten, you will not be able to recreate these profiles.

Another element of many of these laws and regulations is tied to data processing and transfer across country and state lines. If someone is taking an assessment in a different state or country, these regulations may come into play and have to be considered to ensure that assessment results can be tied back to the test taker. Some nuances of these regulations may introduce unexpected challenges that need to be overcome to remain compliant. As a result, it is critical that organizations take an inventory of all personal information being collected, how it is being used, and where the data is stored and in what jurisdiction the data is sourced, collected, processed, and stored. This inventory will help organizations establish appropriate data protection procedures. Because of the complexities, many organizations are only collecting personal information that is relevant to the service being provided, thus simplifying data collection (ATP, 2019).

10.3 Privacy and Online Proctoring

As more and more testing programs move to online proctoring (OP) to deliver their assessments, a practice that was expedited for many during the pandemic, privacy has become an increasingly important concern (Brown, 2021; Cahn & Deng, 2020; Diebert, 2020; Harwell, 2020; Journal Editorial Board, 2020; Patil & Bromwich, 2020). Because video monitoring is a critical component of ensuring the security of the online proctoring experience, some test takers are uncomfortable taking exams while someone can see into their homes or office space, viewing this as an invasion of their privacy. For Microsoft candidates, our research suggests that about 50% of candidates prefer to take exams at a test center. While there may be many reasons for this preference, some candidates certainly prefer test centers for this reason. Further, you cannot record minors in the USA (this is true in most, if not, all countries worldwide), making it even more difficult to maintain the security of the assessment process for many students who are underage. In normal times, this may not be an issue because assessment could be delivered in the classroom, but in pandemics, it is, creating an interesting challenge for testing programs as they try to balance privacy concerns with the need to deliver exams and assessments in the most secure way possible when they cannot control the environment, as is the case with online proctored deliveries.

Although not related to privacy, it is important to remember that even within the USA and Canada, there are internet deserts, meaning that even in these privileged countries not all test takers have the bandwidth or internet access they need to take assessments from home or their office.

In some instances, testing programs are able to provide a way for the test taker to download the assessment to their phone or other device when they do have a connection, take it offline, and upload the results when they reconnect. This is not possible in all situations, however, making access to some assessments extremely difficult for some people even in the USA and Canada. Given the privilege that many of us experience in these countries, that fact is easy to overlook when it comes to online testing.

10.4   Online Proctoring and Artificial Intelligence

Many online proctoring providers use AI to enhance the human proctor or, in some cases, even replace that person in the monitoring process. Unfortunately, organizations may have been overly zealous in using this technology before it was thoroughly trained, and many of these AI solutions are making errors related to race, ethnicity, and other factors that highlight the bias in these models. In fact, in December 2020, some US senators sent an inquiry to several OP providers asking them to address reports that facial recognition and detection software failed to identify students of color and students who wear religious garb (Kelley & Oliver, 2020; Morse, 2020). The memo sent by these Senators to ExamSoft is available: https://www.blumenthal.senate.gov/imo/media/doc/2020.12.3%20Letter%20to%20Ed%20Testing%20Software%20Companies%20ExamSoft.pdf.

Students with disabilities also said online proctoring technology flagged their involuntary movements, such as muscle spasms, as possible signs of cheating (Cahn & Deng, 2020; Patil & Bromwich, 2020). This is not to say that the technology cannot be used for proctoring. Indeed, the future of proctoring would benefit from AI because you can't bribe a machine, machines don't get tired or distracted, and so on. But we need better ways to train the models, and given the political environment around AI and proctoring, the best solution is likely to be using AI to identify and flag anomalies in the exam environment that a human proctor can then review and determine the appropriate steps.

10.5   Accommodations versus Accessibility

A recent trend that is emerging in the assessment industry concerns a shift from "accommodations" to "accessibility." While accommodations were originally embedded into testing programs as a matter of law in Canada in 1977 (Government of Canada, 1977), the United States in 1990 (US

Equal Employment Opportunity Commission, 1990), and Mexico in 2007 via the Committee on the Rights of Persons with Disabilities (Global Disability Rights Now!, n.d.), the emphasis has increasingly been on accessibility and access for all.

Whereas it was acceptable only a few years ago to offer "equal-but-separate" accommodations (e.g., assessments that didn't contain problematic item types, such as drag and drop or hot area), more and more test takers expect to participate in the same testing experience without additional obstacles or modifications because the assessment is completely accessible through assistive technologies, such as keyboard shortcuts, screen readers, text magnifiers, voice to text, and so on. This will require that the assessment industry reimagines its assessment processes from any learning elements through registration, delivery, and score reporting. At a minimum, this means designing exams and item types to be more compatible with assistive technologies and that do not include changes from the "standard" form. This will only be made possible through innovations and enhancements of our assessment process and item types. This will be enabled through technology.

10.6   Opting Out of Testing

Prior to COVID-19, there was a fair amount of criticism and skepticism about the assessment industry, and the pandemic has brought this sentiment into stark relief, underscoring the smallness of the steps we have taken as an industry to leverage technology to change how we assess and measure knowledge, skills, abilities, and other characteristics. The recent decision by California that it will no longer require the ACT or SATs (standardized tests often required as part of the college application/admissions process) in their college application process by 2025 (University of California, 2020) is just one example of this, and I recently learned that some grad programs are considering dropping the GREs (graduate record examinations) from their application process.

COVID has magnified the risk that test takers and other key stakeholders (college admission boards, parents, employers, etc.) will decide that objective measurement is irrelevant, easily replaced, and/or does not provide sufficient benefit for the associated costs. In addition, our reliance on our current item formats (multiple choice); assessment development and delivery processes, and psychometrics that have not evolved to accommodate today's technologies; and the pace with which knowledge is changing are undermining the assessment industry. From the outside looking in, it is hard to convince the average person that multiple-choice questions are effective measures of skill and ability. Further, as an industry, we struggle with innovation in assessment methods because of our overreliance on classic psychometrics that do not account for machine learning and other big data solutions or the pace with which knowledge is changing and growing in most industries. However, this has not stopped AI engineers and data scientists from creating and selling "assessments" that lack psychometric rigor and that most organizations and users do not realize is missing because the solution looks "cool."

We have an opportunity to reimagine our assessments to better meet the needs of our audiences and to minimize the bias that is driving the perception that measurement does not add value. Measurement is important; we need to seize this moment to leverage technology to drive change in our models. This is another place where AI can play a role in assessment and measurement.

Emerging technologies, such as machine learning, artificial and ambient intelligence, gaming, animation, virtual reality, speech/gesture/gaze/voice recognition, blockchain, and bots, just to name a few, can be harnessed to create solutions that have higher authenticity, making them more acceptable to our stakeholders and test takers, and may be more valid and reliable than our more traditional assessments. This begs the question: How can we reimagine the assessment design, development, and delivery processes through the possibilities that technology could enable?

10.7   Telemetry and Instrumentation to Define Competence

Let us start with job analysis, task analysis, position analysis, competency analysis, etc. Quite honestly, this may be one of the easiest places to radically change assessment development, and it may even be easier than we think.

Leveraging telemetry (i.e., automatic recording and transmission of data to a different location for monitoring and analysis that is often used in technology to understand the features that are most used, detect bugs/issues, and providing data-driven visibility into performance) and instrumentation (i.e., measuring equipment that enables telemetry information to be collected), we can truly understand how people are performing their jobs. Today, we rely on (often unreliable) subject matter experts to help us define the job role, tasks performed, and skills and abilities needed for success. However, research consistently shows that true experts in a job often forget to include some of the basic tasks that they perform or even what it was like to be starting in a role, resulting in a list of skills and abilities that misses some of the critical job tasks that we should be evaluating by our exams (Manea, 2020; Woodley, 2015).

If we use telemetry to understand what people are really doing in their jobs and align that to their skill level, we will have a better understanding of what we should be assessing by our exams to determine competence; we will understand the criticality and importance of each task through a data-driven process rather than the subjective nature of subject matter expert (SME)-driven consensus. Constantly monitoring this telemetry will help us identify new and emerging tasks and skills that are needed for success and inform us on when to add those skills to our assessment process. This would also help us identify the frequency with which tasks are performed and their outcomes when not performed correctly. Further, it can help us build a learning culture that is becoming critical to organizational success today by identifying common mistakes and providing learning opportunities in the moment.

Certainly, SMEs will need to be involved in refining the skills into something coherent that we can use for training and assessment development. Still, by building a job analysis (or similar) on telemetry, we will have a much more accurate foundation for our assessment process. Not only will it help us quickly identify emerging tasks and skills and identity important but infrequent tasks, it may allow us to redefine what competence means by helping us better understand aspects of skills that have largely been ignored, such as elegance and efficiency of a solution, the quality of the outcome, speed of implementation or problem-solving, and so on. It should be noted that telemetry will not be able to capture the nuances of how a task was performed or the mental processes required to complete it, but if you know what tasks were performed, with SMEs' help, you may be able to uncover the knowledge, skills, and abilities required to perform those tasks more efficiently and, perhaps, more accurately because you will be focused on the "right" tasks that need to be part of your assessment process. (It should also be noted that jobs that do not require any interactions with technology [few, though, they may be] would not lend themselves to this approach, and even in those jobs that do, there are likely elements of the job that happen away from technology – and our ability measure through telemetry – that will still require the input from SMEs to ensure that those skills are included in the assessment process.)

As an example, think about how work in your organization has changed in a virtual world in the wake of COVID-19. Your employees certainly have more interactions via email, chat, or text; meetings are happening through Teams or Zoom. How has that changed the dynamic of these interactions? Other than virtual meetings, how else has work for your employees changed? Have your assessments – be it for selection or training and development purposes – changed to reflect this new reality? Are your assessments evaluating the skills needed for success in a virtual world? In most cases, our current testing models are not flexible enough to accommodate disruptive changes that fundamentally change the job. Imagine how much more quickly we could respond to changing work requirements and the associated skills and abilities if we could use instrumentation and telemetry to inform us when the work has changed significantly or in unexpected ways.

10.8   AI in Assessment Development

Assessment development can also change radically with these emerging technologies. Imagine a tool that "reads" text, "watches" videos, "completes" tutorials, and then identifies the key concepts to build a series of questions to assess someone's understanding, skill, or ability in only a few minutes or seconds. This goes beyond automatic item generation (AIG), which has been around for years (Gierl & Haladyna, 2013; Gierl et al., 2021), to a solution that is truly automated developing unique items "on the fly" that is not based on the cloning assumptions that are part of the current AIG solutions. AI technologies are making it possible to do this today (see, for example, FineTune Testing's Generate solution at https://www.finetunelearning.com/generate or the work being done by Duolingo [von Davier et al., 2021]).

Azure Cognitive Services, as one example, could also allow testing programs to move from structured response assessment questions to assessment processes that are more open-ended in nature (interviews, written documentation, portfolio reviews, projects, etc.) in scalable, repeatable, cost-effective ways, creating assessments that have higher authenticity and face validity. These cognitive services may also improve and automate the localization of our assessment content at a much lower cost.

10.9   Technology in Assessment Delivery

Ultimately, to prevent the risks that people will begin to see assessment as irrelevant, we need to create experiences that match their expectations in a world where technology is embedded in all that they do. Taking a multiple-choice assessment is "old school." We can deliver more interactive assessments by leveraging technology to provide more reliable and scalable scoring of verbal and written responses; we could even design a "create your own adventure" type of assessment based on personal needs or known strengths and weaknesses. Virtual reality, mixed reality, and similar technologies that immerse the candidate in the experience will provide a more authentic testing experience and will feel less like a test than multiple-choice questions. This sounds like science fiction, but the metaverse is on the horizon (Shaw, 2021); it is up to assessment developers to determine how to leverage it to evaluate skills and abilities.

In addition, advances in technology enable us to think differently about how we are evaluating skills, such as collaboration, communication, writing, etc., especially if we consider the types of data we can capture in a virtual world. As long as we are intentional about the data we collect, we can design an evaluation based on meaningful patterns of behaviors that help us better understand the test taker's engagement, collaboration abilities, and communication styles.

One example of how a company is leveraging the ubiquity of technology and increasing the use of digital assistants in assessments is OpenEyes technologies (https://www.theopeneyes.com/). Recognizing the people want convenient assessment solutions that happen where they are, OpenEyes is working on an AI natural language data collection platform for assessment, surveying, and employment screening. This solution is designed so that not only will test takers (be it students, job applicants, or someone seeking certification or license) not need to leave the comfort of their homes or offices, but they will not even need to sit in front of a computer to take the assessment. The digital assistant will ask the questions, and the test taker will respond verbally. The assistant will note the answer and move to the next question.

Azure Cognitive Services and related technologies leverage powerful algorithms to see, hear, speak, understand, and interpret our needs using natural methods of communication, including emotion and sentiment detection; image and speech recognition; language understanding, etc. They will make it easier and will more accurately assess soft skills (communication, problem-solving, teamwork, collaboration, interpersonal skills, etc.) that are of critical importance to organizations. Although some uses of these technologies have come under attack recently because of their bias (Crumpler, 2020; Valentino-DeVries, 2020), if we understand the limitations and potential pitfalls, we can train the models differently and more responsibly to eliminate much of that bias and minimize the risks of using. We know that humans are biased. We can leverage these technologies to assist humans, resulting in less biased decisions.

These technologies allow testing programs to move from structured (and rigid) response assessment questions to assessment processes that are more open-ended (and flexible) in nature (interviews, written documentation, portfolio reviews, projects, etc.) in scalable, repeatable, cost-effective ways. If we are intentional in identifying the data that is critical to understanding engagement, collaboration, communication, etc., technology can open a whole new world for soft skills assessment.

Further, technology is allowing us to think about other ways to assess relevant skills and abilities indirectly. Could something that evaluates physiological measures, such as modeling of eye movement, keystrokes, etc., be a good predictor of communication or other soft skills that today we are evaluating in low-tech ways? How can fitness trackers, body sensors, and other similar devices change the way we think about measurement and what we can easily measure? We don't have the answers to these questions – yet – but the possibilities are intriguing and worth exploring.

Finally, technology can move assessment delivery beyond computer adaptive testing. Probabilistic modeling allows computers to consider uncertainties and estimate the likelihood that a test taker will complete a task or answer a question correctly. Leveraging technology, we can take computer adaptive testing one step further and present the "right" task or question at the "right" time to determine competence more quickly and foster a continuous learning mindset. This would be a more effective approach to computer adaptive testing because it would optimize the item pool more efficiently.

Going one step further, imagine a tool that is generating items "real time" during the assessment process based on the skills that the test taker has demonstrated up to that point. Every exam is a unique, accurate, and more efficient evaluation of skills. This introduces a number of psychometric challenges that we need to address, meaning we have to reimagine psychometrics, too.

10.10 Computational Psychometrics: The Future of Measurement

Measurement, psychometrics, and exams as we know them today have been around for a millennium. We have evidence of similar approaches to assessment being used in China and ancient Greece thousands of years ago for job placement and educational purposes (Fletcher, 2009; Traub, 1997).

Further, psychometrics is about 150 years old if you start with the work of Galton (Buchanan & Finch, 2005), and even our beloved classical test theory models and item response theory are now 70+ years old (Bock, 1997); we are dealing with a legacy exam design process that is analyzed using legacy processes that have not evolved to keep pace with technology, changing educational models, the explosion of knowledge, and disruptive factors like COVID-19. We are still largely measuring crystallized intelligence – what I know – at a fixed point in time, which is in direct conflict with the fact that knowledge is doubling in some fields every few months and in less than a year in nearly all fields (Alleyne, 2011). It is insufficient to measure knowledge and skills in this way. As a testing industry, we have not shown the world that we can assess skills in modern and relevant ways, and much of this is related to our approach to psychometrics that underlies our ability to say if an item or assessment is valid and reliable. We need to completely rethink our approach to psychometrics to better reflect what and how we should be assessing, especially given the doors that technology advancements have opened for us.

Our current psychometric models cannot handle the changes technology allows in assessment or our need to change in times of disruption. They cannot handle new approaches to assessment that technology enables, telemetry-based evaluations, or solutions that assess all that there is to measure about a skill with a single "item" (SMART items; Foster, 2020; Weiner et al., 2020). With computational psychometrics (ACTNext, 2019), combining traditional psychometrics with measurement techniques from data mining, machine learning, and other computer science fields, we are starting to make inroads into this challenge as well, but it requires a unique set of skills that combines knowledge of machine learning and assessment design and evaluation. By necessity, this means better collaboration between measurement professionals and computer scientists and developers (Polyak et al., 2017; von Davier, 2017).

10.11 Imagining the Future of Assessment

Imagine a world without tests or exams – at least without the traditional definition of a test or exam because the objective evaluation of skills will always be necessary. To truly understand if someone has the skills to be successful in a job, we should assess people as they are doing something as close as possible to that job. When possible, this means that we should be designing "in work" assessments that evaluate skills as people are doing their jobs or performing tasks like what they will doing on the job. xAPIs (a specification for learning technology that enables the collection of data across a wide range of experiences; the data is often used for personalized learning experiences [xAPI.com, 2021]) or similar telemetry could determine if someone has the skills that they need to be considered competent and identify any weaknesses.

Barring that, we need to design assessments that get as close as possible to what they will be doing on the job. These types of assessments are "free form" because there are many ways that people can accomplish the same tasks, and our scoring/evaluation processes need to account for that. Traditional analysis and scoring techniques have not been able to adequately evaluate this type of free-form responses. AI, with its natural language processing techniques and neural networks and machine learning, can increase our ability to evaluate and understand unstructured responses dramatically, but this requires partnering with data and AI engineers and other cognitive and computational science experts.

In addition, we need to expand our definition of assessment to a more integrated learning and assessment experience that combines frequent, planned low- and high-stakes assessments that evaluate competency and guide learning. Why are we not embracing the learning mindset needed to be successful in nearly every job as technology continues to advance so rapidly in the way we think about assessment?

We need to break out of our paradigm of what we think an assessment is. We need to stop creating obstacles that prevent us from thinking differently about assessments. If assessment becomes a seamless and integrated part of our daily experience that drives not only achievement but ongoing learning, not only would we have a more accurate and authentic evaluation of skills, but the odds are good that people will see assessments are relevant and possibly, dare I say, fun.

REFERENCES

ACTNext. (2019). *Computational psychometrics: A field guide.* https://actnext.org/research-and-projects/computational-psychometrics-field-guide/

Alleyne, R. (2011). Welcome to the Information Age – 174 newspapers a day. *Daily Telegraph.* https://www.telegraph.co.uk/news/science/science-news/8316534/Welcome-to-the-information-age-174-newspapers-a-day.html

Anderson, C. (2017). *Cloud skills and organizational influence: How cloud skills are accelerating the careers of IT professionals.* http://download.microsoft.com/download/C/3/0/C3068200–2F9B-4D8D-BF5D-32E1F7ED669A/IDC_Microsoft_How_Cloud_Skills_Are_Accelerating_IT_Pro_Careers_May_2017.pdf

Association for Test Publishers (ATP). (2019). *Privacy in Practice Bulletin: Customer guidance on privacy compliance.* Bulletin 1. Privacy in Practice Bulletin Series (memberclicks.net).

Association for Test Publishers (ATP). (2021, December). Nevada broadens its privacy law… what are the implications? *Test Publishers News and Information from ATP*, 21.

Bock, R. D. (1997). A brief history of item response theory. *Educational Measurement: Issues and Practice, 16*(4), 21–33. https://doi.org/10.1111/j.1745-3992.1997.tb00605.x

Brown, M. F. (2021). *Key challenges to remote proctoring: Communications and technology, security, and privacy.* https://www.credentialinginsights.org/Article/key-challenges-to-remote-proctoring-communications-and-technology-security-and-privacy-1

Buchanan, R., & Finch, S. (2005). History of psychometrics. In B. Everitt & D. Howell (Eds.), *Encyclopedia of statistics in behavioral science.* John Wiley & Sons.

Cahn, A. F., & Deng, G. (2020). *Remote test-taking software is an inaccurate, privacy-invading mess.* https://www.fastcompany.com/90586386/remote-test-taking-software-is-an-inaccurate-privacy-invading-mess

Californians for Consumer Privacy. (2021). *Introducing the California Privacy Rights Act (CPRA) Resource Center.* https://www.caprivacy.org/introducing-the-california-privacy-rights-act-cpra-resource-center/

CCPA. (2018). *California Consumer Privacy Act (CCPA).* https://www.oag.ca.gov/privacy/ccpa

Crumpler, W. (2020). *The problem of bias in facial recognition.* https://www.csis.org/blogs/technology-policy-blog/problem-bias-facial-recognition

Diebert, R. J. (2020). Opinion: We've become dependent on a technological ecosystem that is highly invasive and prone to serial abuse. *Mail.* https://www.theglobeandmail.com/opinion/article-the-pandemic-has-made-us-even-more-dependent-on-a-highly-invasive/

DLA Piper. (2021). *Law in Mexico – DLA Piper global data protection laws of the world.* https://www.dlapiperdataprotection.com/index.html?t=law&c=MX

Faggella, D. (2020). *Everyday examples of artificial intelligence and machine learning.* https://emerj.com/ai-sector-overviews/everyday-examples-of-ai/

Fletcher, D. (2009). *A brief history of standardized testing.* http://content.time.com/time/nation/article/0,8599,1947019,00.html

Foster, D. (2020). *SmartItem™: Stop test fraud, improve fairness, and upgrade the way you test.* https://info.caveon.com/the-smartitem-ebook-promo

GDPR EU. (2021). *GDPR – user-friendly guide to General Data Protection Regulation.* https://www.gdpreu.org/

Gierl, M. J., & Haladyna, T. (2013). *Automatic item generation.* Routledge.

Gierl, M. J., Lai, H., & Tanygin, V. (2021). *Advanced methods in automatic item generation.* Routledge.

Global Disability Rights Now!. (n.d.). *Mexico.* https://www.globaldisabilityrightsnow.org/mexico

Goddard, W. (2020). *Where is AI used today?* https://itchronicles.com/artificial-intelligence/where-is-ai-used-today/

Government of Canada. (1977). *Rights of people with disabilities.* https://www.canada.ca/en/canadian-heritage/services/rights-people-disabilities.html

Harwell, D. (2020, November 12). Students rebel over remote test monitoring during the pandemic. *The Washington Post.* https://www.washingtonpost.com/technology/2020/11/12/test-monitoring-student-revolt/

International Data Corporation. (2020). *Cloud adoption and opportunities will continue to expand leading to a $1 trillion market in 2024, according to IDC.* https://www.idc.com/getdoc.jsp?containerId=prUS46934120

Journal Editorial Board. (2020). *Online proctoring unfairly punishes cheaters & non-cheaters alike.* https://www.queensjournal.ca/story/2020-11-19/editorials/online-proctoring-unfairly-punishes-cheaters-and-non-cheaters-alike/

Kelly, J., & Oliver, L. (2020). *Senators express privacy concerns over proctoring apps.* https://www.eff.org/deeplinks/2020/12/senators-express-privacy-concerns-over-proctoring-apps

Manea, A. I. (2020). Selecting subject matter experts in job and work analysis surveys: Advantages and disadvantages. *Academic Journal of Economic Studies,* 6(2), 52–61. https://link.gale.com/apps/doc/A631140986/AONE?u=anon~aa6ed072&sid=googleScholar&xid=b0778136

MIT Technology Review. (2020). *Ten breakthrough technologies in 2020.* https://www.technologyreview.com/10-breakthrough-technologies/2020/

MIT Technology Review. (2021). *Ten breakthrough technologies in 2021.* https://www.technologyreview.com/2021/02/24/1014369/10-breakthrough-technologies-2021/

Morse, J. (2020). *Online testing is a biased mess, and senators are demanding answers.* https://mashable.com/article/senate-open-letter-remote-proctoring-examsoft-bias-student-privacy/

Office of the Privacy Commissioner of Canada. (2019). *The Privacy Act.* https://priv.gc.ca/en/privacy-topics/privacy-laws-in-canada/the-privacy-act/

Patil, A., & Bromwich, J. E. (2020, September 29). How it feels when software watches you take tests. *The New York Times.* https://www.nytimes.com/2020/09/29/style/testing-schools-proctorio.html

Polyak, S. T., von Davier, A. A., & Peterschmidt, K. (2017). Computational psychometrics for the measurement of collaborative problem-solving skills. *Frontiers in Psychology,* 8. https://doi.org/10.3389/fpsyg.2017.02029

Recio, D. (2017). *Mexico's new public-sector data protection law.* https://iapp.org/news/a/mexicos-new-public-sector-data-protection-law/

Rippy, S. (2021). *US state privacy legislation tracker.* https://iapp.org/resources/article/us-state-privacy-legislation-tracker/

Saeed, F. (2020). *9 powerful examples of artificial intelligence in use today.* https://www.iqvis.com/blog/9-powerful-examples-of-artificial-intelligence-in-use-today/

Shaw, F. X. (2021). *Microsoft Cloud at Ignite 2021: Metaverse, AI, and hyperconnectivity in a hybrid world.* https://blogs.microsoft.com/blog/2021/11/02/microsoft-cloud-at-ignite-2021-metaverse-ai-and-hyperconnectivity-in-a-hybrid-world/

Traub, R. E. (1997). Classical test theory in historical perspective. *Educational Measurement: Issues and Practice, 16*(4), 8–14. https://doi.org/10.1111/j .1745-3992.1997.tb00603.x

University of California. (2020). *University of California Board of Regents unanimously approved changes to standardized testing requirement for undergraduates.* https://www.universityofcalifornia.edu/press-room/university-california-board-regents-approves-changes-standardized-testing-requirement#:~:text=Eliminati on>%20of%20the%20ACT%2FSAT%20test%20requirement%3A%20By %202025%2C,UC-endorsed%20test%20to%20measure%20UC-readiness% 20would%20be%20required

US Equal Employment Opportunity Commission. (1990). *Americans with Disabilities Act of 1990.* https://www.eeoc.gov/americans-disabilities-act-1990-original-text

Valentino-DeVries, J. (2020, January 12). How the police use facial recognition, and where it falls short. *The New York Times.* https://www.nytimes.com/ 2020/01/12/technology/facial-recognition-police.html

von Davier, A. A. (2017). Computational psychometrics in support of collaborative educational assessments. *Journal of Educational Measurement, 54*(1), 3–11. https://doi.org/10.3389/fpsyg.2017.02029

von Davier, A. A., Munson, L., & Lottridge, S. (2021, July). In T. Hembry (Moderator), *Increased automation in our industry: How not to get it wrong.* Panel discussion presented at ATP's New World of Testing (NWT) Digital Series.

Weiner, J., Munson, L. J., & Foster, D. (2020, September). *Test security in the digital age: Advances in design and analytics.* Breakout session accepted at ATP's Global Annual Innovations in Testing Virtual Conference.

Woodley, C. D. (2015, April). *Careful selection of subject matter experts is the key to a successful JTA meeting.* The Item Bank: The Professional Testing Blog. http://www.proftesting.com/blog/2015/04/29/2015429careful-selection-of-subject-matter-experts-is-the-key-to-a-successful-jta-meeting/

xAPI.com. (2021). *What is xAPI aka the Experience API or Tin Can API?* https:// xapi.com/overview/

Technology and Measurement Challenges in Education and the Labor Market in South America

Filip De Fruyt, Toon Devloo, Ana Carolina Zuanazzi, Thais Brandão, Ricardo Primi, Fabiano Koich Miguel, and Juliana Seidl

The past decades witnessed tremendous technological innovations and evolutions that have affected the measurement, reporting, and monitoring of psychological constructs and processes spanning various domains of people's lives from early education to postretirement. The worldwide COVID-19 pandemic has accelerated this development, requiring students and employees to study or work from home temporarily, and some of these alternate ways of teaching and working will likely be continued after the pandemic (Kniffin et al., 2021). This disruption has emphasized the use and distribution of technology to teach and evaluate learning progress in education, run psychological assessments with job applicants online, or develop work performance appraisal and monitoring systems for employees in organizations.

11.1 Impact of Technology on Assessment

The introduction of new measurement technology has affected measurement in pedagogical and psychological sciences in at least four different ways. First, technology fundamentally challenged and changed the relationship between the assessor and assessee, which previously required one or another form of personal contact between both actors in the relationship. Using technology, assessments can be done without an assessor, using (un)proctored electronic assessment platforms (instead of paper and pencil tests), or the assessee may even be unaware of being the subject of assessment when a computer algorithm is analyzing social media behavior. Through technology, assessment and measurement can be conducted anywhere at any time, and this may have consequences for the administration but also the interpretation of assessments. It further induces a series of legal liabilities regarding the use of information that can be retrieved about individuals to protect their privacy (Alexander et al., 2020).

A second major innovation is that the use of technology in measurement significantly changed and expanded the assessment content and methods that can be used. Personality assessments conducted via questionnaires can now be complemented, for example, with an analysis of someone's electronic footprint, revealed in Facebook or Twitter posts, electronic search and buying behavior, or other types of social media activities. Situation descriptions in situational judgment tests can be replaced by virtual reality stimuli. Alternatively, wearable electronic devices and other forms of ambulatory assessments make it possible to monitor and analyze an individual's behavior on a continuous basis. In sum, technological progress has opened a new box of critical questions about human functioning (in various science fields, including education and psychology) that could not be adequately addressed using traditional methods of assessment such as paper and pencil tests or surveys. The availability of cell phones or wearable electronic devices has boosted ambulatory assessment research, for example, enabling the study of within-person fluctuation in personality traits and the experiencing of situations beyond the assessment of between-person differences (Abrahams et al., 2021). The availability of technology to describe fluctuating states and processes in the person permitted us to advance our knowledge on different types of dynamics in the person (Lang et al., 2021) as well as how these dynamics affected consequential outcomes such as learning or job performance (Debusscher et al., 2016; Lievens et al., 2018; Sosnowska et al., 2020). Technological innovations in measurement hence significantly boosted scientific knowledge in various areas.

A third major impact of technology on measurement was on how the results of the psychological assessment are analyzed and reported. Technology not only helped to standardize administration, analysis, and interpretation of assessments (preventing potential biases), it further provided unique opportunities to develop a range of reports for assessees and professionals that could be delivered immediately after test administration. On top of this, technology further helps to save assessment results in databases and swiftly connect this information with other data available on the person. Formative and summative assessment results of students, for example, can now be easily filed and connected with data that are available in school databases, such as information on students' academic achievement, absenteeism data, or social-demographic information.

Finally, technology also heavily impacted what we do with the measurement results and how we can make better use of its results for individual and organizational decision-making. Electronic assessments and various reports can be delivered at the right time to the different stakeholders of assessments serving either formative or summative purposes. For formative assessments, it is often also important that this information comes at the right dosage when the person is "ready" to capture that particular piece of information or input. This makes technology-based assessment an indispensable tool providing input for learning and coaching in education and across the professional career path. Moreover, given that technology has made assessments less dependent on the assessor, it puts the individual student or employee in a responsible position to manage their own learning and development from school into their professional career. At school, students learn knowledge and develop (social-emotional) skills, and this process continues across their professional career path. Technology-driven employee experience systems, slowly finding their way into contemporary organizations, have put the individuals as central in the organization and in the driver's seat of their own development. These systems support employees to keep track of development and consolidate newly acquired knowledge, expertise, and skills, suggest new job opportunities, and also help individuals identify skill gaps and connect them to (electronic) learning modules. Artificial intelligence systems, operating in the background of such tools, support the individual employee in making sense of this information flow sustaining their employability. It is clear that such systems are critically dependent on the utility and validity of the information that is available about the individual, and the results of reliable and valid psychological assessment (via technology) will be the critical fuel for these tools.

11.2 Technology and Measurement in South America

Although technology travels quickly and easily across countries and cultures, South American countries face particular educational, institutional, and social-economic challenges that urge a quick introduction of technology-supported assessment in the worlds of education and work.

Regarding education, several South American countries are facing lower rankings in international comparisons of educational performance (OECD, 2019), necessitating new and efficient monitoring systems to document and diagnose what is happening and take action on how the situation can be optimized. Policymakers and school directors need effective measurement systems to monitor performance differences among school systems (e.g., public versus private education) and states within countries that show variability in academic performance indicators. Educational performance in the city of Sobral (the State of Ceara, North of Brazil), for example, has shown to be substantively higher on an educational quality index (*Índice de Desenvolvimento da Educação Básica*; INEP, 2020), and researchers and policymakers want to investigate the working ingredients of Sobral's education system to implement in other states of the country.

Besides poor performance, also dropout rates from school have been a major concern in many education systems in South America, so close monitoring of educational attendance, belonging at school, and learning progression is primordial from a policy perspective. If students leave education too early, they end up poorly educated and in a bad position to connect with the increasing demands of the current labor market. These two challenges for education in South America underscore the necessity to scale up measurement and monitoring across large groups of students and schools, making technology-based measurement indispensable.

At the level of the South American labor market, there are also notable challenges. First, unemployment has been a major problem in several countries (or parts thereof) already for many years and the COVID pandemic will likely enhance this. At the same time, however, there is a large number of job vacancies or potential job openings (most often requiring specific competencies) that turn out to be difficult to fill. In other words, there is a mismatch between the demand and supply side of the available/required labor force – companies do not find the required competencies on the labor market, not even if they tone down or adjust requirements. In addition to specialist technical expertise and skills, the labor market today is looking for transferable skills, so organizations and their employees are in a better position to deal with the challenges of the volatile, uncertain, complex, and ambiguous world (De Fruyt, 2021). This explicit attention shift to transferable skills has brought new challenges to education that is now explicitly urged to help students acquire and develop social-emotional skills beyond languages and knowledge about STEM (science, technology, engineering, and math) subjects. In Brazil, for example, the attainment of social-emotional skills has been recently formally included in the education curriculum (Base Nacional Comum Curricular; Brasil, 2018), bringing a series of new challenges to education on how to develop such skills and evaluate their attainment. Once on the labor market, employees will have to further develop their transferable skills (life-long learning), so they remain "agile" for the quickly changing labor market and its demands (De Fruyt et al., 2015).

A second major shift in human resources thinking notable across the world is that individual employees are considered more and more as critical and responsible agents of their own career development to ascertain employability across their career paths (Seidl et al., 2020). Employees will have to engage in life-long learning and will become learners across their entire life. Formal education during adolescence and young adulthood is not an end-point of schooling and development anymore, but only a first step in a life-long learning and development trajectory. Once on the labor market, individual employees will have to learn formally and informally across the diversity of jobs they are employed in. Organizations will have to support this learning process, and online systems to track this development will be necessary to support this trajectory within and outside of the organization. Employee-experience tracking systems will play a critical role here to guide this process, helping new employees, for example, to onboard in the organization, receive "tailor-made" learning content and suggestions at a time they need this, and follow their personal learning progression and performance indicators within and outside of the organization.

Finally, a third major challenge that today's societies and labor markets have to deal with is the paradox between the increasing number of mature people (over the age of 50 years) who will have to postpone their retirement and, at the same time, the lack of job opportunities due to the economic crisis that affect all and agism that affects especially older people in Western societies (Seidl & Hanashiro, 2021). In Brazil, for example, the latest pension reform was approved at the end of 2019 and, for those aged 50 and over, the unemployment rate jumped from 2.7% in 2012 to 7.2% at the end of 2020.[1] For many of those who lost jobs (in the pandemic), they can no longer be employed in the kind of jobs they did before because these disappeared, job requirements dramatically changed, or new jobs became available in the novel economies. For other workers (both employed and unemployed), acquired expertise and skill levels need to be consolidated, and employees need support to translate their expertise and experience into the language of new labor market demands. Given the many people involved, technology-based assessment and talent matching algorithms will be necessary to adequately consolidate, unlock, and further develop and manage this enormous potential.

The current chapter will review two of these technology-driven assessment developments, one in education where technology is used to facilitate the learning and development of social-emotional skills in young Brazilian students, the other in human resources where we discuss an

[1] https://economia.uol.com.br/noticias/bbc/2021/03/15/chego-com-experiencia-mas-querem-juventude-desemprego-entre-mais-velhos-dispara-pandemia.htm

employee-experience system developed by an Argentinian team that can be rolled out in organizations to support and monitor an individual's career path, progression, and learning.

11.3   Technology-Supported Assessment of Social-Emotional Skills in Pupils in Brazil

11.3.1   Technology and Social-Emotional Skills

The beginning of the 21st century was marked by accelerated growth of South American scientific production in psychological and educational assessment and testing. An area that has been expanding and developing tremendously is the use of computerized methods and technology to measure psychological constructs and processes (Primi, 2010), such as intelligence and personality, but also social-emotional skills (Shiner et al., 2022) more recently.

Computerization and technology can aid the measurement of psychological constructs in several ways. First, counter to a paper and pencil test, computerization offers the opportunity to present items or answer options in *alternate orders*. In reasoning tests, items traditionally start with the easiest, with increasing levels of item difficulty. For such tests, changing the order of items is not desired, but it is possible to modify the order of answer alternatives. In self-report inventories (such as personality inventories, interest scales, etc.), however, it is very easy with computerized administration to alter the presentation order of items without affecting individuals' self-descriptions, so the item sequence can follow a random order (Miguel, 2017). When it is necessary to assess a construct multiple times to chart learning or development, for example, one often uses the same assessment tool because independent parallel versions are not available. Most often, it is too costly to develop parallel versions, and when alternatives are available, their measurement equivalence is usually not established. Using the same tool across short time intervals includes a considerable risk for memorization effects (Anastasi & Urbina, 2000; Wise & Kingsbury, 2000). Administering randomly ordered versions of the same item set is hence a good alternative when one has to reassess a certain construct over a short time interval.

A second advantage of computerized administration is the possibility of adaptive testing, reducing assessment time, and providing items that are better aligned with the trait level of the assessee. Adaptive tests have been first developed for cognitive assessments to reduce the number of items that have to be administered. Answering an extensive sequence of increasingly difficult items can be tiring or embarrassing for children with lower intellectual capacity. For children with higher intellectual levels, the first items may seem too simple, compromising their concentration or even the validity of the test (Urbina, 2007). Measurement errors are introduced in both cases. There are few printed instruments that overcome this difficulty, usually through specific instructions for starting or ending, such as starting with a more advanced item depending on the age of the person being evaluated or interrupting the application of items after a certain time or number of mistakes. Item response theory and computerized assessment allowed to solve this problem using computerized adaptive testing, where items are presented according to the pattern of correct or wrong answers (or choices, in the case of Likert-type scales), while calculating the level of that subject's ability (Thompson & Weiss, 2011; Wise & Kingsbury, 2000). More recently, adaptive tests are also being developed for assessing personality traits.

A third impactful innovation of technology is the expanded possibilities to present stimulus material using multimedia, that is, animations and/or sounds on the computer (Barak & English, 2002; de Klerk et al., 2018), virtual reality assessments, or games. This feature can make the task more attractive for assessees, often complaining that assessments are boring and giving the impression of being repetitive. In many assessment situations, the motivation of the assessee is an important prerequisite to obtaining a reliable and valid estimate of an individual's level on a trait or ability. Also, for the assessment of children, animations may be very helpful to get them engaged in the task, because they are exposed to new media possibilities already from an early age. Even for the youngest or for those who are not proficient in reading, it is possible to include audio support to help them conduct the assessment with less assessor interaction/interference.

Finally, electronic administration is also very useful to collect additional behavioral variables easily and reliably, such as response time or how many times the assessee changes the response before proceeding to the next item. The assessee can be alerted when the answering of an item is omitted, and the analysis of the results can be conducted without clerical errors ensuring greater reliability and standardization.

The assessment of social-emotional skills in children and pupils is one area where technology in measurement can make a significant step forward. Social-emotional skill assessment usually relies on self-reports using written items requiring already advanced cognitive and social-emotional capacities of students. Respondents first need to be able to read items fluently, encode the information enclosed in the items, retrieve relevant information from their long-term memory, reflect and make a synthetic judgment, and finally respond by selecting among the provided options (Duckworth & Yeager, 2015). Because very young children (6–9 years old) are still developing their verbal skills, it is difficult to use assessments using traditional sentence items. Computerized tests bypass the need for reading and writing skills by using pictorial and sound stimuli, texts and images, or videos to present stimulus material. Children can respond quickly, by touching pictorial response options on tablets, and their spontaneous reactions and behaviors can be registered and analyzed.

11.3.2 SENNA Kids

One example of computerized assessment of socio-emotional skills in young children is the "SENNA kids" tool developed by researchers from eduLab 21 of the Institute Ayrton Senna (Brandão et al., 2021, Zuanazzi et al., 2021). SENNA kids is inspired by the Berkeley Puppet Interview developed by Measelle et al. (2005) and the Teste de Organização de Histórias Emocionais (Emotional Stories Organization Test) of Miguel and Zuanazzi (2020). The tool is designed to assess the social-emotional skills of pupils of 6–11 years, using various technology-supported assessment formats.

One format uses different sets of pictorial items describing various situations accompanied by two potential reactions that are orally presented to pupils by the computer. In this "forced choice" SENNA kids subtest, children are presented with a cartoon-like picture (see the upper part of Figure 11.1) representing the two opposite poles of a social-emotional skill dimension like "engaging with others" or "self-management," for example. In addition, they hear two reaction options such as: "I find it easy to make new friends" versus "I find it hard to make new friends" (for engaging with others), or "When a lesson is difficult, I keep trying until I can do it" versus "I give up when I realize something is difficult" (for self-management). The upper part of Figure 11.1 shows an example of a pictorial forced-choice item assessing "Amity," showing a situation where a child is crying, and the other child (assessee) is observing this. Pupils are subsequently asked to indicate which of these two options best reflects how they usually react in a situation like this. The two potential reactions are also orally presented, that is, "I just realized a friend had a problem after a long time" or "I worry when a friend has a problem." After selecting an option, the student is further presented with a pictorial Likert-type scale asking them

Figure 11.1   Senna Kids socio-emotional skills forced-choice test (upper figure)
and role-playing histories (lower figure)

to indicate the intensity of their choice on a three-point scale (see the right
option in the top part of Figure 11.1).

Another SENNA kids subtest presents five cartoon-like cards (see the
bottom part of Figure 11.1) and asks children to create a story about
themselves in the school, selecting any three cards to fill blank spaces. After
selection, children have to record their stories orally. The produced stories
can be scored and further decoded afterward using algorithms for text
analysis that are currently under development. The kind of cards selected
and their order in the story composition can be analyzed, and the story's
content can be further coded in terms of referrals to, for example, emotional conflicts, social interaction, or self-management issues. The selection

of the used "thematic" pictures may teach us something about how they perceive their environment (Brandão et al., 2021; Zuanazzi et al., 2021).

Cognitive labs conducted in a pilot study showed that children as young as five years could easily understand the procedures and questions used in SENNA kids (Brandão et al., 2021). The first results of a factor analysis of the items learned that children were able to distinguish among at least three broad dimensions of social-emotional skills (Abrahams et al., 2019; Primi et al., 2021), that is, (a) "Learning skills" (i.e., a combination of "self-management" and "open-mindedness" covering motivation to learn and achieve, focus attention, and resist distractions); (b) "Social skills" (i.e., a combination of "engaging with others" and "amity," reflecting making new friends, positive self-esteem, being socially accepted, being empathic, and recognizing rules of interpersonal behavior); and (c) "Emotion regulation skills" (i.e., emotional resilience, representing how one deals with fears, anxieties, irritability, and aggression). These first results showed that technology-aided assessment considerably facilitated the assessment of social-emotional skills in young students. The assessment procedures developed by Measelle et al. (2005) are very time- and labor-intensive, whereas SENNA kids seems to hold a lot of promise because it can easily be scaled up at relatively low costs. SENNA kids is now further tested and refined to be used in formative assessment of social-emotional learning in Brazilian primary education.

11.3.3   Challenges

Although computer-aided assessment of social-emotional skills in education overcomes several limitations of traditional assessment using sentence items, there is still a number of limitations and challenges that are bound to the digital format itself. A first obstacle is the distribution and availability of electronic devices at schools or in students' families. This is certainly a limiting factor in South American societies characterized by large social-economic inequalities. In order to be able to use a tool like SENNA kids for formative assessment in education, one needs the technological infrastructure to roll out assessments at a large scale, requiring enough computers, tablets, or cell phones at school or in the home environment. Moreover, computerized assessment and mobile devices are not always functioning in a stable way – a program can "freeze" or the internet connection can be too weak at times to load programs or can be interrupted. This is a specific challenge, especially when multiple students connect at the same time for an assessment in class in more remote areas in South America.

Familiarity with technology by teachers and students is another critical factor. For teachers and test administrators, care must be taken so that the application proceeds in a standardized way, which includes attention to the brightness of the screen, the fidelity of the colors on the monitor, the screen sizes provided, the sensitivity of the input (keyboard, mouse or touch screen), among other details (Barak & English, 2002). Technology-supported measurement is further dependent on the technological features of the available technological infrastructure. A measurement application may behave differently when installed on devices with different operating system versions. The continuous updating of internet browsers often requires updates of the assessment tool so that it works correctly again (Khomh et al., 2015). From the perspective of the assessed child, one needs to ensure that they know how to handle the device and respond appropriately. Although digital inclusion is increasing quickly, there are still people who are afraid to interact with computers or who simply do not have access to technology, such as people with low purchasing power (Bolzan & Löbler, 2016).

Finally, it is considered that some issues inherent to testing cannot be resolved with computerization. One of them is social desirability, that is, the tendency of the subject to answer the test in order to present more desirable characteristics, a phenomenon that can be present in both printed and digital versions. Another issue may be dedication to the task of answering the test. Some people lack motivation to respond and therefore make mistakes or deliberately respond inappropriately. In fact, computerization can even make this situation worse in cases where the test application is done remotely. Without the test administrator present to verify presence and engagement, some children may feel more comfortable not reading instructions properly, lying, responding inappropriately, answering the test several times until they reach the desired performance, or even asking another person to answer for them (Barak & English, 2002; Miguel, 2017). For these reasons, it is recommended that remote applications are accompanied by a video call or video registration.

11.4   Supporting the Individual's Career via Technology and Assessment

11.4.1   HR Technology and the Future of Work

In part accelerated by the global COVID-19 pandemic, technology has taken a central role in our personal and professional lives. We got used to the fact that platforms such as Amazon or Takeaway.com "understand" our needs as consumers and provide us with services, products, and content that match our interest profile. To a broader extent, machine learning and artificial intelligence enable these personalized, fast, and hassle-free customer experiences. Based on our previous purchases or behavioral preferences, machine-learning algorithms that underlie the technology behind many of these platforms can learn from this recorded data, recognize patterns, and in turn predict what we are more likely to consume or to purchase in the (near) future. Your favorite pizza, from your favorite pizza place, delivered at record speed? It's only one click away on your mobile phone!

Interestingly, these consumer technologies are shaping our expectations and needs as (assessment) professionals as well. As a result, chatbots, recommendation engines, and other artificial intelligence applications are finding their way into the workplace to leverage more fluid, productive, and, above all, more personalized working experiences. This digital transformation at work and adoption of smart technologies entails an enormous opportunity for human resources to shift from being an administrative and process-driven area into a more strategic and people-centric department. Compared to how marketers approach their customers' experience, human resources still have quite some catch-up to do when it comes to creating great and differentiated employee experiences. Experts estimate that technological advancements in employee experience management are still five to eight years behind customer experience (Green, 2021). This is in spite of the fact that good practices around employee experience are likely to be associated with positive business outcomes such as increased probability to obtain financial targets, superior customer satisfaction, higher employee retention, and increased innovation (Bersin, 2021a).

So, what makes for a good employee experience? In his book *The Employee Experience Advantage*, Jacob Morgan (2017) refers to employee experience as the overlap between employee expectations and needs, and the efforts carried out by an organization to design interventions, practices, and processes that meet these employee expectations and needs. According to Morgan, employee experience taps into three distinct environments: the technological environment (i.e., the digital tools to get the job done), the physical environment (i.e., working space of an organization), and the cultural environment (i.e., how employees and teams feel in their organization). This implies that to design an organization that people want to work for and to be able to flourish, companies need to understand what their employees expect. An HR department that takes a "one size fits all" approach to manage the experience of its employees with highly differentiated needs, will not cut it anymore.

To make personalized experiences to all employees scalable, inevitably, technology comes into play. In this regard, there are various examples of HR technology "powered by machine learning" that are being woven into the entire employee life cycle to improve the employee experience. For example, applicant tracking systems seek to maintain candidate engagement throughout the entire hiring process. This can be achieved by sharing relevant information about the progress of the process with a specific candidate or gradually providing more information about the company as the candidate progresses through the selection process, even suggesting other interesting positions within the same organization that could coincide with the candidate's interest profile. HR also has started to implement chatbots to facilitate employee self-service, where employees can change their benefits plan, request vacations, or make inquiries about administrative processes. A clear win-win for both employees and HR. According to recent data, early adopter companies of artificial intelligence tools for HR management are 19% more effective at reducing the time spent executing administrative tasks compared to companies that have not adopted this technology yet (Columbus, 2018).

Another example is learning management systems that have also become important tools to personalize the experience of employees. In this regard, machine learning makes it possible to replicate some key characteristics of successful content consumption platforms such as Spotify or YouTube with the aim of personalizing and improving the training experience of an employee. One very promising path is microlearning, the practice of breaking down learning material into small content capsules that are quick and easy to digest (Leong et al., 2020). These content capsules are suitable for adaptive, personalized, and flexible learning. This type of learning is particularly a natural fit for mobile use, for example for frontline workers who don't always have access to desktops to consume more traditional learning content. Employees can benefit from micro-learning initiatives in order to access performance resources to be used on the job, reflect on their current skillset, or refresh recently completed trainings. Machine learning plays an important role in this evolution since it enables a dynamic selection of these capsules depending on the profile and needs of the employee, resulting in personalized learning tracks.

The strong rise of HR technology is also resulting in an increasing amount of data points that are available to analyze and use to improve data-driven decision-making. For example, the detection of anomalies to identify unexpected events in employee journeys such as an unexpected drop in productivity. In a similar vein, predictive models are being developed to identify employees who are at risk of leaving the company and should be included in an employee retention program or followed up specifically with stay interviews. Furthermore, these increased analytical capabilities may also benefit the development of in-house content, for example, to improve job descriptions, recommend career paths, assign mentors, or develop customized professional development programs. In other words, the data produced and collected through all these different HR platforms and tools represent an additional valuable resource for HR to expand its analytical capacity and design employee experiences based on data-driven criteria.

A lot of HR tasks and processes are built around the different stages of the employee life cycle in a company. A typical example would be the onboarding of new employees, a promotion, or employees leaving the organization. Supervising each step of the onboarding process or accompanying an employee when they change roles or return from long sick leave implies a great investment of time and resources on the part of the HR team (and the employee, for that matter). Each of these processes and tasks tend to be coordinated by different HR subareas such as selection and recruitment, training and development, or compensation and benefits. Furthermore, these subareas are likely to use different systems and communication channels to carry out their core activities. This may result in a fragmented and complex technological environment with different applications and portals through which employees must navigate. In this regard, a new category of technology is emerging that makes it possible to integrate all these different HR systems and apps in an intelligent and user-friendly way. This technology has been described by Josh Bersin as the employee experience platform (Bersin, 2021a).

In the same way that Amazon integrates and consolidates the data of its users to be able to accompany each consumer in a better way, an employee experience platform allows you to do the same for your employees. These types of platforms act as virtual assistants for employees that provide them with all the necessary content, resources, tools, and contact points to make their time spent at work easier. Employee experience platforms aim to provide employees with a single and consistent digital user interface that connects all these different HR back-end systems (i.e., such as the platforms mentioned earlier on: applicant tracking systems, HR information systems, or learning management systems) without interrupting their experience. Strategic and people-centric activities such as designing employee journeys, setting up HR workflows, performing continuous listening activities to monitor employee experience, and sharing personalized content can all take place within an employee experience platform. In other words, this technology enables a more integral approach to managing and streamlining employee experiences throughout the entire employee life cycle.

11.4.2   An Employee Experience Platform in Action

Currently, the HR technology market in Latin America is growing rapidly, particularly in countries such as Mexico, Brazil, Argentina, Colombia, and Chile. From a cultural perspective, work dynamics in Latin America are designed around in-person interactions and physical workspaces. However, with the recent outbreak of coronavirus (COVID-19), organizations have been pushed to explore and adopt solutions that facilitate the rising trend of work-from-home models and tools that can streamline core HR processes and safeguard employee well-being. Given the low levels of employee well-being and workplace health that historically have been reported in Latin American countries such as Mexico or Colombia, these countries have recently started to enact governmental policies that require institutions and private companies to analyze risk factors and take appropriate actions to improve employee well-being (Cardenas, 2019; L&E Global, 2019). This represents another incentive for Latin American companies to increasingly adopt technology that can monitor and improve the experience of their employees and create better and healthier workplaces.

Interestingly, the strongest job creation sector in Latin America still remains the tertiary sector, which includes, among others, community, social and personal services; health and basic services; and commerce, restaurants, and hotels (CEPAL, 2019). In this sector, employees such as frontline staff and the operations team are at the center of customer experience and hence are crucial pillars for the organization. However, to date, most HR technology solutions to improve the experience of employees globally and in Latin America specifically have been developed for office-based workers and not necessarily for employees at the frontline (Bersin, 2021b; Levine, 2021). Hence, it can be expected that HR technology that targets this segment of frontline employees will be in strong demand by Latin American organizations in their pursuit to improve the employee experience for their entire workforce.

An example of the potential that digital solutions may have for improving employee experience is an employee experience platform that has been developed by Bondi X, an HR technology provider that operates in the Latin American region. This employee experience platform operates by means of a conversational virtual assistant for employees. This virtual assistant can carry out a broad range of tasks that facilitate HR service delivery at a large scale, from handling HR-related questions regarding holiday policies or benefit plans, to setting up workflows that automate HR processes such as onboarding or offboarding. Since a conversational assistant can simulate a more human and personal communication style, it is an interesting tool to involve employees more actively in designing their own journey at the company, built around their own needs and expectations. For example, the platform can be used to assist new employees who enter the company by articulating key milestones during their first weeks or months at the organization, such as a welcome message from the CEO, sharing documents for administrative purposes, or planning a meeting with their supervisor and team. These workflows can be entirely customized based on the needs of specific groups of employees. In this regard, perhaps the organization wants to design a different onboarding experience for its employees that enter the R&D versus the commercial department.

Instead of concentrating all this overwhelming amount of information, often accessed through various systems or shared by different facilitators, this virtual assistant can be used to distribute and articulate these milestones in a more dynamic, consistent, and easy-to-digest format. Given that this employee experience platform is backed by machine learning and natural language processing, it can continuously improve its ability to better understand and answer inquiries of employees that normally are addressed individually by the HR team. Furthermore, the platform has the capability to carry out continuous listening activities by reaching out to employees and asking about their current experience at work. In turn, the platform has been engineered through machine-learning algorithms to analyze these open text comments and to recognize potential pain or gain points associated with an employee's journey. For example, if an employee comments about the lack of career opportunities within the company, the platform will identify "career growth" as a potential pain point and will provide the employee with recommendations on how to proactively pursue growth opportunities within the company. These sets of recommendations have been developed by organizational psychologists and are unlocked and articulated by the virtual assistant from the moment an employee addresses a specific touchpoint. This way, the platform seeks to meaningfully engage with employees and to nudge them toward undertaking actions that may benefit their overall experience at work.

This conversational dynamic to track employee experience also results in insights and metrics displayed in a dashboard for the HR department and other stakeholders within the organization. Through this dashboard, the employee experience of the entire workforce can be systematically monitored. Additionally, the platform provides the possibility of sharing content capsules with specific segments of employees for internal communication purposes. That is, small pieces of content regarding specific activities, policies, or other relevant information should come to the attention of specific groups of employees. For example, if an organization is about to change its COVID-19 security measures for all frontline employees, then the virtual assistant can reach out to the adequate group of people in a more personalized way. In a similar way, should the organization have new job opportunities at its commercial department, then these job openings can be brought to the attention of possible internal candidates. Given the various functionalities that this employee experience platform provides, it aims to be the first digital contact point for employees regarding all relevant internal HR services. To do so in an efficient manner, this employee experience platform can be integrated and connected with every human resources information system that an organization might be using. These integrations provide access to relevant employee data and detect relevant events in the employee journey. For example, when an employee changes from department or job title, the platform can provide assistance and relevant information during these critical moments, and workflows can be automatically activated. Furthermore, this employee experience platform has been designed to be an omnichannel experience, as employees can access the virtual assistant through a mobile app, website, or through the main collaboration and communication platforms that a company uses.

11.4.3   (Please Brace Yourselves for) Impact!

Employee experience platforms such as the one that Bondi X has developed can benefit HR and the organization in various ways to a broader extent. First, they provide HR with the ability to automate repetitive and transactional activities, and to make high-quality experiences consistent and scalable to all employees during their time at the organization. Consequently, HR teams can dedicate their time and resources to strategic tasks that add value to their function and department. Furthermore, compared to 10 years ago, AI-based technology has become affordable. In times where most teams have to do more with less, this type of employee experience platform might be a vital resource to reduce bottle-necks and to operate more cost-efficiently. Furthermore, employee experience platforms do not only make HR services and employee experience management more scalable, but it can also make them faster as well. In this regard, conversational agents and other types of virtual assistants are available 24/7, and reduce drastically response time when employees need support or require access to HR resources. As Bersin points out (2020), one of the main challenges for HR is to reduce the distance from capturing employee signals to carrying out adequate action. By adopting modern listening tools based on machine learning and natural language processing, employee comments and suggestions can be captured and analyzed instantly and organically across the entire employee life cycle. In turn, these signals can provide insights on emerging trends and problems, activate suggested actions, and trigger workflows. For example, if a significant number of employees express similar concerns about a lack of leadership and support at their job, HR can move fast to address these problems, design adequate interventions, and capitalize on opportunities. Preliminary results based on a series of pilots with mid-sized organizations in Latin America that are using the platform of Bondi X to measure and streamline the experience of their employees are promising. First of all, participating companies are able to track employee experience in a continuous way, as opposed to yearly engagement surveys which are more static in nature. This is particularly useful to identify sudden changes in the experience of specific segments of employees and to quickly act on these insights. In this regard, we observe that the data collected and processed within the platform are being consulted on a weekly basis by participating HR administrators. This is an important shift in how HR assigns its efforts on continuous listening initiatives: less time on the practical aspects of measuring employee experience (given that it is automated by the platform) and more focus on analyzing and acting on employee experience data. Furthermore, by applying a virtual assistant to collect employee experience data, by means of interactive check-ins, employees are triggered to share their experience on a more regular basis. In this regard, we observe that participating companies report promising response rates of between 30% and 60% of employees that are completing at least one experience check-in each two weeks. However, long-term user interaction beyond a period of six months remains to be tested.

"If you take care of your employees, they will take care of your clients." This famous quote of Richard Branson underlines the importance for companies to offer symmetrical experiences between employees and customers. The rise of HR technology provides organizations with an increasing number of tools and resources to approach employee experience in a similar way to customer experience – personalized, fast, and hassle-free. Consequently, this puts HR in a unique position to embrace employee experience as a key pillar for the organization in its pursuit of success, sustainability, and happy customers.

11.5 Conclusions

In this chapter, we reviewed two technology-supported assessment and monitoring tools developed in South America, one to assess social-emotional skills in elementary school children, the other system supporting and consolidating experiences across employees' careers. Both systems have in common that they use advanced technology to assess, collect, integrate, analyze and report on people's standing on psychological constructs and their development. These tools meet current assessment and monitoring needs in South America that cannot be handled adequately with more traditional methods of measurement and follow-up.

Although these two examples come from two fields that have been considered different and rather separately from each other, the worlds of education and work nowadays get more integrated through the necessity of building expertise and knowledge, together with the development of trans-ferable skills and life-long learning. What we learn from technology-supported systems to assess social-emotional skills in pupils will also help us to build better assessment tools to track transferable skill development in employees. Alternatively, employee-experience systems as described in the current chapter may also inspire student-experience systems to be set up in education. An ultimate goal could be to use the information provided by social-emotional skill assessments at various stages in an individual's trajec-tory as input for a student/employee-experience system that puts the individual in the driver seat of their learning and development across life.

Overall, it is clear that technology-based assessment and measurement has not only substantively affected what and how we measure, but has also radically changed the positions of the assessor and the assessee. Technology-based assessment provides the individual assessee with more autonomy to keep track of learning and development across life and various contexts (education, different jobs, up to postretirement). Artificial intelligence algorithms further help to integrate and make sense of this broad set of inputs and data, and indicate more explicit forms of assessment where necessary to provide better service to the individual (e.g., the suggestion of learning or job opportunities, suggestions to craft job content, or providing well-being recommendations). Finally, technology-supported assessment and monitoring is easily scalable, a necessity in South American countries with a large population living in big cities but also in more remote places. The examples provided here illustrate that technology and assessment should not be perceived as a threat but go hand-in-hand to ascertain the well-being and employability of students, employees, and citizens.

REFERENCES

Abrahams, L., Pancorbo Valdivia, G., Primi, R., Santos, D., Kyllonen, P., John, O., & De Fruyt, F. (2019). Social-emotional skill assessment in children and adolescents: Advances and challenges in personality, clinical and educational contexts. *Psychological Assessment, 31*(4), 460–473. https://doi.org/10.1037/pas0000591

Abrahams, L., Rauthmann, J. F., & De Fruyt, F. (2021). Person-situation dynamics in educational contexts: A self- and other-rated experience sampling study of teachers' states, traits, and situations. *European Journal of Personality, 35*(4), 598–622. https://doi.org/10.1177/08902070211005621

Alexander, L., Mulfinger, E., & Oswald, F. L. (2020). Using big data and machine learning in personality measurement: Opportunities and challenges. *European Journal of Personality, 34*(5), 632–648. https://doi.org/10.1002/per.2305

Anastasi, A., & Urbina, S. (2000). *Testagem psicológica [Psychological testing].* Artes Médicas.

Barak, A., & English, N. (2002). Prospects and limitations of psychological testing on the internet. *Journal of Technology in Human Services, 19*(2–3), 65–89. https://doi.org/10.1300/J017v19n02_06

Bersin, J. (2020). *Employee Experience 4.0: Shortening the distance from signal to action.* https://joshbersin.com/2020/11/employee-experience-4-0-closing-the-loop-from-signal-to-action/

(2021a). *Secrets to employee experience: The definitive guide launches today.* https://joshbersin.com/2021/07/secrets-to-employee-experience-the-definitive-guide-launches-today/

(2021b). *Why service workers are now more important than software engineers.* https://joshbersin.com/2021/08/why-service-workers-are-now-more-impor tant-than-software-engineers/

Bolzan, L. M., & Löbler, M. L. (2016). Socialização e afetividade no processo de inclusão digital: Um estudo etnográfico [Socialization and affection in digital inclusion process: An ethnographic study]. *Organizações & Sociedade, 23*(76), 130–149. https://doi.org/10.1590/1984-9230767

Brandão, T. B., Oliveira, K. S., Zuanazzi, A. C., Marino, R. L. F., Primi, R., Lessa, J. P. A., & Stelko, A. C. (2021). Avaliação das competências socioemocionais: laboratório cognitivo na construção de instrumento para crianças de 6 a 11 anos [Assessment of socio-emotional skills: Cognitive laboratory in the construction of an instrument for children aged 6 to 11 years]. In *Anais do X Congresso Brasileiro de Avaliação Psicológica*. IBAP.

Brasil. (2018). *Base nacional comum curricular*. Ministério da Educação, Brasília. http://basenacionalcomum.mec.gov.br/images/BNCC_EI_EF_110518_ver saofinal_site.pdf

Cardenas, A. (2019). *2019 employment legislation changes in Mexico*. https:// velocityglobal.com/blog/2019-employment-legislation-changes-in-mexico/

CEPAL. (2019). *Employment situation in Latin America and the Caribbean: The future of work in Latin America and the Caribbean – old and new forms of employment and challenges for labour regulation*. https://repositorio.cepal.org/ bitstream/handle/11362/44605/1/S1900308_en.pdf

Columbus, L. (2018). *5 ways AI can help solve today's talent crisis*. https://www .forbes.com/sites/louiscolumbus/2018/09/23/5-ways-ai-can-help-solve-todays-talent-crisis/?sh=7a6b1c3aa386

De Fruyt, F. (2021). Understanding and testing socio-emotional skills. In OECD, *AI and the future of skills: Capabilities and assessments* (Vol. 1, pp. 97–116). OECD Publishing.

De Fruyt, F., Wille, B., & John, O. P. (2015). Employability in the 21st century: Complex (interactive) problem solving and other essential skills. *Industrial and Organizational Psychology – Perspectives on Science and Practice, 8*(2), 276–281. https://doi.org/10.1017/iop.2015.33

de Klerk, S., Veldkamp, B. P., & Eggen, T. J. H. M. (2018). A framework for designing and developing multimedia-based performance assessment in vocational education. *Educational Technology Research and Development, 66*(1), 147–171. https://doi.org/10.1007/s11423-017-9559-5

Debusscher, J., Hofmans, J., & De Fruyt, F. (2016). From state neuroticism to momentary task performance: A person × situation approach. *European Journal of Work and Organizational Psychology, 25*(1), 89–104. https://doi .org/10.1080/1359432X.2014.983085

Duckworth, A. L., & Yeager, D. S. (2015). Measurement matters: Assessing personal qualities other than cognitive ability for educational purposes. *Educational Researcher, 44*(4), 237–251. https://doi.org/10.3102/00131 89X15584327

Green, D. (2021). *Why employee experience and performance management are two sides of the same coin*. https://www.linkedin.com/pulse/why-employee-experi ence-performance-management-two-sides-david-green/ https://joshbersin .com/2019/02/the-employee-experience-platform-a-new-category-arrives/

INEP. (2020). *Índice de Desenvolvimento da Educação Básica*. http://ideb.inep .gov.br/

Khomh, F., Adams, B., Dhaliwal, T., & Zou, Y. (2015). Understanding the impact of rapid releases on software quality: The case of Firefox. *Empirical Software Engineering, 20*(2), 336–373. https://doi.org/10.1007/s10664-014-9308-x

Kniffin, K. M., Narayanan, J., Anseel, F., Antonakis, J., Ashford, S. P., Bakker, A. B., et al. (2021). COVID-19 and the workplace: Implications, issues, and insights for future research and action. *American Psychologist, 76*(1), 63–77. https://doi.org/10.1037/amp0000716

L&E Global. (2019, August). *Colombia: Summary of recent labour and workplace related issues.* https://knowledge.leglobal.org/colombia-summary-of-recent-labour-and-workplace-related-issues/

Lang, J. W. B., Runge, J. M., & De Fruyt, F. (2021). What are agile, flexible, or adaptable employees and students? A typology of dynamic individual differences in applied settings. *European Journal of Personality, 35*(4), 510–533. https://doi.org/10.1177/08902070211012932

Leong, K., Sung, A., Au, D., & Blanchard, C. (2020). A review of the trend of microlearning. *Journal of Work-Applied Management, 13*(1). https://doi.org/10.1108/JWAM-10-2020-0044

Levine, L. (2021). *The HR tech industry is on fire: Why, and what it means for startups in Latin America.* https://www.linkedin.com/pulse/hr-tech-industry-fire-why-what-means-startups-latin-america-levine/?trk=articles_directory

Lievens, F., Lang, J. W. B., De Fruyt, F., Corstjens, J., Van de Vijver, M., & Bledow, R. (2018). The predictive power of people's intraindividual variability across situations: Implementing whole trait theory in assessment. *Journal of Applied Psychology, 103*(7), 753–771. https://doi.org/10.1037/apl0000280

Measelle, J. R., John, O. P., Ablow, J. C., Cowan, P. A., & Cowan, C. P. (2005). Can children provide coherent, stable, and valid self-reports on the big five dimensions? A longitudinal study from ages 5 to 7. *Journal of Personality and Social Psychology, 89*(1), 90–106. https://doi.org/10.1037/0022-3514.89.1.90

Miguel, F. K. (2017). Instrumentos informatizados e testagem adaptativa computadorizada [Computerized instruments and computerized adaptive testing]. In B. F. Damásio & J. C. Borsa (Eds.), *Manual de desenvolvimento de instrumentos psicológicos [Psychological instrument development manual]* (pp. 195–214). Vetor.

Miguel, F. K., & Zuanazzi, A. C. (2020). Estudos de validade e precisão do teste de organização de histórias emocionais [Validity and reliability studies of the emotional stories organization test]. *Revista Iberoamericana de Diagnostico y Evaluacion-e Avaliacao Psicologica, 57*, 27–40. https://doi.org/10.21865/RIDEP57.4.02

Morgan, J. (2017). *The employee experience advantage: How to win the war for talent by giving employees the workspaces they want, the tools they need, and a culture they can celebrate.* John Wiley & Sons.

OECD. (2019). *PISA 2018 results (Vol. I): What students know and can do.* OECD Publishing.

Primi, R. (2010). Avaliação psicológica no Brasil: Fundamentos, situação atual e direções para o future [Psychological assessment in Brazil: Foundations, current situation and future directions]. *Psicologia: Teoria e Pesquisa, 26* (especial), 25–35. https://doi.org/10.1590/S0102-37722010000500003

Primi, R., Santos, D., John, O. P., & De Fruyt, F. (2021). SENNA inventory for the assessment of social and emotional skills in public school students in Brazil: Measuring both identity and self-efficacy. *Frontiers in Psychology*, *12*, 716639. https://doi.org/10.3389/fpsyg.2021.716639

Seidl, J., De Andrade, A. L., & De Fruyt, F. (2020). The impacts of COVID-19 on workers' careers. In M. M. de Moraes (Ed.), *Work and containment measures for Covid-19: The impacts of pandemic on workers and their work relationship* (pp. 69–77). SBPOT Publications.

Seidl, J., & Hanashiro, D. M. M. (2021). Ageism and age diversity management: Concepts and scales. In M. H. Antunes, S. M. T. Boehs, & A. B. Costa (Eds.), *Trabalho, maturidade e aposentadoria: Estudos e intervenções [Work, maturity and retirement: Studies and interventions]* (pp. 49–66). Vetor Editora.

Shiner, R., Soto, C. J., & De Fruyt, F. (2022). Personality assessment of children and adolescents. *Annual Review of Developmental Psychology*, *3*, 113–137. https://doi.org/annurev-devpsych-050620-114343

Sosnowska, J., Kuppens, P., De Fruyt, F., & Hofmans, J. (2020). New directions in the conceptualization and assessment of personality: A dynamic systems approach. *European Journal of Personality*, *34*(6), 988–998. https://doi.org/10.1002/per.2233

Thompson, N. A., & Weiss, D. J. (2011). A framework for the development of computerized adaptive tests. *Practical Assessment Research & Evaluation*, *16*(1), 1–9. https://doi.org/10.7275/wqzt-9427

Urbina, S. (2007). *Fundamentos da testagem psicológica [Fundamentals of psychological testing]*. Artmed.

Wise, S. L., & Kingsbury, G. G. (2000). Practical issues in developing and maintaining a computerized adaptive testing program. *Psicológica*, *21*, 135–155.

Zuanazzi, A. C., Stelko-Pereira, A. C., Lessa, J. P. A., Oliveira, K. S., Primi, R., Hamburg, S., Brandão, T. B., & Padilha, Y. S. (2021). Teste de criatividade emocional em crianças: Proposta de correção e resultados preliminares [Test of emotional creativity in children: Correction proposal and preliminary results]. In *Anais do X Congresso Brasileiro de Avaliação Psicológica* (p. 172). IBAP.

CHAPTER 12

Reflections on Testing, Assessment, and the Future

Fred Oswald and Tara Behrend

Throughout life, most people experience a wide array of tests, whether they are occupational (e.g.., a personality test), educational (e.g., a geometry test), medical (e.g., the Apgar physical wellness test as a newborn), or even tests taken for fun (e.g., a crossword puzzle). Given that tests are omnipresent, and given we live in a moment in history marked by intense debate around testing, what are the social, political, psychological, and organizational factors that determine how – and even whether – we should use tests? How do the benefits and costs of using tests compare to not doing so? While appreciating all of these factors, we also argue that decisions around test use should be guided by professional guidelines that reflect the accumulation of the best science and practice available (e.g., *Standards for Educational and Psychological Testing*, American Educational Research Association et al., 2014; *Principles for the Validation and Use of Personnel Selection Procedures*, Society for Industrial and Organizational Psychology, 2018). We reflected on the chapters in this book with this context in mind. As today's organizations and governments worldwide grapple with important questions of the fairness, validity, privacy, and ethics of testing, we are heartened to see that the essential wisdom of the past century is still highly relevant in solving these modern problems. Yet it is equally clear, through the expert insights of the contributing authors of this book, that we still have many intriguing questions to pursue – and a great deal of continued thinking and work to do.

Testing in its various forms and settings comes with a history fraught with complexity. It is important to start by stating the obvious, because "testing" is not one thing. It does not make sense to say that "testing" is uniformly good or bad. That said, many outspoken segments of society are expressing fear or outright loathing of the very concept of testing. Consider the recent debates taking place in many American universities regarding the use of the Graduate Record Exam (GRE). The University of Pennsylvania, writing in 2018, remarked:

the GRE can be financially burdensome for low-income applicants and offer unfair advantages to wealthy applicants ... GRE scores do not, in general, accurately predict academic performance in graduate school ... significant gaps in GRE performances by women and underrepresented racial and ethnic minorities made it especially difficult for them to be accepted ... nothing of significant epistemic value was gained by our use of the GRE that we couldn't figure out from looking at transcripts, writing samples, etc. ... we will not discriminate against you based on an outdated, expensive, biased, and predictively invalid test.

This press release is consistent with other modern complaints about testing, namely that it discriminates against minority applicants and is not a valid predictor of success. The counterargument is that testing is, in fact, found to be more fair and valid than attempting to "figure out" qualifications based on other measures that reflect greater subjectivity and opportunity biases, such as research experiences (Miller et al., 2021) and reference letters (e.g., Woo et al., 2023). And it is worth noting that college grade-point average is also subject to similar issues as the GRE, regarding racial/ethnic differences that are lower for underrepresented minorities (Roth & Bobko, 2000). Even these types of data are usually not persuasive to people who hold this belief, even among those who lack concrete alternatives for making admissions decisions.

To some extent, this example suggests that testing experts have been losing the battle about the benefits of testing in the court of public opinion. And yet now standardized tests are being reconsidered as part of a college applicant's materials, given that admissions officers need to understand how much knowledge and preparation an applicant has coming into graduate school. This leads to a broader point: Given the power of the press, how can we restore public trust and confidence in the appropriate use of testing to inform difficult decisions that must be made? Some people applying to graduate school will get in, and others will not. Some applying for a job will get a job, and others will not. Decision-makers are therefore forced to distinguish between applicants. What is the most *appropriate* and *ethical* way to do so?

Although statistics cannot answer this critically important societal question, it can usefully inform it and make the benefits and challenges of testing concrete. For example, to evaluate the quality of tests, psychometricians and test developers have long relied on principles of reliability, validity, and fairness. Underlying these principles is a focus on *constructs*, or the underlying characteristics of people we seek to measure (e.g., verbal knowledge, learner engagement, performance, satisfaction).

Without constructs, we cannot usefully interpret what responses to test content mean.

For example, when we have a test of 25 geometry items, this is neither a random collection of items, nor a definitive set of 25 geometry problems. Instead, the items together are intended to measure a more general construct of geometry knowledge, such that someone who shows mastery of those 25 items likely knows (without any guarantee) similar geometry items. Without a construct-based approach to testing like this, we could not make useful inferences about people's psychological characteristics. By extension, we also cannot simply use statistics and data (without an understanding of the construct to be measured) to help us evaluate the fairness and validity of a measure.

Ironically, claims like the one from Penn Philosophy, that "nothing can be learned from tests that can't be learned other ways," is not a testable proposition. It cannot be disproven without understanding constructs and taking a data-driven approach to human decision-making. Moreover, machine-learning professionals and other computer scientists have also muddied the waters by discarding constructs and using language like "ground truth," which implies a focus on the data alone, and a lack of need for constructs in the world of employment, college admissions, medical diagnoses, and other high-stakes prediction. This is essentially why critical issues of bias have arisen in machine-learning contexts because by avoiding a construct-driven focus, sources of variance irrelevant to the constructs have not only crept in, but swept in. Factors such as race/ethnicity, gender, age and other demographics; experience with social media; and the format of one's résumé are all factors that could influence an assessment relying on machine learning, even though none of these factors reflect the constructs that are to be measured. What these machine-learning experts and anti-test university administrators tend to have in common is the need to better appreciate how to understand and control (minimize, estimate) the construct-irrelevant factors in the world that are either systematic (bias) or random (noise). Using tests to predict outcomes such as academic success and job performance is not only hard because we need to define our outcomes carefully; it is also hard because it is difficult to predict the future in a complex world. Tests have many good qualities in this context, because they can be subject to scrutiny (e.g., test item content can be reviewed and revised, vs. what was asked in an employment interview may be unknown), and they are standardized (e.g., everyone receives the same items, vs. an interview which might be "customized" to each applicant in unknown or unfavorable ways).

The chapters in this book grapple with these and other important issues around technology and testing, offering insights about the ways that cultural context can add additional layers of complexity. A number of integrative themes emerged around algorithms, technology, privacy, fairness, and workplace applications.

Algorithms: Regarding algorithms, Song and colleagues (Chapter 1) focused on the nature and complexity of the machine-learning algorithms that mine equally complex big datasets (e.g., social media data, ecological momentary assessment data, audiovisual data), ultimately hoping to yield clusters of cases and/or out-of-sample predictions that are both accurate and useful. Even when predictions from machine learning are shown to be robust in terms of cross-validation within a given dataset, questions regarding the extent of the generalizability of the predictive model loom large, just as they would in traditional data analyses. How do we know that our results will be relevant in different organizations, jobs, regions of the world, points in time, and so on? And as the authors ask, how do the benefits and challenges compare with more traditional approaches (e.g., cross-validated linear regression)?

Moreover, given that we are dealing with big data, what about the generalizability of the data themselves? Given potentially thousands of variables, how confident are we that similar variables will be obtained in other settings? In other words, a big dataset might contain thousands of variables and thousands of participants, and we might ask how *both* are being sampled. The authors' point about "ground truth" is useful when one finds relationships between big data and more traditional measures (e.g., a self-report measure of dutifulness). But when relationships are not found, is it because personality is not found and/or because unique and complex forms of personality are found within big data as discovered through machine learning? To begin answering this question, the thinking and theory of experts must supplement the so-called ground truth of established measures.

No matter how one might think about "ground truth," algorithms that can operationalize standards of fairness become increasingly challenging when dealing with large and messy big datasets, combined with the complexity of machine-learning algorithms. In this context, Phan and colleagues ask (Chapter 6), how do we know whether technical and cultural environments might be contributing to individual differences (and thus biases) in our measures, rather than differences in the relevant psychological constructs that we hope to measure? In traditional measurement settings measurement experts have wrestled with this question – the hallmark of measurement invariance – for at least 50 years (e.g., Meredith, 1964) having made important conceptual and statistical advances in this domain (Somaraju et al., 2022).

Phan and colleagues point out how measurement invariance takes on new challenges for big data, using the analysis of mobile sensing data across cultures as an example. As the authors note, measurement invariance is dependent on multiple factors of importance, for example mobile device, time, and the constructs being inferred from measures of behavior. Here, the authors provide important insight into how cultural differences in why, when, and how a smartphone is used can profoundly influence individual differences in smartphone data that result, and this might even suggest that constructs derived from big data could differ in their *meanings* across cultures (measurement noninvariance), which prevents comparing their means. Working carefully in measure-development efforts to obtain empirical support for similar meaning (measurement invariance) across cultures, mobile devices, time points, etc. is an important effort prior to understanding cultural differences in prediction (though see Millsap, 1997, for the psychometric challenges). This is an especially critical empirical question when attempting to measure constructs in a culture-fair manner using modern technologies.

Technologies: Using Singapore as a contextual example, Chan (Chapter 8) points out how technology is embedded within government, organizations, and societies that, in turn, attempt to govern the very technological benefits and risks that affect them. For example, the successful design of a medical device should not narrowly focus on its benefit to individuals. Its design should consider the entire system on which the technology critically depends (e.g., caregivers, physicians, healthcare policy). These dependencies can be usefully researched using Chan's framework of the "3C's" of context, changes, and collaborations. As such research is conducted, the author emphasizes how a solid approach to measuring constructs (e.g., key aspects of individuals, innovation, and infrastructure) will ensure that good data (and not just big data) inform and improve human-systems interactions with technology. This integrated approach should incorporate strong psychometrics that is sensitive to change over time, model multilevel effects inherent to the system, and involve multidisciplinary collaboration with differences in expertise and opinion.

Song and colleagues (Chapter 7) emphasize how in Asia, dynamics that can be captured with modern technologies are becoming more commonplace on the one hand (e.g., game-based assessments, smartphones) while new technologies are emerging and evolving simultaneously. What strikes us here is how technologies relevant to cognitive domains (e.g., knowledge assessment) and noncognitive domains (e.g., fitness trackers) will allow researchers not only to measure constructs in new and more refined ways than traditional methods do, they will also allow researchers to investigate how cognitive and noncognitive constructs interact over time in major life domains (e.g., work, school, and home) and in ways never before researched (e.g., stress, team, and performance dynamics operating simultaneously).

Privacy: Privacy is a major ethical and legal issue that arises consistently across a wide range of applications and on an international basis. Xu and Zhang (Chapter 3) point out how the richness of big data is generally a force for good (e.g., finding better-fitting jobs, more effective educational interventions, more beneficial medical treatments), but as we know, it may also be a force for evil (e.g., identifying and exploiting a person's specific habits, residence, and personal connections). Balancing such benefits versus risks is a commonplace calculation when designing organizational research to be submitted to an institutional review board. With big data, we can learn similar lessons involving calculations and practices made in addressing vulnerable populations (e.g., children, homeless) and sensitive datasets (e.g., medical records, educational records). Also, pressure-testing the data to see whether people can be reidentified (e.g., merging usernames or zip-code data with other third-party data) might become an important routine before any data are shared publicly. Legislation around AI and big data in the USA continues to arise, often featuring privacy concerns (National Conference of State Legislatures, 2021; Office of Science and Technology Policy, 2022).

Overall, one can easily imagine modern-day tensions between these privacy issues on the one hand that recommend guarding big datasets, and the open science movement and taxpayer-funded granting agencies that recommend sharing those data. As the authors note, managing the *perception* that privacy might be breached is often as important as the actual risks and realities around data privacy. We recognize that anonymizing data is always possible, but then other concerns arise, for example whether doing so detracts from comparisons with findings in real-world datasets and whether doing so might compromise the power of machine-learning algorithms to mine the data for complexity. And in truth, anonymizing data is not nearly as simple as it may seem, given that back-tracing and reidentifying deidentified data can be a trivial programming task when precautions are not taken (Rocher et al., 2019).

Fairness: The meaning of fairness is culturally bound and thus depends on cultural norms, cultural history, country-specific legal guidance, and other contextual factors. A "meritocratic" system that seems fair in one context might be seen to uphold cultural power hierarchies in another context. Moreover, conceptions of fairness are time-bound, and in fact, the very technologies being reviewed in the chapters in this volume speak to the specific challenges of ensuring fairness in testing when expectations vary so widely, and will do so in the future. Rather than identify the aspects of fairness in each chapter, we seek to highlight that fairness is a critical theme underlying all of them, and that the nature of fairness must be appreciated within the context of the work and in light of the reader's own conceptions of fairness.

Workplace Applications: In the arena of personnel assessment, technology has served to enhance traditional assessments in some cases (e.g., interviews, assessment centers, adaptive testing) while extending or even supplanting those assessments in others (e.g., game-based assessment, social media data, resume parsing, real-time work behaviors). Guenole and colleagues (Chapter 9) and Munson (Chapter 10) find that in Europe and in the USA, respectively, professional test standards (e.g., the *Standards* and *Principles* cited in our introduction) and the legal context (e.g., Hamilton & Davidson, 2022) can help push today's technological innovations driving employment test development in many right directions – given the proper guidance – while avoiding many wrong directions. We often hear about the benefits of technology-based assessments in terms of scalability, cost, candidate engagement, time to completion, and rapid scoring and reporting. Still, as the authors note, these aspects of technology-based assessment become decidedly unimportant when they are lacking in the essentials of reliability, validity, and fairness.

In this vein, Landers and colleagues (Chapter 5) dive into game-based assessments (GBAs), noting that GBAs are not merely games, given that their primary goal is to conduct construct-relevant assessments. Of course, just as there are many potential irrelevant sources of variance in traditional tests (e.g., response styles, random responding, social desirability), so might there be irrelevancies that affect GBAs (e.g., due to age and reaction time, visual acuity, prior video-game experience, style of video-game play). In this latter case, a GBA that appears to measure a construct (e.g., personality) might run the risk of also tapping these irrelevances or perhaps even tapping other constructs instead (e.g., cognitive ability instead of personality, as intended; Wu et al., 2022). The authors note how GBAs face issues of implementation, cross-cultural invariance, and privacy concerns in a changing legal landscape. GBAs must continue to be vetted carefully for evidence of job relevance, reliability, validity, and fairness, just as should be done with any other selection test.

What struck us about these themes is that they are simultaneously culturally determined and universal in their importance. Consideration of technology and measurement "around the globe," then, must be similarly globally and locally minded.

12.1   A Way Forward

These chapters, and others that have called for a psychological approach to understanding the world of testing, give us hope. There are several future research directions we think will advance this cause. First, we hope to see more research that tempers the promise of technology-based testing with the skepticism surrounding testing (in both appropriate and naive forms) and engages with these latter ethical and legal concerns head-on. This may include a wide range of possibilities, where we will name only a few: (1) key comparisons of technology-based tests with one another, with traditional alternatives – and with abandoning tests altogether, as some might suggest; (2) qualitative and quantitative studies on the user experience of testing, treating testing as part of a larger sociotechnical system; (3) head-to-head comparisons of various technological tools attempt to balance privacy protection with the transparency required to research and understand how tests and algorithms work.

It will also be important for researchers to hold test vendors accountable for the claims they advertise, ensuring not only adherence to all relevant laws and regulations, but ethical standards of conduct. For example, AI-based assessments might be engaging (a game), scalable (in the cloud), convenient (fast to take, easy to make decisions from), and fair to all. But remember that a coin flip is fast and unbiased – surely, we expect something more than that in AI-based assessments. As we ask with all assessments, are they measuring relevant constructs we care about? What data and psychometric evidence would help answer this question? We should assume a position of skepticism, and set the expectation that vendors participate in audits of their measures to provide paying organizations with reassurance of not only the fairness of measures, but of their construct relevance in terms of reliability and validity. To be clear, audits may vary in their systematic approach and are bound to context, for example, an essential part of psychological audits (Landers & Behrend, 2023) is to consider the cultural context explicitly in evaluating claims.

In some cultures, testing may be seen as a key means of evaluating and comparing student performance, and may be closely linked to ideas of merit and achievement. In other cultures, testing may be viewed more skeptically, with an emphasis on holistic, experiential learning rather than on standardized measures of performance.

- Some cultures may place a greater value on group cooperation and collaboration, while others may place a greater emphasis on individual achievement and competition. These differing values can shape attitudes towards testing and the ways in which tests are designed and administered.
- The purposes and functions of testing may vary across cultures. In some cultures, testing may be seen as a tool for guiding and supporting student learning while in others it may be more closely tied to ideas of accountability and control.
- The role of technology in testing can also vary across cultures. In some contexts, technology may be seen as a valuable tool for enhancing the efficiency and fairness of testing, while in others it may be viewed with skepticism or resistance.

An additional challenge that will be faced by test developers has to do with innovation in large language models (LLMs), which are capable of producing human-sounding responses to questions, such as the ones asked during job interviews. As a demonstration of the power of these models, consider the preceding paragraph of this chapter (beginning with "in some cultures" and ending in "skepticism or resistance"), which was produced by ChatGPT, a large language model developed by OpenAI, as a response to the prompt, "Explain how people's perceptions about testing may vary as a result of their culture." The ability of LLMs to produce responses that, for example, can pass standardized tests (e.g., SAT, ACT, LSAT, MCAT), requires new research efforts to understand the limits and possibilities, as well as the implications for test developers, especially for remote and unproctored tests.

In sum, like the contributing authors of this book, we are struck with the power, potential, and cautions of emerging technologies that together are already challenging and altering the practice and science of testing in fundamental ways. We are equally sure, though, that the fundamentals of psychometrics and construct-oriented testing, developed and refined over the past hundred years, will continue to serve us well as an anchoring framework as we strive, together and in earnest, to improve the future of technology-based testing and the society it serves. Given that technology is intended to improve human welfare, technology-based testing should be subjected to our highest ethical, legal, practical, and scientific standards and aspirations.

REFERENCES

American Educational Research Association, American Psychological Association, & National Council on Measurement in Education, & Joint Committee on Standards for Educational and Psychological Testing. (2014). *Standards for educational and psychological testing*. AERA.

Hamilton, R. H., & Davidson, H. K. (2022). Legal and ethical challenges for HR in machine learning. *Employee Responsibilities and Rights Journal, 34*, 19–39. https://doi.org/10.1007/s10672-021-09377-z

Landers, R. N., & Behrend, T. S. (2023). Auditing the AI auditors: A framework for evaluating fairness and bias in high stakes AI predictive models. *American Psychologist, 78*(1), 36–49. https://doi.org/10.1037/amp0000972

Meredith, W. (1964). Notes on factorial invariance. *Psychometrika, 29*, 177–185. https://doi.org/10.1007/BF02289699

Miller, A., Crede, M., & Sotola, L. K. (2021). Should research experience be used for selection into graduate school: A discussion and meta-analytic synthesis of the available evidence. *International Journal of Selection and Assessment, 29*, 19–28. https://doi.org/10.1111/ijsa.12312

Millsap, R. E. (1997). Invariance in measurement and prediction: Their relationship in the single-factor case. *Psychological Methods, 2*(3), 248–260. https://doi.org/10.1037/1082-989X.2.3.248

National Conference of State Legislatures. (2021, September 15). *Legislation related to artificial intelligence*. https://www.ncsl.org/research/telecommunications-and-information-technology/2020-legislation-related-to-artificial-intelligence.aspx

Office of Science and Technology Policy. (2022). *Blueprint for an AI bill of rights: Making automated systems work for the American people* ("AI Blueprint"). Executive Office of the President. https://www.whitehouse.gov/wpcontent/uploads/2022/10/Blueprint-for-an-AI-Bill-of-Rights.pdf

Rocher, L., Hendrickx, J. M., & de Montjoye, Y. A. (2019). Estimating the success of re-identifications in incomplete datasets using generative models). *Nature Communications, 10*, Article 3069. https://doi.org/10.1038/s41467-019-10933-3

Roth, P. L., & Bobko, P. (2000). College grade point average as a personnel selection device: Ethnic group differences and potential adverse impact. *Journal of Applied Psychology, 85*(3), 399–406. https://doi.org/10.1037/0021-9010.85.3.399

Society for Industrial and Organizational Psychology. (2018). *Principles for the validation and use of personnel selection procedures* (5th ed.). https://www.apa.org/ed/accreditation/about/policies/personnel-selection-procedures.pdf

Somaraju, A. V., Nye, C. D., & Olenick, J. (2022). A review of measurement equivalence in organizational research: What's old, what's new, what's next? *Organizational Research Methods, 25*(4), 741–785. https://doi.org/10.1177/10944281211056524

Woo, S. E., LeBreton, J. M., Keith, M. G., & Tay, L. (2023). Bias, fairness, and validity in graduate-school admissions: A psychometric perspective. *Perspectives on Psychological Science, 18*(1), 3–31. https://doi.org/10.1177/17456916211055374

Wu, F. Y., Mulfinger, E., Alexander III, L., Sinclair, A. L., McCloy, R. A., & Oswald, F. L. (2022). Individual differences at play: An investigation into measuring Big Five personality facets with game-based assessments. *International Journal of Selection and Assessment, 30*(1), 62–81. https://doi.org/10.1111/ijsa.12360

Index

Milton Keynes UK
Ingram Content Group UK Ltd.
UKHW020039081123
432178UK00019B/115